Popular Culture in American History

BLACKWELL READERS IN AMERICAN SOCIAL AND CULTURAL HISTORY

Series Editor: Jacqueline Jones, Brandeis University

The *Blackwell Readers in American Social and Cultural History* series introduces students to well-defined topics in American history from a socio-cultural perspective. Using primary and secondary sources, the volumes present the most important works available on a particular topic in a succinct and accessible format designed to fit easily into courses offered in American history or American studies.

Popular Culture
in American History

Edited by

Jim Cullen

BLACKWELL
Publishers

Copyright © Blackwell Publishers Ltd 2001; editorial matter and organization
copyright © Jim Cullen 2001

First published 2001

2 4 6 8 10 9 7 5 3 1

Blackwell Publishers Inc.
350 Main Street
Malden, Massachusetts 02148
USA

Blackwell Publishers Ltd
108 Cowley Road
Oxford OX4 1JF
UK

Library of Congress Cataloging-in-Publication Data

Popular culture in American history / edited by Jim Cullen.
    p. cm—(Blackwell readers in American social and cultural history; 1)
Includes bibliographical references and index.
ISBN 0–631–21957–9 (acid-free paper)—ISBN 0–631–21958–7 (pbk.: acid-free paper)
    1. Popular culture—United States—History. I. Cullen, Jim, 1962– II. Series.

E161. P66 2000
306'.0973—dc21
                                                                    00–028935

British Library Cataloguing in Publication Data
A CIP catalogue record for this book is available from the British Library.

Typeset in 10 on 12pt Plantin
by Kolam Information Services Pvt. Ltd, Pondicherry, India
Printed in Great Britain by TJ International, Padstow, Cornwall

This book is printed on acid-free paper.

In loving memory of
Rita Cullen (1910–98)
and
Elizabeth Del Dotto (1914–99),
who knew and loved the sidewalks of New York;

and in loving anticipation for
Grayson Cullen
and
Ryland Cullen,
who arrived, uptown, as their forebears departed

Contents

Notes on Contributors

Jim Cullen teaches in the Expository Writing Program at Harvard University. He is the author of *The Civil War in Popular Culture: A Reusable Past* (1995), *The Art of Democracy: A Concise History of Popular Culture in the United States* (1996), and *Born in the U.S.A.: Bruce Springsteen and the American Tradition* (1997).

Daniel J. Czitrom is Professor and Chair of the History Department at Mount Holyoke College. He is author of *Media and the American Mind: From Morse to McLuhan* (1982), is co-author, with John Mack Faragher and Mari Jo Buhle, of *Out of Many: A History of the American People* (multiple editions through 1999), and is currently completing *Mysteries of the City: Culture, Politics, and the Underworld in New York, 1870–1920*.

Michael Denning is Professor of American Studies at Yale University. He is the author of *Mechanic Accents: Dime Novels and Working Class Culture in America* (1987), *Cover Stories: Narrative and Ideology in the British Spy Thriller* (1987), and *The Cultural Front: The Laboring of American Culture in the Twentieth Century* (1997).

Lawrence Levine is Professor of History at George Mason University. He is a 1983 recipient of the MacArthur Prize and has served as President of the Organization of American Historians. Among his many books are *Black Culture and Black Consciousness: Afro-American Folk Thought from Slavery to Freedom* (1977), *Highbrow/Lowbrow: The Emergence of Cultural Hierarchy in America* (1988), and *The Opening of the American Mind: Canons, Culture, and History* (1996).

W. T. Lhamon, Jr. is University Distinguished Teaching Professor, Department of English, Florida State University. He is the author of *Deliberate Speed: The Origins of a Cultural Style in the American 1950s* (1990) and *Raising Cain: Blackface Performance from Jim Crow to Hip Hop* (1998).

David Marc has taught at Brown University, Brandeis University, and the University of Southern California. His books include *Demographic Vistas: Television in American Culture* (1984), *Comic Visions: Television Comedy and American Culture* (1989), and *Bonfire of the Humanities: Television, Subliteracy, and Long-Term Memory Loss* (1998).

Victor Neuberg has taught at universities in England, Canada, and the United States. Among his many books are *The Penny Histories* (1968) and *Popular Press* (1983).

Kathy Peiss is Professor of History at the University of Massachusetts at Amherst. Her works include *Cheap Amusements: Working Women and Leisure in Turn-of-the-Century New York* (1986); *Passion and Power: Sexuality in History*, co-edited with Christina Simmons and Robert A. Padgug (1989), and *Hope in a Jar: The Making of America's Beauty Culture* (1998).

Tricia Rose is Acting Director of Africana Studies at New York University. She is the author of *Black Noise: Rap Music and the Black Culture in Contemporary America* (1994) and co-editor, with Andrew Ross, of *Microphone Fiends: Youth Music and Youth Culture* (1994).

Susan Smulyan is Associate Professor in the Department of American Civilization at Brown University. She is the author of *Selling Radio: The Commercialization of American Broadcasting, 1920–1934* (1994). She is also a principal figure in the creation of a website, "Whole Cloth: Discovering Science and Technology Through American Textile History," developed by the Society for the History of Technology in collaboration with teachers (http://www.si.edu/lemelson/centerpieces/whole_cloth).

Series Editor's Preface

The purpose of the Blackwell Readers in American Social and Cultural History is to introduce students to cutting-edge historical scholarship that draws upon a variety of disciplines, and to encourage students to "do" history themselves by examining some of the primary texts upon which that scholarship is based.

Each of us lives life with a wholeness that is at odds with the way scholars often dissect the human experience. Anthropologists, psychologists, literary critics, and political scientists (to name just a few) study only discrete parts of our existence. The result is a rather arbitrary collection of disciplinary boundaries enshrined not only in specialized publications but also in university academic departments and in professional organizations.

As a scholarly enterprise, the study of history necessarily crosses these boundaries of knowledge in order to provide a comprehensive view of the past. Over the last few years, social and cultural historians have reached across the disciplines to understand the history of the British North American colonies and the United States in all its fullness. Unfortunately, much of that scholarship, published in specialized monographs and journals, remains inaccessible to undergraduates. Consequently, instructors often face choices that are not very appealing – to ignore the recent scholarship altogether, assign bulky readers that are too detailed for an undergraduate audience, or cobble together packages of recent articles that lack an overall contextual framework. The individual volumes of this series, however, each focus on a significant topic in American history, and bring new, exciting scholarship to students in a compact, accessible format.

The series is designed to complement textbooks and other general readings assigned in undergraduate courses. Each editor has culled particularly innovative and provocative scholarly essays from widely scattered books and journals, and provided an introduction summarizing the major themes of the essays and documents that follow. The essays reproduced here were chosen because of the authors' innovative (and often interdisciplinary) methodology and their ability to reconceptualize historical issues in fresh and insightful ways. Thus students can appreciate the rich complexity of an historical topic and the way that scholars have explored the topic from different perspectives, and in the process transcend the highly artificial disciplinary boundaries that have served to compartmentalize knowledge about the past in the United States.

Also included in each volume are primary texts, at least some of which have been drawn from the essays themselves. By linking primary and secondary material, the editors are able to introduce students to the historian's craft, allowing them to explore this material in depth, and draw additional insights – or interpretations contrary to those of the scholars under discussion – from it. Additional teaching tools, including study questions and suggestions for further reading, offer depth to the analysis.

Jacqueline Jones
Brandeis University

Preface: About This Book

Popular Culture in American History is a narrative anthology of sources. It may be worthwhile to take a moment for an explanation about just what this means.

The book is narrative in the sense that it proceeds in a loosely chronological manner, and describes the evolution of economic, technological, and social structures that mediate between the creators and audiences of popular culture. Every story has its omissions, and this one may well have more than most. That's partly a function of its editor's biases, and partly a function of its design as a collection of disparate writings rather than a seamless stretch of prose. But even one-author narrative accounts of popular culture (which I myself have written) can never hope to be comprehensive; the subject is just too large. The goal here, in any case, is not simply to present a collection of data to be absorbed and regurgitated on a multiple-choice exam. It is, rather, meant to offer a series of case studies that can deepen and broaden understanding of a world of popular culture which, almost by definition (a definition I'll try to refine in the introduction), we already know quite well.

An anthology, or collection of selected pieces or passages, lends itself quite well to such a purpose. To put it in terms of a television metaphor, I think each of the featured pieces in this book focuses on an episode in the hit series "the history of popular culture." (Some of the first television series, which were often loosely connected by their sponsor or genre, were in fact called anthologies.) Very often, a detailed look at an aspect of a particular topic teaches one more than a broad survey of it, much in the way that a close reading of a novel set in the Great

Depression reveals things about the 1930s that a general American history textbook usually does not. This premise was central to the way this book was conceptualized and assembled.

In a sense, to call *Popular Culture in American History* an anthology of *sources* is redundant – what anthology isn't? But it nevertheless seems useful to do so because the word "sources" helps emphasize just what kind of anthology this is: a scholarly one, and more specifically, a historical one. Sources are the very tissue of scholarship; while a novelist or poet can at least theoretically invent from the imagination, any kind of historical writing – even the most imaginative historical writing – must nevertheless rely on some kind of previously recorded information. Occasionally, such information may have been observed directly by a historian (though it's more common for, say, a journalist or anthropologist to do so). More often than not, though, the historian relies on the first-hand accounts of those who are no longer living – and builds on the work of other historians, living and dead.

Historians customarily distinguish between such first-hand and subsequent accounts by calling them "primary" and "secondary" sources. A primary source might be anything from a store receipt to a memoir; a secondary source would be an academic monograph that quotes from either. *Popular Culture in American History* includes both primary and secondary sources. The emphasis here is on the secondary sources – sources which are typically more accessible and informative for those not deeply knowledgeable about a subject, and which place them in a broader context – but each secondary source is accompanied by primary sources like photographs, fiction, advertisements, and other materials. Space considerations and the costs associated with the intensifying commodification of copyrighted material have limited the amount of sources included here. But one hopes there's enough here to invite useful reflection – and further investigation.

The featured essays in this volume were not chosen because they necessarily represent the most cutting-edge scholarship or represent the last word on the topic in question. My primary criterion in choosing them was pedagogical rather than theoretical or methodological: the emphasis here is on informative, readable prose that doesn't assume the reader has been immersed in scholarly debates or is planning on writing a dissertation. At the same time, the writers in this collection have all distinguished themselves as historians of popular culture, and my pleasure in collecting these various pieces, which were published over a span of two decades, is something akin to putting together a tape of my favorite songs for a friend. (I've indulged my prerogative as editor by including a new piece of my own, which I hope won't hurt the overall quality of the album.)

A few words about organization. Each chapter of this book consists of three main parts. The first is a brief introductory section that offers a broad overview or immediate context for a period, form, or issue in pop culture history. The second is an essay, often a chapter from a longer book, by an established scholar in the field. The last section, "Consider the Source," includes companion primary sources, discussion questions, and suggestions for further reading. Whether read straight through or in any combination of chapters or sections, the hope here is that the book will enliven the study of popular culture in a course on the subject, in a related field or survey course, or in a personal plan of study.

The inspiration for this approach toward *Popular Culture in American History* came from *The Puritans in America: A Narrative Anthology* edited by Alan Heimert and Andrew Delbanco (Cambridge, Mass.: Harvard University Press, 1985). The core of that book is sixteenth- and seventeenth-century primary sources, and does not include discussion questions, photographs, and some of the other ancillary materials included here. But the example of judiciously chosen, abridged, and sequenced sources – and especially the superb headnotes that accompany each section – served as a powerful example for which I am grateful from the standpoint of a reader as well as the editor of a volume of my own. My hope is that I can perform a similar service for those who thumb through these pages.

Jim Cullen
Bronxville, New York
January 2000

Acknowledgments

Allow me to acknowledge some debts: to the scholars whose work appears in this volume; to series editor Jackie Jones; and to Susan Rabinowitz and Ken Provencher of Blackwell Publishers. I also benefited from the competence and grace of copy editor Juanita Bullough, and from the work of Leanda Shrimpton on the cover.

My work was also facilitated by a number of librarians and archivists, among whom I would like to thank Tom Ford of the Houghton Library at Harvard University; Holly Hinman of the New-York Historical Society; Jonathan Hyams of the Michael Ochs Archive; and Judy Kicinski and the staff of the Sarah Lawrence College Library, which served as my intellectual base of operations during a key phase of work on this project. Nancy Sommers, director of the Expository Writing Program at Harvard, has been notably gracious for a number of years now in accommodating a somewhat complicated personal and professional life, and I will always be grateful to her and my colleagues for the great experience I've had at "Expos."

Closer to home, my in-laws, Ted and Nancy Sizer, have continued to offer good advice, generous support, and the example of their important body of work. My wife, Lyde Cullen Sizer, has tolerated me through this project just as she has every previous one, and managed to finish her own book, earn tenure, give birth to twin boys, grow lots of tomatoes and bake lots of bread at the same time. (Not bad, huh?) Last but not least, I'm grateful for the cooperation and good company of my eldest son, Jay, and his twin brothers, Grayson and Ryland, who spent much of the time I was framing these chapters in my lap. It's become a cliché to say that books are collaborative enterprises, but in this case it seems especially true and necessary to do so.

J. C.

Introduction: The Worldwide Web of Popular Culture

Here's some history for you:

The words you are now reading were first sequenced on a computer keyboard in the summer of 1999. My computer, a mid-line IBM Aptiva, was purchased in January of 1997 for about $1500, and had a 166-megahertz processor with 16 megabytes of memory (I added another 16 MB for a speech recognition program that never performed as well as I'd hoped). Connected to the Internet by a traditional phone line, I frequently had to wait to download data, and usually avoided doing so for anything but written text. At the moment I was writing this paragraph in Microsoft Word 7.0, a row of small rectangular boxes displayed at the bottom of my monitor by my Windows 95 operating system told me that I had Microsoft's Encarta 98 Encyclopedia in my CD-ROM drive and that my Netscape browser was on my home page, the CNN website.

I'm telling you all of this because I expect it'll all sound fairly dated by the time you read it. My point is to illustrate how the restless pace of change renders once cutting-edge technology obsolete – that is, it turns the future into history – with what I regard as startling rapidity. Nevertheless, as someone born before 1980, I'm still inclined to be amazed by what even my old-fashioned equipment can do, especially in regard to a multimedia resource like the Internet. From that CNN website, I could:

- read new stories;
- view photos;
- vote in polls;
- download video streams of television broadcasts;

- scan advertisements;
- make links to other websites (and buy just about anything).

In short, the new communications media I'm using to assemble this book on the history of popular culture are *themselves* a compendium of older popular culture. These new media take the best of what came before and make them components of a more powerful whole. Under such circumstances, you might say, what happened yesterday seems far less complicated, interesting or decisive than what's happening today – or tomorrow. Indeed, back in the 1990s, the phrase "that's history" was a way of dismissing something as irrelevant.

But the reach of the past is more subtle and powerful than many of us may realize. I can illustrate this point by some of the very terms we use with our PCs. At some level, we all know we don't actually press "buttons," "pull down" menus, or "open" visual spaces we call "windows." There are technical terms that describe such functions (like "graphical user interface"), but we instead use metaphors – metaphors drawn from our collective previous experience – to understand and use technology that might otherwise seem formidably complex or alien. The connected power lines we know as the World Wide Web aren't exactly a web; they just seem like one – or did at one point. Some people, perhaps dissatisfied about the way the Internet has been commercialized, might lament it's less like a web than a flow chart – a metaphor with much more hierarchical implications than a "web" or "net." If enough people come to think the same way, such a perception may well lead us to adopt different terms from our collective memory to describe our experiences.

The Internet has also developed on lines laid down by historical precedent. To a great extent, its development closely resembles its technological grandfather, radio broadcasting. Like the Internet, radio began with clusters of technical innovators whose work increasingly converged. Like radio, too, the Internet owed much of its initial growth to the federal government – especially the Defense Department – which provided funding in the (realized) hope it would have useful military applications. Eventually, private interests emerged ascendant in both media. But both went through protracted periods of uncertainty as to how commerce could actually make money from them. Radio's eventual answer, advertising (a subject discussed in more depth in Chapter 7), laid down developmental tracks rapidly adopted by television in the 1950s and the Internet in the 1990s.

That's not to say that history is destiny. Indeed, around the time this introduction was written, there was a strong concern among advertisers that their messages could be filtered out much more systematically by web users than magazine readers or radio listeners, a situation that raised questions about the economic viability of the Internet as it was then constituted. The particular – and in some cases, unique – circumstances or qualities surrounding any historical development can often lead to unexpected and even unprecedented outcomes. It is this very unpredictability – an alchemy of precedent and contingency – that makes history such a fascinating (and, in some cases, frustrating) form of inquiry.

As with any form of inquiry, though, it helps to define some terms.

What Is Popular Culture?

"Popular culture" is a term – like "love," "art," or, to name one that will explored in more detail in chapter 8, "the American Dream" – that is almost willfully imprecise. Indeed, that is often what makes such concepts useful; the familiar assertion that "I may not be able to define art, but I know it when I see it" captures the utility of an elastic definition. And popular culture is nothing if not elastic, encompassing everything from baseball box scores to political cartoons and seemingly everything in between.

But the value of any term rests on some sense of limits; only by knowing what something is *not* can one really get a firm sense of what something *is*. Let's begin with "culture." That CD-ROM encyclopedia I mentioned a minute ago defines it as "the beliefs, behavior, language, and entire way of life of a particular time or group of people."[1] That covers a lot. But there are things it *doesn't* cover: weather; properties of magnesium; sexual reproduction by penguins. To put it another way, culture deals with objects, ideas and processes produced by human effort. Things like weather, magnesium, and penguins can get along fine without people (indeed, they may well be better-off without them). Of course, humans have been affected by all three, and have intervened to manipulate their actions and/or effects. To that extent, one could call research on penguins, for example, a form of culture. But not *popular* culture (so far, anyway).

One can begin to get a sense of what popular culture is all about when one juxtaposes it with *unpopular* culture – not necessarily in the sense of "disliked," but rather relatively limited in scope. Research on the sexual behavior of penguins, even in esteemed scientific journals read by thousands of people, is nevertheless considered something of an acquired taste. So, for that matter, is opera. Indeed, popular culture is sometimes juxtaposed against *elite* culture, that is, that culture – particularly artistic productions – that embodies what the nineteenth-century British critic Matthew Arnold famously defined as "the best that has been thought and said." Elite culture is typically produced for (and often by) the rich and powerful. It usually draws on what is considered the most valuable resources available at any given time, as well as the talents of individuals deemed most successful at producing artifacts for the enjoyment of the privileged.

It's important to note that what's considered elite culture can change. As chapter 2 explains, Shakespeare was once considered a playwright for the rich as well as the poor, the college-educated along with the illiterate. For much of the twentieth century, however, Shakespeare's plays have usually been considered an elite affair as likely to studied at a library as witnessed in a theater. On the other hand, the Bard's emergence in a series of major motion pictures in late 1990s – including *Hamlet, Othello, Richard III, A Midsummer Night's Dream,* and the Academy Award-winning *Shakespeare in Love,* all of which took liberties with the original plays in ways comparable to early nineteenth-century productions – suggests that Shakespeare made something of a comeback in popular culture at the turn of this century.

Perhaps it's time to put the matter in more positive terms. The definition of popular culture that guided this book comes from Lawrence Levine, the man who portrays Shakespeare's role in chapter 2. In a 1992 article in *the American Historical Review,* Levine defined popular culture as "the folklore of industrial society."[2] Our trusty Encarta defines folk-lore as a "general term for the verbal, spiritual, and material aspects of any culture that are transmitted orally, by observation, or by imitation."[3] Industrial society, which tends to reproduce and disseminate culture through mechanical means, allows it to reach people who might not necessarily experience it from person to person (e.g. by reading about it in a book or website). As Levine notes, the line between folklore and popular culture, like the line between elite and popular culture, is not fixed. The blues, for example, began as a form of folk music, became an important idiom in popular music, and continues to be played in small, private settings. But allowing for some imprecision, popular culture does seem to be a discrete phenomenon in its own right, in part because the very act of reproducing and disseminating a cultural artifact *in itself* has important effects and ramifications – as when, for example, the huge success of Harriet Beecher Stowe's 1851 novel *Uncle Tom's Cabin* inflamed sectional tensions in the decade before the Civil War (and shaped white perceptions of African Americans for decades to come).

There is an important corollary to Levine's definition of popular culture that is worth spelling out here. In the United States, among other nations, the folklore of *industrial* society is also *capitalistic* – that is, it operates in an economic system premised on private (as opposed to government or collective) ownership. Not all industrial societies are capitalistic; the Soviet Union, for example, was not, and China's relationship with capitalism at the start of the twenty-first century is ambivalent and incomplete at best. Both have had (an often shadowy) popular culture.

As in so many other ways, the impact of capitalism on popular culture has been mixed. On the one hand, it has shown a notable efficiency in manufacturing and distributing popular artifacts, thus fostering a kind of cultural democracy. On the other, its tendency to concentrate power and wealth in a few hands, coupled with the unceasing search for profit, can just as easily stifle as promote the spread of ideas. No discussion of popular culture – and no stance *toward* popular culture – can get very far without considering the role of capitalism.

A few other definitions:

- For the purposes of this book, the term *medium* (and its plural, *media*) refers to a means of technological communication that connects otherwise separate creators and audiences of popular culture. Printing presses; film projectors, the Internet: these are media. So is a stage in a theater.
- A *form* consists of an established series of cultural conventions within a medium that can accommodate seemingly infinite variations. The novel is a form within the print medium; plays and concerts are forms within the medium of the stage. You go to them with some notion of what you're going to get (a story with a beginning, middle and end; lines recited by actors; notes played by musicians) without knowing how things will turn out – or which general "rules" may get bent or even broken, like a novel where beginning, middle, and end are scrambled out of order.
- A *genre*, which can exist in more than one medium, is a form that has more specific expectations surrounding it. The western is a *kind* of novel or film; so is the situation comedy, which originated in radio but became a staple of television. The rules can get bent or broken here, too, but they're stiffer: you can't have a Western set in Tokyo, and while you might laugh in a horror movie, it just won't work if nobody gets scared.
- Finally, a *format* is the specific organization a form takes within a medium. Dime novels were published as newspapers or pamphlets; a jazz album is distributed on CD as well as audiotape, among other formats. Formats tend to be more ephemeral than forms. In the twentieth century, movies are available on film, videotape, and a plethora of disk formats (CD-ROM, DVD, and so on). Sometimes forms and formats get conflated – people refer to "films" when they really mean movies they watched on videotape – but the distinction is

real and can be helpful when you're trying to map popular culture and get a sense of the big picture.

Some General Themes

Even given the boundaries I've tried to sketch here, the domain of popular culture remains far broader than can be done full justice in a book of this sort. There are many aspects of the subject – sports and fashion come to mind as two obvious examples – that are very much part of that realm but are not discussed in the chapters that follow. As noted in the Preface, however, the point here is not to comprehensively survey the field. It is, instead, to offer a series of compelling case studies whose resonance extends beyond their immediate context. Considered solely on its own terms, turn-of-the-century dance halls (chapter 5) is a fairly arcane topic. But as a snapshot in women's struggle to achieve sexual and personal autonomy, or as subtle illustration of the ways class conflict shapes people's lives even when they're not at working, it makes for worthwhile reading. If a look at this book, in whole or in parts, gives you some sense of that patterns that *link* various kinds of popular culture, then I, for one, think it will have served a useful purpose.

What are some of those links? Ideally you yourself, perhaps in discussions with others, will figure a few out. But I'll enumerate some here, all of which are interrelated:

- *Popular culture as the art of democracy.* By definition, "popular" means widely shared, something of "the many" as opposed to "the few." While words like "many" and "few" can be relative (sell 100,000 books and you usually have a hit; sell 100,000 movie tickets and you usually have a flop), popular culture in any form is usually designed to appeal to as broad an audience as possible. It has an egalitarian spirit about it, and it is surely no accident that popular culture has a particular force and presence in representative democracies like the United States.

  That's not to say that popular culture always lives up to that spirit. For one thing, the individualist cast of American democracy in particular gives it a strongly hierarchical spin, as in the case of a remote superstar adored by millions, or a record company that oppresses musicians with onerous contracts and fans with overpriced records. For another, popular culture, like other institutions in society, is afflicted with evils like racism, which belie the fondest principles of those who profess to believe in representative democracy.

From another standpoint, though, the problem with popular culture is precisely that it *is* democratic, and thus reflects the less attractive aspects of democracy: endless pandering to the lowest common denominator; persistent difficulties in articulating shared standards (who gets to decide?); tiresome assertiveness and self-absorption on the part of people who are basically indistinguishable from each other; a thrill-seeking mentality that leads to decadence. One of the ironies of democracy, in this view, is that its tendencies toward chaos make it susceptible to a conformist, even fascist, mentality by those in positions of power to manipulate it. This is why some scholars prefer the term "mass culture," with its connotations of undifferentiated size, to "popular culture." I, like many of the writers of this book, tend to have a more optimistic outlook about popular culture. But I'm not unaware of its problems – and you shouldn't be, either.

• *Popular culture as a target of criticism by suspicious elites.* The issues I've just raised are not simply abstract philosophical problems; they're complaints that have a long history. From the proliferation of novels read by white women in the late eighteenth century to the proliferation of rap songs listened to by black men in the late twentieth century, there have been consistent – and strikingly similar – criticisms of popular culture. Arguments that it expresses the brazen excesses of urban life; seduces and corrupts young people who need to be quarantined from it; and functions as an enervating substitute for "serious" forms of culture are made again and again in a variety of contexts (among them presidential elections). In many cases, such criticism reflects class, racial, religious, or other investments in the status quo threatened by new media or genres of pop culture, like movies and rock-and-roll. Such concerns should not be dismissed out of hand; to say that popular culture has no negative effects also denies its potentially positive effects and thus negates its power altogether. Certainly, some popular culture *is* repellent and even dangerous. But in such cases indignant outrage is generally less useful than an attempt to account for its appeal and underlying causes.

• *Popular culture as a gateway for marginalized outsiders.* In the United States at least, the democratic majority is not uniform, but diverse. To speak of the American working class, for example, is to speak of a panoply of religions, races, regions, and sexual orientations. Moreover, while the United States was born amid assertions that all men are created equal, it has always been true, to paraphrase George Orwell, that some men have been more equal than others – and that most men have been more equal than most women. But far more than in the labor market, government or (especially) residential patterns, there has long been a sense of openness about popular culture sorely lacking in other areas in American life. The success of women in popular literature, homosexuals in theater, and African Americans in popular music has given them kinds of social, political, and economic power they could get nowhere else. Admittedly, only small minorities of minorities become visible stars. But their impact is disproportionately great, not only in offering solace and inspiration to others, but in providing some of the only glimpses others might have about what it means to be an outsider in America.

Popular culture, then, is not only an interconnected web of media, formats, genres, and formats, but an integral part of society as a whole. Trying to understand what makes something fun – whether for you or someone in another time and place – can be a real learning experience. That's a good reason to study it in school. But beyond that, a richer sense of popular culture can also heighten your talents in mastering the art of everyday life.

Suggested Further Reading

Some of the best general sources of information on the history of popular culture are reference books (and CD-ROMs). Among the most import-ant are the *St. James Encyclopedia of Popular Culture*, edited by Tom and Sara Pendergast (Detroit: St. James Press, 1999) and the *Encyclopedia of American Cultural and Intellectual History*, edited by Mary Kupiec Cayton and Peter W. Williams (New York: Scribner, 2000). See also Cayton, Williams, and Elliot J. Gorn's *Encyclopedia of American Social History* (New York: Scribner, 1993), which includes pop culture topics, and *The Handbook of Popular Culture*, 2nd edition, edited by Thomas Inge (West-port, CT: Greenwood Press, 1989). For a brief one-volume treatment, see Jim Cullen, *The Art of Democracy: A Concise History of Popular Culture in the United States* (New York: Monthly Review Press, 1996). For a more theoretical overview, see John Storey, *An Introductory Guide to Critical Theory and Popular Culture* (Athens, Ga.: University of Georgia Press, 1993).

Notes

1   "Culture," *Microsoft® Encarta® 98 Encyclopedia*. © 1993–7 Microsoft Cor-poration.

2   Lawrence Levine, "The Folklore of Industrial Society: Popular Culture and Its Audiences," *American Historical Review* 97:5 (December 1992): 1369–99. The piece is also included in Levine's collection of essays, *The Unpredictable Past: Explorations in American Cultural History* (New York: Oxford University Press, 1993).

3   "Folklore," *Microsoft® Encarta® 98 Encyclopedia.*

1
In the Beginning

1517	Martin Luther posts his 95 theses in Wittenburg, Germany
1534	Henry VIII of England breaks with the Roman Catholic Church
1607	Jamestown settled
1620	Pilgrims arrive in Plymouth; Mayflower Compact
1630	Massachusetts Bay Colony founded
1639	First printing press in North America established in Cambridge
1640	First publication of the *Bay Psalm Book*
1642–9	English Civil War
1660	Restoration of English monarchy under Charles II
1682	First publication of *Narrative of the Captivity of Mrs. Mary Rowlandson*
1688	Glorious Revolution
1724	First (?) Richard Rum chapbooks published
1756–63	English, French, and Indians fight in North America as part of Seven Years War
1776	Thomas Paine's *Common Sense* published; Declaration of Independence signed

Introduction

As in so many other ways, the Protestant Reformation that transformed Europe in the sixteenth and seventeenth centuries was pivotal in the rise of popular culture. In their attempt to overthrow what they viewed as an irredeemably corrupt Catholic clergy, Protestant leaders put new emphasis on the word of God as divinely transmitted to the writers of the Bible – and a new emphasis on individuals experiencing that word for themselves by reading it. For no one was this faith more passionate than for the early settlers of colonial British North America, particularly New England. While no one knows for sure just how many people could read, most scholars agree that New England had one of the highest rates of literacy in the entire seventeenth-and eighteenth-century world.

The ministers who promoted this religious individualism would find it had unintended consequences. In some cases, they found their *own* authority in question, as when, for example, early New Englander Anne Hutchinson challenged the teachings of Puritan ministers a mere seven years after the founding of Boston in 1630 (she was tried and banished by colonial authorities, and eventually killed by Indians). Far more subtle – but cumulatively more powerful – were less direct assertions of independence, as when members of a congregation privately disagreed with a minister's interpretation of scripture they could read for themselves. Moreover, the Bible, while undoubtedly a fixture of many a colonial household, wasn't always the *only* thing these people were reading. Indeed, long before contemporary religious leaders and politicians denounced the sex and violence of Hollywood movies and rap music, Puritan clergy were complaining about the corrupting influence of the plays, poetry, and music of colonial America.

A key site of this emerging popular culture was the printing press. The first one in the American colonies was established in Cambridge, Massachusetts in 1639. This press, like others to follow – and like many back home in London, which remained the capital of American publishing well into the nineteenth century – were established primarily for religious reasons. An early publication of the Cambridge press, *The Whole Book of Psalms* (popularly known as *The Bay Psalm Book*), became a bestseller on both sides of the Atlantic. But this press and others soon began publishing more secular material as well. Sheet music, almanacs, sermons, political tracts: by the time of the American Revolution, the colonies could legitimately be called a culture of print.

Ministers, planters, and merchants prized expensive leather-bound books imported from abroad. This elite culture of church, state, and countinghouse was relatively well preserved in public and private libraries passed down through generations. Alongside, and occasionally intertwining, was a more ephemeral print culture for those with less time, money, and aptitude for reading. This culture was commodified in a growing network of publishers, peddlers, and retailers that disseminated different forms and genres of print media in a variety of formats. Among the most popular of these formats were chapbooks.

In this excerpt from a 1989 anthology of essays exploring the scholarly subdiscipline known as "history of the book," literary historian Victor Neuberg offers an evocative sketch of chapbooks: what they were, how they were produced and distributed, and the kind of reading material typically found in them. Ironically, he notes, the very familiarity of chapbooks in their time has made them elusive in ours: "the majority of them were read to pieces." Moreover, while it's one thing to know what a chapbook is, it's another to know just who read them and how these readers understood them. In part, this reflects the scarcity of primary source material on American colonial life (and it is another irony that the current repository for once-commonplace chapbooks are necessarily restricted archives like the American Antiquarian Society in Worcester, Massachusetts, where Neuberg did much of his research). But the complexities of popular culture audiences and responses remain vexing – and fascinating – issues even for that most recent heir of the chapbook, the rack-sized paperback available at drugstores and airports.

Chapbooks: Reconstructing the Popular Reading of Early America

Victor Neuberg

Within the context of the American colonies, chapbooks are best defined as the cheap, ephemeral booklets that were offered for sale in the bookstores and printing offices of Boston, New York, and Philadelphia, and were also hawked around the streets by itinerant traders – often characterized as Yankee peddlers – who carried them as a regular part of their stock in trade to the small towns and settlements that lay inland beyond the eastern seaboard. Like so much in the early days of colonial America, they originated in England. There, from about the middle of the seventeenth century, they constituted a major element in popular literature, rivaling both almanacs and broadside ballads as widely selling items. Numerically this trade in popular literature was considerable, and some light is thrown upon the extent of it if we recall that during the 1660s as many as four hundred thousand almanacs were sold in a year, while Charles Tias, publisher and member of a consortium, left ninety thousand chapbooks in stock when he died in 1664.[1] Because almanacs and broadsides depended for their appeal to the purchaser very largely upon local and topical factors, they were produced by printers in the colonies

Excerpt from Victor Neuberg's "Chapbooks in America: Reconstructing the Popular Reading of Early America" included in *Reading in America: Literature and Social History*, edited by Cathy N. Davidson, pp. 81–4, 102–8, 111–13. © 1989 The Johns Hopkins University Press.

THE

HISTORY

of

Sir Richard Whittington

THRICE

Lord-Mayor of London.

Printed and Sold at the Printing-Office in Bow-
Church-Yard,

Good character   A 1763 chapbook cover of the much-fictionalized "history" of the plucky Dick Whittington, who – with the help of his rat-catching cat – rose from obscurity to wealth and fame in medieval London. The story circulated widely in England's American colonies. *Photo by permission of the Houghton Library, Harvard University*

long before there was any substantial production of chapbooks, and right up to the outbreak of the War of Independence in 1775 chapbooks were being imported in large numbers from England.

Before considering these aspects of the trade, we should look briefly at the content of chapbooks. According to the *Shorter Oxford English Dictionary*, the term "chapbook" did not come into general use until 1824;[2] until then most contemporaries used various terms for them, the commonest of which were "small books," "chapmen's books," "small histories," or simply "histories." Tradition was the keynote. In chapbooks were to be found abridged versions of the romances of knights and maidens that, in lengthier and rather more sophisticated versions, had delighted medieval audiences. There were tales of giants, monsters, and fairies, many of them the residue of an oral peasant culture rooted in a long-distant past. There were songs, riddles, jokes, anecdotes of pirates and highwaymen; there was fortunetelling, divination, primitive weather forecasting; there were cookbooks and household manuals; and during the eighteenth century there were versions of *Robinson Crusoe* and *Moll Flanders*. Such richly varied material was published in small books measuring roughly 8.5 centimeters by 16 centimeters, often with uncut edges, comprising twenty-four, or less usually sixteen or thirty-two pages. Many were illustrated with crude though lively woodcuts – usually relevant to the printed text, but sometimes a woodcut might be used on an ad hoc basis to fill a page when the text ran out. Printed on coarse rag paper, they were sufficiently tough to withstand much of the handling that came their way, though inevitably the majority of them were read to pieces.

This, then, was the nature of the chapbooks that found their way to America. The state of printing in the original colonies was patchy, and not until 1762, with the establishment of a press in Savannah, Georgia,[3] did all of the thirteen colonies have printing plants. Few American printers, however, were able to invest money or resources in substantial enterprises. There was a fairly restricted market in the colonies for literary products, and the publishing of books, particularly those in several volumes, involved considerable risk. It was very much easier, and more profitable to the trade in both countries, to import books from England, and there was a thriving traffic in them until the War of Independence – and even after hostilities had commenced it does not seem to have died out completely.

Charles Evans in his *American Bibliography* records, between 1639 (when Stephen Days set up the first press in America at Cambridge, Massachusetts) and 1799, thirty-six thousand separately printed items, these not including tradesmen's letterheads or the blank forms that made up a considerable part of the printer's output. In Philadelphia, for example, the printing firm of Franklin and Hall lists in its Work Book for 1755 such items as "700 Vestrey Notices," "200 Advertisements desiring Landlords to pave their Footways," "1000 Way Bills," "50 Invitations on Cards," "250 Certificates for loading foreign Melasses";[4] and it is apparent that such items formed an important element in the work of many local printers well into the nineteenth century.

Among what might, in the widest possible terms, be called the "literary" productions of the early colonial press were almanacs, broadsides, newspapers, medical handbooks, letter writers, and practical manuals of all kinds. Ready reckoners were especially important in a country where not every storekeeper might be adept in adding up a column of figures; and such difficulties were compounded by the fact that the pound sterling might differ in value between neighboring colonies, and there were those in which Spanish currency was widely used. Then too, among the output of the printing offices were schoolbooks, devotional works, and chapbooks.

It is with the latter that we are concerned, and at the outset there is a problem. Because of their ephemeral nature, few chapbooks have survived, and a good deal – though by no means all – of our knowledge of them comes from booksellers' advertisements, which do not as a rule specify whether the chapbooks were printed in America or imported from England. The majority, however, almost certainly were imported until after the Revolution. A wide range of titles with woodcut illustrations was readily and cheaply available to the American book trade at wholesale prices; and because they were easy to transport and did not, unlike almanacs, go out of date, importing chapbooks was an easy option. There was, in the early days of America, one other factor that told decisively against the production of chapbooks in large numbers, and this was the endemic shortage of paper throughout the eighteenth century. There was a constant demand for rags to be turned into paper. As one poet put it, "Kind friends when thy old shift is rent / Let it to th' paper mill be sent."[5] A story is also told that in 1748 a Spanish ship sailing westward was captured by an English warship and brought into Boston, where her cargo was discharged and sold. Included in it were several bales of papal bulls or indulgences destined for the Spanish colonies, printed on one side only of small sheets of good paper. The printer Thomas Fleet bought the lot cheaply and printed popular songs and broadsides on the backs of the sheets.[6]

Despite such a windfall, the problem of paper and its manufacture continued to bedevil the book trade. A New York printer, Hugh Gaine, was offering in 1760 "Ready Money for clean Linnen Rags," and eleven years later "The highest Price for clean Linen Rags".[7] Because so many colonists lived frugally and kept their clothes as long as they held together, the chronic scarcity of rags for the papermaking mill continued. In the early years of the Revolution, up to 1777, the price paid for rags was three pence per pound; in 1778, eight pence; in 1779 twelve pence or one shilling; in 1780, three shillings; and in 1781, ten shillings. In 1787, when rags were being sold for twelve shillings a pound, paper cost six pounds per ream, and the problem of paper was not finally solved in America until William Megaw of Meadville, Pennsylvania, established in 1828 a mill that made paper from straw pulp. This process brought the price down considerably, and meant that the two hundred or so paper mills at that period were no longer competing for scarce supplies of rags.[8] . . .

There were three quite specific American contributions to the chapbook tradition. One was the Indian captivity theme; the second, Richard Rum; and the last, the career of the felicitously named Chapman Whitcomb.

Indian captivities were stories about, and almost always by, dwellers on the frontier or in the wilderness who had been captured by Indians from whom, after a lapse of years, they escaped in various ways.[9] One of the earliest of these, first published at Cambridge, Massachusetts, in 1682, was Mary Rowlandson's captivity. It was often reprinted. Some of the other popular titles dealt with such captives as Peter Williamson, Mary Jemison, and Benjamin Gilbert. The Indians were always ready to kidnap white settlers in these stories, and their victims were of all ages and both sexes.

Two authors who wrote captivities that were published in chapbook style were Josiah Priest (1788–1851), who combined authorship with coach trimming and harness making, and the pseudonymous Abraham Panther.[10] The latter was responsible for *A very surprising narrative of a young woman, discovered in a rocky-cave, after having been taken by the savage Indians of the wilderness in the year 1777, and seeing no human being for the space of nine years. In a letter from a gentleman to a friend.* Between about 1786 and 1816 various editions were published under this title or variations of it in a number of places. The story is simple and gives a good idea of what captivities were like. "A most beautiful young Lady sitting near the mouth of a cave" is seen by two travelers in the wilderness. When she sees them she faints, and on recovering shortly afterward exclaims, "Heavens! Where am I?" She tells the sad story of a quarrel with her father and flight to the wilderness where her lover was murdered by the Indians who captured her. She spurned the advances of one brave, and was tied up overnight so that she might ponder the choice between submission to him and death. Resourcefully she chewed through her walnut bark bonds, but realizing that she could not escape she took matters into her own hands: "I did not long deliberate but took up the hatchet he had brought and, summoning resolution I, with three blows, effectually put an end to his existence." She then cut off his head, sliced the corpse into quarters, dragged it for about half a mile, and buried it under foliage. She returned to the cave and made it her home, growing Indian corn to feed herself, for nine years until the travelers happened by. They listen to her story and eventually reunite her with her aged father, who hears her account of what has happened to her and then dies, leaving her a handsome fortune.

Narratives of this sort, with all kinds of variations, were extremely popular until the end of the eighteenth century and for several years into the nineteenth. The pattern of their publication in many different locations suggests that they became part of a common heritage, and grew to be as much a feature of the American chapbook tradition as stories to Tom Thumb and Guy of Warwick, say, were of the English one.

The Richard Rum chapbook was American in origin and, so far as I am aware, unknown in England. It is generally entitled *At a Court held at Punch-Hall, in the Colony of Bacchus. The Indictment and Trial of Sir Richard Rum....* Editions with this title are recorded in 1724 (the first?), 1750, 1770, 1774, 1775, 1785, 1791, and 1793.[11] There are a few versions called *The Indictment and Tryal of Sir Richard Rum at a Court...*, dated 1765, 1794, and 1796; and there is a related chapbook, *A Dialogue between Sam, Sword and Richard Rum* (1794).

The subject is temperance, and the full title of an early edition – effectively a summary of its contents – is worth quoting in full:

> At a Court held at Punch-Hall in the Colony of Bacchus. The Indictment and Tryal of Sir Richard Rum a Person of noble Birth and Extraction, well known both to Rich and Poor throughout all America. Who was accused for several Misdemeanours against his Majesty's Liege people, viz. killing some, wounding others, bringing thousands to Poverty, and many good Families to utter Ruin. It is not the Use, but the Abuse of any good thing, that makes it hurtful. The Fourth Edition, with a Preface, and a Song, compos'd by Sir Richard, immediately after his Discharge, not in former Editions. Boston: Printed and sold at the Heart and Crown in Cornhill. 1750.

The publisher was Thomas Fleet, mentioned earlier, who had advertised what was probably the first edition in the *New England Courant* of March 2, 1724, at a price of six pence for a single copy or four shillings a dozen. There was a similar advertisement in the same paper on March 9, but no mention is made of a second edition, although on March 16 there is an announcement of a third edition. It appears that two editions were sold out, and a third announced, within two weeks of first publication.

The fourth edition – the title quoted in full above – was advertised in the *Boston Evening Post* of March 5 and 12, 1750. It contains a preface that reads,

TO THE
READER

The following Tract has sufficiently recommended it self to the World, by the Sale of three large Impressions, the last of which went off in a little more than a Fortnights Time, a few Years ago, and so gave Birth to this Fourth Edition.[12]

It went through several more editions, one of which was printed in Philadelphia in 1796 "for Robert Stewart, travelling Bookseller," and cost eight pence.[13] What was probably the last edition appeared in Boston in 1835.

The text recounts the trial of Sir Richard before Sir Nathan Standfast and Sir Solomon Stiffrump. Among the jurors are Timothy Tosspot, Benjamin Bumper, John Neversober, and Edward Emptypurse. The indictment is read, and Sir Richard pleads not guilty. One of the witnesses, William Shuttle the Weaver, testifies, "I can never sit at my Loom, but this wicked Companion is enticing me from my Work and is never quiet till he gets me to the Tavern." Among other witnesses are "Barbadoes With the Leeward Islands," who say that "without the Help of Sir Richard we that live in the Islands could not subsist; for he is the best Branch of our Trade." John Friend, the Quaker, speaks up for Sir Richard too, saying that "he hath many times comforted me, both at Sea and Land." In his address to the court Sir Richard claims, "I have done good Service to the Common Wealth, of which I am a good and loyal Member." He is acquitted, and the implication is very clearly that rum should be drunk in moderation. A nicely ambivalent verdict, this, which reflects the conflicting economic and social demands of colonial society. It is, moreover, one that reflects an ambiguity that has characterized North American attitudes toward alcohol well into our own time.

Sir Richard's creator is not known – the chapbook was always issued anonymously. John W. Farwell suggests rather tentatively that it might have been Matthew Adams, a minister who wrote for the *New England Courant*, had a good library, and was an early friend of Benjamin Franklin.[14] In his day Adams was a popular writer, but his claim to the authorship of this bestseller must remain uncertain.[15]

Rather less uncertainty surrounds the career of Chapman Whitcomb (1765–1833), author and traveling bookseller in Massachusetts at the turn of the eighteenth and nineteenth centuries. What we know of Whitcomb is almost entirely due to the researches of J. C. L. Clark over a period of more than twenty years. His *Notes on Chapman Whitcomb*, reprinted from a series of newspapers, was privately published in a small edition in 1911. Then, after many references to Whitcomb in a series of unpublished letters to C. S. Brigham at the American Antiquarian Society, he wrote two further articles, published in the *Clinton Courant*, December 4, 1931, and April 1, 1932, which added a few details to the material he had already published.[16]

The man revealed to us – partly, at least – by Clark was a graduate of Dartmouth College, New Hampshire, in 1785. He was something of an eccentric, and turned up, dressed in green, at the wedding of a young lady who had jilted him in favor of another. He married Rhoda Willard in 1793, but the marriage does not seem to have been altogether successful, for on one occasion, Clark reports, Whitcomb publicly disclaimed any responsibility for the debts of his wife. Clark was doubtful whether, when Mrs. Whitcomb went as a widow to look after her orphaned grandchildren, she took with her the books and papers of her late husband. "I don't imagine," he wrote, "Mrs Whitcomb was very literary, or had much sympathy with her husband's tastes."[17]

Few other details of Whitcomb's family life or personality emerge, though in one of the last letters that he wrote on the subject, Clark did speculate interestingly – and, I suspect, perceptively – about Whitcomb's set of mind: "I am 'handicapped' by very slight knowledge of Whitcomb's early manhood. A certain tone about his satirical verse leads me to a conjecture, which I have hardly touched upon in my articles, that he may have attempted the ministry and failed on account of some natural limitation, leaving him rather embittered on the subject."[18]

We are on very much more certain ground when we come to consider Whitcomb's publications, of which the American Antiquarian Society possesses what must be a virtually complete collection – it is certainly the largest. As the then librarian, R. W. G. Vail, put it in a letter to H. G. Rugg of the Dartmouth College Library,

> We have perhaps the best collection of Chapman Whitcomb material, but I do not believe that we have a single duplicate. His chap books are all exceedingly rare and some of them very important. In fact, there is no other early printing town in New England as interesting as Leominster. I notice that you speak of Whitcomb as a printer. Many items were issued with his imprint, but they were almost always described as printed for Chapman Whitcomb. I doubt whether he was himself a printer, but he must have been a very attractive and interesting character. I suspect that his Christian name describes him pretty accurately.[19]

At one time he was a teacher; at another he was engaged in ragpicking; and from these occupations he seems to have drifted into becoming a traveling bookseller whose stock in trade was the chapbooks that, with one or two exceptions, he had printed by Charles and John Prentiss, who started printing in the town in 1795.[20] The titles are generally undated and bear the imprint "Leominster: Printed for Chapman Whitcomb."

Among the twenty-four Whitcomb publications in the possession of the American Antiquarian Society there are four captivities, including the adventures of Mary Rowlandson and the story by the pseudonymous Abraham Panther. One of his most interesting titles is *The Farmer's Daughter: Being a History of the Life and Suffering of Miss Clarissa Dalton*, an adaptation of an English chapbook based upon an actual robbery that took place in 1785.[21] The story was popular in America, where it was reprinted several times.[22] Whitcomb, however, gave the characters a new set of names – the leading one became Miss Clarissa Dalton[23] – and he also changed the name of the author from James Pen to William Penn. The American Antiquarian Society copy has the usual imprint, but there is also a manuscript note in a contemporary hand after the author's name, which reads, "Printed for Chapman Whitcomb the old book peddeller."

All of Whitcomb's publications were intended for the popular market. In 1795 he published at Worcester, Massachusetts, a twelve-page chapbook of his own poetry entitled *Miscellaneous Poems*. Eight of the pages are devoted to a poem of over three hundred lines called "A Concise View of Antient and Modern Religion." The verse is not great, but it is readable,[24] and his facility in prose and verse suggests comparison with the popular English writer of the later seventeenth century, John Taylor, the "Water Poet," who was equally at home with prose and verse in his chapbooks. Taylor in fact had an American namesake, Amos Taylor (1748–1813?), a traveling bookseller. Having failed to gain entry to Dartmouth College in 1779, Amos Taylor became a teacher, and then peddled through New England books that he had written himself. Many of his twenty-eight recorded titles[25] were religious, and in general his work belongs only marginally to the chapbook tradition.

Popular religious tracts were circulated in colonial days, and in much larger numbers during the early years of the Republic. Hannah More's "Cheap Repository Tracts" had something of a vogue from about 1797;[26] but religious tracts belonged only in a very marginal sense, I believe, to the chapbook tradition. Indeed, although the worthy men and women on both sides of the Atlantic who founded tract societies used hawkers and peddlers to distribute their evangelical wares, they saw their endeavors as being directly opposed to more secular popular literature. An anonymous American writer noted with approval the efforts of the Religious Tract Society in London: "In August 1805, moved by the overwhelming influence which a flood of infidel and other publications was exerting upon the lower orders of society, they conceived the idea of publishing a distinct series of Tracts, adapted to gain their attention, and to supplant the mischievous publications with which they were furnished in great profusion by unprincipled men, for mere purposes of gain." The author went on to say that seventy-five thousand copies of the series were circulated, with the result that "about three hundred thousand of the profane and immoral books, commonly sold to Hawkers, were known to have been kept out of circulation by this series of Tracts having been purchased instead of them."[27]

Leaving aside the enviable certainty of this conclusion, there is no doubt that tracts circulated in large numbers in the United States. Between May 23, 1814, and May 1, 1824, the American Tract Society published over four million tracts, at an average cost of one dollar per five hundred of a single title.[28] These figures are impressive – but they are hardly firm evidence of readership. Promotional zeal on the part of the organizers may well have outrun reality; and, more important, it would be rash to conclude that every tract distributed was read by its recipient. What the figures do indicate, in a more general way, is a large reading public at the bottom end of the social scale.[29]

The extent to which chapbooks helped to make and to shape the tastes of this reading public, some of whom could afford the few coppers charged for them,[30] is still a matter for discussion. What does seem beyond argument is that chapbooks provide us with one of the major threads that lead us to the common reader of the eighteenth and early nineteenth centuries. By about 1825 they had dwindled in popularity as adult fare, but for children they remained in demand until the end of the century and beyond. The reason for their decline among adult readers was almost entirely cultural, and was connected with the new sophistication of a working class called into being by the Industrial Revolution.

There are, however, some continuities, for we find in chapbooks the earliest stories of the American frontier (precursors of the dime novel western and the fiction of Zane Grey) and chronicles of crime, both of which, in differing forms, have remained popular down to our own times. It would not be too difficult to find other interesting, if less immediately obvious, connections between past and present. In a more ideological sense we should remember too the reprinting in America of the English chapbook account of Dick Whittington.[31] The presentation – even if somewhat inaccurate – of Whittington as a poor boy who achieved wealth, fame, and high office through his own efforts became a forerunner of the stream of novels written by Horatio Alger in the nineteenth century about making good – *Struggling Upward* and *Strive and Succeed* are typical titles – that helped to perpetuate the myth that any boy (not girl!) could, if he were honest, intelligent, and hard-working, become either a millionaire or president of the United States. The persistence of such a myth over so long a period is a remarkable tribute to the role of popular literature, which from chapbooks onward has provided significant elements in the theoretical underpinning of a free enterprise culture.

Notes

I am grateful to the American Antiquarian Society (AAS), which made me a Simon Foster Haven Fellow in summer 1984. Its hospitality and resources made this essay possible. I dedicate this essay to Liz Reilly, in love and admiration.

1 Bernard Capp, "Popular Literature," in *Popular Culture in Seventeenth Century England*, ed. Barry Reay (London, 1985), 199.
2 But it was used before then. A Thomas Longman invoice dated August 10, 1773, among the Henry Knox Papers in the Massachusetts Historical Society, Boston, lists "Chap Books." I am deeply grateful to Liz Reilly, who drew my attention to the Knox Papers and lent me relevant photocopies.
3 L. C. Wroth, *The Colonial Printer* (1931; rpt. Charlottesville, Va., 1964), 15.
4 Ibid., 218–19.
5 John Holme, "A True Relation of the Flourishing State of Pennsylvania," quoted in L. H. Weeks, *History of Paper Manufacture in the United States* (New York, 1916), 5–6. First published in 1847, the poem is about Wm. Bradford, who was printing in Oxford, near Philadelphia, from 1685 to 1693.
6 Weeks, *History of Paper Manufacture*, 45.
7 See P. L. Ford, ed., *The Journals of Hugh Gaine, Printer*, 2 vols. (New York, 1902), 1:44.
8 See *Paper Trade Journal* (November 28, 1940), sec. 2, pp. 7–8.
9 The best survey of them is still R. W. G. Vail, *The Voice of the Old Frontier* (Philadelphia, 1949). See also C. A. Smith, *Narratives of Captivity among the Indians of North America* (Chicago, 1912) and *Supplement I* (Chicago, 1928).
10 See Winthrop H. Duncan, "Josiah Priest, Historian of the American Frontier," *Proceedings of the American Antiquarian Society* (April 1934); and R. W. G. Vail, "The Abraham Panther Indian Captivity," *American Book Collector* 2 (1932).
11 C. K. Shipton and J. E. Mooney, eds., *National Index of American Imprints through 1800: The Short Title Evans* (Worcester, Mass., 1969). See also J. A. L. Lemay, "Recent Bibliographies in Early American Literature," *Early American Literature* 8, no. 1 (Spring 1973).
12 The preface is identical to that of the third, except that in the earlier the words were "gave Birth to the Third Edition."
13 Copy in John Carter Brown Library, Providence, RI.
14 J. W. Farwell, "Sir Richard Rum," *Publications of the Colonial Society of Massachusetts* 17 (1915): 234–44. I have drawn heavily upon this printed version of a talk given by Farwell to the society. He showed members a copy of the fourth edition, which is now in the possession of the AAS.
15 In *North American Almanack . . . 1776* (Worcester, Watertown, and Cambridge, Mass.), 17 (unnumbered), there is a plea by "Sir Richard Rum" for less drunkenness in the army.
16 In an unpublished letter to the secretary of Dartmouth College dated April 18, 1932 (now in the Dartmouth College archives, Hanover, NH), Clark spoke of five articles in all, the last of which was to be "as complete a bibliography as possible"; but the project was never completed.

17 J. C. L. Clark to C. S. Brigham, July 11, 1927, AAS.
18 Clark to the secretary of Dartmouth College, April 18, 1932.
19 R. W. G. Vail to H. G. Rugg, April 23, 1932, Dartmouth College archives.
20 Clark to Brigham, January 15, 1913, AAS.
21 See *Annual Register* (September 3, 1785).
22 On at least five occasions between 1797 and 1814 – once in Hartford, Conn., and by three different publishers in New York.
23 See Clark to Brigham, June 18, 1927, AAS.
24 See, for example, his view of the Shakers, who had several communities in New England and elsewhere:

The Shaker thinks that all are blind but he,
And wonders at their gross stupidity;
In the old lady [Mother Anne Lee, the founder], firmly, does believe,
Devoutly pins her faith upon her sleeve,
And thinks that none true faith nor grace possess,
Till to her elders, they their sins confess.

25 See M. A. McCorison, "Amos Taylor, a Sketch and Bibliography," *Proceedings of the American Antiquarian Society* (April 1959).
26 See M. G. Jones, *Hannah More* (Cambridge, 1952), ch. 6 passim; and H. B. Weiss, *Hannah More's Cheap Repository Tracts in America* (New York, 1946), rpt. from *Bulletin of the New York Public Library* (July and August 1946).
27 *Proceedings of the First Ten Years of the American Tract Society Instituted at Boston, 1814* (Boston, 1824), 181. The best account of the tract movement in America is in S. E. Slocum, Jr., "The American Tract Society: 1825–1975. An Evangelical Effort to Influence the Religious and Moral Life of the United States," diss., New York University, 1975. It is very good on the early years.
28 *Proceedings of the First Ten Years*, 178 (unnumbered).
29 See, for example, W. J. Gilmore, *Elementary Literacy on the Eve of the Industrial Revolution: Trends in Rural New England, 1760–1830* (Worcester, Mass., 1982).
30 The economics of chapbook production, in both Britain and the United States, are impossible to reconstruct. Such publications were cheap – whatever that description may mean – and were designed for as many readers as could afford them. How many could? How long were print runs? To the former question there are some partial answers in US Department of Labor, *History of Wages in the United States from Colonial Times to 1928* (Washington, DC, 1929). So far as chapbook print numbers are concerned, it is hazardous even to guess at totals.
31 The real Richard Whittington (who died in 1423) became Lord Mayor of London on several occasions. See *Dictionary of National Biography*; also S. Lysons, *The Model Merchant of the Middle Ages* (London, 1860); and W. Besant and J. Rice, *Sir Richard Whittington*, new ed. (London, 1902).

Consider the Source

I   In his description of common chapbook types, Victor Neuberg describes captivity narratives as especially popular, particularly the *Narrative of the Captivity of Mrs. Mary Rowlandson*. Three excerpts from that narrative are quoted below: the title page of the first edition; the opening four paragraphs of the narrative, and the closing paragraph. Do you have any ideas as to why this book was popular for well over a century – and is now regarded as a classic of early American literature?

Excerpts from *Narrative of the Captivity of Mrs. Mary Rowlandson* (1682)

The Soveraignty and Goodness of GOD, Together With the Faithfulness of His Promises Displayed; Being a Narrative Of the Captivity and Restauration of Mrs. Mary Rowlandson. Commended by her, to all that desires to know the Lords doings to, and dealings with Her. Especially to her dear Children and Relations. The second Addition Corrected and amended. Written by Her own Hand for Her private Use, and now made Publick at the earnest Desire of some Friends, and for the benefit of the Afflicted.
*   Deut. 32.29. See now that I, even I am he, and there is no God with me; I kill and I make alive, I wound and I heal, neither is there any can deliver out of my hand.*
Cambridge, Printed by Samuel Green, 1682.[1]

A Narrative of the Captivity and Restauration of Mrs. Mary Rowlandson

On the tenth of February 1675,[2] Came the Indians with great numbers upon Lancaster: Their first coming was about Sun-rising; hearing the noise of some Guns, we looked out; several Houses[3] were burning, and the Smoke ascending to Heaven. There were five persons[4] taken in one house, the Father, and the Mother and a sucking Child, they knockt on the head; the other two they took and carried away alive. Their were two others, who being out of their Garison upon some occasion were set upon; one was knockt on the head, the other escaped: Another their was who running along was shot and wounded, and fell down; he begged of them his life, promising them Money (as they told me) but they would not hearken to him but knockt him in head, and stript him naked, and split open his Bowels. Another seeing many of the Indians about his Barn, ventured and went out, but was quickly shot down. There were three others belonging to the same Garison[5] who were killed; the Indians getting up upon the roof of the Barn, had advantage to shoot down upon them over their Fortification. Thus these murtherous wretches went on, burning, and destroying before them.

At length they came and beset our own house, and quickly it was the dolefullest day that ever mine eyes saw. The House stood upon the edg of a hill; some of the Indians got behind the hill, others into the Barn, and others behind any thing that could shelter them; from all which places they shot against the House, so that the Bullets seemed to fly like hail; and quickly they wounded one man among us, then another, and then a third, About two hours (according to my observation, in that amazing time) they had been about the house before they prevailed to fire it (which they did with Flax and Hemp, which they brought out of the Barn, and there being no defence about the House, only two Flankers[6] at two opposite corners and one of them not finished) they fired it once and one ventured out and quenched it, but they quickly fired it again, and that took. Now is the dreadfull hour come, that I have often heard of (in time of War, as it was the case of others) but now mine eyes see it. Some in our house were fighting for their lives, others wallowing in their blood, the House on fire over our heads, and the bloody Heathen ready to knock us on the head, if we stirred out. Now might we hear Mothers and Children crying out for themselves, and one another, Lord, What shall we do? Then I took my Children (and one of my sisters, hers) to go forth and leave the house: but as soon as we came to the dore and appeared, the Indians shot so thick that the bulletts rattled against the House, as if one had taken an handfull of stones and threw them, so that we were fain to give back. We had six stout Dogs belonging to our Garrison, but none of them would stir, though another time, if any Indian had come to the door, they were ready to fly upon him and tear him down. The Lord hereby would make us the more to acknowledge his hand, and to see that our help is always in him. But out we must go, the fire increasing, and coming along behind us, roaring, and the Indians gaping before us with their Guns, Spears and Hatchets to devour us. No sooner were we out of the House, but my Brother in Law[7] (being before wounded, in defending the house, in or near the throat) fell down dead, wherat the Indians scornfully shouted, and hallowed, and were presently upon him, stripping off his cloaths, the bullets flying thick, one went through my side, and the same (as would seem) through the bowels and hand of my dear Child in my arms. One of my elder Sisters Children, named William,[8] had then his Leg broken, which the Indians perceiving, they knockt him on head. Thus were we butchered by those merciless Heathen, standing amazed, with the blood running down to our heels. My eldest Sister being yet in the House, and seeing those wofull sights, the Infidels haling Mothers one way, and Children another, and some wallowing in their blood: and her elder Son telling her that her Son William was dead, and my self was wounded, she said, And, Lord, let me dy with them; which was no sooner said, but she was struck with a Bullet, and fell down dead over the threshold. I hope she is reaping the fruit of her good labours, being faithfull to the service of God in her place. In her younger years she lay under much trouble upon spiritual accounts, till it pleased God to make that precious Scripture take hold of her heart, 2 Cor. 12.9. *And he said unto me, my Grace is sufficient for thee.* More then twenty years after I have heard her tell how sweet and comfortable that place was to her. But to return: The Indians laid hold of us, pulling me one way, and the Children another, and said, Come go along with us; I told them they would kill me: they answered, If I were willing to go along with them, they would not hurt me.

Oh the dolefull sight that now was to behold at this House! *Come, behold the works of the Lord, what dissolations he has made in the Earth.*[9] Of thirty seven persons who were in this one House, none escaped either present death, or a bitter captivity, save only one,[10] who might say as he, Job 1. 15, *And I only am escaped alone to tell the News.* There were twelve killed, some shot, some stab'd with their Spears, some knock'd down with their Hatchets. When we are in prosperity, Oh the little that we think of such dreadfull sights, and to see our dear Friends, and Relations ly bleeding out their heart-blood upon the ground. There was one who was chopt into the head with a Hatchet, and stript naked, and yet was crawling up and down. It is a solemn sight to see so many Christians lying in their blood, some here, and some there, like a company of Sheep torn by Wolves, All of them stript naked by a company of hell-hounds, roaring, singing, ranting and insulting, as if they would have torn our very hearts out; yet the Lord by his Almighty power preserved a number of us from death, for there were twenty-four of us taken alive and carried Captive.

I had often before this said, that if the Indians should come, I should chuse rather to be killed by them then taken alive but when it came to the tryal my mind changed; their glittering weapons so daunted my spirit, that I chose rather to go along with those (as I may say) ravenous Beasts, then that moment to end my dayes; and that I may the better declare what happened to me during that grievous Captivity, I shall particularly speak of the severall Removes we had up and down the Wilderness. . . .

Before I knew what affliction meant, I was ready sometimes to wish for it. When I lived in prosperity, having the comforts of the World about me, my relations by me, my Heart chearfull, and taking little care for any thing; and yet seeing many, whom I preferred before my self, under many tryals and afflictions, in sickness, weakness, poverty, losses, crosses, and cares of the World, I should be sometimes jealous least I should have my portion in this life, and that Scripture would come to my mind, Heb. 12.6. *For whom the Lord loveth he chasteneth, and scourgeth every Son whom he receiveth.* But now I see the Lord had his time to scourge and chasten me. The portion of some is to have their afflictions by drops, now one drop and then another; but the dregs of the Cup, the Wine of astonishment, like a sweeping rain that leaveth no food, did the Lord prepare to be my portion. Affliction I wanted, and affliction I had, full measure (I thought) pressed down and running over; yet I see, when God calls a Person to any thing, and through never so many difficulties, yet he is fully able to carry them through and make them see, and say they have been gainers thereby. And I hope I can say in some measure, As David did, *It is good for me that I have been afflicted.* The Lord hath shewed me the vanity of these outward things. That they are the Vanity of vanities, and vexation of spirit; that they are but a shadow, a blast, a bubble, and things of no continuance. That we must rely on God himself, and our whole dependance must be upon him. If trouble from smaller matters begin to arise in me, I have something at hand to check my self with, and say, why am I troubled? It was but the other day that if I had had the world, I would have given it for my freedom, or to have been a Servant to a Christian. I have learned to look beyond present and smaller troubles, and to be quieted under them, as Moses said, Exod. 14.13. *Stand still and see the salvation of the Lord.*

Finis.

Notes

1 Title-page of the original.
2 Thursday, February 10, 1675/6.
3 The houses mentioned were those of John White, Thomas Sawyer, John Prescott, and the Rowlandson and Wheeler garrisons. The site of the Rowlandson garrison is indicated on a picture in Ellis and Morris, *King Philip's War* (New York, 1906), opposite p. 171.
4 The family of John Ball, the tailor.
5 The garrison of Richard Wheeler, on the southern side of George Hill.
6 Flankers were projections from which blank walls (curtains) could be enfiladed.
7 John Divoll had married Hannah, the youngest sister of Mrs. Rowlandson.

8 William Kerley was the son of Mrs. Rowlandson's sister Elizabeth White, who had married Henry Kerley.
9 Psalm xlvi.8.
10 The person escaping was Ephraim Roper. The size of the garrison as given by contemporary writers varies from 37 to 55, of whom three Kettle children escaped in some way unknown to Mrs. Rowlandson.

2. "... religious tracts belonged only in a very marginal sense, I believe, to the chapbook tradition," Neuberg writes (p.20). Other scholars are more inclined to believe otherwise. One such scholar is religious historian David Hall, who in *Worlds of Wonder, Days of Judgment: Popular Religious Belief in Early New England*, describes a series of such books published in the 1650s with titles like *The Dreadful Character of a Drunkard*, *The Devil's Disease*, and *Morbus Satanicus*. Yet Hall himself notes that many clergymen felt ambivalent at best about chapbooks such as these. Do you have any idea why they might object to detailed examinations of drinking, infidelity, or devil-worship? Can you think of parallel examples in, say, the topics of songs by your favorite musicians?

3. Confronting a shortage of source material, scholars must sometimes resort to unusual – even ingenious – ways of understanding the past. (Archeologists of colonial America, for example, sometimes have used discarded tobacco pipes, whose width varied over time, as a means of dating historical sites.) Much of what Neuberg learned about chapbooks came from sources other than the books themselves – advertisements, shipping records, wills. Imagine, for a moment, that you are living 400 years in the future and wished to gain knowledge about, say, websites that have long since vanished into thin air. What kinds of strategies would you use?

4. Neuberg ends his piece by citing the popularity of Dick Whittington chapbooks. (The cover of one such chapbook opens this chapter.) The real Richard Whittington was the son of a medieval knight who became a merchant selling clothes and velvets. In 1397, 1406, and 1419, he was elected lord mayor of London. Whittington was wealthy enough to lend money to the English kings Richard II, Henry IV, and Henry V, and upon his death in 1423 left his estate to charity (some funds were used for rebuilding a prison and the establishment of a college in his name).

A somewhat different Richard Whittington – actually, a series of different Whittingtons – inhabit the pages of chapbooks. In one common version (Dick) Whittington is a poor boy who goes to work as a dishwasher in London. Tired of abusive treatment, he is about to leave the city, but hears church bells that seem to say "Turn again, Whittington, Lord Mayor of London." Dick returns to work, but sends his cat aboard a ship, where it kills so many rats that Whittington is able to sell it for a small fortune to an African prince. Dick marries and lives happily ever after, attaining his prophesied post of mayor.

Why might the story of Richard Whittington – fabled as well as factual – resonate with colonial American readers? Neuberg names Horatio Alger as Whittington's spiritual heir. Can you think of others?

Suggested Further Reading

Neuberg's piece can be read in its entirety – along with a number of other intriguing pieces on the print culture of the early American history – in *Reading in America: Literature and Social History*, edited by Cathy N. Davidson (Baltimore: The Johns Hopkins University Press, 1989). Neuberg is also the author of *The Penny Histories: A Study of Chapbooks Over Two Centuries for Young Readers* (New York: Harcourt, Brace & World, 1968). David Hall takes up the subject of chapbooks in the first chapter of *Worlds of Wonder and Days of Judgment: Popular Religious Belief in Early New England* (Cambridge: Harvard University Press, 1996) and *Cultures of Print: Essays in the History of the Book* (Amherst: University of Massachusetts Press, 1996). See also *The Other Print Tradition: Essays on Chapbooks, Broadsides, and Related Ephemera*, edited by Cathy Lynn Preston and Michael J. Preston (New York: Garland, 1995).

2
The World of the Stage

Introduction

Puritan New England may have been the center of print culture in American life, but the primary energy for another major form of early popular culture, theatrical entertainment, came from elsewhere. While religious leaders across the colonies took a very dim view of theater – "the synagogue of Satan," in the words of one minister – plays and other forms of live entertainment were popular, particularly among the elite classes, throughout the South and Middle Atlantic colonies. (New England finally gave up what was an increasingly rearguard action when a Massachusetts state law against theatricals was repealed in 1792.) Royall Tyler's popular 1787 play *The Contrast* – whose title referred to the difference between sturdy American republicans and effete British degenerates – typified the nationalist spirit that animated the quest for a native cultural idiom in the infant United States. In the decades following the Revolution, a number of high-minded reformers in the nineteenth century went so far to suggest that plays could be an instrument for the civic reform and edification of the lower classes, particularly those in rapidly growing cities.

Those classes, however, had other ideas. After the War of 1812, a period coinciding with Andrew Jackson's rise to power, a new theatrical culture took root in the United States. Unmoored from the social and familial traditions of the countryside, a mobile urban population turned to live entertainment as a release from the ravages of wage-earning labor. Playhouses were built to accommodate this new audience, and priced themselves to maximize profits. New York City's Park Theatre, which opened in the late eighteenth century, charged between $1 and $2 for one of its 300 seats; its replacement, completed in 1821, was over eight times larger and charged between $37\frac{1}{2}$ and 75 cents. The new Park, in turn, was expensive compared to the 4,000-seat Bowery Theatre, which opened in 1826. Then, as now, New York was the center of the theatrical world, but its reach was literally continental, and surfaced in some surprising outposts.

Also surprising was the entertainment these people came to see. Some kinds – notably minstrel acts, where white actors comically masqueraded as African Americans – would be considered offensive now. Others, like opera, are now so thoroughly identified with elite culture that it seems almost laughable to imagine mechanics and factory workers humming Mozart or Verdi. (The 1850 American tour of Swedish opera star Jenny Lind, which was promoted by the famed impresario P. T. Barnum, caused mass hysteria comparable to the hype surrounding contemporary pop singers.)

In a similar vein, twenty-first-century Americans are likely to regard playwright William Shakespeare as a towering – but somewhat remote – cultural figure. But as the eminent cultural historian Lawrence Levine explains in this excerpt from his 1988 book *Highbrow/Lowbrow: The Emergence of Cultural Hierarchy in America*, nineteenth-century Americans knew the Bard on a much more familiar basis – and were not afraid to "improve" him for their own purposes. For Levine, the popularity of Shakespeare in the antebellum era is not only, or even primarily, testimony to the playwright's remarkably enduring appeal. It is also a revealing window into American cultural history: who we were, who we are, and what we have gained – and lost – in becoming a society whose art has become much more ordered and segmented than it used to be.

William Shakespeare in America

Lawrence Levine

Mark Twain's treatment of Shakespeare in his novel *Huckleberry Finn* helps us place the Elizabethan playwright in nineteenth-century American culture. Shortly after the two rogues, who pass themselves off as a duke and a king, invade the raft of Huck and Jim, they decide to raise funds by performing scenes from Shakespeare's *Romeo and Juliet* and *Richard III*. That the presentation of Shakespeare in small Mississippi River towns could be conceived of as potentially lucrative tells us much about the position of Shakespeare in the nineteenth century. The specific nature of Twain's humor tells us even more. Realizing that they would need material for encores, the "duke" starts to teach the "king" Hamlet's soliloquy, which he recites from memory:

> To be, or not to be; that is the bare bodkin
> That makes calamity of so long life;
> For who would fardels bear, till Birnam Wood
>   do come to Dunsinane,
> But that the fear of something after death
> Murders the innocent sleep,
> Great nature's second course,
> And makes us rather sling arrows of outrageous fortune
> Than fly to others that we know not of...[1]

Twain's humor relies on his audience's familiarity with *Hamlet* and its ability to recognize the duke's improbable coupling of lines from a variety of Shakespeare's plays. Twain was employing one of the most popular forms of humor in nineteenth-century America. Everywhere in the nation burlesques and parodies of Shakespeare constituted a prominent form of entertainment.

Hamlet was a favorite target in numerous travesties imported from England or crafted at home. Audiences roared at the sight of Hamlet dressed in fur cap and collar, snowshoes and mittens; they listened with amused surprise to his profanity when ordered by his father's ghost to "swear" and to his commanding Ophelia, "Get thee to a brewery"; they

Reprinted by permission of the Publisher from *Highbrow/Lowbrow: The Emergence of Cultural Hierarchy in America* by Lawrence Levine, Cambridge, Mass.: Harvard University Press. Copyright © 1988 by the President and Fellows of Harvard College.

Wild about Bill   "Great Riot at Astor Place," a lithograph by Nathaniel Currier, ca.1850. The immediate cause of the riot, which took place in May of 1849, involved a controversy between celebrated American and English actors over the proper portrayal of the lead in William Shakespeare's *Macbeth*. Currier, with his partner J. Merritt Ives, formed the core of the tremendously successful lithographic publishing firm of Currier & Ives, whose celebrated prints documented American life for much of the nineteenth century. *Photo from the Collection of the New-York Historical Society*

heard him recite his lines in black dialect or Irish brogue and sing his most famous soliloquy, "To be, or not to be," to the tune of "Three Blind Mice." In the 1820s the British comedian Charles Mathews visited what he called the "Nigger's (or Negroe's) theatre" in New York, where he heard "a black tragedian in the character of Hamlet" recite "To be, or not to be? That is the question; whether it is nobler in *de* mind to suffer, or tak' up arms against a sea of trouble, and by *opossum* end 'em." "No sooner was the word *opossum* out of his mouth," Mathews reported, "than the audience burst forth, in one general cry, '*Opossum! opossum! opossum!*'" – prompting the actor to come forward and sing the popular dialect song "Opossum up a Gum Tree". On the nineteenth-century American stage, audiences often heard Hamlet's lines intricately combined with those of a popular song:

> Oh! 'tis consummation
> Devoutly to be wished

To end your heart-ache by a sleep,
When likely to be dish'd.
Shuffle off your mortal coil,
Do just so,
Wheel about, and turn about,
And jump Jim Crow.[2]

No Shakespearean play was immune to this sort of mutilation. *The Comedy of Errors* was performed as *Ye Comedie of Errours, a Glorious, Uproarous Burlesque. Not Indecorous nor Censorous, with Many a Chorus, Warranted Not to Bore Us, now for the First Time Set before Us*. *Richard III*, the most popular Shakespearean play in the nineteenth century, was lampooned frequently in such versions as *Bad Dicky*. In one New York production starring first-rank Shakespearean actors, a stuttering, lisping Othello danced while Desdemona played the banjo and Iago, complete with Irish brogue, ended their revelries with a fire hose. The comedic form made it possible to touch upon extremely sensitive issues. In a southern parody of *Othello*, for example, Othello and Desdemona were allowed to sing together, "Dey say dat in the dark all cullers am de same." In Kenneth Bangs's version of *The Taming of the Shrew*, Kate ended up in control, observing that, although "Shakespeare or Bacon, or whoever wrote the play . . . studied deeply the shrews of his day . . . the modern shrew isn't built that way," while a chastened Petruchio concluded, "Sweet Katharine, of your remarks I recognize the force: / Don't strive to tame a woman as you would a horse." Serious or slapstick, the punning was endless. In one parody of the famous dagger scene, Macbeth continues to put off his insistent wife by asking, "Or is that dagger but a false Daguerreotype?" Luckily, Desdemona had no brother, or Othello "might look black and blue," a character in *Othello* remarked, while one in *The Merchant of Venice* observed of Shylock, "This crafty Jew is full of *Jeux d'esprit!*" Throughout the century, there was an impressive number of parodies with such titles as *Julius Sneezer, Roamy-E-Owe and Julie-Ate, Hamlet and Egglet, Desdemonum*, and *Much Ado about a Merchant of Venice*.[3]

These full-fledged travesties reveal only part of the story. Nineteenth-century Shakespearean parody most frequently took the form of short skits, brief references, and satirical songs inserted into other modes of entertainment. In one of their routines, for example, the Bryant's Minstrels playfully referred to the famous observation in Act II of *Romeo and Juliet*:

Adolphus Pompey is my name,
But that don't make no difference,
For as Massa Wm. Shakespeare says,
A name's of no significance.

The minstrels loved to invoke Shakespeare as an authority: "you know what de Bird of Avon says 'bout 'De black scandal an' de foul faced reproach!'" And they constantly quoted him in appropriately garbled form: "Fust to dine own self be true, an' it must follow night and day, dou den can be false to any man." The significance of this national penchant for parodying Shakespeare is clear: Shakespeare and his drama had become by the nineteenth century an integral part of American culture. It is difficult to take familiarities with that which is not already familiar; one cannot parody that which is not well known. The minstrels' characteristic conundrums would not have been funny to an audience lacking knowledge of Shakespeare's works:

> When was Desdemona like a ship?
> When she was Moored.[4]

It is not surprising that educated Americans in the eighteenth and nineteenth centuries knew their Shakespeare so well that John Quincy Adams, who was born in 1767, could write, "at ten years of age I was as familiarly acquainted with his lovers and his clowns, as with Robinson Crusoe, the Pilgrim's Progress, and the Bible. In later years I have left Robinson and the Pilgrim to the perusal of the children; but have continued to read the Bible and Shakespeare." What is more interesting is how widely Shakespeare was known to the public in general. In the last half of the eighteenth century, when the reading of Shakespeare's plays was still confined to a relatively small, educated elite, substantial numbers of Americans had the chance to see his plays performed. From the first documented American performance of a Shakespearean play in 1750 until the closing of the theaters during the American Revolution*, Shakespeare emerged as the most popular playwright in the colonies. Fourteen to fifteen of his plays were presented at least one hundred and eighty – and one scholar has estimated perhaps as many as five hundred – times. Following the Revolution, Shakespeare retained his position as the most widely performed dramatist, with five more of his plays regularly performed in an increasing number of cities and towns.[5]

Not until the nineteenth century, however, did Shakespeare come into his own – presented and recognized almost everywhere in the country. In the cities of the Northeast and Southeast, Shakespeare's plays

---

* In 1774 the Continental Congress discountenanced and discouraged "every Species of Extravagance and Dissipation, especially all Horse Racing, and all Kinds of Gaming, Cock Fighting, Exhibitions of Shews, Plays, and other expensive Diversions and Entertainments."

dominated the theater. During the 1810–11 season in Philadelphia, for example, Shakespearean plays accounted for twenty-two of eighty-eight performances. The following season lasted one hundred and eight nights, of which again one-quarter – twenty-seven – were devoted to Shakespeare. From 1800 to 1835, Philadelphians had the opportunity to see twenty-one of Shakespeare's thirty-seven plays. The Philadelphia theater was not exceptional; one student of the American stage concluded that in cities on the Eastern Seaboard at least one-fifth of all plays offered in a season were likely to be by Shakespeare. George Makepeace Towle, an American consul in England, returned to his own country just after the Civil War and remarked with some surprise, "Shakespearian dramas are more frequently played and more popular in America than in England." Shakespeare's dominance can be attested to by what Charles Shattuck has called "the westward flow of Shakespearean actors" from England to America. In the nineteenth century, one prominent English Shakespearean actor after another – George Frederick Cooke, Edmund Kean, Junius Brutus Booth, Charles Kemble, Fanny Kemble, Ellen Tree, William Charles Macready – sought the fame and financial rewards that awaited them in their tours of the United States.[6]

It is important to understand that their journey did not end with big cities or the Eastern Seaboard. According to John Bernard, the English actor and comedian who worked in the United States from 1797 to 1819, "If an actor were unemployed, want and shame were not before him: he had merely to visit some town in the interior where no theatre existed, but 'readings' were permitted; and giving a few recitations from Shakespeare and Sterne, his pockets in a night or two were amply replenished." During his travels through the United States in the 1830s, Tocqueville found Shakespeare in "the recesses of the forests of the New World," and observed, "There is hardly a pioneer's hut that does not contain a few odd volumes of Shakespeare. I remember that I read the feudal drama of *Henry V* for the first time in a log cabin." Five decades later, the German visitor Karl Knortz made a similar observation:

> There is, assuredly, no other country on earth in which Shakespeare and the Bible are held in such general high esteem as in America, the very country so much decried for its lust for money. If you were to enter an isolated log cabin in the Far West and even if its inhabitant were to exhibit many of the traces of backwoods living, he will most likely have one small room nicely furnished in which to spend his few leisure hours and in which you will certainly find the Bible and in most cases also some cheap edition of the works of the poet Shakespeare.

Even if we discount the hyperbole evident in such accounts, they were far from inventions. The ability of the illiterate Rocky Mountain scout

Jim Bridger to recite long passages from Shakespeare, which he had learned by hiring someone to read the plays to him, and the formative influence that the plays had upon young Abe Lincoln growing up in Salem, Illinois, became part of the nation's folklore.[7]

But if books had become a more important vehicle for disseminating Shakespeare by the nineteenth century, the stage remained the primary instrument. The theater, like the church, was one of the earliest and most important cultural institutions established in frontier cities. And almost everywhere the theater blossomed Shakespeare was a paramount force. In his investigation of the theater in Louisville, Cincinnati, St. Louis, Detroit, and Lexington, Kentucky, from 1800 to 1840, Ralph Leslie Rusk concluded that Shakespeare's plays were performed more frequently than those of any other author. Chicago, with slightly more than four thousand inhabitants, was barely incorporated in 1837 when productions of *Richard III* were being given in a theater improvised in the dining room of the deserted Sauganash Hotel. In Mississippi between 1814 and the outbreak of the Civil War, the towns of Natchez and Vicksburg, with only a few thousand inhabitants each, put on at least one hundred and fifty performances of Shakespeare featuring such British and American stars as Ellen Tree, Edwin Forrest, Junius Brutus Booth, J. W. Walleck, Charles Kean, J. H. Hackett, Josephine Clifton, and T. A. Cooper. Stars of this and lesser caliber made their way into the interior by boat, along the Ohio and Mississippi rivers, stopping at towns and cities on their way to New Orleans. Beginning in the early 1830s, the rivers themselves became the site of Shakespearean productions, with floating theaters in the form first of flatboats and then of steamboats bringing drama to small river towns.[8]

By mid-century, Shakespeare was taken across the Great Plains and over the Rocky Mountains and soon became a staple of theaters in the Far West. During the decade following the arrival of the Forty-niners, at least twenty-two of Shakespeare's plays were performed on California stages, with *Richard III* retaining the predominance it had gained in the East and South. In 1850 the Jenny Lind Theatre, seating two thousand, opened over a saloon in San Francisco and was continuously crowded: "Miners ... swarmed from the gambling saloons and cheap fandango houses to see *Hamlet* and *Lear.*" In 1852 the British star Junius Brutus Booth and two of his sons played *Hamlet, Macbeth, Othello*, and *Richard III* from the stage of the Jenny Lind and packed the house for the two weeks of their stay. In 1856 Laura Keen brought San Franciscans not only old favorites but such relatively uncommon productions as *Coriolanus* and *A Midsummer Night's Dream*. Along with such eminent stars from abroad, American actors like McKean Buchanan and James Stark kept the hunger for Shakespeare satisfied.[9]

But Shakespeare could not be confined to the major population centers in the Far West any more than he had been in the East. If miners could not always come to San Francisco to see theater, the theater came to them. Stark, Buchanan, Edwin Booth, and their peers performed on makeshift stages in mining camps around Sacramento and crossed the border into Nevada, where they brought characterizations of Hamlet, Iago, Macbeth, Kate, Lear, and Othello to miners in Virginia City, Silver City, Dayton, and Carson City. Walter M. Leman recalled the dearth of theaters in such California towns as Tod's Valley, Chip's Flat, Cherokee Flat, Rattlesnake, Mud Springs, Red Dog, Hangtown, Drytown, and Fiddletown, which he toured in the 1850s. In the Sierra town of Downieville, Leman performed *Richard III* on the second story of a cloth and paper house in a hall without a stage: "We had to improvise one out of the two billiard tables it contained, covering them with boards for that purpose." Such conditions were by no means confined to the West Coast. In earlier years, Leman had toured the Maine towns of Bangor, Belfast, Orono, and Oldtown, not one of which had a proper theater, necessitating the use of church vestries and other improvisations. In 1816 in Lexington, Kentucky, Noah Ludlow performed *The Taming of the Shrew*, *Othello*, and *The Merchant of Venice* in a room on the second floor of an old brewery, next door to a saloon, before an audience seated on backless, cushionless chairs. In the summer of 1833, Sol Smith's company performed in the dining room of a hotel in Tazewell, Alabama, "on a sort of landing-place or gallery about six feet long, and two and a half feet wide." His "heavy tragedian" Mr. Lyne attempted to recite the "Seven Ages of Man" from *As You Like It* while "persons were passing from one room to the other continually and the performer was obliged to *move* whenever any one passed."[10]

Thus Shakespeare was by no means automatically treated with reverence. Nor was he accorded universal acclaim. In Davenport and neighboring areas of eastern Iowa, where the theater flourished in both English and German, Shakespeare was seldom performed and then usually in the form of short scenes and soliloquies rather than entire plays. As more than one theater manager learned, producing Shakespeare did not necessarily result in profits. Theatrical lore often repeated the vow attributed to Robert L. Place that he would never again produce a play by Shakespeare "no matter how many more he wrote." But these and similar incidents were exceptions to the general rule: from the large and often opulent theaters of major cities to the makeshift stages in halls, saloons, and churches of small towns and mining camps, wherever there was an audience for the theater, there Shakespeare's plays were performed prominently and frequently.[11] Shakespeare's popularity in frontier communities in all sections of the country may not fit Frederick

Jackson Turner's image of the frontier as a crucible, melting civilization down into a new amalgam, but it does fit our knowledge of human beings and their need for the comfort of familiar things under the pressure of new circumstances and surroundings. James Fenimore Cooper had this familiarity in mind when he called Shakespeare "the great author of America" and insisted that Americans had "just as good a right" as Englishmen to claim Shakespeare as their countryman. At the dedication of Shakespeare's statue in Central Park in 1872, his familiarity to Americans was taken for granted. "Old World, he is not only thine," the inscription on the temporary pedestal proclaimed, and Bayard Taylor, in his commemorative poem, declared:

> He came, a household ghost we could not ban:
> He sat, on Winter nights, by cabin-fires;
> ....
> He preached within the shadow of our spires;
> ...and became
> The Master of our Thought, the Land's first Citizen![12]

Shakespeare's popularity can be determined not only by the frequency of Shakespearean productions and the size of the audiences for them but also by the nature of the productions and the manner in which they were presented. Shakespeare was performed not merely alongside popular entertainment as an elite supplement to it; Shakespeare was performed as an integral part of it. Shakespeare *was* popular entertainment in nineteenth-century America. The theater in the first half of the nineteenth century played the role that movies played in the first half of the twentieth: it was a kaleidoscopic, democratic institution presenting a widely varying bill of fare to all classes and socioeconomic groups.

During the first two-thirds of the nineteenth century, the play may have been the thing, but it was not the only thing. It was the centerpiece, the main attraction, but an entire evening generally consisted of a long play, an afterpiece (usually a farce), and a variety of between-act specialties. In the spring of 1839, a playbill advertising the appearance of William Evans Burton in *As You Like It* at Philadelphia's American Theater announced, "Il Diavolo Antonio And His Sons, Antonio, Lorenzo, Augustus And Alphonzo will present a most magnificent display of position in the Science of Gymnastics, portraying some of the most grand and imposing groups from the ancient masters ... to conclude with a grand Horizontal Pyramid." It was a characteristically full evening. In addition to gymnastics and Shakespeare, "Mr. Quayle (by Desire)" sang "The Swiss Drover Boy," La Petite Celeste danced "a New Grand Pas Seul," Miss Lee danced "La Cachuca," Mr. Quayle returned to sing "The Haunted Spring," Mr Bowman told a "Yankee Story," and "the Whole" concluded "with *Ella Rosenberg* starring Mrs. Hield."[13]

Thus Shakespeare was presented amid a full range of contemporary entertainment. During the Mexican War, a New Orleans performance of *Richard III* was accompanied by "a new and ORIGINAL Patriotic Drama in 3 Acts . . . (founded in part on events which have occurred during the Mexican War,) & called: Palo Alto! Or, Our Army on the Rio Grande! . . . TRIUMPH OF AMERICAN ARMS! Surrender of Gen. Vega to Capt. May! Grand Military Tableau!" It would be a mistake to conclude that Shakespeare was presented as the dry, staid ingredient in this exciting menu. On the contrary, Shakespearean plays were often announced as spectacles in their own right. In 1799 the citizens of Alexandria, Virginia, were promised the following in a production of *Macbeth*: "In Act 3d – A Regal Banquet in which the Ghost of Banquo appears. In Act 4th – A Solemn incantation & dance of Witches. In Act 5th – A grand Battle, with the defeat & death of Macbeth." At mid-century, a presentation of *Henry IV* in Philadelphia featured the "Army of Falstaff on the March! . . . Battlefield, Near Shrewsbury, Occupying the entire extent of the Stage, Alarms! Grand Battle! Single Combat! DEATH OF HOTSPUR! FINALE – Grand Tableau."[14]

Shakespeare's position as part and parcel of popular culture was reinforced by the willingness of Shakespearean actors to take part in the concluding farce. Thus Mr. Parsons followed such roles as Coriolanus, Othello, Macbeth, and Lear by playing Ralph Stackpole, "A Ring-Tailed Squealer & Rip-Staver from Salt River," in *Nick of the Woods*. Even Junius Brutus Booth followed his celebrated portrayal of Richard III with the role of Jerry Sneak in *The Mayor of Garrat*. In the postbellum years Edward L. Davenport referred to this very ability and willingness to mix genres when he lamented the decline of his profession: "Why, I've played an act from *Hamlet*, one from *Black-Eyed Susan*, and sung 'A Yankee Ship and a Yankee Crew' and danced a hornpipe, and wound up with a 'nigger' part, all in one night. Is there any one you know of today who can do that?" It is clear that, as much as Shakespearean roles were prized by actors, they were not exalted; they did not unfit one for other roles and other tasks; they were not elevated to a position above the culture in which they appeared. Although David Garrick's *Catherine and Petruchio*, a condensation of *The Taming of the Shrew*, or his *Shakespeare's Jubilee*, consisting of scenes from a number of Shakespeare's plays concluding with a grand procession, were popular afterpieces, more frequently the final word of the evening was not Shakespeare's. *Hamlet* might be followed by such farces as *Fortune's Frolic* and *The Sultan; or, A Peep Into the Seraglio*, *The Merchant of Venice* by *The Lottery Ticket*,

Richard III by *The Green Mountain Boy*, *King Lear* by *Chaos Is Come Again* on one occasion and by *Love's Laughs at Locksmiths; or, The Guardian Outwitted* on another, and, in California, *Romeo and Juliet* by *Did You Ever Send Your Wife to San Jose?*[15]

These afterpieces and *divertissements* most often are seen as having diluted or denigrated Shakespeare. I suggest that they may be understood more meaningfully as having *integrated* him into American culture. Shakespeare was presented as part of the same milieu inhabited by magicians, dancers, singers, acrobats, minstrels, and comics. He appeared on the same playbills and was advertised in the same spirit. This does not mean that theatergoers were unable to make distinctions between Shakespearean productions and the accompanying entertainment. Of course they were. Shakespeare, after all, was what most of them came to see. But it was a Shakespeare presented as part of the culture they enjoyed, a Shakespeare rendered familiar and intimate by virtue of his context.

In 1843 the curtain of the rebuilt St. Charles Theatre in New Orleans featured an arresting bit of symbolism: it depicted Shakespeare in a halo of light being borne aloft on the wings of the American eagle. Shakespeare was not only domesticated; he was humanized. Henry Norman Hudson, the period's most popular Shakespearean lecturer, hailed Shakespeare as "the prodigy of our race" but also stressed his decency, his humility, his "true gentleness and lowliness of heart" and concluded that "he who looks the highest will always bow the lowest." In his melodrama *Shakespeare in Love*, Richard Penn Smith pictured the poet not as an awesome symbol of culture but as a poor, worried, stumbling young man in love with a woman of whose feelings he is not yet certain. In the end, of course, he triumphs and proclaims his joy in words that identify him as a well-rounded human being to whom one can relate: "I am indeed happy. A poet, a lover, the husband of the woman I adore. What is there more for me to desire?" Nineteenth-century America swallowed Shakespeare, digested him and his plays, and made them part of the cultural body. The nature of his reception by nineteenth-century audiences confirms this conclusion.[16]

While he was performing in Natchez, Mississippi, in 1835, the Irish actor Tyrone Power observed people on the road hurrying to the theater. Their fine horses, ornate and often antique saddles, and picturesque clothing transported him back to Elizabethan England and "the palmy days of the Globe and Bear-garden." Power's insight was sound; there *were* significant similarities between the audiences of Shakespeare's own day and those he drew in America. One of Shakespeare's contemporaries commented that the theater was "frequented by all sorts of people old and younge, rich and poore, masters and servants, papists and puritans, wise men etc., churchmen and statesmen." The nineteenth-century American audience was equally heterogeneous. In both eras the various classes saw the same plays in the same theaters – though not necessarily from the same vantage point. Until mid-century, at least, American theaters generally had a tripartite seating arrangement: the pit (orchestra), the boxes, and the gallery (balcony). Although theater prices fell substantially from 1800 to 1850, seating arrangements continued to dovetail with class and economic divisions. In the boxes sat, as one spectator put it, "the dandies, and people of the first respectability and fashion." The gallery was inhabited largely by those (apprentices, servants, poor workingmen) who could not afford better seats or by those (Negroes and often prostitutes) who were not allowed to sit elsewhere.* The pit was dominated by what were rather vaguely called the "middling classes" – a "mixed multitude" that some contemporaries praised as the "honest folks" or "the sterling part of the audience."[17]

All observers agree that the nineteenth-century theater housed under one roof a microcosm of American society. This, the actor Joseph Jefferson maintained, was what made drama a more difficult art than painting, music, or writing, which "have a direct following, generally from a class whose taste and understanding are pretty evenly balanced, – whereas a theater is divided into three and sometimes four classes." And all of those classes had to be addressed, as Jefferson also noted: "There must be no vagueness in acting. The suggestion should be unmistakable; it must be hurled at the whole audience, and reach with unerring aim the boys in the gallery and the statesmen in the stalls." Walt Whitman warmly recalled the Bowery Theatre around the year 1840, where he could look up to the first tier of boxes and see "the faces of the leading authors, poets, editors, of those times," while he sat in the pit surrounded by the "slang, wit, occasional shirt sleeves, and a picturesque freedom of looks and manners, with a rude, good-nature and restless movement" of cartmen, butchers, firemen, and mechanics. Others spoke of the mixed audience with less enthusiasm. Washington Irving wrote a series of letters to the *New York Morning Chronicle* in 1802 and 1803 describing his theater experiences. The noise in the gallery he found "is somewhat similar to that which prevailed in Noah's Ark; for we have an imitation of the whistles and yells of every kind of animal." When the "gallery gods" were roused for one reason or another, "they commenced a discharge of apples, nuts & ginger-bread, on the heads of

---

* The *Daily Picayune* in New Orleans commented on March 14, 1844, "The playgoing portion of our negro population feel more interest in, and go in greater numbers to see, the plays of Shakespeare represented on the stage, than any other class of dramatic performance."

the honest folks in the pit." Throughout the evening there was a chorus of "coughing and sneezing... *whistling and thumping*... The crackling of nuts and the craunching of apples saluted my ears on every side."[18]

Little had changed by 1832 when the English visitor Frances Trollope attended the theater in several American cities. In Cincinnati she observed coatless men with their sleeves rolled up, incessantly spitting, reeking "of onions and whiskey." She enjoyed the Shakespeare but abhorred the "perpetual" noises: "The applause is expressed by cries and thumping with the feet, instead of clapping; and when a patriotic fit seized them, and 'Yankee Doodle' was called for, every man seemed to think his reputation as a citizen depended on the noise he made." Things were no better in Philadelphia and, if anything, worse in New York theaters, where she witnessed "a lady performing the most maternal office possible... and a general air of contempt for the decencies of life." When he published his reminiscences in 1836, Tyrone Power tried to counter such accounts by praising the attentiveness and intelligence of his American audiences, but it appears that what differed was less the audience than Power's tolerance for it. For instance, in hailing the "degree of repose and gentility of demeanour" of the audience he performed for in New Orleans in 1835, he wrote:

> The least prolonged tumult of approbation even is stilled by a word to order: and when it is considered that here are assembled the wildest and rudest specimens of the Western population, men owning no control except the laws, and not viewing these over submissively, and who admit of no *arbiter elegantiarum* or standard of fine breeding, it confers infinite credit on their innate good feeling, and that sense of propriety which here forms the sole check on their naturally somewhat uproarious jollity.[19]

Evidence of this sort makes it clear that an understanding of the American theater in our own time is not adequate grounding for a comprehension of American theater in the nineteenth century. To envision nineteenth-century theater audiences correctly, one might do well to visit a contemporary sporting event in which the spectators not only are similarly heterogeneous but are also – in the manner of both the nineteenth century and the Elizabethan era – more than an audience; they are participants who can enter into the action on the field, who feel a sense of immediacy and at times even of control, who articulate their opinions and feelings vocally and unmistakably. Washington Irving wryly observed, "The good folks of the gallery have all the trouble of ordering the music." When the orchestra's selection displeased them, they stamped, hissed, roared, whistled, and groaned in cadence until the musicians played "*Moll in the wad, Tally ho the grinders,* and several other *airs* more suited to their tastes." In 1833 the *New York Mirror* reported that during a recent evening at the American Theatre the audience was unhappy with the overture, loudly called for "Yankee Doodle," "and its melting tones forthwith breathed forth in mellifluous harmony. The pit were gratified, and evinced their satisfaction by a gentle roar." The audience's vociferousness continued during the play itself, which was punctuated by expressions of disapproval in the form of hisses or groans and of approval in the form of applause, whistles, and stamping to the point that a Virginia editor felt called upon to remind his readers in 1829 that it was not "a duty to applaud at the conclusion of every sentence." A French reporter, attending a production of Shakespeare in California in 1851, was fascinated by the audience's enthusiasm: "The more they like a play, the louder they whistle, and when a San Francisco audience bursts into shrill whistles and savage yells, you may be sure they are in raptures of joy." Audiences frequently demanded – and got – instant encores from performers who particularly pleased them. "Perhaps," a New York editor wrote sarcastically in 1846, "we'll flatter Mr. Kean by making him take poison twice." As late as the 1870s an observer reported that while "the fashionable portion of the audience" in a small northeastern manufacturing city watched quietly as a dramatic troupe led by the great Italian actor Tommaso Salvini presented a "spiritless, dragging" version of *Hamlet,*

> the gallery made up in good humor and liveliness whatever was lacking of those qualities on the part of the actors themselves. When the ghost of Hamlet's father rose majestic from the underworld and caught his mosquito-net in the trap-door, they cheered him through all his frantic efforts to jerk himself loose; they manifested their sympathy with Hamlet's psychological difficulties by the groans with which they accompanied the immortal soliloquy; ... and when, in the final act, the festal goblet was brought upon the stage, they called clamorously but good-naturedly upon the king to "set up the crowd."[20]

Like the Elizabethans, a substantial portion of nineteenth-century American audiences knew their Shakespeare well. Sol Smith reported that in 1839, when he wanted to put on an evening of acts from various Shakespearean plays in St. Louis, he had "no difficulty in finding Hamlets, Shylocks and Richards in abundance, very glad of the opportunity to exhibit their hidden powers." Constance Rourke has shown that as far west as California, from miners' camps to the galleries of urban theaters, there were many who knew large parts of the plays by heart. This knowledge easily became an instrument of control, as more than one hapless actor found out. In the winter of 1856 Hugh F. McDermott's depiction of Richard III did not meet the critical expectations of his

Sacramento audience. During the early scenes of Act I "a few carrots timidly thrown, had made their appearance," but the full ardor of the audience was roused only when Richard's killing of Henry included a thrust, *a posteriori,* after Henry had fallen." Then, the *Sacramento Daily Union* reported, "Cabbages, carrots, pumpkins, potatoes, a wreath of vegetables, a sack of flour and one of soot, and a dead goose, with other articles, simultaneously fell upon the stage." The barrage woke the dead Henry, who fled followed by Richard, "his head enveloped in a halo of vegetable glory." Pleas from the manager induced the audience to allow the play to go on – but not for long. In Act II, McDermott's inept wooing of Lady Anne again exhausted the patience of the audience. "When Richard placed the sword in her hand," a reporter observed, "one half the house, at least, asked that it might be plunged in his body." This storm of shouts was followed by a renewal of the vegetable shower accompanied this time by Chinese firecrackers. As poor Richard fled for the second time, "a well directed pumpkin caused him to stagger, and with still truer aim, a potato relieved him of his cap, which was left upon the field of glory, among the cabbages."[21]

Scenes like this account for the frequent assurance on playbills that "proper officers are appointed who will rigidly enforce decorum." Proper officers or not, such incidents were common enough to prompt a nineteenth-century gentleman to note in his diary, "The egg as a vehicle of dramatic criticism came into early use in this Continent." Despondency over the use of such critical "vehicles" by audiences in Philadelphia's Chestnut Street Theatre led the actor Richard Fullerton to drown himself in the Delaware River in the winter of 1802. "He was annoyed by anonymous and cutting criticisms," a contemporary observed, "and by contemptible hissing and other open demonstrations directed to him personally when on the stage." Here was literal proof of the continued validity of Samuel Johnson's prologue:

> The drama's laws,
> the drama's patrons give,
> For we that live to please,
> must please to live.

"The public," an American critic agreed in 1805, "in the final resort, govern the stage." It was of course a two-edged sword; the same California audiences capable of driving King Richard from the stage could pay homage to a performance they recognized as superior. Irish-born Matilda Heron's portrayal of Juliet on New Year's night 1854 "so fascinated and entranced" the "walnut-cracking holiday audience," according to the *San Francisco Chronicle,* that "they sat motionless and silent for

some moments after the scene was done; and then suddenly recovering themselves from the thraldom under which they had been placed, they came down in a shower of applause that shook the house."[22]
These frenetic displays of approval and disapproval were signs of engagement in what was happening on the stage – an engagement that on occasion could blur the line between audience and actors. At a performance of *Richard III* with Junius Brutus Booth at New York's Bowery Theatre in December 1832, the holiday audience was so large that some three hundred people overflowed onto the stage and entered into the spirit of things, the *New York Mirror* reported. They examined Richard's royal regalia with interest, hefted his sword, and tried on his crown; they moved up to get a close look at the ghosts of King Henry, Lady Anne, and the children when these characters appeared on stage; they mingled with the soldiers during the battle of Bosworth Field and responded to the roll of drums and blast of trumpets by racing across the stage. When Richard and Richmond began their fight, the audience "made a ring round the combatants to see fair play, and kept them at it for nearly a quarter of an hour by 'Shrewsbury's clock.' This was all done in perfect good humor, and with no intention to make a row." When Dan Rice came on to dance his famous Jim Crow, the on-stage audience made him repeat it some twenty times, "and in the afterpiece, where a supper-table [was] spread, some among the most hungry very leisurely helped themselves to the viands." Frequently, members of the audience became so involved in the action on stage that they interfered in order to dispense charity to the sick and destitute, advice to the indecisive, and, as one man did during a Baltimore production of *Coriolanus* and another during a New York production of *Othello*, protection to someone involved in an unfair fight. In a wonderful instance of how nineteenth-century American audiences tended to see drama as both reality and representation simultaneously, a canal boatman screamed at Iago in a production of *Othello* in Albany, New York, "You damned-lying scoundrel, I would like to get hold of you after the show and wring your infernal neck."[23]

Notes

1 Mark Twain, *The Adventures of Huckleberry Finn* (New York, 1884), 190.
2 Laurence Hutton, *Curiosities of the American Stage* (New York, 1891), 157, 181–6; Stanley Wells, ed., *Nineteenth-Century Shakespeare Burlesques*, V (London, 1978), xi–xii; Charles Mathews, *Trip to America* (Baltimore, 1824), 9, 25; Charles Haywood, "Negro Minstrelsy and Shakespearean Burlesque," in Bruce Jackson, ed., *Folklore and Society: Essays in Honor of Benj. A. Botkin* (Norwood, Pa., 1976), 88; and Ray B. Browne,

"Shakespeare in America: Vaudeville and Negro Minstrelsy," *American Quarterly*, 12 (Fall 1960), 381–2. For examples of parodies of *Hamlet*, see *An Old Play in a New Garb: Hamlet, Prince of Denmark*, in Wells, ed., *Nineteenth-Century Shakespeare Burlesques*, V; and *Hamlet the Dainty*, in Gary D. Engle, ed., *This Grotesque Essence: Plays from the Minstrel Stage* (Baton Rouge, 1978). For the popularity of parodies of *Hamlet* in the United States, see Ralph Leslie Rusk, *The Literature of the Middle Western Frontier*, 2 vols. (New York, 1925), II, 4n; Louis Marder, *His Exits and His Entrances: The Story of Shakespeare's Reputation* (Philadelphia, 1963), 295–6, 316–17; and Esther Cloudman Dunn, *Shakespeare in America* (New York, 1939), 108–12, 215–16.

3   For examples, see Wells, ed., *Nineteenth-Century Shakespeare Burlesques*, V, and Engle, ed., *This Grotesque Essence*. For a contemporary view of nineteenth-century parodies, see Hutton, *Curiosities of the American Stage*, 145–204. Also see Marder, *His Exits and His Entrances*, 316–17; Alice I. Perry Wood, *The Stage History of Shakespeare's King Richard the Third* (New York, 1909), 158; Browne, "Shakespeare in America," *American Quarterly*, 12 (Fall 1960), 380, 385–90; David Grimsted, *Melodrama Unveiled: American Theater and Culture, 1800–1850* (Chicago, 1968), 240; Constance Rourke, *Troupers of the Gold Coast* (New York, 1928), 221; Russell Nye, *The Unembarrassed Muse* (New York, 1970), 172; and Charles B. Lower, "Othello as Black on Southern Stages, Then and Now," in Phillip C. Kolin, ed., *Shakespeare in the South: Essays on Performance* (Jackson, Miss., 1983), 211.

4   Haywood, "Negro Minstrelsy and Shakespeare Burlesque," in Jackson, ed., *Folklore and Society*, 80, 86–7; and Browne, "Shakespeare in America," *American Quarterly*, 12 (Fall 1960), 376–9.

5   Adams to James H. Hackett, printed in Hackett, *Notes and Comments upon Certain Plays and Actors of Shakespeare, with Criticisms and Correspondence* (New York, 1864), 229. See Alfred Van Rensselaer Westfall, *American Shakespeare Criticism, 1607–1865* (New York, 1939), 45–6, 50–5; Wood, *The Stage History of Shakespeare's King Richard the Third*, 134–5; Charles H. Shattuck, *Shakespeare on the American Stage: From the Hallams to Edwin Booth* (Washington, DC, 1976), 3, 15–16; and Hugh Rankin, *The Theater in Colonial America* (Chapel Hill, 1960), 191–2.

6   Arthur Hobson Quinn, *A History of the American Drama* (New York, 1943), 162; Dunn, *Shakespeare in America*, 133, 171–2; and Carl Bode, *The Anatomy of American Popular Culture, 1840–1861* (Berkeley and Los Angeles, 1960), 16–17. For the reception of Shakespeare in specific eastern and southern cities, the following are useful: T. Allston Brown, *A History of the New York Stage from the First Performance in 1732 to 1901*, 3 vols. (New York, 1903); James H. Dorman, Jr., *Theater in the Ante-Bellum South, 1815–1861* (Chapel Hill, 1967); W. Stanley Hoole, *The Ante-Bellum Charleston Theatre* (Tuscaloosa, Ala., 1946); Reese Davis James, *Cradle of Culture, 1800–1810: The Philadelphia Stage* (Philadelphia, 1957); Martin Staples Shockley, *The Richmond Stage, 1784–1812* (Charlottesville, Va., 1977); Eola Willis, *The Charleston Stage in the Eighteenth Century* (Columbia, SC, 1924); Joseph Patrick Roppolo, "Hamlet in New Orleans," *Tulane Studies in English*, 6 (1956), 71–86; and the essays in Kolin, ed., *Shakespeare in the South*. For tables showing the popularity of plays in the first half of the nineteenth century, see Grimsted, *Melodrama Unveiled*, apps. 1–2. Towle's observation was made in his *American Society*, II (London, 1870), 22. The migration

of English stars to America is demonstrated throughout Shattuck's *Shakespeare on the American Stage: From the Hallams to Edwin Booth.*

7   Bernard, *Retrospections of America, 1797–1811* (New York, 1887), 263; Tocqueville, *Democracy in America*, pt. 2 (Vintage edn., New York, 1961), 58; Knortz, *Shakespeare in Amerika: Eine Literarhistorische Studie* (Berlin, 1882), 47. For Bridger and Lincoln, see James G. McManaway, "Shakespeare in the United States," *Publications of the Modern Language Association of America*, 79 (December 1964), 514; and Bernard De Voto, *Mark Twain's America* (Boston, 1932), 142–3.

8   Rusk, *The Literature of the Middle Western Frontier*, I, 398–400, 411–14; Louise Taylor, "Shakespeare in Chicago, 1837–1900" (Ph.D. diss., 2 vols., Northwestern University, 1981), I, 5–12; William Bryan Gates, "Performances of Shakespeare in Ante-Bellum Mississippi," *Journal of Mississippi History*, 5 (January 1943), 28–37; Ashley Thorndike, "Shakespeare in America," in L. Abercrombie et al., eds., *Aspects of Shakespeare* (Oxford, 1933), 116–17; Westfall, *American Shakespearean Criticism*, 59; William G. B. Carson, *The Theatre on the Frontier: The Early Years of the St. Louis Stage* (1932; repr., New York, 1965); West T. Hill, Jr., *The Theatre in Early Kentucky, 1790–1820* (Lexington, Ky., 1971); Joseph Gallegly, *Footlights on the Border: The Galveston and Houston Stage before 1900* (The Hague, 1962); Sol Smith, *Theatrical Management in the West and South for Thirty Years* (New York, 1868); and Noah Ludlow, *Dramatic Life as I Found It* (St. Louis, 1880).

9   Rourke, *Troupers of the Gold Coast*, 33, 44, 101–2, George R. MacMinn, *The Theater of the Golden Era in California* (Caldwell, Idaho, 1941), 23–4.

10 Leman, *Memories of an Old Actor* (San Francisco, 1886), 212–13, 260–2, 276–7; Ludlow, *Dramatic Life as I Found It*, 89–90, 113, 116, 242–3, 256, 258, 303; and Smith, *Theatrical Management in the West and South for Thirty Years*, 90–1.

11 Joseph S. Schick, *The Early Theater in Eastern Iowa: Cultural Beginnings and the Rise of the Theater in Davenport and Eastern Iowa, 1836–1863* (Chicago, 1939). Schick's appendixes contain a list of all plays performed in either English or German in Iowa during these years. Place is quoted in Dormon, *Theater in the Ante-Bellum South*, 257n.

12 James Fenimore Cooper, *Notions of the Americans*, II (London, 1828), 100, 113. The dedication of Shakespeare's memorial was covered in the *New York Times*, May 24, 1872. Bayard Taylor's poem was printed in the *New York Tribune*, May 23, 1872.

13 Playbill, American Theatre, Philadelphia, May 13, 1839, Folger Shakespeare Library, Washington, DC. For the prevalence of this format in the eighteenth century, see Rankin, *The Theater in Colonial America*, 150, 193–4; Kenneth Silverman, *A Cultural History of the American Revolution* (New York, 1976), 62; and Garff B. Wilson, *Three Hundred Years of American Drama and Theatre* (Englewood Cliffs, NJ, 1973), 19–27.

14 Playbills, St. Charles Theatre, New Orleans, November 30, 1846, Alexandria, Virginia, July 12, 1799, and Arch Street Theatre, Philadelphia, March 2, 1857, Folger Shakespeare Library.

15 Playbills, American Theatre, Philadelphia, August 30, 31, 1838, September I, II, 1838, June 24, 1839, Walnut Street Theater, Philadelphia, November 30, 1821, Military Hall, Newark, NJ, August 15, 1852, Montgomery Theatre, Montgomery, Ala., March 21, 1835, and American

Theatre, Philadelphia, June 25, 1839, December 14, 1837, Folger Shakespeare Library. See also Arnold Aronson, "Shakespeare in Virginia, 1751–1863," in Kolin, ed., *Shakespeare in the South*, 30 and MacMinn, *The Theater of the Golden Era in California*, 90. Davenport is quoted in Lloyd Morris, *Curtain Time: The Story of the American Theater* (New York, 1953), 205. For examples of *Catharine and Petruchio* being used as an afterpiece, see playbills, American Theatre, New Orleans, April 20, 1827, American Theatre, Philadelphia, September 26, 1838, and St. Charles Theatre, New Orleans, March 25, 1864, Folger Shakespeare Library. *Catharine and Petruchio* also served as an afterpiece when plays other than Shakespeare's were presented; see playbills, American Theatre, New Orleans, April 20, 1827, and American Theatre, Philadelphia, September 26, 1838, December 8, 1838, Folger Shakespeare Library.

16 John S. Kendall, *The Golden Age of the New Orleans Theater* (Baton Rouge, 1952), 210; Hudson, *Lectures on Shakespeare*, I (New York, 1848), 1–41; and Smith, *The Sentinel and Other Plays*, ed. Ralph H. Ware and H. W. Schoenberger (Bloomington, Ind., n.d.), 101–14.

17 Power, *Impressions of America*, 2 vols. (London, 1836), II, 189–192. Shakespeare's contemporary is quoted in Alfred Harbage, *Shakespeare's Audience* (New York, 1941), 84–5. The *Times Picayune* quote comes from Joseph Patrick Roppolo, "Shakespeare in New Orleans, 1817–1865," in Kolin, ed. *Shakespeare in the South*, 126n7. For an excellent discussion of theater audiences in the first half of the nineteenth century, see Grimsted's indispensible *Melodrama Unveiled*, chap. 3. For a comparison with audiences in eighteenth-century England, see James T. Lynch, *Box, Pit and Gallery: Stage and Society in Johnson's London* (New York, 1971). Claudia Johnson deals with a neglected part of the American audience in "That Guilty Third Tier: Prostitution in Nineteenth-Century Theaters," *American Quarterly*, 27 (1975), 575–84.

18 *The Autobiography of Joseph Jefferson*, ed. Alan S. Downer (Cambridge, Mass., 1964), 286; Benjamin McArthur, *Actors and American Culture, 1880–1920* (Philadelphia, 1984), 171; Whitman, "The Old Bowery," in Justin Kaplan, ed., *Walt Whitman: Poetry and Prose* (New York, 1982), 1189–90; and Irving, *Letters of Jonathan Oldstyle*, ed. Bruce I. Granger and Martha Hartzog (Boston, 1977), 12–25.

19 Trollope, *Domestic Manners of the Americans*, 2 vols. (London, 1832), I, 179–84, and II, 87–8, 194–5; Power, *Impressions of America*, I, 171–4; also see I, 62–6, 87–9, 123–6, 210–11.

20 Irving, *Letters of Jonathan Oldstyle*, 14; *New York Mirror*, June 8, 1833; the Virginia and New York editors are quoted in Grimsted, *Melodrama Unveiled*, 63–4; the French reporter's account is reprinted in Barnard Hewitt, *Theatre U.S.A., 1665 to 1957* (New York, 1959), 164–6; and the account of Salvini's *Hamlet* appeared in "The Old Cabinet," *Scribner's Monthly*, 9 (January 1875), 379.

21 Smith, *Theatrical Management*, 137–8; Rourke, *Troupers of the Gold Coast*, 149–50, 209–10; *Sacramento Daily Union*, December 8, 1856.

22 For an example of the warning of law enforcement, see playbill, Walnut Street Theatre, Philadelphia, November 30, 1821, Folger Shakespeare Library; the gentleman is quoted in Nancy Webb and Jean Francis Webb, *Will Shakespeare and His America* (New York, 1964), 84; Fullerton's suicide is described and the America critic is quoted in James S. Bost, *Monarchs of*

*the Mimic World, or, The American Theatre of the Eighteenth Century through
the Managers – The Men Who Made It* (Orono, Me., 1977), 84–5, 103; the
San Francisco Chronicle, January 1854, is quoted in MacMinn, *The Theatre of
the Golden Era in California,* 100.

23   The Bowery Theatre scenes are described in *New York Mirror,* December
29, 1832. Edwin Forrest portrayed the Iago who so infuriated the canal
boatman; see William Rouseville Alger, *Life of Edwin Forrest, the American
Tragedian,* 2 vols. (1877; repr., New York, 1972), I, 477. Constance Rourke's anecdote is contained in her *American Humor: A Study of the National
Character* (1935; repr., New York, 1953), 96–7. The other examples of
audience engagement and interference, can be found in Grimsted, *Melodrama Unveiled,* 60, and *Harper's New Monthly Magazine,* 28 (December
1863), 133.

Consider the Source

I.   Poet, essayist, and a principal figure in the nineteenth-century philosophical movement of Transcendentalism, Ralph Waldo Emerson inhabited a much
more refined world than the typical member of the gallery as described by
Lawrence Levine. But like such theatergoers, Emerson was a fan of Shakespeare, and his views on the Bard are particularly interesting when juxtaposed
with theirs. Emerson devoted a chapter of his 1850 book *Representative Men*
to Shakespeare, from which the following excerpt is taken. What is the basis
of Emerson's admiration of Shakespeare? How would you compare it to the
words – and actions – of the audiences Levine depicts? Can you imagine
Emerson in a New York theater? In what ways would, and wouldn't, it be a
plausible scene (where, for example, would he be likely to sit)?

Excerpt from *Representative Men* by Ralph Waldo Emerson (1850)

Shakspeare; or, the Poet

Great men are more distinguished by range and extent, than by originality. If we require the originality which consists in weaving, like a spider,
their web from their own bowels; in finding clay, and making bricks, and
building the house; no great men are original. Nor does valuable originality consist in unlikeness to other men. The hero is in the press of

knights, and the thick of events; and, seeing what men want, and sharing their desire, he adds the needful length of sight and of arm, to come at the desired point. The greatest genius is the most indebted man. A poet is no rattlebrain, saying what comes uppermost, and, because he says every thing, saying, at last, something good; but a heart in unison with his time and country. There is nothing whimsical and fantastic in his production, but sweet and sad earnest, freighted with the weightiest convictions, and pointed with the most determined aim which any man or class knows of in his times.

The Genius of our life is jealous of individuals, and will not have any individual great, except through the general. There is no choice to genius. A great man does not wake up on some fine morning and say, 'I am full of life, I will go to sea, and find an Antarctic continent: to-day I will square the circle: I will ransack botany, and find a new food for man: I have a new architecture in my mind: I foresee a new mechanic power:' no, but he finds himself in the river of the thoughts and events, forced onward by the ideas and necessities of his contemporaries. He stands where all the eyes of men look one way, and their hands all point in the direction in which he should go. The church has reared him amidst rites and pomps, and he carries out the advice which her music gave him, and builds a cathedral needed by her chants and processions. He finds a war raging: it educates him, by trumpet, in barracks, and he betters the instruction. He finds two countries groping to bring coal, or flour, or fish, from the place of production to the place of consumption, and he hits on a railroad. Every master has found his materials collected, and his power lay in his sympathy with his people, and in his love of the materials he wrought in. What an economy of power! and what a compensation for the shortness of life! All is done to his hand. The world has brought him thus far on his way. The human race has gone out before him, sunk the hills, filled the hollows, and bridged the rivers. Men, nations, poets, artisans, women, all have worked for him, and he enters into their labors. Choose any other thing, out of the line of tendency, out of the national feeling and history, and he would have all to do for himself: his powers would be expended in the first preparations. Great genial power, one would almost say, consists in not being original at all; in being altogether receptive; in letting the world do all, and suffering the spirit of the hour to pass unobstructed through the mind.

Shakspeare's youth fell in a time when the English people were importunate for dramatic entertainments. The court took offence easily at political allusions, and attempted to suppress them. The Puritans, a growing and energetic party, and the religious among the Anglican church, would suppress them. But the people wanted them. Inn-yards, houses without roofs, and extemporaneous enclosures at country fairs, were the ready theatres of strolling players. The people had tasted this new joy; and, as we could not hope to suppress newspapers now, – no, not by the strongest party, – neither then could king, prelate, or puritan, alone or united, suppress on organ, which was ballad, epic, newspaper, caucus, lecture, punch, and library, at the same time. Probably king, prelate, and puritan, all found their own account in it. It had become, by all causes, a national interest, – by no means conspicuous, so that some great scholar would have thought of treating it in an English history, – but not a whit less considerable, because it was cheap, and of no account, like a baker's-shop. The best proof of its vitality is the crowd of writers which suddenly broke into this field; Kyd, Marlow, Greene, Jonson, Chapman, Dekker, Webster, Heywood, Middleton, Peele, Ford, Massinger, Beaumont, and Fletcher.

The secure possession, by the stage, of the public mind, is of the first importance to the poet who works for it. He loses no time in idle experiments. Here is audience and expectation prepared. In the case of Shakspeare there is much more. At the time when he left Stratford, and went up to London, a great body of stage-plays, of all dates and writers, existed in manuscript, and were in turn produced on the boards. Here is the Tale of Troy, which the audience will bear hearing some part of every week; the Death of Julius Cæsar, and other stories out of Plutarch, which they never tire of; a shelf full of English history, from the chronicles of Brut and Arthur, down to the royal Henries, which men hear eagerly; and a string of doleful tragedies, merry Italian tales, and Spanish voyages, which all the London prentices know. All the mass has been treated, with more or less skill, by every playwright, and the prompter has the soiled and tattered manuscripts. It is now no longer possible to say who wrote them first. They have been the property of the Theatre so long, and so many rising geniuses have enlarged or altered them, inserting a speech, or a whole scene, or adding a song, that no man can any longer claim copyright on this work of numbers. Happily, no man wishes to. They are not yet desired in that way. We have few readers, many spectators and hearers. They had best lie where they are.

Shakspeare, in common with his comrades, esteemed the mass of old plays, waste stock, in which any experiment could be freely tried. Had the *prestige* which hedges about a modern tragedy existed, nothing could have been done. The rude warm blood of the living England circulated in the play, as in street-ballads, and gave body which he wanted to his airy and majestic fancy. The poet needs a ground in popular tradition on which he may work, and which, again, may restrain his art within the due temperance. It holds him to the people, supplies a foundation for his edifice; and, in furnishing so much work done to his hand, leaves him at leisure, and in full strength for the audacities of his imagination. In short, the poet owes to his legend what sculpture owed to the temple. Sculpture in Egypt, and in Greece, grew up in subordination to architecture. It was the ornament of the temple wall: at first, a rude relief carved on pediments, then the relief became bolder, and a head or arm was projected from the wall, the groups being still arranged with reference to the building, which serves also as a frame to hold the figures; and when, at last, the greatest freedom of style and treatment was reached, the prevailing genius of architecture still enforced a certain calmness and continence in the statue. As soon as the statue was begun for itself, and with no reference to the temple or palace, the art began to decline: freak, extravagance, and exhibition, took the place of the old temperance. This balance-wheel, which the sculptor found in architecture, the perilous irritability of poetic talent found in the accumulated dramatic materials to which the people were already wonted, and which had a certain excellence which no single genius, however extraordinary, could hope to create.

In point of fact, it appears that Shakspeare did owe debts in all directions, and was able to use whatever he found; and the amount of indebtedness may be inferred from Malone's laborious computations in regard to the First, Second, and Third parts of Henry VI, in which, "out of 6043 lines, 1771 were written by some author preceding Shakespeare; 2373 by him, on the foundation laid by his predecessors; and 1899 were entirely his own." And the proceeding investigation hardly leaves a single drama of his absolute invention. Malone's sentence is an important piece of external history. In Henry VIII, I think I see plainly the cropping out of the original rock on which his own finer stratum was laid. The first play was written by a superior, thoughtful man, with a vicious ear. I can mark his lines, and know well their cadence. See Wolsey's soliloquy, and the following scene with Cromwell, where, – instead of the metre of Shakspeare, whose secret is, that the thought constructs the tune, so that reading for the sense will best bring out the rhythm, – here the lines are constructed on a given tune, and the verse has even a trace of pulpit eloquence. But the play contains, through all its length, unmistakable traits of Shakspeare's hand, and some passages, as the account of the coronation, are like autographs. What is odd, the compliment to Queen Elizabeth is in the bad rhythm.

Shakspeare knew that tradition supplies a better fable than any invention can. If he lost any credit of design, he augmented his resources; and, at that day, our petulant demand for originality was not so much pressed. There was no literature for the million. The universal reading, the cheap press, were unknown. A great poet, who appears in illiterate times, absorbs into his sphere all the light which is any where radiating. Every intellectual jewel, every flower of sentiment, it is his fine office to bring to his people; and he comes to value his memory equally with his invention. He is therefore little solicitous whence his thoughts have been derived; whether through translation, whether through tradition, whether by travel in distant countries, whether by inspiration; from whatever source, they are equally welcome to his uncritical audience. Nay, he borrows very near home. Other men say wise things as well as he; only they say a good many foolish things, and do not know when they have spoken wisely. He knows the sparkle of the true stone, and puts it in high place, wherever he finds it. Such is the happy position of Homer, perhaps; of Chaucer, of Saadi. They felt that all wit was their wit. And they are librarians and historiographers, as well as poets. Each romancer was heir and dispenser of all the hundred tales of the world, –

> Presenting Thebes' and Pelops' line
> And the tale of Troy divine.

The influence of Chaucer is conspicuous in all our early literature; and, more recently, not only Pope and Dryden have been beholden to him, but, in the whole society of English writers, a large unacknowledged debt is easily traced. One is charmed with the opulence which feeds so many pensioners. But Chaucer is a huge borrower. Chaucer, it seems, drew continually, through Lydgate and Caxton, from Guido di Colonna, whose Latin romance of the Trojan war was in turn a compilation from Dares Phrygius, Ovid, and Statius. Then Petrarch, Boccaccio, and the Provençal poets, are his benefactors: the Romaunt of the Rose is only judicious translation from William of Lorris and John of Meun: Troilus and Creseide, from Lollius of Urbino: The Cock and the Fox, from the *Lais* of Marie: The House of Fame, from the French or Italian: and poor Gower he uses as if he were only a brick-kiln or stone-quarry, out of which to build his house. He steals by this apology, – that what he takes has no worth where he finds it, and the greatest where he leaves it. It has come to be practically a sort of rule in literature, that a man, having once shown himself capable of original writing, is entitled thenceforth to steal from the writings of others at discretion. Thought is the property of him who can entertain it; and of him who can adequately place it. A certain awkwardness marks the use of borrowed thoughts; but, as soon as we have learned what to do with them, they become our own.

Thus, all originality is relative. Every thinker is retrospective. The learned member of the legislature, at Westminster, or at Washington, speaks and votes for thousands. Show us the constituency, and the now invisible channels by which the senator is made aware of their wishes, the crowd of practical and knowing men, who, by correspondence or conversation, are feeding him with evidence, anecdotes, and estimates, and it will bereave his fine attitude and resistance of something of their impressiveness. As Sir Robert Peel and Mr. Webster vote, so Locke and Rousseau think for thousands; and so there were fountains all around Homer, Menu, Saadi, or Milton, from which they drew; friends, lovers, books, traditions, proverbs, – all perished, – which, if seen, would go to reduce the wonder.

2.   The illustration that opens this chapter – a lithograph published by the famous firm of Currier and Ives – depicts one of the most notorious episodes in New York City history: the Astor Place Riot of 1849. Most historians agree that the underlying cause for the riot was class conflict, but the immediate spark was a dispute between British actor Charles Macready and his American antagonist Edwin Forrest over proper portrayals of Shakespeare's *Macbeth*. Macready's relatively cerebral approach to Shakespeare was derided by some as elitist, even snobbish; Forrest's more expressive style was deemed blustery overacting by others. As it turned out, both men were performing *Macbeth* in New York City in May of 1849 – Forrest in the notoriously boisterous Bowery Theatre, and Macready in the upscale Astor Place Opera House. On the night of May 9, a large, hostile crowd gathered outside the Opera House. At the end of his performance – for which he received a standing ovation – Macready slipped out of the building by hiding amid the exiting audience. The scene outside was chaotic: flying rocks and pressing crowds alarmed the police, who called on the help of the local militia. When Macready left the theater, the militia fired over the heads of the crowd. Believing the soldiers were shooting blanks, the crowd surged forward, with tragic consequences: 22 dead and 150 wounded.

Look closely at the Currier and Ives rendition of the event. How does this print depict the rioting? How would you describe the people involved and the setting in which they are fighting? It seems almost unimaginable now that people would riot over Shakespeare. But can you think of other people, places or things in popular culture that would make people so mad? How and why?

3.   "Whatever Shakespeare's own designs, philosophy, and concept of humanity were, his plays had meaning to a nation that placed the individual at the center of the universe and personalized the large questions of the day," Levine writes elsewhere in this book. "Shakespeare's characters – like the Davy Crocketts and Mike Finks that dominated American folklore and the Jacksons, Websters, Clays and Calhouns who dominated its politics – were larger than life: their passions, appetites, and dilemmas were of epic proportions." Just how central *is* individualism in American popular culture? What would popular culture that *wasn't* individualistic look and sound like?

Suggested Further Reading

The best treatment of the antebellum theater world – one that includes extensive discussion of Shakespeare – is David Grimsted's *Melodrama Unveiled: American Theater and Culture, 1800–1850*; first published in 1968, it was reissued with a new introduction by Lawrence Levine in 1987 by the University of California Press. See also Howard Taubman, *The Making of American Theater* (New York: Coward McCann, 1965) and Robert Toll, *On with the Show: The First Century of American Show Business* (New York: Oxford University Press, 1976).

3
The Racy Appeal of the Minstrel

1820	Compromise of 1820 eases sectional conflict over slavery
ca.1828	Thomas D. Rice jumps Jim Crow
1837	Panic of 1837 plunges US into economic depression
1843	Premiere of Dan Emmett's Virginia Minstrels
1848–9	Mexican War
1850	Compromise of 1850 defers sectional crisis over slavery
1851	Publication of Harriet Beecher Stowe's *Uncle Tom's Cabin* (minstrel versions and parodies follow)
ca.1855	First black minstrel troupe forms
1857	US Supreme Court decides slaves have no legal rights in *Dred Scott v. Sandford*
1859	John Brown leads unsuccessful interracial insurrection at federal arsenal at Harper's Ferry, Virginia
1861–5	American Civil War
1893	Bert Williams begins show business career in minstrelsy
1928	*Amos 'n' Andy* begins run as radio (and later television) series

Introduction

It stands as one of the more bizarre rituals in American history: a group of men, their faces blackened with burnt cork, singing, dancing, and telling jokes in a highly stylized manner. Although they are white, they are pretending to be black, and pride themselves on the verisimilitude with which they re-create African-American life and customs. But these are not simple acts of imitation or homage – the routines they enact are wildly, even grotesquely, exaggerated. Nor are these rites the habit of some obscure cabal. They are, instead, elements of one of the most popular genres, if not *the* most popular genre, of stage entertainment in the nineteenth century: the minstrel show.

Like later kinds of popular culture (among them the vaudeville show and the first movies), the minstrel show did not emerge all at once, but rather evolved as a component of other kinds of theater. As Lawrence Levine noted in chapter 2, an evening at the theater in the nineteenth century was a varied affair that included a series of between-act, or "entr'acte," routines along with the featured play. This tradition, which can be traced back to medieval minstrels who entertained in court, continued into nineteenth-century America, where imitations of African-American slaves and free blacks became part of the minstrel repertoire. The motives of such performers – and the reactions of audiences – are impossible to gauge; it seems likely that some combination of genuine admiration for the African-American folk culture jostled with obvious racist ridicule. Legend has it, in any event, that dramatic history was made when, sometime around 1828, a previously obscure stage carpenter and actor named Thomas D. Rice began performing a striking dance he said he had learned by watching an old black man who sang, "Wheel about and turn jus' so/Every time I wheel about, I jump Jim Crow." In the decade that followed, Rice and a series of other performers began elaborating and consolidating such routines until they became a stage genre in its own right: the minstrel show.

Between the mid-1840s and the Civil War, the minstrel show evolved into a three-part structure that would define its course for the rest of the century. In the first part, an ensemble of actors formed a semicircle, with the star performers, called "Tambo" and "Bones" for the instruments they played (tambourine and drums), at either end. Individual minstrels sang or danced, while the rest of the troupe sang choruses. Such numbers were presided over by a non-blackfaced master-of-ceremonies known as the interlocutor. The first part ended with a group song-and-dance number.

The second part of the show, known as the "olio," was a variety section that included any number of acts, many of them featuring ribald sexual humor. One important element of the olio was the stump speech, usually given by Tambo or Bones, who spoke in the pretentious language of a black man "putting on airs." Such stock figures – among them the foppish Jim Dandy, the buffoonish Zip Coon, and the slow-witted Sambo – were fixtures of the minstrel show as a whole.

The final part of the show was a one-act skit. These generally had Southern plantation settings and featured slapstick comedy. Pie fights and explosions literally ended the show with a bang; such climaxes were typical of stage entertainment generally in the nineteenth century, when even Shakespearian tragedies were followed with a farce to lighten the audience's mood. A final "walk-around" by the troupe – which was almost always male and played to a male audience – closed the show.

Yet broad humor represented only one side of minstrelsy. The other was a melancholy strain that took a variety of forms in minstrel songs. Some were laments for lost family members; others expressed nostalgia for plantation life. The most famous composer of such music was Stephen Foster, who began his career as a blackface singer before selling a series of songs to minstrel troupes in the 1840s and 1850s. His "Old Folks at Home" and "Massa's in the Cold, Cold Ground" were great crowd pleasers, while other songs like "O! Susannah!" and "Hard Times Come Again No More" have entered the canon of American popular music. Many of Foster's songs described dying or dead lovers, which intensified their impact. He drank himself to death during the Civil War.

In the years before and during the war, minstrelsy increasingly became a vehicle for more direct political commentary. A series of shows invoked (and more commonly parodied) Harriet Beecher Stowe's *Uncle Tom's Cabin,* while others used the genre as a means of pointing out the class bias that often accompanied white abolitionism. While many minstrel acts were avowedly racist, others critiqued the plantation order; the famous song "Blue Tail Fly," for example, was sung from the point of view of a slave slyly celebrating the death of his master from an insect bite. Yet one of the ironies of minstrelsy was that its focus on Southern settings and issues belied that fact that most minstrels and much of the audience for minstrel shows were Northern. A minstrel song by the native Ohioan Dan Emmett, "Dixie's Land" ("I wish I were in the land of cotton/Old times there are not forgotten"), ultimately became the Confederate national anthem.

The ironies became even more complex and bizarre after the Civil War when *black* men became minstrels – and *also* corked their faces. A series of African-American performers, among them Sam Lucas, Billy Kersands, and James Bland (writer of "Carry Me Back to Old Virginny," the Virginia state anthem from 1940 until 1997, when protests over its celebration of slavery led to its revocation), found minstrel shows to be both a source of financial and cultural empowerment – and an oppressive racial straitjacket. Unlike their white counterparts, black minstrels tended not to pine nostalgically for the good old days under slavery, and their songs tapped more directly into a powerful African-American musical tradition rooted in church music. But in their attempt to satisfy white audiences that would accept nothing else, they perpetrated old stereotypes that hardly could be said to enhance the status of their people. And yet all these men had large black followings. By the end of the century, these tensions were powerfully captured in the life and work of Bert Williams, who with his partner George Walker, and later on his own, gave minstrelsy an expressive power that won him worldwide fame (even if he had to stay in segregated hotels while on tour).

The career of Williams is also suggestive in explaining what happened to minstrelsy in the twentieth century: it dissolved back into other forms of entertainment. Williams and Walker adapted minstrel routines for ambitious black musicals, for example, and Williams himself incorporated elements into relatively highbrow revues, like the Ziegfeld Follies, in which he starred in the 1910s. Minstrel acts also became part of vaudeville shows. And minstrel humor also became an important source for stand-up comedy and the situation comedy, most obviously in the case of the wildly popular radio serial *Amos 'n' Andy*. Minstrelsy's influence has been pervasive, even as it has become increasingly invisible to subsequent generations more inclined to scratch their heads – or be offended – when learning about its conventions.

But while the minstrel show has become obscure to the general public, the genre has been the subject of increasing scholarly interest. Beginning in the 1960s, a series of black and white writers (among them the legendary novelist Ralph Ellison) have explored its complex, even contradictory meanings. This commentary intensified still further in the 1990s, when a series of books paid special attention to the class dynamics of minstrelsy, and the strands of envy, admiration, and even solidarity that characterized white usage and adaptation of black culture.

Perhaps the most emphatic assertion of minstrelsy as a thoroughly interracial art comes from W. T. Lhamon, Jr., author of this excerpt from his 1998 book *Raising Cain: Blackface Performance from Jim Crow to Hip Hop*. Lhamon's study, which ranges from the antics of "Bobolink Bob," a slave who danced for eels at New York's Catherine Market in the 1820s, to the elaborate choreography of M. C. Hammer's music videos in the 1990s, argues for a view of minstrelsy rooted in a working-class refusal to accept the so-called "respectable" values of upwardly mobile and elite Americans. Central to this ongoing refusal is what he calls "the blackface lore cycle," a series of expressive behaviors – moans, narratives, steps, gestures – that function as racial shorthand that gets used, adapted, forgotten and recovered from generation to generation. This avowed embrace of stereotypes is both highly decentralized and (surprisingly) widespread and resilient. And, as Lhamon learns first-hand on the other side of what he (and others) call "the black Atlantic," you never know where it's going to turn up.

The Blackface Lore Cycle

W. T. Lhamon, Jr.

In one of its simplest forms, the argument about the beginning of the minstrel show revolves around whether its initial instance was in late January or early February 1843 at the Chatham Theatre when Dan Emmett's Virginia Minstrels first performed. Emmett remembered the preliminary for this coming together in a letter. "I was residing at No. 37 Catherine Street, and one day, while playing upon my violin, and accompanied by Billy Whitlock on the banjo, the door opened and Frank Brower entered." Eureka, Frank Brower walked fully formed through a door to play the funny bones on stage. When the door opened again, and Dick Pelham brought them his tambourine and dancing, the Virginia Minstrels would be complete. A few more days of practice and they would go to the Chatham Theatre for the first formulaic minstrel show – a benefit for Pelham, a boon for the depressed New York theatre, a defining wedge for the construction of whiteness, and an albatross around the neck of black culture that has yet to be lifted. That's the way the story still goes.[1]

But there are many reasons *not* to consider this the beginning either of minstrelsy in general or the formulaic minstrel show in particular. Why should the Virginia Minstrels be said to have started things when Micah Hawkins, George Washington Dixon, T.D. Rice, and many performers imitating them had been delineating "Ethiopians" in the western Atlantic for more than a quarter-century? Perhaps, you might say, because these forebears did not call themselves minstrels, and the bands in the early 1840s did. Naming is hardly beginning, however. It merely emphasizes one dimension of the whole.

A better reason is that there was a difference between creating an entr'acte character, inserting a blackface performer into a melodrama, or even writing a farce as a vehicle for his specialties, as Dixon did in the 1820s and Rice did more elaborately in the 1830s, and aiming to organize a whole evening's entertainment around songs, dances, and patter purporting to be the behavior of southern plantation field hands.

Excerpt from "The Blackface Lore Cycle" reprinted by permission of the Publisher from *Raising Cain: Blackface Performance from Jim Crow to Hip Hop*, by W. T. Lhamon, Cambridge, Mass.: Harvard University Press. Copyright © 1998 by the President and Fellows of Harvard College.

Color lines An 1854 poster for Christy's Minstrels. Originally formed in Buffalo in 1842 by E. P. Christy, who played the Interlocutor, the Christy Minstrels became one of the most successful of all Minstrel troupes, its fame stretching from London (where they were particularly popular) to San Francisco (site of the shows advertised here). *Photo by permission of the Harvard Theatre Collection, Houghton Library, Harvard University*

That is what the minstrel troupes tried to do in the 1840s. Dixon and Rice were still operating within the framework of the compromise conventions worked out in the English "illegitimate" theatres. Those warped conventions had translated largely intact across the Atlantic to the popular theatres of Chatham Square and the Bowery, Louisville and Cincinnati, Pensacola and Mobile. In the west Atlantic their forms were enforced by neither the same class system nor its entrenched privileges, so were ripe for modification if not supplanting.

It is a commonplace that the depression of the late 1830s crippled the American stage, opening up possibilities – by the early 1840s – for ever more vulgar acts. But this partially plausible argument does not account for either the lag between the depression in 1837 and its effect in 1843 or the fact that the vulgar acts were targeting precisely those people with the least capacity to pay for their seats. The depression argument ought to explain why poor people, who could not afford theatrical luxuries, were filtered out of the audience. It ought to account for a performance tradition refined toward literate standards. But that is not what happened as the 1830s became the 1840s. Instead, while literate drama held its own, the most surprising growth occurred in the poor audience – who were spending their money to discover their identity on the stage. Blackface was the first Atlantic mass culture.

Too, its performance was shifting from scripted toward improvised theatre. The former mayor and lifelong diarist Philip Hone confirms these trends when he notes that while the Park Theatre did well during this period, the Bowery drew full houses "with Jim Crow, who is made to repeat nightly almost *ad infinitum* his balderdash song." Moreover, in the 1840s American performers trained in the circus rather than in English theatrical conventions successfully shouldered their rougher performance tradition into the established patterns of tragedy, entr'acte, and farce. Adding to the paradox, in the western Atlantic this possibility for circus acts in theatrical spaces had London precedents. The same tendency had been under way in England before it appeared in the Americas. Thus even the form taken by the 1840s minstrel show was in part a variant of imperial practice.[2]

The depression was important, therefore, not for its affordable theatre tickets but because it so drastically increased the critical mass of people aware of their community and their lack of cultural franchise. The depression focused the formation of a new working class that would seek images of itself chiefly on the stage. On both sides of the Atlantic theatrical producers underwrote novelty that would quench the apparently fickle – but perhaps simply unknown, perhaps gargantuan – appetites of the new populations in the rapidly industrializing Atlantic economies. That's why, in London, at the Royal Surrey Theatre in the summer and fall of 1836, T. D. Rice's Jim Crow alternated in the bills with "The Real Bedouin Arabs," a North African acrobatic troupe imported via Paris, who had a run of some ninety nights.[3]

Why has blackface performance lasted? Why has minstrelsy produced a lore cycle with legs that have run and run, while tumbling Bedouin Arabs no longer have currency in Atlantic culture? Because the Arab tumblers were imported as novelty, while blackface was built up in the Atlantic markets and other working places where men and women rubbed against each other under the stresses that produce cultural form. This blackface form was a long time coming. It grew out of the way actors copied and adapted the dances of New York markets and plantation frolics. It grew out of the way they proved those gestures in theatres across all regions of the United States and, across the Atlantic, from London to Dublin. It grew out of the way the blackface figure always resisted, or did not easily fit into, other peoples' forms – and so gradually forced a form that gave it room of its own. The Real Bedouin Arabs did not produce that interest in the nineteenth century.

Yankee Peddler, Kentucky Rifleman, and Jim Crow – Constance Rourke's comic trio – had all been pushed into European drawing-room dramas. And each of these produced a flurry of further formal activity – the Sol Smith plays, the Davy Crockett almanacs. But it was only Jim Crow who disturbed the culture enough, and was sufficiently seized as a broad champion of metropolitan working spirits, to create a genre of his own. Looking back on the 1840s, one sees an apparently independent *form* taking shape on the western Atlantic stage as early postcolonial consciousness. Despite its international parallels in circus trends, its apparent independence is the reason cultural historians keep trying to validate the Virginia Minstrels' claim of beginning their pastiche. But the Virginia Minstrels were not the only and not even the first assemblers of this bricolage. The troupe of Emmett, Brower, Pelham, and Whitlock were not even the first to take the name "Virginia Minstrels."

Just as T. D. Rice did not first dance Jim Crow in New York City but in a score of provincial theatres from Pensacola to Pittsburgh, so the first minstrel show was not in New York City but in provincial Buffalo. That's where E. P. Christy formed his band and gave his first concert in June 1842 – six months before the Emmett group in New York City. As reported in its earliest clippings, Christy's band was originally three performers: E. P. Christy, George Harrington (who later changed his name to Christy and became a favorite endman, bones player, and female impersonator); and T. Vaughn. They called themselves, then, the Virginia Minstrels.[4]

The size of the minstrel band, supposedly fixed by either of the troupes calling themselves the Virginia Minstrels, was always a sliding affair, in fact. For all the years since Rice's grand successes, accompanists and companions had augmented the dances of the single blackface performers. Theatre bills from the Franklin, Chatham, and Bowery theatres all show there was nothing fixed about two, three, four, five, or more performers.[5]

Therefore, the minstrel show that appeared in the 1840s was not a New York City form, as such. Nor was it fixed at four performers. It did not have specific instrumentation. It did not have a fixed format. It did not yet have an interlocutor. It did not yet have the endman convention. All that was in continual flux. Certainly a commercial minstrel show with distinctive postcolonial features did appear in the 1840s. But we have to find features other than number, format, or fixed roles to define the form.

> Freely depicted in his own vocation . . . the Canaller would make a fine dramatic hero, so abundantly and picturesquely wicked is he . . . A terror to the smiling innocence of the villages through which he floats; his swart visage and bold swagger are not unshunned in cities . . . Nor does it at all diminish the curiousness of this matter, that to many thousands of our rural boys and young men born along its line, the probationary life of the Grand Canal furnishes the sole transition between quietly reaping in a Christian corn-field, and recklessly ploughing the waters of the most barbaric seas.
>
> – Herman Melville, *Moby-Dick*

A big part of the problem in the history of minstrelsy is the triple prejudice in favor of New York City. The meager records have often been kept there, are about there, and have been analyzed by writers there. Buffalo as a goad to minstrelsy? The idea is outrageous to anyone believing in either a plantation or a metropolitan concept of blackface origins. Being neither a plantation nor (in the early nineteenth century) a large metropolis, Buffalo is well worth a pause as we consider this sliding beginning of the blackface lore cycle.

How and why did the gestural elements of minstrelsy travel from plantations and such postcolonial markets as that at Catherine Slip, to be reassembled with panache in remote heartland places like Buffalo? How is it that the early minstrel show could seem to emerge at the same time in two places well over five hundred miles apart, connected by water that could be traversed no faster than five miles an hour?[6] In one word: canals. In two: canal laborers.

Canallers and the conditions of their work underpin both Buffalo, as a city, and minstrelsy, the first popular culture along the Lakes. During the

1820s, when the Erie's construction was climaxing, population grew more rapidly in the canal region than anywhere else in the country: "Albany gained 96 per cent, Utica 183, Syracuse 282, Buffalo 314, and Rochester 512.[7] After they dug Clinton's ditch, canallers became sailors, plying the waterways and the Lakes.

The early canals in North America, including the Erie (1817–25), were dug largely by unfree labor. Slaves built southern canals. Slaves working alongside indentured laborers bought from European boats docking in Philadelphia, Baltimore, and other eastern ports, shoveled canals in the mid-Atlantic and northern states. In the early days of canal work, free workers also contracted to work alongside the slaves and the indentured workers. But that changed during the years of the Erie's construction. "Increasingly, the work became stigmatized as the roughest of rough labor," writes Peter Way, who has looked at canal work from the point of view of the workers themselves. Their work was

> performed by the lowest of the low, Irish immigrants and slaves. These two pariah groups, pushed into the worst kinds of work as the most disadvantaged of labourers, pulled canal construction further down in the estimation of potential workers from the late 1820s. Republican freemen soon lost their appetite for canalling, making it one of the first truly lumpen proletarian professions in North America. In sum, the various "Corktowns" and "Slabtowns" were hardly Lowells, Lynns, or even St. Clairs. They were environments that left little scope for self-determination.[8]

There is a fissure in the history of work in the Atlantic community that corresponds with the completion of the Erie Canal in 1825. After this break, the world of work had a distinct schism between navvy and republican, apprentice and artisan, slave and freeman that had been less marked in earlier dispensations. Until this schism it is possible to generalize a mutuality in common labor. The schism can be overemphasized – I think *has* been overemphasized. But there is much less danger of pushing the mutuality too hard, because its story has hardly been broached.

The mutuality of miscellaneous labor is a virtually untold story in the cultural history of the Atlantic world. What I call *mudsill mutuality* is the shared experience of sweating at hard material work, digging and cleaning, cutting and cropping, sailing and herding, while all along being stepped on and despised for the work others disdain. Mudsill mutuality existed alongside, and in vivid tension with, the gradually increasing internal opposition along ethnic lines. Although an internal schism becomes quite pronounced in the Atlantic world around 1825, this break does not mean that the shared experience of despised labor disappeared. On the contrary, its consciousness increased proportionately with its increased embattlement. Ethnic divisions and mudsill mutuality are not necessarily in a hydraulic relationship, one rising as the other falls. They can increase or decrease together. I believe they hyped each other.[9]

I do not deny the racism that also increased along with the schism. The racism is a fact. It had real costs for the life of laborers, and particularly that of black people. It became an intra-class distinction of tragic proportions.

Even as we learn to reconstruct and admit this working-class racism, however, we need to remember that there were virile instances of it more than a century before the earliest blackface performance. During worker and slave revolts in 1712 and 1741 in New York, public authorities appealed to "white" unity to try to divide workers, and workers themselves used "white" in a very different cant sense to refer to "privileged" or "rich" people.[10] Details like these remind us that no class is one-dimensional, that not everyone was pushed into or chose the same route, that change was gradual, fitful, and lapsing rather than immediate, monolithic, and steady. Multiple fissures remain in the course of labor consciousness. Not only inter-and intra-class arguments exist, and not only black-white animosities, but also white on white and black on black, generation on generation, gender on gender (just to point at the gross cracks). In this reassessment the difficulty is to hear and score all the tones. Many of those tones are blue notes, sliding uncertainly between their fixed notations.

The dominant historiography describes the poignant decline of artisanal labor, and its struggle to organize into trade unions. But what of the mass of workers who had no trade and no license, the journeymen and their sisters, the diggers and haulers, cleaners and cooks, navvies and slaves, pressed sailors and convicted soldiery, the *hogler* (or lowest field laborer) of England who became the *hoggee* digging the canal? What about Melville's "piebald parliament," that unacknowledged but surely ultimate legislature of history? What about that *lumpen* stir from which all culture springs?[11]

The *lumpen* stir is the mass which even Karl Marx disdained, feared, and memorably defined in 1851, the same year Melville centered it as castaway culture, calling it the "Anacharsis Clootz deputation" in *Moby-Dick*.[12] Rightly conceived, blackface performance gives us more clues to this suppressed but ultimately powerful force than we have yet traced. The blackface lore cycle is what held together in useful tension the conflicted voices of this class.

The rule of thumb is that rough laborers did not then and do not now organize. They left few records of their own in the eighteenth and nineteenth centuries and they do not leave many more now. For they have never been warranted by a "moral economy" providing them a safety net of traditional protocols.[13] The comments made about them by journalists and diarists are dangerous to take at face value. What cultural creations they have been historically allowed to claim have been either oral or so cheaply produced that they long ago sifted to smudge. There is a long looping logic of disdain that makes rough labor seem to have no discrete consciousness. If rough labor is not rooted as artisanal toil is, according to this logic, if mudsill work does not manifest inherited organizational forms and customs, then it has not had cultural existence. But what if its tracings are more fugitive than sturdy? What if these light-fingered, light-footed tracings have more ultimate staying power than those middle-class phenomena thought to be "permanent" because they stand erect to be counted? What if, as Ralph Ellison's narrator noticed in *Invisible Man*, your castaway population is characteristically found "running and dodging the forces of history instead of making a dominating stand"?[14]

What if the lumpen alliance of rough labor has found ways to propagate itself as a parasite precisely on those acts and cultural marks that oppose it? To understand the dispersal and survival of a rough culture that leaves no monuments to itself that can be attacked or buried, it helps to think of it as burrs attaching themselves to the passing pants of the very planter who would stamp them out. Vernacular culture circulates and survives like weed seeds. It obeys no boundaries, personal or state. It sifts its way across the abstract fictions of borders as readily as it stays put. Going and staying are the same to the burrs of rough culture. They combine with whatever keeps them going. That's the way vernacular history really moves.

Despite these biological images, there is of course real difference between cultural and biological ecology. One important difference is this: extinguished species are rare in the ecology of culture. Vernacular culture adapts rather than disappears. It hangs on the very acts that seem to erase or efface it. Because of these mutations blackface performance has been able to survive past its apparent initial containment. Thus despite the few records mudsill labor has left behind, tracing its genealogy back through the adaptations of minstrelsy is one way to return mutuality – along with schism – to our history of the formation of the working class in the western Atlantic.

The movement of men and capital, and the stories of their engagement up the Hudson River, then massively west from Rome toward Buffalo, and from Rome east toward Albany, between 1817 and 1825; the digging of 363 miles of canal by pick and barrow; the hardening of attitudes toward the hierarchy of work and those who would do it; the industrializing of the old rural tasks of moving soil and water – all this was ripening in the lyrics and gestures and especially the mask of minstrelsy a few years later.

Peter Way notes that foremen commonly shaved marks on those diggers who fled their labor. Shaved eyebrows and bald strips and crosses on the skull: these traditional harlequin signs were becoming by the 1840s "the visage of labour." Repeat offenders had iron collars forged around their necks.[15] These details suggest a mutuality among disdained workers extending from the stooping work they did, digging and picking, to the way they were marked. Employers marking men they owned or rented across race is important.

The self-marking of blackface minstrelsy – a mark we are still learning to *see*, rather than look through – had one of its beginnings in transfiguration of these historical marks. Minstrels on the move as performers mark their solidarity with journeymen by accepting the marks borne by the journeymen in the minstrel audience as the theme of their own acting. Employers marked the visage of labor; minstrels made a sign of that visage. And it is not just the face of labor or the face of Jim Crow that they thereby made meaningful. The whole stopped posture of the hoggee, permanently bent by the shovel and barrow, and still evident in day laborers to this day, is caught in Jim Crow's gimp. Jim Crow embodies common labor, face to foot.

Finally, when I say that canalling experience shows up in the lyrics and mask of minstrelsy, I mean that the songs of this formal minstrel period of the 1840s and 1850s are everywhere about the distance from *home*, emphasized in its characteristic rhyme with "roam." The lyrics are about the daily scramble that gave journeymen their name. It was no accident when the Christy Minstrels sang, "Old Massa gave us money / And sent us on our journey."[16] George Christy (né Harrington), who performed this song, was a multiply masked man from Buffalo, who had changed his name, performed blacked-up and cross-dressed, and here negotiated the in-between problem of licensed-but-enforced roaming. Slaves and other workers forced to middle passages without their families for war, for sugar, or for canalling were characteristically caught in this quandary. What too often has seemed like sentimental rhyming is also a way of declaring within the surveillance of the minstrel theatre the terrible exhaustion, loneliness, and privation forced onto the lowest workers of the Atlantic.

It makes a gnarled sense that the cultural song and dance representing back-stopping labor of shoveling and carting dirt, of building locks and being uprooted from family and home for long periods of time, should appear at the same moment on Lake Erie and along the Atlantic coast. What looks like polygenesis, simultaneous generation of the same form in more than one place, is really the appearance of that form at about the same time at both ends of the waterway whose making matured the symbolism of the labor. The activity that became known as minstrelsy was largely the cultural symbolism of this mutual labor. The fate of this symbolism is a lore cycle. The fate is not fixed. The cultural symbolism of blackface performance, like other contentious cycles of lore, is sometimes disdained, other times fetishized, sometimes buried, other times enhanced and elaborated. Along the way it has absorbed its warped interpretations, folding them also into its effects.

INGREDIENTS: Dried Potato, Vegetable Oil, Potato Starch, Salt & Vinegar Flavour (acidity regulators E262, 262; Flavour Enhancer – 621, Malic Acid, Citric Acid), Salt, Emulsifier (E471), Colour (E160c). Best Before 27 May 95.
   – Rippled Potato Snack packet, dustbin, British
   Museum, 1995

The forecourt of the British Museum, lunchtime. I am among schoolchildren. They are spilling, tossing, swapping crisps, that most processed of contemporary foods. The British crisp, eaten in the United States as a potato chip, is one far-gone fate for the western Atlantic potato. The crisp has several functions in these circles as an individual and group indulgence with a short shelf life, indoor frisbee, token of trade, and trash feed for sparrows and pigeons. These many unintended effects constitute a parable for other slicings and deep fryings on equally casual display here in the broad border area between the street and terminal curation.

Italian, German, French, Hindi, and Dutch vowels are caroming among more local consonants from the Old Kent Road south of the Thames to Kentish Town on its north. I have spent the morning deciphering Jim Crow plays in the manuscript room. Now, drinking tea and unwinding with a sandwich, I am wondering, Why are these plays locked up here on Great Russell Street in London? Why not in Pensacola or Pittsburgh or New York, to which places one might plausibly trace their definitive coming together and their apparent erasure from history?

The Jim Crow scripts are curated here in this place, and in no other, because of accidents of disdain in the west Atlantic and, in the east Atlantic, accidents of arrest. In North America most associations with Jim Crow were long ago suppressed. (But not of course expunged. The gross effects of Jim Crow cartooning linger in a sub rosa half-life. Some private collectors perversely prize its grossest emblems as camp artifacts:

the ceramic Jemimas whose grins functioned as ashtrays, the stamped-tin Uncle Bens that advertised rice on roadside fence rails.) Across the Atlantic in London, the Lord Chamberlain's censorship, imperial collections, and a Victorian confidence that all details may someday fit the grand jigsaw – these have united to keep manuscripts of Jim Crow plays from the 1830s locked up with mummies, Parthenon friezes, and a few lyrics scrawled in John Lennon's hand to McCartney's "Yesterday."

Such are the thoughts possessing me while I avoid these kinetic children, their shirttails akimbo, flushing one-legged pigeons in my direction. Frowning Chinese couples photograph each other before the steps rising toward the polished brass in the Museum pediment. American students come and go by twos and threes, with their hightop sneakers and flat vowels, buying postcards. Scholars hurry, guards search for bombs in bags, vendors hawk faux scarabs in "Egyptian" blue wash spread on tarps at their feet.

In all this crowd a group of young Japanese arrests my eye. These tourists are more assured and urbane than others. They clearly have the means and liberty to elaborate themselves as they will. Men and women alike are dressed casually in jeans and pastel running shoes. Some wear baseball caps backward betokening favored mascots from far edges of North America: Blue Devils, Seminoles, Huskies. These Japanese tourists have carefully assembled their signs of who they would be. But their caps and jeans are not what hold my eye. The meaning of their hair is what produces my double-take. Even such a rooted entity as hair has been routed.

These flourishing young Japanese have tightly curled and matted their formerly shiny straight hair into varying forms of the dreadlock. Raga-muffin question marks tumble topsy-turvy on some. Cornrows plait symmetrical patterns over others. Beaded dreadlocks, tied in African scarves, drape yet others to their shoulders. These Pacific young men and women have closely studied the variety of black Atlantic styles.[17]

In the early summer of the mid-1990s they are lifting those styles from across the world, as they have increasingly listened to Charlie Parker, Little Richard, and Prince. Their liftings are not brazen or aggressive, but routine. Their seamless absorption of the Atlantic strange into the Pacific conventional, but with the simultaneous persistence of blackness – that's what focuses my double-take. I register this global circulation and continuity, and it all seems appropriate. I am wondering, Why haven't these visitors tied their hair in tea-lead or eel skin? Such details, I realize, are obscured by the paradox of curation: what's kept inside is kept from circulating outside. But had these eastern visitors penetrated the inner chambers of the West's archives, had merchants with the right labels marketed eel skins with sufficient cachet, surely these youths would have blazoned them gracefully and proudly.

Returning inside to the manuscript room, to *Bone Squash Diavolo*, *Jim Crow in His New Place*, and *The Peacock and the Crow*, I am reinforced in my conviction that these plays traced a moving force older and newer than the scripts I am reading. Like those Japanese dreadlocks outside, Jim Crow plays are waystations for lore circulating ever wider. What I noticed in the forecourt of the British Museum was the extension of routes: the black Atlantic gone global.

There are important sights on both sides of the walls of the British Museum. Sights like the Jim Crow manuscripts, on the inside where "Infinity goes up on trial," as Bob Dylan sang, are set in the amber of public warranty. On the outside, the sights still "flow like de seeds ob de squash," as Dan Emmett used to preach in his stump sermons.[18] Constantly rechosen, they are continually reanimated. If we were talking about folktales, we would call this reanimation "tale maintenance." But I seek terms for a process that, although it parallels folktales, is more furtive and difficult to trace. My topic is the choosing and the enlivening of gestures and style signatures. So I call it lore maintenance. These choices constitute the fundamental practice of identity. In this practice, identity finds its proof and reproof.

The door opens and Bobolink Bob comes among us . . . alive as you or me . . . but this time he speaks Japanese and he rides a tour bus. These are late turns in the minstrel lore cycle.

Notes

1   Letter from Dan Emmett to Frank Dumont, quoted in the *New York Commercial*, "The Story of Negro Minstrelsy," n.d., in the Emmett folder of the Museum of the City of New York. Carl Wittke: "The first minstrel show, in which a troupe of burnt cork performers monopolized the whole performance and thereby constructed an entirely new and distinctively American form of entertainment [was when] the famous 'Virginia Minstrels' made their debut." *Tambo and Bones*, pp. 38–9. Hans Nathan: "The Virginia Minstrels deserve to be called the first minstrel band – one consisting of four blackface musicians playing the violin, banjo, tambourine, and bones." *Dan Emmett and the Rise of Early Negro Minstrelsy* (Norman: University of Oklahoma Press, 1962), p. 146. Nathan dates the first performance of a minstrel show by the Virginia Minstrels as 31 Jan. 1943. Robert Toll: "In February 1843, four blackfaced white men, wearing ill-fitting, ragtag clothing, took the stage in New York City, to perform for the first time an entire evening of the 'oddities, peculiarities, eccentricities, and comicalities of that Sable Genus of Humanity.'" *Blacking Up: The Minstrel Show in Nineteenth-Century America* (New York: Oxford University Press, 1974), p. 30. His quotation is from a poster the Virginia Minstrels used in Dublin in 1844, when their program

was far more settled and they were, indeed, filling the theatre's whole night. They did not do so at first.

2   *The Diary of Philip Hone, 1828–1851*, ed. Allan Nevins (New York: Dodd, Mead, 1927), pp. 272–3. A. H. Saxon, *Enter Foot and Horse: A History of Hippodrama in England and France* (New Haven: Yale University Press, 1968).

3   British Library Playbill Collection, catalogue 313, sample bills on 22 Aug. 1836, 18 Sept. 1836, and 24 Oct. 1836. Their performance was described by Charles Rice, an audience member: " 'the real Bedouin Arabs,' as they are largely designated in the bills, exhibited some of the best somersets, and other descriptions of tumbling, ever witnessed even in this metropolis; but, as is always the case in this species of entertainment, there is a dwelling on the various tricks which prolongs the performance of them longer than is pleasant." *The London Theatre in the Eighteen-Thirties*, ed. Arthur Colby Sprague and Bertram Shuttleworth (London: Society for Theatre Research, 1950), p. 5.

4   H. P. Grattan, "The Origin of the Christy's Minstrels," *The Theatre* (London) (March 1882), citing details which E. P. Christy first published 30 Jan. 1848 in the *New York Age*. Nathan, *Dan Emmett*. E. P. Christy's troupe had a nearly ten years' run at Mechanics' Hall in New York City. George Harrington Christy became one of the most influential minstrel performers. Son of an Erie Canal roadhouse hostess, he began dancing jigs in blackface at age 12 in Buffalo. There is a drawing of him as Topsy in *Christy's and White's Ethiopian Melodies* (Philadelphia, 1854), wearing calico and boots and playing a four-string banjo. A fourth member of the early troupe may have been L. Durand.

5   One instance: on 27 Jan. 1843 the Chatham featured itself as having "Lower Prices than any Theatre in the City!" Specifically, "Pit, 6 1/4 cts. Second and Third Tier Boxes, 12 1/2 cts. First Tier, 25 cts." Fairly far down the page came this announcement: "The Ethiopian Dancers and the King of the Banjo Players, Messrs. Frank Diamond, Pelham, and W. Whitlock, in Three ORIGINAL EXTRAVAGANZAS." Diamond was one of the best blackface dancers. But the next Wednesday Pelham and Whitlock would become half of the Virginia Minstrels. At the bottom of the playbill appears this announcement: "A GREAT VARIETY OF EXTRAVAGANZAS! VIZ: – 'Lucy Long,' 'Dan Tucker,' 'Smoke House,' 'Farewell My Dinah Gal,' 'Grape Vine Twist,' 'Celeste,' 'Fanny Elssler,' 'Napolean Buonaparte,' &c. &c." Many of these songs would become staples of Emmett's troupe and, like "Dan Tucker," which he claims to have written at age 13, forever associated with them. For further evidence of the sliding size of the minstrel band see Nathan, *Dan Emmett*.

6   Thomas L. Nichols, *Forty Years of American Life*, I (London, 1864).

7   Whitney R. Cross, *The Burned-over District: The Social and Intellectual History of Enthusiastic Religion in Western New York, 1800–1850* (Ithaca: Cornell University Press, 1950), p. 56.

8   Peter Way, *Common Labour: Workers and the Digging of North American Canals, 1780–1860* (Cambridge: Cambridge University Press, 1993), pp. 1, 10–11.

9   Sean Wilentz's masterly history of New York City labor in this period is nevertheless the history of the artisanry, without catching much of the voice of mudsill mutuality: *Chants Democratic: New York City and the Rise of the American Working Class, 1788–1850* (New York: Oxford University Press,

1984). Alexander Saxton, in *The Rise and Fall of the White Republic: Class Politics and Mass Culture in Nineteenth-Century America* (London: Verso, 1990), David Roediger, in *The Wages of Whiteness: Race and the Making of the American Working Class* (London: Verso, 1991), and Eric Lott, in *Love and Theft*, all persuasively trace this dividing wedge. Peter Quinn's novel *Banished Children of Eve* (New York: Viking, 1994) gives an imaginative narrative of the conflict. I am trying to uncover and decode the submerged evidence of cross-"racial" attractions that worked against this wedge and have survived it.

10   I am grateful to Marcus Rediker for showing me his " 'The Outcasts of the Nations of the Earth': The New York Conspiracy of 1741 in Atlantic Perspective," now published in Peter Linebaugh and Marcus Rediker, *The Many Headed Hydra* (Boston: Beacon, 1998).

11   Hoggee: Lionel D. Wyld, *Low Bridge! Folklore and the Erie Canal* (Syracuse: Syracuse University Press, 1962), p. 19. Herman Melville, *The Confidence Man*, ed. Harrison Hayford (1857; New York: Library of America, 1984), p. 848.

12   Karl Marx, *The Eighteenth Brumaire of Louis Bonaparte*, in *The Marx–Engels Reader*, ed. Robert C. Tucker (New York: Norton, 1972). Melville *Moby-Dick; or, The Whale* (1851; New York, Penguin, 1992), p. 132.

13   When E. P. Thompson outlined "The Moral Economy of the Crowd," he meant a "particular equilibrium" achieved over time between paternalist authority and those workers with deeply rooted traditions. Their self-regulating economy was ending at the beginning of the nineteenth century. However, the moral economy had never warranted the lowest, most nomadic, workers – and never appreciated their expression. Thompson's crowd was upright in a market they could be proud of because they shaped it. I seek the slippery gestures created within the uncongenial market conditions of industrial capital – an amoral economy. The groups I am after must find themselves in a place where they are afraid of being caught. Without license of the moral economy, rough workers were constantly having not only to find out who they were, what a just society for them would be, but also act without legitimacy. Thus, it is no accident that much of the evidence of the blackface lore cycle surfaces in the illegitimate theatres of London and their equivalent American low stages. But the great poet of this orphaned condition is Ishmael, imagining Ahab's interior monologue: "Where is the foundling's father hidden? Our souls are like those orphans whose unwedded mothers die in bearing them: the secret of our paternity lies in their grave, and we must there to learn it." *Moby-Dick*, p. 535.

14   Ralph Ellison, *Invisible Man* (1952; New York: Random House, 1982), p. 333. Sure, rough laborers built the skyscrapers, sailed the ships, and laid the rails. But their traces in that labor will forever be organized and unjustly claimed by the people who front the capital – in the way the Erie Canal became "Clinton's Ditch." I am trying to shift the ground of the argument to emphasize the anti-monumentality of lumpen culture. I want to find the features of this fugitive culture made by invisible men and women.

15   Way, *Common Labour*, p. 3.

16   *Christy's Plantation Melodies*, no. 2 (Philadelphia, 1853), p. 60.

17   The classic study of "black" hair as a sign system is Kobena Mercer, "Black Hair/Style Politics," *New Formations*, 7, no. 3 (1987).

18   Dylan, "Visions of Johanna." Nathan, *Dan Emmett*, p. 411.

Consider the Source

1. The following are excerpted routines from nineteenth-century minstrel shows. Why might some Americans have found them funny? Do you? Why or why not?

A. Song

A nigger come from Arkansaw   He went to shell corn in de shed
De biggest fool I eber saw   He shell'd his shins all bare instead
At mornin when this nigger rose   He went to feed de horse at de barn
He put his mittens on his toes   He put himself in de trough for corn

B. Duet

He: O Miss Fanny let me in
    for the way I lub you is a sin
She (spoken): O no I cannot let you in . . .
He: Oh when I set up an oyster cellar,
    you shall wait upon de feller
    Sell hot corn and ginger pop
    You be de lady ob de shop
She: Oh Sam, if dat's de trufe you tell . . .
    Oh, Sam Slufheel, you may come in.
He: Oh, Miss Fanny, I'se a comin' in

C. Song by James Bland, an African American, 1875

Carry me back to old Virginny,
There's where the cotton and the corn and 'tatoes grow,
There's where the birds warble sweet in the springtime,
There's where the old darkey's heart am long'd to go,
There's where I labored so hard for old massa,
Day after day in the field of yellow corn,
No place on earth do I love more sincerely
Than old Virginny, the state where I was born.

D. Joke

Mr. Bones: Mr. Interlocutor, sir!
Interlocutor: Yes, Mr. Bones?

Mr. Bones: Mr. Interlocutor, sir. Does us black folks go to hebbin? Does we go through dem golden gates?
Interlocutor: Mr. Bones, you know the golden gates is for white folks.
Mr. Bones: Well who's gonna be dere to open dem gates for you white folks?

E. Stump Speech

When I got a little piece from the shore, de man axed me if I knowed anything about frenologism [phrenology, the now-discredited nineteenth-century science of mapping the brain]. I told him no. Ah, says he, den one quarter of your life is gone. Finally he says, does you know anything about grammar. I told him no. Ah, says he, den one half ob your life am gone . . . He axed me if I knowed anything about dicksionary. I told him no and he say tree quarters of your life is gone. We hit a rock and den I axed him if he knowed how to swim. He said no. Den says I, de whole four quarters of your life am gone – shure.

2.   In the photograph on page 62, the program lists a "burlesque lecture" on the rights of women to close the olio section. Given what you know of minstrel humor – and the way female figures are shown in the advertisement – how do you imagine Christy's troupe would depict the emerging suffrage movement of the mid-nineteenth century? How might it relate to the race and class attitudes of (cross-dressing male) minstrel performers and their overwhelmingly masculine audiences?
3.   At one point in this excerpt, W. T. Lhamon pauses in his discussion to list the ingredients in a package of potato crisps (or chips, as they're known in the United States). Why does he do so? How do the crisps function as a metaphor? (Consider, for example, the phrase "terminal curation" in light of his research on minstrel scripts at the British Museum.)
4.   All major recent studies of minstrelsy see racism as an important component of the genre. At issue is how much. "Was minstrelsy monolithic in its justification of slavery?" asks Alexander Saxton his 1990 book *The Rise and Fall of the White Republic*. "Almost, but not quite," he answers, acknowledging that critiques of the plantation order sometimes lingered in songs borrowed from black culture. Lhamon, by contrast, does not deny the racism that suffused minstrelsy, but nevertheless emphasizes the way minstrelsy tended to subvert many taboos, including white supremacy, a matter in which many white Americans had a tremendous investment (literal and figurative). Given this basic consensus but difference in emphasis, and the primary and secondary

evidence at hand in this chapter, are you more inclined to focus on obvious racism or subtle solidarity? Why?

Suggested Further Reading

One of the first serious treatments of minstrelsy came from folklorist Constance Rourke in her classic study *American Humor* (New York: Harcourt, Brace, 1931), which discusses blackface humor in the broader context of early American history. Ralph Ellison makes a more racially nuanced exploration in his 1958 essay "Change the Joke and Slip the Yoke," included in his collection *Shadow and Act* (New York: Random House, 1964), as does Nathan Irvin Huggins in the final chapter of *Harlem Renaissance* (New York: Oxford University Press, 1971). Among historians, Robert Toll's *Blacking Up: The Minstrel Show in Nineteenth Century America* (New York: Oxford University Press, 1974) remains influential in the field. So is Alexander Saxton's "Blackface Minstrelsy and Jacksonian Ideology," a 1975 article in the academic journal *American Quarterly* that was later incorporated into his *The Rise and Fall of the White Republic: Class Politics and Mass Culture in Nineteenth Century America* (London: Verso, 1990). David Roediger makes a comparably Marxist-influenced analysis in a chapter on minstrelsy in *The Wages of Whiteness: Race and the Making of the American Working Class* (London: Verso, 1991). Other recent treatments include Eric Lott's highly theoretical *Love and Theft: Blackface Minstrelsy and the American Working Class* (New York: Oxford University Press, 1993); the essay collection *Inside the Minstrel Mask: Readings in Nineteenth-Century Blackface Minstrelsy*, edited by Annemarie Bean, James V. Hatch, and Brooks McNamara (Middletown, CT: Wesleyan University Press 1996), Dale Cockerell, *Demons of Disorder: Early Blackface Minstrels and Their World* (Cambridge: Cambridge University Press, 1997), and William J. Mahar, *Behind the Burnt Cork Mask: Early Blackface Minstrelsy and Antebellum American Popular Culture* (Urbana: University of Illinois Press, 1998). Two other books which deal with minstrelsy only incidentally, but which are a rich treasure-trove of African-American humor, are worth mentioning here. The first is Mel Watkins's *On the Real Side: Laughing, Lying and Signifying – the Underground Tradition of African-American Humor that Transformed American Culture, From Slavery to Richard Pryor* (New York: Simon and Schuster, 1994). Finally, no discussion of African-American music and humor would be complete without Lawrence Levine's *Black Culture and Consciousness: Afro-American Thought from Slavery to Freedom* (New York: Oxford University Press, 1977).

4
Literature for the Million

1690	First newspaper appears in the American colonies
1733–57	Benjamin Franklin publishes *Poor Richard's Almanac* in Philadelphia
1741	Franklin launches *American Magazine* in Philadelphia
1801	Alexander Hamilton founds the *New York Evening Post*
1833	*New York Sun* first published
1851–2	Harriet Beecher Stowe's *Uncle Tom's Cabin* serialized in the *National Era*, a political/religious newspaper
1855	First story paper, the *New York Ledger*, first published
1860	*Beadle's Dime Novels* series inaugurated in New York (millions distributed to US soldiers during the Civil War)
1868	Horatio Alger's first novel, *Ragged Dick*, published
1873	Comstock Law prohibits mailing of "obscene" books, dime novels, and story papers
1875	Lakeside Library, the first cheap library, begins publication in Chicago
1877	Great Railroad Strike heightens class tensions
1900	"The Extinction of the Dime Novel" published by *Bookman* trade magazine
1900s	*Argosy, All-Story Weekly, Cavalier* and other magazines publishing "pulp fiction" carry on dime novel tradition

Introduction

In the excerpt from *Representative Men* included in Chapter 2 of this book, Ralph Waldo Emerson says of William Shakespeare's England, "There was no literature for the million. The universal reading, the cheap press, was unknown." The same could not be said of Emerson's United States. The trickle of print that began with the publication of the *Bay Psalm Book* in 1640 had become a steady stream by 1776, when Thomas Paine's *Common*

Sense (which sold 100,000 copies between January and March alone) urged the colonies to revolt. But by the 1830s – the very moment the minstrel show and other stage entertainments were also transforming American culture – the flow of printed matter had become a veritable flood which gushed for the remainder of the nineteenth century. Never before, and never again, would the published word matter so much to so many people.

The pivotal medium in this literature for the million was newspapers. The first newspaper was published in the American colonies on September 25, 1690 in Boston, though it was suppressed four days later by Massachusetts authorities because its publisher had not received permission to operate. Newspapers became increasingly common over the course of the eighteenth century – as did magazines, one of the first of which was published by Benjamin Franklin out of Philadelphia in 1741 – but they tended to have a relatively elite readership (newspapers in particular had a mercantile orientation with a particular emphasis on the shipping industry so central to international trade). At the turn of the nineteenth century, papers became increasingly political in their outlook; Alexander Hamilton, for example, founded the *New York Evening Post* in 1801 with the help of wealthy patrons as a vehicle to attack the policies of his rival, Thomas Jefferson.

By the time of Andrew Jackson's presidency, technological and demographic changes fueled the creation of a new kind of newspaper – and a new kind of readership. Faster and cheaper presses, along with the advent of the telegraph, made an inexpensive daily newspaper feasible on a mass basis (many sold for as little as a penny a day). The first such paper was the *New York Sun*, founded in 1833 by printer-turned editor Benjamin Day. It was followed in rapid succession by a number of other papers, among them the *New York Herald* (1835), the *Philadelphia Public Ledger* (1836), and the *Baltimore Sun* (1837). Newspapers also rapidly penetrated the nation's interior; by 1860, Illinois had over 400 newspapers, with eleven dailies in Chicago alone.

And just what did readers find in their pages? "The object of this paper is to lay before the public, at a price within the means of every one, ALL THE NEWS OF THE DAY, and at the same time afford an advantageous medium for advertising," Benjamin Day told readers of the first issue of the *New York Sun*. Tens of thousands of buyers read what he published daily, in large part because the *Sun* and other penny dailies defined "the news of the day" in ways working people found arresting: political scandals, sensational disasters, titillating stories, even outrageous hoaxes. In some ways, this freewheeling newspaper culture was very unlike what came later: not even the *New York Times* (founded in 1851) strived for anything resembling scientific objectivity. On the other hand, the reader of any tabloid today – notably Alexander Hamilton's *New York Post*, which has changed in ways that would mortify its founder – can recognize the continuity in style and content with these early newspapers.

But newspapers were only one format in this raucous new culture of print – and we *are*, until the advent of inexpensive photographic reproduction transformed it in the latter part of the nineteenth century, talking about a culture of *print* (though ink illustrations, particularly cartoons, were common). Magazines, religious tracts, political pamphlets: all were part of the blizzard of paper that blanketed the young United States. Moreover, many forms of writing that are somewhat compartmentalized today, like church sermons or song lyrics, might appear in any number of formats.

One of the most important forms of writing that crossed such barriers was the novel. Often formatted into serialized narratives – Harriet Beecher Stowe's *Uncle Tom's Cabin* is the most famous example – novels, along with short stories and poetry, were often featured in newspapers and magazines. In fact, such prose was so popular that by the time of the Civil War a series of publications were running it exclusively in a newspaper format. These "story papers," as they were known, laid the foundation for one of the most beloved genres of popular culture in American history: the dime novel.

In this opening chapter to his 1987 book *Mechanic Accents: Dime Novels and Working-Class Culture in America*, Yale historian Michael Denning describes what he calls the "figure" of dime novels: their form, their content, and the meanings some observers have attached to them. For Denning, the dime novel has been a site of selective memory and unconscious forgetting in American history. His book, which recovers the "accents" of class conscious-ness and conflict in the genre, represents an important chapter in the recon-struction of working-class life central to the academic scholarship of the late twentieth century.

The Figure of the Dime Novel in American Culture
Michael Denning

The dreadful damage wrought to-day in every city, town, and village of these United States by the horrible and hideous stuff set weekly before the boys and girls of America by the villainous sheets which pander greedily and viciously to the natural taste of young readers for excitement, the irreparable wrong done by these vile publications, is hidden from no one.

Brander Matthews, 1883

The saffron-backed Dime Novels of the late Mr. Beadle, ill-famed among the ignorant who are unaware of their ultra-Puritan purity, ... began to appear in the early years of the Civil War; and when I was a boy in a dismal boarding school at Sing Sing, in the winters of 1861–1863, I reveled in their thrilling and innocuous record of innocent and imminent danger. ... I make no doubt that if the Dime Novels of my school-days had been in circulation in Shakespeare's boyhood the Bard would have joyed in them.

Brander Matthews, 1923

Cheap thrills Cover of *Shadow Bill, The Scout,* a dime novel in the series launched by George Munro in 1864. Such 4-x-6-inch pamphlets of about 100 pages found a large audience among Civil War soldiers, and typically focused on western characters and settings. *Photo from the Collection of the New-York Historical Society*

Dime novels: this figure conjures powerful images in American culture. Standing for the whole of nineteenth-century cheap sensational fiction, it evokes nostalgic images of boys' books, read on the sly, but fundamentally harmless and wholesome: tales of the west in the adventures of Buffalo Bill and Deadwood Dick, of rags-to-riches in the Horatio Alger saga and of the schoolboy fun of Frank Merriwell at Yale. Within a few years of their demise in the 1890s they were recalled as signs of a lost innocence, unspoiled fragments of an age before mass culture; the nineteenth-century debates about their immoral and disreputable nature seemed a comic extravagance of Victorian gentility. As the two quotations from Brander Matthews – an influential American literary critic of the time – demonstrate, the immediate menace of cheap sensational fiction to genteel culture was repressed, generating a screen memory of thrilling and innocuous boyhood pleasures. And through the twentieth century, dime novels have been kept alive more by collectors and enthusiasts than by literary critics or cultural historians. In the face of this memory, it is necessary to unravel the synecdoche: to see what is the part, and what the whole, and to see the history of its construction. For though I will refer to the entire body of commercial, mass-produced, sensational fiction of the nineteenth century as "dime novels," to use the term uncritically can lead us to mistake drastically the nature of nineteenth-century popular fiction.

Popular fictional narratives appeared in three main formats between the 1840s and the 1890s: the story paper, the dime novel, and the cheap library. Though the formats overlapped in history and content – at some times all three sorts were on the market and many novels appeared in all three formats – they do mark three different moments in the cheap fiction publishing of the nineteenth century.

The story paper was an eight-page weekly newspaper, which cost five or six cents, and contained anywhere from five to eight serialized stories, as well as correspondence, brief sermons, humour, fashion advice, and bits of arcane knowledge. They were published mainly in New York and Philadelphia for a national audience, having emerged out of a gradual but incomplete separation of the news and story functions of the newspaper. They first appeared at the tail end of the newspaper revolution of the 1830s, when the penny press was established. The penny press – the *New York Sun* (founded 1833), *New York Herald* (founded 1835), and *Philadelphia Public Ledger* (founded 1836), among others – was, as Michael Schudson summarizes, "distinctive economically – in selling cheaply, in its distribution by newsboys, and in its reliance on advertising; politically – in its claims to independence from party; and substantively – in its focus on news, a genre it invented."[1] The conditions for the success of the penny press also contributed to the beginning of the story papers: technological developments in production and distribution with the emergence of the steam-driven cylinder press and an extensive rail and canal network, and social changes in the emergence of a new reading public, the artisans and mechanics of the eastern cities. The first story papers were *Brother Jonathan*, founded in New York by Park Benjamin and Rufus Griswold in 1839, and *New World*, founded by Benjamin and Griswold a few months later after leaving *Brother Jonathan* in a dispute. "Both journals," the historian James Barnes notes, "far exceeded the circulation of other American periodicals, with the exception of *Graham's Magazine* and a few of the leading daily newspapers."[2] In Boston, the *Nation* and the *Universal Yankee Nation* soon entered the field. These early story papers were competitive and short-lived, relying largely on pirated European novels despite their nationalist rhetoric. The foundations for longer-lasting story papers came in the 1850s with the establishment of Robert Bonner's *New York Ledger* (1855) and Street & Smith's *New York Weekly* (1859). Their success established a format that was imitated by competitors for the next forty years: Beadle & Adams's *Saturday Journal* (1870) (which became *Beadle's Weekly* in 1882 and *Banner Weekly* in 1885); James Elverson's *Saturday Night* (1865); George Munro's *Fireside Companion* (1867); and Norman Munro's *Family Story Paper* (1873). These papers, which had circulations in the hundreds of thousands, were aimed at the entire family, containing a carefully-balanced mixture of serialized adventure stories, domestic romances, western tales, and historical romances.[3]

The second main format for cheap, sensational fiction was the pamphlet novel, also pioneered by Park Benjamin when he issued a twelve-and-a-half-cent "shilling novelette" as an "extra" for readers of the *New World* in 1842. These fifty-page, 5-inch-by-$8\frac{1}{2}$-inch pamphlets were widely imitated until increased postal rates put many of them out of business in 1845.[4] Nevertheless, the practice had been established well enough for a small New York publisher of ten-cent song-and etiquette books to issue a weekly series of pamphlet novels in 1860 under the title "Beadle's Dime Novels." Within four years the *North American Review* saw fit to review the Beadle books, and the reviewer found their sales to be "almost unprecedented in the annals of booksellers. A dime novel is issued every month and the series has undoubtedly obtained greater popularity than any other series of works of fiction published in America."[5] These dime novels, 4-inch-by-6-inch pamphlets of about 100 pages each known as "yellow-backs," found a large part of that unprecedented audience among soldiers in the Civil War. Beadle and Adams had published four million dime novels by 1865; sales of individual titles ranged from 35,000 to 80,000.[6] Competitors sprang up quickly; among the more successful series were Sinclair Tousey's American Tales (1863), Elliott, Thomas & Talbot's Ten Cent Novelettes (1863), George Munro's Ten Cent Novels (1864), and Robert DeWitt's Ten Cent Romances (1867).

The third main format for popular fiction was the cheap library. These were series of nickel and dime pamphlets of about 8 inches by 11 inches, consisting of either 16 or 32 pages of two-or three-columned print. They were introduced in 1875 when Donnelly, Lloyd & Co., a Chicago publisher, issued their Lakeside Library. When *Publisher's Weekly* surveyed the field in late 1877, they found "fourteen 'libraries' or series of these broadsheets, of which one outreaches a hundred numbers, while another is increasing just now at a regular rate of eight a week." They continue:

> It is difficult to generalize as to what classes of readers buy these broadsheets, but we are inclined to believe, from what we can learn, that they are very largely the *clientele* of the weekly story papers. These have not been pushed of late years as they used to be, and their readers perhaps are ready for something new. The new libraries are also said to have pretty nearly disposed of what little remained of the dime-novel business.[7]

Not only were the readers the same, but so were the publishers. Beadle and Adams issued a Fireside Library, George Munro a Seaside Library, and Norman Munro a Riverside Library; but the field was dominated by Street & Smith, whose many series included the Log Cabin Library (1889) and the Nick Carter Library (1891); and Frank Tousey, who published the Five Cent Weekly Library (1878–93) and the New York Detective Library (1883–98), among others.

So, despite the changing formats, the continuities of readership, publishers, and the fiction itself – many stories were first serialized in the story papers, then printed as dime novels, and eventually reprinted in the libraries – justify the use of "dime novels" to describe this body of narratives, a body quite separate from the genteel fiction of the Victorian middle classes, the novels reviewed and serialized in the major periodicals: *Century*, *Scribner's*, *Harpers* and *The Atlantic*.

If this period can be said to have begun with the newspaper revolution that brought forth the penny press and its new reading public, its end is probably marked by several circumstances of the 1890s: John Lovell's attempt to create a cheap book trust by buying out many of the libraries for his US Book Company in 1891, and his failure in the Panic of 1893; the International Copyright Agreement of 1891, which ended the pirating of British and European fiction that had generated much of the profit of the cheap books and series; the development of the Sunday newspaper; and the "magazine revolution," the emergence of inexpensive slick and pulp magazines in the 1890s. By 1900, the *The Bookman* was noting "the extinction of the dime novel."[8]

If that is the whole for which the "dime novel" stands as a synecdoche, the emphasis on the early westerns, tales of the frontier and of Indian fighting, as the dominant, most characteristic, and most interesting genre has established a prevalent view of that whole. The shift toward outlaw tales, tales of urban life, and detective stories is usually considered a degeneration of the dime novel.[9] In addition, dime novels are characteristically thought of as books for boys and men; cheap romances for women are rarely read or studied.

This view, which dominated the first wave of studies and appreciations of nineteenth-century popular fiction, was triggered by Frank P. O'Brien's large collection of Beadle's dime novels. Part of this collection was auctioned to the public in 1920, while most of it was donated to the New York Public Library and purchased by the Huntington Library in the early 1920s. As Philip Durham points out, "realizing the tendency to look down on cheaply-printed popular literature, Dr. O'Brien was careful not to refer to his books as dime novels; the descriptive title of the catalogue was *American Pioneer Life*."[10] In the New York Public Library catalogue of the O'Brien collection, one finds a classic formulation of the "dime novel." They are

> literally saturated with the pioneer spirit of America. It [the collection] portrays the struggles, exploits, trials, dangers, feats, hardships, and daily lives of the American pioneers. . . . It is a literature intensely nationalistic and patriotic in character; obviously designed to stimulate adventure, self-reliance and achievement; to exalt the feats of the pioneer men and women who settled the country; and to recite the conditions under which those early figures lived and did their work.

They are considered realistic novels:

> It has finally come to be realized that the pictures of pioneer life in the Far West, as presented by the Beadle books, are substantially accurate portrayals of the strange era and characters therein depicted. . . . The Beadle books present a more accurate and vivid picture of the appearance, manner, speech, habits and methods of the pioneer western characters than do the more formal historians. We find in this introduction the folk wisdom that "uncounted armies of boys who lived between the Mississippi and the Atlantic were taken to the woodsheds by their fathers, and there subjected to severe physical and mental anguish as a result of the parental discovery that they were reading such 'impossible trash' ". And we find the sense that the cheap libraries of the 1880s and 1890s are "degenerate and feeble imitations of the earlier Beadle publications". There is no attention to the romances published for girls and women.[11]

Most subsequent considerations of the dime novel were based on the O'Brien collection and this view of the lineaments of nineteenth-century popular fiction. Newspaper humorist Irwin Cobb, in his "A Plea for Old Cap Collier,"[12] defends the dime novels by comparing them to the style and substance of nineteenth-century school readers, and concludes: "Read them for the thrills that are in them. Read them, remembering that if this country had not had a pioneer breed of Buckskin Sams and Deadwood Dicks we should have had no native school of dime novelists. Read them for their brisk and stirring movement; for the spirit of out-door adventure and life which crowds them; for their swift but logical processions of sequences; for the phases of pioneer Americanism they rawly but graphically portray, and for their moral values." In 1929, Edmund Pearson, a librarian, published the first book-length account of dime novels: *Dime Novels: or, Following an Old Trail in Popular Literature*. This slight, entertaining history, interspersed with liberal quotations and plot summaries, exemplifies the combination of nostalgia and nationalism that characterized many of these treatments. Such discussions are also marked by a disdain for their contemporary popular culture, measuring present degeneration against past glory;[13] they share this contempt with the more substantial contemporary treatments of popular fiction in Britain: Q. D. Leavis's *Fiction and the Reading Public* (1932) and George Orwell's "Boys' Weeklies" (1939).

This view of dime novels also informed the first major scholarly and critical studies: Albert Johannsen's two-volume *The House of Beadle and Adams and its Dime and Nickel Novels* (1950), which contains lists of novels, indexes, and biographies of writers, and remains the finest bibliographic guide to dime novels; and Henry Nash Smith's essays on dime novel westerns in *Virgin Land* (1950). They too focused on a single publisher, Beadle and Adams; a single genre, the western; and a primarily male reading public.[14]

Furthermore, it is important to realize the centrality of the collecting and sale of dime novels to our understanding of them. A small group of collectors has been responsible for the physical preservation of this ephemeral literature and for all of the indexes and catalogs of stories that exist. Most of the major research library collections owe their existence to these collectors, not to library initiative. The main periodical dealing with nineteenth-century popular fiction, *Dime Novel Round-Up*, has been published since 1931 as a collector's journal. The bibliographic work of its present editor, Edward T. LeBlanc, is the foundation for any scholarly or critical examination.

However, when Albert Johannsen writes at length on the "value" of dime novels, he is referring to their exchange value. He writes that "another factor in determining the value of a novel . . . is the story itself.

Opinions differ as to the relative importance of the different groups of novels." Johannsen goes on to list types, in order of descending "value": early colonial and pioneer tales, western tales of scouts and Indian fighters, tales of Buffalo Bill and Calamity Jane, sea tales, tales of city life, detective stories. He concludes: "And love stories, I presume, should go at the bottom of the list."[15] My reason for citing this is less to disagree with Johannsen (I assume that his was a relatively accurate sense of the rare book market of the late 1940s) than to point out its effects on historical writing. When dealing with an immense body of narratives – Beadle and Adams alone published 3,158 separate titles[16] – certain kinds of selection are necessary. And the kind of selection that has structured our understanding – the kind of synecdoche "dime novel" is – has an historical and ideological foundation.

This is why I rehearse this history. For Beadle and Adams, though important, did not entirely dominate sensational fiction. Their success with tales of pioneers and the frontier must be balanced against the wider range of fiction – aristocratic costume romances, detective tales, working-girl stories, tales of the American Revolution, mysteries of the city, outlaw stories – which was published in the story papers, cheap libraries, and pamphlet novels, both before and after the heyday of Beadle's Dime Books. Several central judgements about dime novels are the result more of collectors' tastes than of historical analysis, tastes that owe much to the myths and ideologies of the "western" in twentieth-century popular culture. Indeed the relative fading of westerns from contemporary popular culture may allow us to recognize the other genres and types that existed in the nineteenth century; there are signs that the dime novel detective tale is replacing the dime novel western in critical favor.[17]

Moreover, the sense that there was a shift in the dime novel from western themes to urban themes is belied by the tremendous popularity of the "mysteries of the city" in the 1840s; and the judgment of degeneration seems an unwillingness to deal with the relation of the dime novel to the immigrant working classes. One can see this in a lament of the late 1920s:

> The period between 1870 and 1900 witnessed the rise of the train-robber and detective as the protagonists in paper-covered literature. It marks also the decline of the House of Beadle and the triumph of the cheaper elements in dime novel publishing. . . . As more competitors entered the field, which was still lucrative, the quality of the "dimes" and "half-dimes" was lowered until they became flaring atrocities. No longer was it possible for a Henry Ward Beecher to commend the editor of a dime novel. Presidents of the United States no longer pored over the yellow-backs. The pulpit and the polite press trained its heaviest "grape" on the

sub-literary weeklies, and in the last fifteen years [1913–28] they have been harried and hunted off the news-stands into the dismal murk of second-hand speakeasies.[18]

However, the picture of the dime novel changes if we think of its readers not as small-town Tom Sawyers sneaking a "read" behind the woodshed but as young factory workers; the nationalism and chauvinism of the cheap stories takes on a different cast when considered in relation to young immigrants. And any attention to the story papers shows the importance of girls' and women's reading in a picture of cheap sensational fiction of the nineteenth century. Finally, far from being an uncorrupted moment before the onset of mass culture, the dime novel industry is a central component of the emerging culture industry: Robert Bonner, Park Benjamin, and Erastus Beadle stand with P. T. Barnum and Albert Spaulding as early entrepreneurs of leisure. Therefore my concern will be with the "mechanic accents" of these stories, with the intersection of the new mass culture and the culture of the new masses, with the place of dime novels within working class life. To view these books that collectors prize through the culture of craftworkers, factory operatives, and laborers rescues them from a kind of patronizing and patriotic nostalgia, and situates them not in a pastoral golden age but in the class conflicts of the gilded age.

Notes

1   Michael Schudson, *Discovering the News: A Social History of American News-papers* (New York: Basic Books, 1978), p. 30.
2   James Barnes, *Authors, Publishers and Politicians: The Quest for an Anglo-American Copyright Agreement, 1815–1854* (Columbus: Ohio State University Press, 1974), p. 11.
3   For an account of the business history and circulation of the early story papers, see Barnes, pp. 1–29. The *Ledger* claimed a circulation of 377,000 by 1869, and the *New York Weekly* had a circulation of 350,000 in 1877 (Mary Noel, *Villains Galore: The Heyday of the Popular Story Weekly* [New York: Macmillan, 1954], pp. 130, 138). Later in the century, the competition was keen; in 1892, the *Weekly* had a circulation of 250,000, the *Fireside Companion* 200,000, the *Family Story Paper* 150,000, and the *Ledger* 100,000 (*N. W. Ayer & Sons Newspaper Annual, 1892*).
4   Frank L. Schick, *The Paperbound Book in America* (New York: R. R. Bowker & Co., 1958), p. 49.
5   William Everett, "Critical Notices: Beadle's Dime Books," *North American Review* 99 (July 1864), pp. 303–9.
6   Schick, p. 51.
7   "The Cheap Libraries," *Publisher's Weekly* 12 (October 6, 1877), pp. 396–7.

8 Fermin Dredd, "The Extinction of the Dime Novel," *The Bookman* 11 (March 1900), pp. 46–8.
9 Robert Peabody Bellows, "The Degeneration of the Dime Novel," The Writer 12 (July 1899), pp. 97–9; Henry Nash Smith, *Virgin Land: the American West as Symbol and Myth* (Cambridge, Mass.: Harvard University Press, 1950), pp. 119–20.
10 Philip Durham, ed., *Dime Novels* (New York: Odyssey Press, 1966), p. ix.
11 *The Beadle Collection of Dime Novels* (New York: New York Public Library, 1922), pp. 3–4, 7, 17.
12 Irvin Cobb, *Irvin Cobb at His Best* (Garden City, NY: Doran & Co., 1929), pp. 194–5.
13 For examples of this kind of commentary, see Edmund Pearson, *Dime Novels; or, Following and Old Trail in Popular Literature* (Boston: Little, Brown, 1929); Brander Matthews, "Certain Books in Black and Red," *Literary Digest Book Review* 1 (June 1923), pp. 33–5; and two articles by Henry Morton Robinson: "The Dime Novel is Dead, But the Same Old Hungers Are Still Fed," *The Century Magazine* 116 (May 1928), pp. 60–7 and "Mr. Beadle's Books," *Bookman* 69 (March 1929), pp. 18–24.
14 This emphasis is continued in Daryl Jones's *The Dime Novel Western* (Bowling Green, Ohio: Bowling Green University Press, 1978) as well as the first major microform collection of University Microfilms International's *Dime Novel Fiction: Popular Escape Fiction of the Nineteenth Century.*
15 Albert Johansen, *The Nickel Library: Bibliographic Listing* (Fall River, Mass.: Edward T. LeBlanc, 1950), Vol. II, p. 325.
16 Durham, p. vi. As a comparison, Lyle Wright's bibliographies of American fiction for 1850–1900 (San Marino, California: The Huntington Library, 1969–78), which omit all dime novels and serialized fiction, have 9,003 entries.
17 See Will Wright, *Six Guns and Society: A Structural Guide to the Western* (Berkeley: University of California Press, 1975) for a fine discussion of the western in twentieth-century culture. Gary Hoppenstand's edited collection *The Dime Novel Detective* (Bowling Green, Ohio: Bowling Green University Popular Press, 1982) is a recent reprinting and reassessment of dime novel detectives.
18 Robinson, "The Dime Novel Is Dead," pp. 64–5.

Consider the Source

1. Soldier, scout, and rider on the fabled Pony Express, William F. Cody (1846–1917) had a colorful career years before he became a fixture of dime novels – and a legend of the American stage – as "Buffalo Bill." Like Davy Crockett and John Wayne, Buffalo Bill was more a legend than a man, a collection of stories whose factual verification was largely beside the point for fans who passionately embraced the varied (and sometimes conflicting) values he seemed to embody.

The following excerpt comes from the 1899 book *Last of the Great Scouts: The Life of Col. William F. Cody* "as told by" his sister, Helen Cody Wetmore. Though not published in the dime novel formats described by Michael Denning, the story, style, and language of Wetmore's book – right down to its purported "authentic" status as a biography – comes straight out of the dime novel tradition. What, as far as you can tell, are the characteristics of that tradition? Why might this kind of story have particular appeal to American boys? Can you imagine why anyone would object to it (or why someone would remember it fondly)?

Excerpt from *Last of the Great Scouts* by Helen Cody Wetmore (1899)

How the Sobriquet of "Buffalo Bill" Was Won

In frontier days a man had but to ask for work to get it. There was enough and to spare for every one. The work that paid best was the kind that suited Will, it mattered not how hard or dangerous it might be...work on the Kansas Pacific Railroad was pushing forward at a rapid rate, and [Will] saw a new field of activity open for him – that of buffalo-hunting. Twelve hundred men were employed on the railroad construction, and Goddard Brothers, who had undertaken to board the vast crew, were hard pressed to obtain fresh meat. To supply this indispensable, buffalo-hunters were employed, and as Will was known to be an expert buffalo-slayer, Goddard Brothers were glad to add him to their "commissary staff." His contract with them called for an average of twelve buffaloes daily, for which he was to receive five hundred dollars a month. It was "good pay," the desired feature, but the work was hard and hazardous. He must first scour the country for his game, with a good prospect always of finding Indians instead of buffalo; then, when the game was shot, he must oversee its cutting and dressing, and look after the wagons that transported it to the camp where the workmen messed. It was while working under this contract that he acquired the sobriquet of "Buffalo Bill." It clung to him ever after, and he wore it with more pride than he would have done the title of prince or grand duke. Probably there are thousands of people to-day who know him by that name only.

At the outset he procured a trained buffalo-hunting horse, which went by the unconventional name of "Brigham," and from the government he obtained an improved breech-loading needle-gun, which, in testimony of its murderous qualities, he named "Lucretia Borgia."

Buffaloes were usually plentiful enough, but there were times when the camp supply of meat ran short. During one of these dull spells, when the company was pressed for horses, Brigham was hitched to a scraper. One can imagine his indignation. A racer dragging a street-car would have no more just cause for rebellion than a buffalo-hunter tied to a work implement in the company of stupid horses that never had a thought above a plow, a hay-rake, or a scraper. Brigham expostulated, and in such plain language, that Will, laughing, was on the point of unhitching him, when a cry went up – the equivalent of a whaler's "There she blows!" – that a herd of buffaloes was coming over the hill.

Brigham and the scraper parted company instantly, and Will mounted him bareback, the saddle being at the camp, a mile away. Shouting an order to the men to follow him with a wagon to take back the meat, he galloped toward the game.

There were other hunters that day. Five officers rode out from the neighboring fort, and joined Will while waiting for the buffaloes to come up. They were recent arrivals in that part of the country, and their shoulder-straps indicated that one was a captain and the others were lieutenants. They did not know "Buffalo Bill." They saw nothing but a good-looking young fellow, in the dress of a working man, astride a not handsome horse, which had a blind bridle and no saddle. It was not a formidable-looking hunting outfit, and the captain was disposed to be a trifle patronizing.

"Hello!" he called out. "I see you're after the same game we are."

"Yes, sir," returned Will. "Our camp's out of fresh meat."

The officer ran a critical eye over Brigham. "Do you expect to run down a buffalo with a horse like that?" said he.

"Why," said Will, innocently, "are buffaloes pretty speedy?"

"Speedy? It takes a fast horse to overhaul those animals on the open prairie."

"Does it?" said Will; and the officer did not see the twinkle in his eye. Nothing amuses a man more than to be instructed on a matter that he knows thoroughly, and concerning which his instructor knows nothing. Probably every one of the officers had yet to shoot his first buffalo.

"Come along with us," offered the captain, graciously. "We're going to kill a few for sport, and all we care for are the tongues and a chunk of the tenderloin; you can have the rest."

"Thank you," said Will. "I'll follow along."

There were eleven buffaloes in the herd, and the officers started after them as if they had a sure thing on the entire number. Will noticed that the game was pointed toward a creek, and understanding "the nature of the beast," started for the water, to head them off.

As the herd went past him, with the military quintet five hundred yards in the rear, he gave Brigham's blind bridle a twitch, and in a few jumps the trained hunter was at the side of the rear buffalo; Lucretia Borgia spoke, and the buffalo fell dead. Without even a bridle signal, Brigham was promptly at the side of the next buffalo, not ten feet away, and this, too, fell at the first shot. The maneuver was repeated until the last buffalo went down. Twelve shots had been fired; then Brigham, who never wasted his strength, stopped. The officers had not had even a shot at the game. Astonishment was written on their faces as they rode up.

"Gentlemen," said Will, courteously, as he dismounted, "allow me to present you with eleven tongues and as much of the tenderloin as you wish."

"By Jove!" exclaimed the captain, "I never saw anything like that before. Who are you, anyway?"

"Bill Cody's my name."

"Well, Bill Cody, you know how to kill buffalo, and that horse of yours has some good running points, after all."

"One or two," smiled Will.

Captain Graham – as his name proved to be – and his companions were a trifle sore over missing even the opportunity of a shot, but they professed to be more than repaid for their disappointment by witnessing a feat they had not supposed possible in a white man – hunting buffalo without a saddle, bridle, or reins. Will explained that Brigham knew more about the business than most two-legged hunters. All the rider was expected to do was to shoot the buffalo. If the first shot failed, Brigham allowed another; if this, too, failed, Brigham lost patience, and was as likely as not to drop the matter then and there.

It was this episode that fastened the name of "Buffalo Bill" upon Will . . .

2. As Denning notes, western stories, while most familiar to collectors and historians, represent only one strand of the dime novel tradition. The following is an advertisement for *A Knight of Labor; or Job Manly's Rise in Life. A Story of a Young Man in the Country* by the highly popular Beadle & Adams author Frederick Whittaker:

Another *speaking* story of work life and struggle – of man and master – of handy hands and sturdy purpose – of country boy fighting his way in the world, with a hammer and will, and out of whose step by step from the village blacksmith shop to the proprietorship of a great carriage manufactory is taught A Splendid Lesson with a Big Moral That, to the young American mechanic, will be a kind of revelation. As a romance of workingman's life it is exceeding full of interest, both personal and associate. In Job, the rough, untutored, hard-headed, almost desperate apprentice, the reader literally has a rough diamond which takes severe cutting to bring out the *facets* of a fine character. That A Woman Does It does not lessen the young blacksmith's heroism, nor detract from the great workman's achievements; and we know the audience interested in Captain Whittaker's previous creations will give this new work a cordial greeting.

What accents do you detect here? How are the qualities celebrated in this advertisement similar to, and different than, Wetmore's account of Buffalo Bill?

3.   Boys weren't the only subject of dime novel fiction. Can-do dime novel heroines like Calamity Jane and Leonie Locke appeared regularly – though often in disguise as men – in many dime novels. The following excerpt from the 1872 novel *A Hard Crowd; or Gentleman Sam's Sister*, describes the character of Iola (that is, Gentleman Sam's sister), who is "quite an Amazon" capable of shooting down any man who insults her. But Iola has something quite different in mind when she tends the wounded hero of the story:

> Unconsciously she yielded to the persuasive clasp of his arms, until she rested, almost fainting, on his breast, and felt the throbbing of his heart, and his warm breath on her cheek.
>
> Their love sought no expression in words. But the woman, whose free heart had been little curbed by the conventionalities of artificial society, let her arms glide around his neck, as was most natural that she should, and clasped him closer and closer until their lips met.
>
> Thus lip to lip they drank in the first incense of mutual love. . . .

How would you describe the portrayal of Iola here: Realistic? Sexy? Sexist? For whom do you imagine it would have the most appeal?

4.   Denning opens this chapter with two epigraphs from Brander Matthews, a professor and playwright described by the *Dictionary of American Biography* as "the last of the gentlemanly school of critics and essayists that distinguished American literature in the last half of the nineteenth century." (Matthews also makes a cameo appearance in Daniel Czitrom's discussion of movies in chapter 6.) Why do you think Denning chose to begin the piece this way? What do you think he gains from doing so? What may explain the seeming divergence of the views Matthews expresses between 1883 and 1923?

Suggested Further Reading

Much of the discussion of dime novel fiction is fragmented and specialized, usually conducted as part of a discussion of other subjects. Any investigator of the topic would do well to begin with one of the great works in American studies scholarship: Henry Nash Smith's *Virgin Land: The American West as Symbol and Myth* (Cambridge, Mass.: Harvard University Press, 1950), which includes a highly influential chapter on dime novels. Also highly regarded is John Cawelti's *The Six-Gun Mystique* (1970; Bowling Green, O.: The Popular Press, 1984) and his *Adventure, Mystery, Romance: Formula Stories as Art and Popular Culture* (Chicago: University of Chicago Press, 1976). See also the latter two volumes of Richard Slotkin's trilogy on the American West: *The Fatal Environment: The Myth of the Frontier in the Age of Industrialization* (New York: Atheneum, 1985) and *Gunfighter Nation: The Myth of the Frontier in Twentieth-Century America* (New York: Atheneum, 1992). A more recent source is a collection of essays, *Pioneers, Passionate Ladies, and Private Eyes: Dime Novels, Series Books, and Paperbacks*, edited by Larry E. Sullivan and Lydia Cushman Schurman (New York: Haworth Press, 1996).

5

The Romance of the Dance Hall

1870s	Thomas Edison and Alexander Graham Bell work on technology for recording sound
1878	Edison receives patent for phonograph
1893	World Columbian Exposition opens in Chicago
1890s	Jazz begins to emerge in New Orleans and other cities
1895	Sea Lion Park opens on Coney Island, followed by other amusement parks that feature dance pavilions
1898	Spanish-American War
ca.1900	The Cakewalk, Turkey Trot and other dance crazes popular among American youth
1901	Theodore Roosevelt becomes president after the assassination of William McKinley (1901–9)
1914	*Modern Dancing* by Vernon and Irene Castle published
1912	Women participate in major strike in textile mills in Lawrence, Massachusetts
1914–18	World War I
1920	Nineteenth Amendment to the US Constitution gives women the right to vote

Introduction

As a means of religious worship, communal celebration, or artistic expression, dance is as old as human civilization. But it only became part of popular culture when it was commodified, i.e., when it became an experience that could be bought and sold on a mass basis. For much of the nineteenth century, this experience, however intensely felt, usually took the form of spectatorship: dancing was an important, though usually subsidiary, component of plays, operas, minstrel shows, and other kinds of stage entertainment.

In the last third of the century, dancing was particularly prominent in the emerging stage genres of vaudeville and burlesque. Vaudeville (the term comes from nineteenth-century French pastoral plays, even though it was very much an urban American form of entertainment) was a variety show that regularly featured many kinds of dancers, from minstrel-show antics to refined ballet. Dancing was more central to the burlesque show, which in the United States began after the Civil War as a kind of musical theater performed by an all-woman cast, but which, in the twentieth century, was increasingly associated with the striptease act.

The decades surrounding 1900 also marked the advent of dancing as a form of popular culture in which men and women could not only experience vicarious pleasure, but actually participate themselves. One key development in this process was the invention of sound recording, which made it possible to practice dancing in the home as well as in public. Like other technologies, sound recording was a group invention; two key players were Alexander Graham Bell and Thomas Edison, who worked independently and in rivalry with each other in the 1870s and 1880s. Both men thought that records – which were originally made on cylinders until the German-born American inventor Emile Berliner developed more user-friendly flat plates – would be used as dictation devices by businessmen. But by the 1890s, arcades were featuring record players along the lines of movie kinescopes (a matter to be discussed in the next chapter). And by 1901 the Columbia Phonograph and Victor Talking Machine Company were competing to provide phonographs for home use. Thus it was that a new medium could promote new forms of popular culture.

Meanwhile, new cultural sites like amusement parks offered visitors open pavilions in which live and recorded music invited people to express themselves in ways that were both private and public at the same time. Dancing had long been associated with bars and clubs where alcohol was consumed, but the owners and managers of these establishments now promoted dancing – and specific techniques like "ladies' nights" – to attract the growing numbers of working-class women untethered from the rhythms of traditional community and family life. The appeal of dancing was so great for women in particular that another new institution, the dance hall, sprang up to meet the demand.

In this chapter from her 1986 book *Cheap Amusements: Working Women and Leisure in Turn-of-the-Century New York*, Kathy Peiss, a women's historian at the University of Massachusetts at Amherst, describes the culture of dance halls. As Peiss explains, social dancing was something of a double-edged sword for young women, offering freedom from work and family constraints – and even some power over the men who courted them – but also revealing the limits of that power both in the forms it could take and the extent of its reach. As such, dance halls are a revealing indicator not only of the gender politics of turn-of-century New York, but also of more lasting dilemmas for all women who continue to navigate between the desire for sexual equality and the appeal of sexual difference.

Dance Madness

Kathy Peiss

Of all the amusements that bedazzled the single working woman, dancing proved to be her greatest passion. After the long day laboring in a factory or shop, young women dressed themselves in their fanciest finery, put on their dancing shoes, and hurried out to a neighborhood hall, ballroom, or saloon equipped with a dance floor. The gaily decorated hall, riveting beat of the orchestra, and whirl of dance partners created a magical world of pleasure and romance. Thousands of young women and men flocked to such halls each week in Manhattan. By the 1910s, over five hundred public dance halls opened their doors each evening throughout greater New York, and more than one hundred dancing academies instructed 100,000 neophytes yearly in the latest steps. As one reformer exclaimed, "the town is dance mad."[1]

The dance hall was the favorite arena in which young working women played out their cultural style. Their passion for the dance started early, often in childhood, as girls danced on the streets to the tunes of itinerant musicians. In a 1910 survey of one thousand public school children aged eleven to fourteen, nearly nine out of ten girls reported that they knew how to dance, in contrast to only one-third of the boys. By the time they were teen-agers, dancing had become a pervasive part of women's social life. The vast majority of women attending dance halls were under twenty years of age, and some were only twelve or thirteen. Their male dance partners tended to be slightly older; dancing was even more popular with them than were saloons and pool halls.[2] For both sexes, going to the city's dance halls marked a particular stage in the life cycle. Participation rose during adolescence, when dance halls offered "the only opportunity in the winter for unrestrained, uncramped social intercourse between the young people of the two sexes."[3] Attendance at the

Hot spot   Exterior of Aly's Dance Hall and Dancing Studio, located at East 125th Street, New York City, May, 1912. Evenings and weekends transformed such unprepossessing settings into sites of drama, romance, and, in some cases, danger. *Photo from the Collection of the New-York Historical Society*

halls lessened considerably when girls started "keeping company" with a beau and ceased upon marriage. Josie, a sixteen-year-old habitué of the dance halls, told Ruth True, "When I'm eighteen or nineteen I won't care about it anymore. I'll have a 'friend' then and won't want to go anywheres."[4]

Young women's attendance at dance halls followed the general patterns of their participation in street life and social clubs. The evidence is too limited to show the specific social composition of the dancers – their ethnicity, family life, or work experience. No ethnic enclave seems to have had a monopoly on dancing. The lower East Side was riddled with dance halls, and Russian and Polish Jews delighted in balls and affairs. In the heart of this district – between Houston and Grand Streets and east of the Bowery – a settlement worker counted thirty-one dance halls, one for every two-and-a-half blocks, more than any other area in the city.[5] Other surveys indicate that dancing was popular throughout Manhattan's working-class neighborhoods, whether the locale was an upper East Side block of Italians and Jews or a West Side tenement district inhabited by American, German, and Irish working people. Although we cannot enumerate the occupations of the dancers, women who worked in typical female jobs, including garment workers, domestic servants, and saleswomen, were commonly seen in the city's halls.[6]

What was the role of the dance hall in the lives of young working-class women? From an anthropological perspective, dance is a form of structured, expressive movement that articulates and conveys cultural information to its participants, helping them to make sense of their world. While dance hall culture is only a piece of working-class experience, and a relatively small one, it is a window on cultural issues and social dynamics that are usually obscured.[7] Ethnographic description of dance halls – dance steps, ballroom etiquette, drinking customs, clothing styles – illuminate aspects of the cultural construction of gender among working-class Americans. These forms of expression dramatize the ways in which working-class youth culturally managed sexuality, intimacy, and respectability.

This dance hall culture, and its embodiment of sexual ideology and gender relations, must also be situated in a broader social context. The organization of dancing underwent important changes in the late nineteenth century, as the commercialization of leisure challenged older patterns of working-class recreation. Once a family amusement and neighborhood event, dancing was transformed as its setting changed. New ballrooms and dance palaces offered a novel kind of social space for their female patrons, enhancing and legitimating their participation in a public social life. The commercial culture of the dance halls meshed with that of working-class youth in a symbiotic relationship, reinforcing emergent values and "modern" attitudes toward leisure, sexuality, and personal fulfillment.

The Social Organization of Working-class Dance

Dance madness thrived in the back rooms of dingy saloons, in large neighborhood halls, and in the brightly lit pavilions of amusement parks. The character of working-class dances from 1880 to 1920 varied considerably with the type of hall, the organization of the dance, and the social composition of the participants.[8] The traditional working-class dance of the late nineteenth and early twentieth centuries, however, was the "affair" held in a rented neighborhood hall. At public dance halls, "receptions, 'affairs,' weddings, and balls are given or take place three or four nights a week in a majority of them and on Saturday and Sunday afternoons," observed the University Settlement. "These are given by reputable organizations and the weddings are usually family parties."[9] Local fraternal lodges, mutual aid societies, political associations, and unions "ran off" dances on an annual or occasional basis. The affair not only raised money for charitable purposes, but strengthened group spirit for members and their families.

Many of these dances originated in kinship ties and Old World customs. Weddings held in neighborhood halls provided frequent opportunities to dance and visit among family and friends. At the East Side's Liberty Hall, which held three weddings each week, young and old danced at the receptions to Russian melodies until the early hours of the morning.[10] Traditional folk dances, such as the annual Bohemian Peasant Ball, were transplanted to New York, reinforcing immigrant bonds. Those in attendance wore national costumes, with some participants representing folk characters. A receiving line of Bohemian societies was formed, and a mock marriage ceremony performed, followed by a dance that lasted until dawn.[11] In addition, the immigrant residents of lower Manhattan often gathered in the back room of corner saloons for dancing, drinking, and socializing. The saloon dance hall, observed one settlement worker, was a "veritable neighborhood rallying-place, where young and middle-aged of both sexes crowd in the stuffy room together; where English is little spoken; and mental and physical atmosphere suggest a medieval inn."[12]

Organization affairs and traditional balls took place in an environment controlled at least partially by familial supervision and community ties, although without the strict properties and chaperonage of a middle-class dance. This was particularly the case at smaller dances, observed one settlement worker, where "greater respectability is maintained, because there is a closer acquaintance among those who attend."[13] Usually the sponsoring organization issued formal invitations and sometimes appointed floor managers to oversee the dancing and drinking. For example, when the Hudson River Railroad Association held a ball at the Manhattan Casino, they hired a special officer to prevent shimmying and improper dancing.[14]

Young women attended affairs or weddings with their families or an approved escort, expecting to see friends and neighbors. With the exception of Italian immigrants, who sharply restricted the public activities of women, most parents considered these dances relatively safe for their daughters. West Side girls whose Irish and native-born parents strictly guarded them were permitted nevertheless to go to an occasional lodge sociable, church dance, or wedding. Similarly, in the lower East Side, "an invitation to a public ball or wedding once in two weeks may reasonably be expected by the unmarried girls of the district." Sarah Wiseman recalls travelling to lower Manhattan to attend the balls of different societies and clubs: "I was going downtown, those years it was customary [to have] balls on Saturday night, each *landsmanschaft*."[15]

The traditional affair, linked to the extensive network of working-class voluntary organizations, remained a common form of amusement well into the twentieth century. In the 1890s, however, new ways of organizing dancing, spurred by the growth of a working-class youth culture, developed alongside the traditional ball and affair. The "racket," a dance organized by social clubs and amusement societies, increasingly enticed young pleasure-seekers. In the tenement districts, the Barn Stormers, Fly-by-Nights, Lady Sheriffs, and other clubs vied with each other to hold the best ball of the social season.[16]

Rackets differed greatly from the lodge affair or benefit society ball, in which dancing was associated with neighborhood supervision, philanthropy, and intergenerational sociability. Clubs evinced little interest in controlling admissions and chaperoning the dance floor. Promotional posters like the following, advertising a dance of the Schiller Young Men's Benevolent Association, plastered tenement walls and saloon windows:

Full dress and Civic Ball
given by
Schiller
Y – M – B – A
Grand Living Broome Street,
March 25,
Music by Prof. L. Uberstein,
Brass Band
Dancing commencing at 7:30 o'clock sharp.[17]

Observed a social investigator, "One day in walking not more than three blocks on Grand and Clinton Streets, I counted nineteen different posters advertising nineteen different balls and entertainments which were to be given in the near future."[18] Extensive advertising and the indiscriminate sale of tickets often brought crowds of seven hundred to eight hundred dancers to a single event. "Almost any one may buy a ticket," young women from the West Side informed Elsa Herzfeld. "If the racket is to be a large one you must expect 'a mixed crowd.'"[19] At such dances, proper working-girls in their neat shirtwaists might find themselves mingling with the flashily dressed and "tough."

Participating in this social round became a familiar practice for the young women and men who belonged to clubs and amusement societies. One reformer observed that "the same people are frequently found at the different dance halls.... It appears that the boxes are all reserved by different 'clubs.'"[20] Rackets offered not only pleasure but profit: the sale of tickets produced enough money to finance excursions and vacations for club members. The Rounder Social Club, for example, ran an affair every year in order to rent a bungalow at Rockaway Beach each summer.[21] With these incentives, the club dance became increasingly widespread throughout the working-class sections of the city.

The Commercialization of Dancing

An interlocking network of commercial institutions and voluntary societies structured working-class dancing. Whether the dances were lodge affairs or club "blow-outs," the dance craze was intensified by the expansion and commercialization of Manhattan's public halls. For the working-class population packed into small tenement apartments, large halls that could be rented for dances, weddings, mass meetings, and other gatherings were a requirement of social life. The number of public halls in Manhattan rose substantially in a short period; business directories listed 130 halls in 1895 and 195 in 1910, an increase of 50 percent. While some of these, like Carnegie Hall, were cultural spaces of the privileged, most were located in working-class districts. The largest East Side halls, such as the New Irving, Progress Assembly Rooms, and Liberty Hall could hold five hundred to twelve hundred people and were always in great demand.[22] Moreover, the directories do not include countless saloons that expeditiously added a back room or upstairs hall for dancing and meetings. In the Trinity Church area of downtown Manhattan, for example, investigators found many private dance halls situated over saloons, even though public dance hall licenses from the city had been denied.[23]

The "liquor interests" spurred the growth of large public halls that could accommodate dances for hundreds of people. In the lower East Side, 80 percent of the dance halls surveyed in 1901 were adjacent to saloons, and the sale of alcohol formed in the foundation of their business. A social club could hire New Irving Hall, for example, for thirty dollars a night, and if its dances were known to be money-making ventures, the owner might offer it free for the next engagement. The club would sell tickets and hat checks to swell its coffers, while the hall owner dispensed liquor to enlarge his. Other halls based their rentals on a sliding scale, determined by the amount of alcohol consumed.[24] With the hall owner's profits pegged to alcohol consumption, dancing and drinking went hand in hand, as typical dance programs suggest. In the small saloon dance hall with no admission fee, a dance might last three or four minutes, followed by a fifteen-to twenty-minute intermission period devoted to drinking. In a respectable dancing academy or lodge affair, ten minutes were permitted for dancing, with a shorter intermission for rest and refreshment.[25] Quenching the thirst of dancers became a profitable business, and amusement resorts rushed to rent spaces to clubs, lodges, and benefit societies. As a waiter at the Central Casino observed, "They have about four balls a week and that[']s what makes this place pay."[26]

By the 1910s, the old multiple-purpose neighborhood hall and saloon no longer could meet the demand for dance space, and huge metropolitan halls and ballrooms designed specifically for dancing sprang up. The first dance palace, the Grand Central, was built in 1911, and five others, including Roseland Ballroom, followed in the next ten years. Ranging in capacity from five hundred to three thousand patrons, the large halls were usually located in the commercial amusement zones of the city, in such areas as 42nd Street and Broadway, 14th Street, and 125th Street, serving a city-wide clientele. Dance palaces attracted people of all nationalities, but they appealed more to factory and office workers than to middle-class and elite amusement-seekers, who flocked to Gotham's cabarets and restaurants. Large working-class organizations often rented these halls for their yearly gatherings. In the 1910s, at least twenty unions held annual balls with over three thousand people in attendance. Huge affairs by such groups as the Metropolitan Street Railway Employees or the Stationary Firemen packed the Palm Garden, Terrace Garden, Manhattan Casino, and other dance resorts.[27]

In the large commercial halls, the continuing presence of a sponsoring club or organization conferred legitimacy on the dance, even as the activity moved away from its traditional working-class form. Hall managers even created their own clubs to encourage a steady clientele and add a veneer of respectability to the dance. The Manhattan Casino, for example, formed the Tiger Social Club, which held basketball games and rackets every Sunday afternoon.[28] The illusion of sponsorship remained important to hall owners, who hoped to bury the unsavory reputation of the commercial dance house, which dated back to the Victorian era. These had been part of an extensive male subculture with links to prostitution, gambling, and the "sporting" life. In the mid-nineteenth century, for example, numerous dance halls run by Germans and frequented primarily by sailors could be found in the 1st Ward; these employed "decoy dancers" or "taxi-dancers" as female companions for the patrons. Dressed in scanty costumes, some of the women also earned money as prostitutes, soliciting the men's business as they waltzed. Prominent commercial dance houses of the 1860s and 1870s, such as John Allen's and Harry Hill's, also were primarily the cultural territory of men. These drew female curiosity-seekers and the demimonde, but respectable women anxious to preserve their reputations would not attend.[29]

The gulf between commercial and sponsored dances lessened by 1900, and hall owners increasingly ran dances without the mediation of an organization or club, throwing open their doors to anyone paying the price of admission. A popular strategy was to advertise the hall as a dancing academy, teach the latest steps during the day, and offer open public "receptions" in the evenings and on Sunday afternoons. Such East Side halls as the Apollo and the Golden Rule, for example, operated primarily as dancing schools.[30]

Commercial dance halls remained morally suspect to some parents and their daughters. Irma Knecht, for example, differentiated between the respectable social evenings of the *landsmanschaft* societies and the promiscuous public halls: "We didn't go to these dance halls, [we] used to go to organization affairs."[31] Others, however, had no qualms about attending the public halls. Ruth Kaminsky, for example, exclaimed, "As single girls we went dancing...in dancing halls, we went dancing, we used to have a nice time, to meet fellows."[32] Girls who were not closely supervised by their parents went to public dances and social club parties at least one evening a week, and some attended as many as three or four. Hutchins Hapgood noticed that some East Side shopgirls "dance every night, and are so confirmed in it that they are technically known as 'spielers.'"[33] For these women, the emergence of the large commercial dance hall, whether run through general admission fees, through social club rentals, or as a dancing academy, created an alternative to the traditional affair of the fraternal lodge and benefit society. The intergenerational integration that was possible in the locally based dance rarely occurred in the new ballrooms and dance palaces. Rather, this expanding network of commercial dance halls became the territory of working-class youth.

Dance Hall Culture

With the commercialization of dancing, hall owners and entrepreneurs especially promoted the participation of young women. Halls lowered their admission prices for unescorted women, charging ten to fifteen cents, as opposed to the usual fee of twenty-five or fifty cents per couple; some even admitted women free. Charges for checking hats and coats show a similar differential: "Ladies ten cents, gentlemen a quarter."[34] This policy implicitly recognized the subordinate economic status of women, at the same time that it urged them to attend ballrooms with or without an escort.

The hall owners' pitch was not primarily an appeal to thrift, however, but rather a promise of excitement, glamour, and romance. In the late nineteenth century, working-class dances had often taken place in small, dingy saloons, crowded with dancers who simply ignored the unpleasant surroundings. The new commercial dance halls, however, were large structures that enticed their patrons with bright lights, blaring music, and a festive atmosphere. "The sounds of a waltz or two step pounded on the piano and emphasized by an automatic drum flow out to a passer-by," while hall managers stood in the streets and declaimed, like circus barkers, upon the splendors inside.[35] In the hall, a large, polished dance floor, bounded by a stage at one end and a bar at the other, drew crowds of youth. Often a balcony ringed the dance floor, containing chairs and tables for patrons to relax and watch the dancers. Banners and mirrors gave a festive air to the halls, and the "Professor" and his band warmed up the crowd with the latest ragtime tunes. As one investigator observed at a lively ball, "Everybody was full of joy asking them to repeat the same dance."[36] Weekday dances ended no earlier than one or two o'clock, and on a Saturday night they continued well into the early morning.

Where young women saw an aura of sensual pleasure, middle-class observers of the commercial halls found immorality, drawing a lurid connection between working girls' recreation and vice. The press was filled with dramatic accounts of innocent daughters tempted by glittering dance halls, seduced and drugged by ruthless "cadets" or pimps, and held against their will in brothels. Beyond the sensationalism, their views had some basis in fact. As historian Ruth Rosen has shown, incidents of white slavery did occur in the nation's large cities. The Committee of Fourteen, a reform agency formed to battle urban prostitution and vice, sent undercover investigators to the city's saloons and dance houses in the 1910s. While their primary concern lay in the clean-up of notorious resorts, their reports reveal in rare detail the culture of many commercial dance halls frequented by working-class youth.[37]

The large public halls they described were territories where the promiscuous interaction of strangers was normative behavior. Classes and cultures mingled in New York's commercial halls. At a Turnverein ball in 1917, for example, a vice investigator reported the entrance of two gentlemen in evening dress and top hats seeking prostitutes at what was primarily a working-class dance.[38] Indeed, by the 1910s, it was often difficult to distinguish the dress and style of respectable women from prostitutes at dances. As one waiter explained to a vice investigator who wished to be "introduced" to any available women, "The way women dress today they all look like prostitutes and the waiter can some times get in bad by going over and trying to put some one next to them, they may be respectable women and would jump on the waiter."[39]

Clearly the middle-class distinction between respectable working-class women and prostitutes polarized a more complex social reality. At the Turnverein ball, for example, the investigator acknowledged that the crowd was a more reputable one than the usual patrons of Remey's, but his description belied the usual bourgeois standards of conduct. He described the scene in the hall's barroom, as patrons sought refreshment between dances:

> I saw one of the women smoking cigarettes, most of the younger couples were hugging and kissing, there was a general mingling of men and women at the different tables, almost every one seemed to know one another and spoke to each other across the room, also saw both men and women leave their tables and join couples at different tables, they were all singing and carrying on, they kept running around the room and acted like a mob of lunatics let lo[o]se.[40]

At a dance hall frequented by Irish domestic servants and motormen, the investigator noted that the easy familiarity of asking strange women to dance or drink did not indicate vice or prostitution: "This changing of tables was not a case of open soliciting but just a general mixing." To prove his point, he exclaimed with some frustration that he had tried for forty-five minutes to pick up some of the women, "but there was nothing doing."[41] At another dance, held under the auspices of the National Brotherhood of Bookbinders, kissing, hugging, singing, shouting, and other familiarities were simply accepted as routine conduct. The presence of several young girls, twelve to fourteen years of age, who "appeared to be respectable and came here with their parents or guardians," attests to the normality of these scenes.[42]

Ribald language and bawdy behavior were encouraged by many commercial halls and social clubs. These dances could be distinguished by their advertising, which took the form of "throwaways" or "pluggers." The sponsoring club or hall would flood the neighborhood with small printed cards announcing the particulars of the dance, accompanied by snatches of popular songs or rhymes. As vice reformer George Kneeland described the throwaway:

> These latter intimate the character of the proposed frolic. They all appeal to the sex interest, some being so suggestive that they are absolutely indecent. During the progress of a dance in St. Mark's Place, a young girl, hardly above seventeen years of age, presented a boy with a printed card advertising a ball soon to be held. When the card is folded, it forms an obscene picture and title.[43]

Although his sensibilities were sorely offended, these suggestive advertisements were carefully preserved and valued as mementos of dances by their young patrons.

Dancing Styles

The sexual expressiveness of working-class youth at the commercial halls was particularly apparent in the styles of dancing. Anxious to maintain their good reputations with working-class parents and placate civil authorities, many hall owners sought to contain promiscuous sexuality by patrolling the dance floor. The Women's Municipal League praised a respectable dance hall in the Murray Hill district, patronized by people of different nationalities: "Signs are displayed calling attention to the fact that orderly demeanor must be observed in the dancing and the patrons appear to be well-disposed and well behaved. The dances taught are the waltz, two-step, etc."[44] These dances, which required specific body positions and had established standards to recommend them, symbolized respectability to parents and reformers.

In the unrestrained commercial halls, however, dancing styles took less traditional forms. In the 1890s and early 1900s, "pivoting" or "spieling" captivated working women. " 'Spieling' is the order of the evening," observed a West Side Study in 1906.[45] In this dance, the couple, held tightly together, would twist and spin in small circles on the dance floor. One observer at a Coney Island dance house described two stereotypical pivoters:

> Julia stands erect, with her body as rigid as a poker and with her left arm straight out from her shoulder like an upraised pump-handle. Barney slouches up to her, and bends his back so that he can put his chin on one of Julia's shoulders and she can do the same by him. Then, instead of dancing with a free, lissome, graceful, gliding step, they pivot or spin, around and around with the smallest circle that can be drawn around them.[46]

Pivoting, which was a loose parody of the fast waltz, was diametrically opposed to the waltz in intention. In nineteenth-century high society, the waltz was initially scandalous because it brought the sexes into closer contact than in dances of previous eras, but the dance form itself countered that intimacy with injunctions toward stiff control and agile skill. The speed of the dance demanded self-control and training to achieve the proper form. The major innovation of the dance was that a woman and man placed their hands on each other, but instructors insisted that partners' shoulders be three to four inches apart and that the distance between their bodies should increase downward. The proper position for the waltz meant that "each dancer will be looking over the other's right shoulder," not directly into each other's eyes.[47]

The spieling dance, in parodying this form, was performed not with self-control, but as a dance out of control, its centrifugal tendencies unchecked by proper dance training or internalized restraint. Instead, the wild spinning of couples promoted a charged atmosphere of physical excitement, often accompanied by shouting and singing. Reformer Julia Schoenfeld, reporting on working girls' amusements, observed that in New York halls "vulgar dancing exists everywhere, and the 'spiel,' a form of dancing requiring much twirling and twisting, . . . is popular in all." In her view, spieling "particularly cause[d] sexual excitement" through "the easy familiarity in the dance practiced by nearly all the men in the way they handle the girls."[48]

The sexual emphasis of the dance was even more pronounced in a style known as "tough dancing," which became popular after 1905. Tough dancing had its origins in the houses of prostitution on San Francisco's Barbary Coast and gradually spread, in the form of the slow rag, lovers' two-step, turkey trot, and bunny hug, to the "low resorts" and dance halls of major metropolitan areas. Ultimately much transformed and tamed, it became by the 1910s the mainstay of the middle-class dance craze, the one-step. In the commercial dance halls, however, unrestrained versions of the grizzly bear, Charlie Chaplin wiggle, "shaking the shimmy," and dip would be joyously danced to the popular ragtime tunes of the day.[49]

Though dances differed significantly from earlier dances like the waltz or two-step, in which partners held each other by the hands or around the waist. "Bodily contact has been conventionalized to an inprecedented degree," observed one reformer, while another elaborated, "Couples stand very close together, the girl with her hands around the man's neck, the man with both his arms around the girl or on her hips; their cheeks are pressed close together, their bodies touch each other."[50] The dancers' movements ranged from a slow shimmy, or shaking of the shoulders and hips, to boisterous animal imitations that ridiculed middle-class ideals of grace and refinement. Performed in either a stationary or a walking position, such dances were appropriate for a small, crowded dance floor. Moreover, they were simple to learn, requiring little training or skill, while permitting endless variations on the basic easy steps. Indeed, one of the common complaints of reformers was that these dances had no standard positions, and dancers could simply walk and glide over the dance floor.[51]

Tough dancing not only permitted physical contact, it celebrated it. Indeed, the essence of the tough dance was its suggestion of sexual intercourse. As one dance investigator noted obliquely, "What particularly distinguishes this dance is the motion of the pelvic portions of the body, bearing in mind its origins [i.e., in houses of prostitution]." What troubled such reformers was that the dance, whether wild or tame, became an overt symbol of sexual activity, which the dancers, operating outside the usual conventions of dance, were free to control: "Once learned, the participants can, at will, instantly decrease or increase the obscenity of the movements, lowering the hands from shoulders to the hips and dancing closer and closer until the bodies touch."[52] More than other dances, the tough dance allowed young women to use their bodies to express sexual desire and individual pleasure in movement that would have been unacceptable in any other public arena.

Working girls were not the only New Yorkers who revelled in the modern dances, for the new dance steps also charmed members of the elite and middle classes. "Everybody's Overdoing It," complained one writer, punning on a popular song title of the day.[53] The dancing mania that swept segments of the middle class points to a new level of sensuality and expressiveness within the dominant culture. As Lewis Erenberg observes, however, these cultural forms did not give vent to unrestrained expression, but rather were carefully controlled and refined to meet middle-class standards of respectability.[54]

The contrast in class attitudes toward the new dances is suggested by the frontal attack on tough dancing made by leading dance masters. Irene and Vernon Castle, who most popularized expressive dance forms of the teens, insisted that their Castle Walk, or one-step, bore "no relation or resemblance to the once popular Turkey Trot, Bunny Hug, or Grizzly Bear." Restraining the creative and individualistic qualities of these dances, the Castle Walk eliminated "all hoppings, all contortions of the body, all flouncing of the elbows, all twisting of the arms, and above everything else, all fantastic dips."[55] Bodily contact between dancers was unnecessary, observed one instructor, proclaiming that the "new dances do not require 'hugging' and crossed arms to make them enjoyable. Insist that the couples stand from 1 to 4 inches apart." Another commanded imperiously, "Do not rag these dances."[56]

The intention of these instructions was to reduce the sexual symbolism and individual expression inherent in the dance, setting clear boundaries for behavior in the promiscuous environment of the dance floor. Dancing masters hoped to fend off criticism from religious and civic leaders, at the same time fearing the infectious popularity of the new dances among liberal members of the middle class. "Our girls will spend hundreds of dollars taking grace lessons, and as soon as a ragtime piece of music starts up, they will grasp a "strange' man in any outlandish position that often will put the lowest creature to shame," one complained.[57] Maintaining class distinctions as well as respectable relations between the sexes could be achieved through proper dance form. "Our aim is to uplift dancing, purify it and place it before the public in its proper light," asserted the Castles.[58]

Given their criticism of middle-class daughters' unbecoming dance steps, it is clear that dance masters' prescriptions should not be equated with behavior. However, tough dancing remained a controversial form within the middle class, the boundary at which most people drew the line. While more sensual than earlier dances, the middle-class dances of the 1910s did not exhibit the blatant sexuality expressed in tough dancing. The subtle distinctions in dance styles may be seen, for example, in a description of a businessman and his respectable date at the Ritz Cabaret: "They dance, the girl with her arm about the fellow's neck – the way many society girls do it now a days. It is not exactly tough but it brings the cou[pl]e rather close together."[59] Similarly, the Committee on Amusements and Vacation Resources of Working Girls, concerned that working women were finding legitimation for tough dancing in the society pages of the newspapers, went to a debutante's ball to see for themselves. They saw no tough dancing at the ball they attended, although they did report hearsay "evidence of *modified* 'turkey trot' and 'grizzly bear' being danced by members of the younger set" at other affairs.[60] While such modifications were also practiced at smaller, chaperoned dances in the tenement districts, in the anonymous spaces of the commercial dance halls neither floor managers nor social conventions restrained the sexual implications of the dance movement.

Constructing Heterosexuality in the Public Halls

Control over dancing styles was only one aspect of the larger problem of regulating heterosexual relations at dances. The popular middle-class resorts, cabarets, and cafés tended to mediate promiscuous contact by imposing elaborate rules on their clientele. Many cabarets not only outlawed suggestive dancing, but often barred unescorted women and men from the premises. The intermingling of strangers was taboo at the Parisien, a fashionable resort that did not allow "men from different tables to take women for a dance and won't allow any one to change tables."[61] After a vice raid, another cabaret did not permit women into the hall alone, prevented sensual dancing, and stopped the music precisely at 12:55 a.m. Nor were performers permitted to mix with the crowd: "The lady entertainers were sitting on the platform with the musicians and didn't drink or dance with any of the men here."[62] The careful scrutiny of vice squads led to increasingly subtle markers of respectability. The owner of the Park View Hotel, for example, did not "allow the men to put their arms around a girl[']s chair and don[']t allow the women to put their hands on men[']s] chair."[63] Moreover, as Lewis Erenberg cogently argues, the placement of tables and the stage in middle-class cabarets created a structure that limited contacts between unacquainted women and men. These measures placed barriers between friends and strangers, as well as audience and performers, and censured the presence of the lone individual, who still connoted the prostitute or her customer.[64] The "couple on a date" became an increasingly important cultural construct for the middle class, since it provided a way to structure potentially promiscuous heterosocial relations at the new resorts.

The commercial dance halls frequented by working-class youth varied in the types of behavior their managers would tolerate, particularly those concerned with vice raids. Unlike the middle-class resorts, however, many hall owners simply ignored the unruly revelry of the crowds and the close physical contact of women and men. At one wild New Year's Eve party at the Princes Café, a dance hall and saloon, an undercover investigator observed that "the manager was on the floor all the time but did not interfere or prevent them from doing what ever they pleased."[65] Investigations by the Committee on Amusements and Vacation Resources of Working Girls cited numerous instances of dance halls with little supervision by the management, concluding that "the proprietors of these places not only permit the young men and women who visit the places to go about as they please, but often encourage their lascivious and immoral tendencies."[66] Balconies, for example, were accepted zones of free behavior, and women could be observed on men's laps, hugging and kissing in the dark corners of the hall.

In contrast to the pleasure-seekers at middle-class cabarets, working-class youth often did not attend dances as heterosexual couples, heightening the problem of control. When a working-class woman or man found a "steady," attendance at balls tended to drop. Instead, young people arrived at the halls alone or with members of their own sex, expecting to "couple off" during the dance. At a huge ball held by the Mohawk Club, for example, the vice investigator thought that "the majority of the women came here unescorted and got doubled up in here."[67] The halls themselves devised schemes to facilitate heterosocial interaction. A number of downtown dance academies and halls employed men called "spielers" who danced with unattached women. "It is the business of the spieler to attract and interest young girls," observed Belle Israels. Waiters were also encouraged to play a role in matching up and introducing young women and men.[68]

More commonly, finding a partner occurred through the custom of "breaking" women on the dance floor. At the beginning of a dance, women would dance together, with men watching them from the sidelines; then "the boys step out, two at a time, separate the girls, and dance off in couples – the popular form of introduction in the popular dance hall." The Committee of Fourteen investigators confirmed this practice, often reporting that they "saw women dance alone on the floor and saw men break these girls while on floor."[69] The etiquette of the hall required that a woman remain with this partner at least until the end of the dance.

The scorn for proper introductions reflects the widespread practice of "picking up" unknown women or men in amusement resorts or the streets, an accepted means of gaining companionship for an evening's entertainment. Indeed, some working-class social clubs apparently existed for this very purpose. In his endless search for prostitutes and loose women, an undercover vice investigator was advised by a waiter to "go first on a Sunday night to 'Hans'l & Gret'l Amusement Society' at the Lyceum 86th Str & III Ave, there the girls come and men pick them up." The waiter carefully stressed, however, that these were respectable working women, not prostitutes.[70] Nor was the "pick-up" purely a male prerogative. Journalist Hutchins Hapgood found that "tough" girls "will go to some dance-hall, which may or may not be entirely respectable, and deliberately look for men to dance with."[71]

Such social customs as "picking up" and "breaking" suggest the paradoxical nature of dance hall culture for women. Women enjoyed dancing for the physical pleasure of movement, its romantic and sensual connotations, and the freedom it allowed them. The commercial dance halls were public spaces they could attend without escorts, choose companions for the evening, and express a range of personal desires. Nevertheless, the greater freedom of expression women found in the dance halls occurred in a heterosocial context of imbalanced power and privileges. Picking up women and breaking dancers were more often male prerogatives in a scenario where women displayed themselves for the pleasure of male eyes. "Two men are sure to 'break' provided the girls are good looking and dance well," observed Ruth True.[72] Moreover, the custom of treating, which enabled many women to participate in the life of the dance hall, undercut their social freedom. Women might pay trolley fare out to a dance palace, or purchase a dance ticket and hat check, but they often relied on men's treats to see them through the evening's entertainment. Making a virtue out of economic necessity, young women learned to prize male gifts and attentions. As Belle Israels remarked, the announcement to one's friends that "he treated" was "the acme of achievement in retailing experiences with the other sex."[73] Under these conditions, the need to strive for popularity with men came to be a socially defined – and ultimately restricting – aspect of female expressiveness and desire.

To win male attention in the dance halls, working women fully elaborated their eye-catching style. Chicago women, for example, placed powder puffs in their stocking tops and ostentatiously flourished them to attract male attention on the dance floor.[74] Their New York sisters could hardly be outdone, wearing high-heeled shoes, fancy ball gowns, elaborate pompadours, hair ornaments, and cosmetics. Louisa, who so distressed her Irish working-class mother, proudly wore her "flossy attire" to the West Side dance halls. "She cannot boast a ball dress to be sure. But her scant suit of brown serge with its sateen collar is trim and new," Ruth True observed. "A great encircling hat of cheap black straw reaches to the middle of her back and bends under the weight of an enormous willow."[75] Fancy dress and masquerade balls were held frequently in the middle West Side during the winter months, with prizes given for the best costume or prettiest woman, subsidized by the hall management or social club. This practice reinforced women's objectification, but it also allowed them an outrageous expressiveness prohibited in other areas of their lives. Significantly, Louise de Koven Bowen found that many Chicago girls attended masquerade balls in male attire, cross-dressing being perhaps the most assertive fashion statement they could make.[76]

Women's popularity was also predicated on willingness to drink. In many dance halls and saloons, economic considerations militated against abstinence, and any woman not drinking or encouraging others to imbibe was made unwelcome by the manager or waiters. In some places, prizes were offered the woman who had the most drinks to her credit.[77] Inventive cocktails helped to make drinking a more acceptable female activity. "Beer and other five-cent drinks are not fashionable at these places," observed Belle Israels. "The young man wants to make an impression and therefore induces the girl to drink Mamie Taylors, cock-tails and other insidious mixtures." Women who refused to drink might also be obstracized by men. The connection between popularity and drinking in the company of a male companion put an observable social pressure on women; Israels noted that between dances "girls not being entertained at the tables rush over to the dressing-rooms to avoid being seen on the floor."[78]

The approved cultural style of dance hall women involved other forms of uninhibited behavior as well. Loud talk, boisterous laughter, and cigarette smoking all helped women gain attention and status in the halls. Smoking was still a controversial form of female behavior in the 1910s, symbolic of the modern and somewhat risqué woman. While some lit their cigarettes in the open, others, like the young women at the Grand Union Hotel's dance hall, smoked covertly: "The men held the cigarettes and the women snatched a puff now and then."[79] Participation in kissing rituals was also emblematic of the "game girl." "Now the kissing parties are starting in," observed a waiter at Remey's New Year's Eve dance, "it appeared to be contagious, when one started kissing they all started." The search for popular attention even led to aggressive and frank sexual advances to men. At another end-of-the-year ball, for example, "one of the girls while in the middle of a dance stopped on [the] floor and went to different tables and kept saying 'You didn't kiss me for New Year's.' "[80]

Treating and Sexuality

For these women, treating was not always a one-way proposition, but entailed an exchange relationship. In the male subculture of the saloon, treating rounds of beer asserted workingmen's independent status while affirming common ties among a group of equals. Women, however, were financially unable to reciprocate in kind and instead offered sexual favors of varying degrees. Most commonly, capitalizing on their attractiveness and personality, women volunteered only flirtatious companionship. "Pleasures don't cost girls so much as they do young men," asserted one saleswoman. "If they are agreeable they are invited out a good deal, and they are not allowed to pay anything." Reformer Lillian Betts observed that working girls held themselves responsible for failing to finagle men's invitations, believing that "it is not only her misfortune, but her fault; she should be more attractive."[81] Not all working-class women simply played the coquette, however. Engaging in treating ultimately involved a negotiation between the desire for social participation and adherence to cultural sanctions that strongly discouraged premarital sexual intimacy. One investigator captured the dilemma women faced in their dependency on men in their leisure time: "Those who are unattractive, and those who have puritanic notions, fare but ill in the matter of enjoyments. On the other hand, those who do become popular have to compromise with the best conventional usage."[82]

The extent of sexual intimacy involved in treating and the nature of the social relations surrounding it are difficult to establish. Dualistic middle-class categories of "respectability" and "promiscuity" do not adequately describe the complexity and ambiguity of working-class sexual norms, norms that were complicated further by ethnic, religious, and generational differences. The Italian daughter who stayed out late at ballrooms or an unmarried Irish girl who became pregnant might equally be stigmatized by their respective communities. Reformer Lillian Betts, for example, cites several cases of women turning their backs on co-workers or neighbors whom they suspected of immorality. Settlement workers observed, however, that for many young women, censure was more instrumental than moralistic. "The hardness with which even the suggestion of looseness is treated in any group of working girls is simply an expression of self-preservation," Betts observed.[83] Another investigation found a profound ambivalence in young women's attitudes toward premartial pregnancies, their criticism of the wrongdoer being more "conventional than sincere and deep-seated; and . . . not always unmixed with a certain degree of admiration for the success with the other sex which the difficulty implies."[84]

Working-class women received conflicting messages about the virtues of virginity in their daily lives. Injunctions about chastity from parents, church, and school might conflict with the lived experience of urban labor and leisure. Working in factories and stores often entailed forms of sexual harassment that instructed women to exchange sexual favors for economic gain, while talk about dates and sexual exploits helped to pass the working day. Crowded tenement homes caused working-class daughters to pursue their social life in the unprotected spaces of the streets, while those living in boarding homes contended with the attentions of male lodgers. The pleasure and freedom young women craved could be found in the social world of dance halls, but these also carried a mixed message, permitting expressive female sexuality within a context of dependency and vulnerability.

Negotiating this world produced a range of responses. While many women carefully guarded their reputations, attended chaperoned dances, and deflected the attentions of men, others engaged in looser forms of behavior. Women who had steady male friends they intended to marry might justify premarital sexual intimacy: "A girl can have many friends," explained one woman, "but when she gets a 'steady,' there's only one way to have him and to keep him; I mean to keep him long."[85]

Other women fully bought into the culture of treating, trading sexual favors of varying degrees for male attention, gifts, and a good time. These women were known in underworld slang as "charity girls," a term that differentiated them from prostitutes because they would not accept money in their sexual encounters with men. As vice reformer George Kneeland found, they "offer themselves to strangers, not for money, but for presents, attention and pleasure, and, most important, a yielding to sex desire." A thin line divided these women from "occasional prostitutes," women who slipped in and out of prostitution when unemployed or in need of extra income. Many respectable working women apparently acted like Dottie: "When she needed a pair of shoes she had found it easy to 'earn' them in the way that other girls did."[86]

Charity girls were frequent patrons of the city's large public dance halls, finding in them the pleasure and freedom they craved, and perhaps the anonymity they needed. Undercover vice investigators were informed by a waiter at one racket that the women present were "game" and "lively," but not prostitutes, and that the "majority . . . are here every week, they take in every affair that takes place at this hall." Often they comprised more than half of the dancers: "Some of the women . . . are out for the coin but there is a lot that come in here that are charity." At La Kuenstler Klause, a restaurant with music and dancing, a waiter confided to the investigator, "girls could be gotten here, but they don't go with men for money, only for [a] good time." The latter sketched the cultural style of such women, reporting that "most of the girls are working girls, not prostitutes, they smoke cigarrettes, drink liquers [sic] and dance dis[orderly] dances, stay out late and stay with any man, that pick them up first." Meeting two women at a bar, another investigator remarked, "They are both supposed to be working girls but go out for a good time and go the 'Limit.' "[87] These women flocked to the dance halls not necessarily as an environment for courtship, but for the pleasures of dancing, flirtation, and sexual encounters.

This evidence points to the presence of charity girls at dance halls, but it tells us little about their numbers, social background, working lives, and relationship to family and community. The vice reports suggest that the women were young, some not over fifteen or sixteen; as one investigator indicated, "Some of these girls had their hair down in a braid." The jobs they held were typical of other working women – waitresses, domestic servants, garment-makers. While some lived alone, others resided with their families, which made sexual encounters difficult. One man, who picked up charity girls at a dance hall, remarked, for example, that "he sometimes takes them to the hotels, but sometimes the girls won[']t go to [a] hotel to stay for the night, they are afraid of their mothers, so he gets away with it in the hallway."[88]

It is important to note that the vice investigators generally attended the larger halls, such as the Manhattan Casino and the Harlem River Casino, oriented to a metropolitan rather than a neighborhood clientele. Not knowing the extent to which charity girls chould be found at the smaller rented halls in the tenement districts makes it impossible to assess how visible or tolerated this behavior was within Manhattan's working-class communities. Nor is there evidence about pregnancy and birth control, and what occurred to these women as they aged. Whether they took the "downward path" toward prostitution, as reformers warned, or married into respectability can only be a matter for speculation.

Whatever the specific numbers of charity girls, many more women must have been conscious of the need to negotiate sexual encounters if they wished to participate in commercial amusements. Clara Laughlin, for example, reported the story of an attractive but decorous working girl who could not understand why men dropped her after a few dates. Finally a co-worker gave her the worldly advice that social participation involved an exchange relationship: "Don't yeh know there ain't no feller goin' t'spend coin on yeh fer nothin'? Yeh gotta be a good Indian, Kid – we all gotta!" While some women self-consciously defined their own respectability against the culture of treating, others clearly relished the game of extracting gifts and favors. A vice investigator offered to take one woman, a department store clerk and occasional prostitute, to the Central Opera House at 3:00 A.M.; he noted that "she was willing to go if I'd take a taxi; I finally coaxed her to come with me in a street car." Sociologist Frances Donovan found similar concerns in the conversations of waitresses, "talking about their engagements which they had for the evening or for the night and quite frankly saying what they expected to get from this or that fellow in the line of money, amusement or clothes."[89]

The intricacies of this negotiation – the balancing act between social respectability, female desire, and male pressures – created subtle and flexible standards for personal conduct. The hat check girl at Semprinis dance hall carefully walked this line in a conversation with a vice investigator, who noted that "she appears to be game and ... is not a church member." Answering his proposal for a date, she "said she'd be glad to go out with me but told me there was nothing doing [sexually]. Said she didn't like to see a man spend money on her and then get disappointed." Commenting on the charity girls who frequented the hall, she remarked:

> These women get her sick, she can't see why a woman should lay down for a man the first time they take her out. She said it wouldn't be so bad if they went out with the men 3 or 4 times and then went to bed with them but not the first time.[90]

The culture of the commercial dance hall – the anonymity of its spaces, tolerance of uninhibited behavior, aura of romance, and peer pressure to conform – supported the social relationship of treating. It induced young women to engage in freer forms of sexuality and perhaps glamorized the notion of a sexual exchange. While treating gave some women opportunities for social participation they otherwise would have lacked, it remained a situation of vulnerability and potential exploitation.

One way women exerted some control over their interactions with men was by attending dances and other leisure activities in the company of a "lady friend." Young working-class women's friendships were structured relationships between girls who usually met at school, at work, or on the streets. Unlike their brothers, who often joined gangs or clubs, young women would cultivate a single friend, or at most a small clique. The formality of these relationships was observed by Ruth True: "It is very constant and means that the two share most of their pleasures together. There are distinct requirements; one must 'call up' and 'wait in' and not 'go round' too much with anyone else."[91] The lady friend enhanced social occasions, as a companion to share the fun of a dance and a confidante for whispered gossip. At the same time, she performed another function, serving as an implicit protector whose presence helped to deflect unwanted sexual attentions. At a racket for the Drivers' Sick and Benevolent Fund, the Committee of Fourteen investigator "tried to get next to some of the women but couldn[']t, they travel in pairs and it[']s hard for one man to pick any of them up." Even when a woman had a steady, outings might include a lady friend for pleasure and protection; Lillian Betts reported that "one would rarely hear of plans that did not include two beside the couple engaged or willing to be. Sometimes two girls were to complete the party."[92] However, True notes that the special obligations of lady friends to be with each other fell by the wayside when one woman began keeping company with her gentleman friend.[93]

The lady friend symbolically drew the line of respectability at a time in women's lives when heterosexual contact was at its most promiscuous and dangerous, when meeting men in dance halls, amusement resorts, and the streets. The single woman alone might be taken for a prostitute, but hunting in pairs permitted women to maintain their respectability in the aggressive pursuit of pleasure. The function of working-class lady friends clearly differs from the nineteenth-century pattern of middle-class female friendships, which emerged in the shared experience of a woman-centered realm, fed by the rituals of the home and the female life cycle.[94] The working women's friendships as described by reformers and settlement workers occurred in a context that strengthened women's ability to negotiate the public, heterosocial world of commercial amusements rather than maintain a privatized female one.

In the commercial dance halls, single working-class women found a social space that reinforced their emergent cultural style and offered an opportunity to experiment with unconventional sexual and social roles. In a few hours of dancing and camaraderie, they could seemingly escape the social relationships and expectations tying them to their household responsibilities, jobs, and ethnic communities. What mattered in the dance hall – popularity, dancing ability, fashionable clothes, and male attention – was a modern style that promised independence, romance, and pleasure. Nevertheless, the realities of working-class life persistently intruded; women's situation in the labor force and family undercut their social freedom, and treating underscored their material dependency. And within the halls, an ideology took shape that fused notions of female autonomy and pleasure with heterosexual relationships and consumerism. This formulation, which ultimately limited female possibilities and power, increasingly defined the cultural construction of gender in the twentieth century.

Notes

1   Belle Lindner Israels, "The Way of the Girl," *Survey* 22 (3 July 1909): 494; Michael M. Davis, Jr., *The Exploitation of Pleasure: A Study of Commercial Recreations in New York City* (New York, n.d.), p. 15, estimated over one hundred dance halls in Manhattan alone.

2   For women's attendance, see Davis, *Exploitation of Pleasure*, pp. 12–13; John M. Oskison, "Public Halls of the East Side," in University Settlement Society of New York, *Report* (New York, 1899), p. 39; Hutchins Hapgood, *Types from City Streets* (New York, 1910), pp. 134–5; A. S. Gilbert to James G. Wallace, 23 Nov. 1912, p. 5, Box 28, Parks and Playgrounds Correspondence, Lillian D. Wald Collection, Rare Book and Manuscript Library, Columbia University, New York; Helen Campbell et al., *Darkness and Daylight, or Lights and Shadows of New York Life* (Hartford, Conn., 1897), p. 230. On dancing's popularity with men, see George E. Bevans, *How Workingmen Spend Their Spare Time* (New York, 1913), pp. 27, 33; movies and theaters were the only forms of commercial amusement more popular among young men aged seventeen to twenty-four.

3   Oskison, "Public Halls," p. 38.

4   Ruth S. True, *The Neglected Girl* (New York, 1914), p. 72; Oskison, "Public Halls," pp. 39–40.

5   Belle L. Mead, "The Social Pleasures of East Side Jews" (M. A. Thesis, Columbia University, 1904), p. 6; Verne M. Bovie, "The Public Dance Halls of the Lower East Side," in University Settlement Society of New York, *Report* (New York, 1901), pp. 31–2.

6   Elsa G. Herzfeld, *Family Monographs: The History of Twenty-four Families Living in the Middle West Side of New York City* (New York, 1905), p. 18; Thomas Jesse Jones, *Sociology of a New York City Block* (Studies in History, Economics and Public Law, vol. 21, no. 2; New York, 1904), p. 45; Israels, "Way of the Girl," p. 494; "Report of Murray Hill Committee on Dance Halls," *Yearbook of the Women's Municipal League*, Nov. 1911, pp. 20–1.

7   See the useful discussion in Anya Peterson Royce, *The Anthropology of Dance* (Bloomington, Ind., 1977), p. 98; Frances Rust, *Dance in Society* (London, 1969).

8   Belle Lindner Israels, "Diverting a Pastime," *Leslie's Weekly* 113 (27 July 1911): 94, 100; George J. Kneeland, *Commercialized Prostitution in New York City* (New York, 1913), p. 56. The range of dance halls emerges particularly in the individual Investigator's Reports, Records of the Committee of Fourteen, Rare Books and Manuscripts Division, New York Public Library, Astor, Lenox and Tilden Foundations (hereafter cited as COF).

9   Bovie, "Public Dance Halls," p. 32; Herzfeld, *Family Monographs*, pp. 17–18; True, *Neglected Girl*, pp. 68–9.

10   Oskison, "Public Halls," p. 39. See also Hapgood, *Types from City Streets*, p. 135; Trinity Church Men's Committee, *A Social Survey of the Washington Street District of New York City* (n.p., Oct. 1914), p. 48.

11   Ruth I. Austin, "Teaching English to Our Foreign Friends, Pt. I: Among the Bohemians," *Life and Labor* 1 (Sept. 1911): 261.

12   Davis, *Exploitation of Pleasure*, p. 15.

13   Oskison, "Public Halls," p. 40.

14 Investigator's Report, Manhattan Casino, 2926 Eighth Avenue, 30 June 1919, COF.
15 Oskison, "Public Halls," pp. 39–40; tapes 1–6 (side B) and IV-12 (side A), New York City Immigrant Labor History Collection of the City College Oral History Project, Robert F. Wagner Archives, Tamiment Institute Library, New York University; True, *Neglected Girl*, pp. 68–9.
16 Bovie, "Public Dance Halls," p. 32; "Modern industry has produced...," n.d., p. 8, in Box 7, Community Center Work, People's Institute Collection, Rare Books and Manuscripts Division, New York Public Library, Astor, Lenox and Tilden Foundations; Israels, "Diverting a Pastime," p. 100; Davis, *Exploitation of Pleasure*, pp. 15–16.
17 Mead, "Social Pleasures," p. 6.
18 *Ibid.*
19 Herzfeld, *Family Monographs*, p. 17; Bovie, "Public Dance Halls," pp. 32–3.
20 Gilbert to Wallace, 23 Nov. 1912, p. 6. See also Kneeland, *Commercialized Prostitution*, p. 56.
21 Investigator's Report, Manhattan Casino, 26 May 1917, COF.
22 *Trow Business Directory of New York City* (New York, 1895), pp. 449–50; *Trow Business Directory of New York City* (New York, 1910), pp. 446–7; Oskison, "Public Halls," p. 39.
23 Trinity Church Men's Committee, *Social Survey*, p. 48.
24 Bovie, "Public Dance Halls," p. 32; Oskison, "Public Halls," p. 39. See also Louise de Koven Bowen, *The Public Dance Halls of Chicago* (Chicago, 1917).
25 Israels, "Way of the Girl," p. 496; Davis, *Exploitation of Pleasure*, p. 16.
26 Investigator's Report, Central Casino, 103/107 McCombs Place, 25 Jan. 1917, COF.
27 Maria Ward Lambin, *Report of the Advisory Dance Hall Committee of the Women's City Club and the City Recreation Committee* (New York, 1924), pp. 1, 6–8; "Suggestions of Mrs. Orrin S. Goan," box 120, Recreation, National Civic Federation Papers, Rare Books and Manuscripts Division, New York Public Library, Astor, Lenox and Tilden Foundations.
28 Investigator's Reports, Manhattan Casino, 10 March 1917, and Park View Hotel, 2137/2139 Boston Road, 18 March 1917, COF.
29 Mathew Hale Smith, *Sunshine and Shadow in New York* (Hartford, Conn., 1869), pp. 228, 435–41, 632; William Sanger, *History of Prostitution* (New York, 1869), p. 524.
30 Oskison, "Public Halls," p. 38; Davis, *Exploitation of Pleasure*, pp. 13, 15; Israels, "Way of the Girl," p. 494, and "Diverting a Pastime," p. 94.
31 Tape 1–59 (side B), Immigrant Labor History Collection.
32 Tape 1–51 (side B), Immigrant Labor History Collection.
33 Hapgood, *Types from City Streets*, pp. 134–5; True, *Neglected Girl*, pp. 69–72; Dorothy Richardson, *The Long Day: The Story of a New York Working Girl* (1905), in *Women at Work*, ed. William L. O'Neill (New York, 1972), pp. 94–5.
34 Herzfeld, *Family Monographs*, p. 18; Lillian W. Betts, *The Leaven in a Great City* (New York, 1902), p. 142.
35 Israels, "Diverting a Pastime," p. 94. On the atmosphere of saloon-dance halls, see Campbell et al., *Darkness and Daylight*, p. 230.
36 Investigator's Report, Excelsior Cafe, 306 Eighth Avenue, 16 Dec. 1916, COF.

37 Ruth Rosen, *The Lost Sisterhood: Prostitution in America, 1900–1918* (Baltimore and London, 1982), pp. 112–36.
38 Investigator's Report, Remey's, 917 Eighth Avenue, 11 Feb. 1917, COF.
39 Investigator's Report, Weimann's, 1422 St. Nicholas Ave., 11 Feb. 1917, COF.
40 Investigator's Report, Remey's, 11 Feb. 1917, COF.
41 Investigator's Report, Jim Coffey's, 2923 Eighth Avenue, 17 Feb. 1917, COF.
42 Investigator's Report, Manhattan Casino, 19 Aug. 1917, COF.
43 Kneeland, *Commercialized Prostitution*, p. 68; Louise De Koven Bowen, "Dance Halls," *Survey* 26 (3 June 1911): 384.
44 "Report of Murray Hill Committee," p. 21; see also Belle Lindner Israels, "The Dance Problem," *Proceedings of the National Conference of Charities and Corrections, 1912* (Fort Wayne, Ind., 1912), p. 144.
45 Herzfeld, *Family Monographs*, p. 18.
46 Julian Ralph, "Coney Island," *Scribner's* 20 (July 1896): 18.
47 [Mrs. Edna Witherspoon], *The Perfect Art of Modern Dancing* (London and New York, 1894), pp. 19–20.
48 Richard Henry Edwards, *Popular Amusements* (New York, 1915); see also Bovie, "Public Dance Halls," p. 33.
49 Bowen, *Public Dance Halls of Chicago*, p. 4; Mathew S. Hughes, *Dancing and the Public Schools* (New York, 1917), p. 20. For a superb analysis of the middle-class dance craze, see Lewis A. Erenberg, *Steppin' Out: New York Nightlife and the Transformation of American Culture, 1890–1930* (Westport, Conn., 1981), pp. 146–75.
50 Edwards, *Popular Amusements*, p. 79; Bowen, *Public Dance Halls of Chicago*, p. 5.
51 Israels, "Dance Problem," p. 144. See also "Turkey Trot and Tango – A Disease or a Remedy?" *Current Opinion* 55 (Sept. 1913): 187.
52 Committee on Amusements and Vacation Resources of Working Girls, two-page circular, box 28, Parks and Playgrounds Correspondence, Wald Collection, Columbia University. See also Julian Street, *Welcome to Our City* (New York, 1913), pp. 9–10; Bovie, "Public Dance Halls," p. 33.
53 Street, *Welcome to Our City*, p. 169.
54 Erenberg, *Steppin' Out*, pp. 146–75; see also James R. McGovern, "The American Woman's Pre-World War I Freedom in Manners and Morals," *Journal of American History* 55 (Sept. 1968): 315–33; Henry F. May, *The End of American Innocence* (Chicago, 1959), pp. 334–47.
55 Vernon and Irene Castle, *Modern Dancing* (New York, 1914), foreword.
56 Frank Leslie Clendenen, *Dance Mad; or the Dances of the Day* (St. Louis, 1914), p. 8; J. S. Hopkins, *The Tango and Other Up-to-Date Dances* (Chicago, 1914), p. 39. See also Troy and Margaret West Kinney, *Social Dancing of Today* (New York, 1914), pp. 2–3.
57 Clendenen, *Dance Mad*, p. 8.
58 Castle and Castle, *Modern Dancing*, foreword.
59 Investigator's Report, Ritz Cabaret, 2114/2118 Seventh Avenue, 9 June 1917, COF.
60 "Welfare Inspector at Society Dance," *New York Times* clipping (n.d.), Subject Papers, Policies Concerning Sex Motion Pictures, 1912, 1913, National Board of Review of Motion Pictures Collection, Rare Books and

Manuscripts Division, New York Public Library, Astor, Lenox and Tilden Foundations (my emphasis).
61 Investigator's Report, Parisien, 945 Eighth Avenue, 18 May 1917, p. 2, COF.
62 Investigator's Report, Central Casino, 25 Jan. 1917, COF.
63 Investigator's Report, Park View Hotel, 28 April 1917, COF.
64 Erenberg, *Steppin' Out*, pp. 135–7. On the cultural ideal of companionate relationships, see Christina Simmons, " 'Marriage in the Modern Manner': Sexual Radicalism and Reform in America, 1914–1941" (Ph.D. diss., Brown University, 1982), pp. 105–49.
65 Investigator's Report, Princess Café, 1203 Broadway, 1 Jan. 1917, COF.
66 Gilbert to Wallace, 23 Nov. 1912, p. 7. See also Investigator's Report, Excelsior Café, 21 Dec. 1916, COF; Kneeland, *Commercialized Prostitution*, p. 70.
67 Investigator's Report, Manhattan Casino, 17 Feb. 1917, COF.
68 Israels, "Diverting a Pastime," p. 95. On the waiter's role, see, for example, Investigator's Report, Weimann's, 27 Jan. 1917, COF.
69 Israels, "Dance Problem," p. 141; Investigator's Report, Manhattan Casino, 19 Aug. 1917, COF; True, *Neglected Girl*, pp. 70, 72; Herzfeld, *Family Monographs*, p. 18.
70 Investigator's Report, La Kuenstler Klause, 1490 Third Avenue, 19 Jan. 1917, COF.
71 Hapgood, *Types from City Streets*, pp. 134–5. See also Rollin L. Hartt, *The People at Play* (Boston, 1909), p. 200.
72 True, *Neglected Girl*, p. 70.
73 Israels, "Way of the Girl," p. 489. See also Oskison, "Public Halls," pp. 39–40.
74 Bowen, "Dance Halls," p. 385.
75 True, *Neglected Girl*, pp. 54–5.
76 Bowen, *Public Dance Halls of Chicago*, p. 7; Herzfeld, *Family Monographs*, p. 18; J. G. Phelps Stokes, "Hartley House and Social Reform," *New York Times*, 27 June 1897, Illustrated Magazine, p. 4.
77 Kneeland, *Commercialized Prostitution*, p. 70; Israels, "Diverting a Pastime," p. 100; Juvenile Protective Agency, Chicago, *Our Most Popular Recreation Controlled by the Liquor Interests: A Study of Public Dance Halls* (Chicago, 1911).
78 Israels, "Diverting a Pastime," p. 100.
79 Investigator's Report, Grand Union Hotel, 1815–1817 Park Ave., 15 June 1917, COF.
80 Investigator's Reports, Remey's, 1 Jan. 1917; Princess Café, 1 Jan. 1917, COF. See also Investigator's Report, Remey's, 9 March 1917, COF; Frank Streightoff, "Eight Dollars a Week," *Consumer's League Bulletin* 4 (Nov. 1914): 38.
81 "A Salesgirl's Story," *Independent* 54 (July 1902): 1821; Betts, *Leaven*, pp. 251–2; Robert A. Woods and Albert J. Kennedy, *Young Working Girls: A Summary of Evidence from Two Thousand Social Workers* (Boston, 1913), pp. 8, 106.
82 New York State Factory Investigating Commission, *Fourth Report Transmitted to Legislature, Feb. 15, 1915* (S. Doc. no. 43; Albany, NY, 1915), vol. 4, pp. 1585–6; Clara E. Laughlin, *The Work-a-Day Girl: A Study of Some Present-day Conditions* (New York, 1913), p. 50.

83   Betts, *Leaven*, pp. 81, 219; True, *Neglected Girl*, p. 69.

84   Woods and Kennedy, *Young Working Girls*, p. 87.

85   *Ibid.*, p. 85.

86   "Memoranda on Vice Problem: IV. Statement of George J. Kneeland," New York Factory Investigating Commission, *Fourth Report*, vol. 1, p. 403; Frances R. Donovan, *The Woman Who Waits* (1920; rpt. New York, 1974), p. 71. See also Committee of Fourteen in New York City, *Annual Report* (New York, 1917), p. 15, and *Annual Report* (New York, 1918), p. 32; Woods and Kennedy, *Young Working Girls*, p. 85. Cf. occasional prostitution, discussed in US Senate, *Report on the Condition of Woman and Child Wage-Earners in the United States, Vol. 15: Relation between Occupation and Criminality in Women* (S. 645, 61st Cong., 2d sess.; Washington, DC, 1911), p. 83; Laughlin, *Work-a-Day Girl*, pp. 51–2.

87   Investigator's Reports, Manhattan Casino, 17 Feb. 1917; Clare Hotel and Palm Garden/McNamara's, 2150 Eighth Avenue, 12 Jan. 1917; La Kuenstler Klause, 19 Jan. 1917; Bobby More's, 252 W. 31st St., 3 Feb. 1917, COF.

88   Investigator's Reports, Manhattan Casino, 26 May 1917; Clare Hotel and Palm Garden/McNamara's, 12 Jan. 1917, COF; see also Investigator's Reports, Manhattan Casino, 10 March 1917; La Kuentsler Klause, 19 Jan. 1917, COF.

89   Laughlin, *Work-a-Day Girl*, p. 50; Investigator's Report, Remey's, 23 Dec. 1916, COF; Donovan, *The Woman Who Waits*, p. 55.

90   Investigator's Report, Semprinis, 145 West 50th St., 5 Oct. 1918, COF.

91   True, *Neglected Girl*, p. 60.

92   Investigator's Report, Manhattan Casino, 20 May 1917, COF; Betts, *Leaven*, pp. 205–6. See also Investigator's Report, Excelsior Café, 23 Dec. 1916, COF; Israels, "Diverting a Pastime," p. 94; Woods and Kennedy, *Young Working Girls*, pp. 8, 35; Hapgood, *Types from City Streets*, p. 131; Herzfeld, *Family Monographs*, p. 18; Richardson, *Long Day*, p. 66 and passim.

93   True, *Neglected Girl*, p. 61.

94   On middle-class female friendships, see Carroll Smith-Rosenberg, "The Female World of Love and Ritual: Relations Between Women in Nineteenth Century America," *Signs* 1 (Autumn 1975): 1–29.

Consider the Source

1.   One source Kathy Peiss cites in her essay is *Modern Dancing*, a 1914 book by Vernon and Irene Castle (see notes 55 and 58). The Castles were the premier dancers of their day, famous not only for their eagerly attended performances, but also for their role as originators and/or popularizers of dances like the one-step and Castle-walk. The Castles were also dance instructors, and *Modern Dancing* was their manual that explained (in words and pictures) how to perform such dances.

Modern Dancing featured an introduction by the couple's theatrical agent, Elisabeth Marbury, a transatlantic socialite who also represented many important writers at the turn of the century (among them Oscar Wilde and George Bernard Shaw). The following excerpt comes from that introduction. As you read it, you might consider the values and assumptions that underlie Marbury's – and, it seems safe to say, the Castles' and many other "enlightened" individuals' of the time – view of the people who attend dance halls. Who is this introduction actually addressing? How does Marbury see young working-class women? What role is she promoting in such women's lives? How do you feel about Marbury's message?

Excerpt from Elisabeth Marbury's Introduction to *Modern Dancing* by Vernon and Irene Castle (1914)

I may be wrong, but it seems to me very improbable that the majority of boys and girls who go to public dances are guilty of harboring and of fostering the thoughts that are imputed to them by those who proclaim against dancing. I believe that only a small number of them dance vulgar steps, some perhaps impulsively, but chiefly because they do not know any better. They want to dance; they want pleasure and excitement, and they take it as it comes to them, the bad with the good. It is our duty to eliminate the bad and encourage the good.

Surely there cannot be as great moral danger in dancing as there is in sitting huddled close in the darkness of a sensational moving-picture show or in following with feverish interest the suggestive sex-problem dramas. Nor from my point of view is there as much harm in dancing as in sitting home in some dreary little hall bedroom, beneath the flaring gas, reading with avidity the latest erotic novel or the story which paints vice in alluring colors under the guise of describing life as it really is.

The Maxixe and the Tango are only two of the so-called modern dances. The Innovation, introduced at a ball recently given by Mrs. Stuyvesant Fish, is in my opinion more graceful, as it is a dance where the partners need not even touch hands in certain of its steps. In the One Step the man must hold his partner loosely if he does the pretty measure where he steps to one side of her as they dip; and in the Hesitation Waltz the steps require that the man and the woman be slightly apart. The

Turkey Trot was a dance which deserved much of the abuse it received; but it died a natural death, because more attractive dances were offered in its place. So will the objectionable features of all modern dances be thrust aside as the statelier and more graceful steps are danced.

I believe dancing to be a useful as well as a beautiful art, and I think that the women of every city should open properly conducted dancing-halls for young people where they can dance to good music under refined supervision.

Give them clean fun to offset the hard work of the day. Give them exercise for tired muscles; give them instructors to teach them, without charge, the correct positions and the correct steps for the popular dances, and every girl and boy you teach in this fashion will teach their friends, until by constructive elimination we have done away with what is vulgar by giving our young people something better.

We are planning now to have classes for girls who work, under the direction of volunteer teachers from Castle House, and I feel that it is a venture whose success is assured, and one which will be copied by men and women of leisure all over the country. It is easy to make the young happy and easy to rob them of joy. It is our privilege, as experienced, responsible guardians, to put within their reach every means of innocent amusement. Otherwise they will fill the void in their lives by amusements of a more questionable character.

The child of the tenement would be delighted if put into a beautiful, clean, and airy play-room; so will be the men and women of all ages when we show them how to dance the modern dances gracefully and modestly. I may be a very gullible person, but I have talked to hundreds of girls about their dancing, and they have put into my hand the golden key to the situation by saying with a puzzled smile and questioning eye: "We're dancing wrong? Well, maybe; but we don't know any other way to dance. Do you?"

We do, and we can teach them. That is really the situation in a nut-shell. They must dance. The lure of the rhythm, the sense of flinging aside the weariness of the working-day, is as strong in the heart of the girl behind the counter as in that of the girl in the private ball-room. The man who labors in the humbler callings is as interested in his girl friend and as anxious to dance with her as the young man in what we call "society." And what is more, I do not and will not believe that all those young persons, the fathers and mothers of to-morrow, who are working and striving to earn honest livings and to rise in the world connect their moments of recreation with suggestive ideas and unworthy ideals.

To them dancing means a stretching of the mental muscles as well as those which are physical. It means something different from the dull daily round; it is almost as natural as the desire for food and sleep. The forbidding of the modern dances in public centers is dangerous. It sets that alluring sign "Forbidden fruit" upon what otherwise would arouse no prurient curiosity. We are told that the new dances encourage too much freedom, and, while "all right if properly danced," are all wrong in a public dancing-room. These would-be reformers never see that they are tacitly admitting that it is ignorance of the dances, not knowledge of them, that does the harm.

It is not difficult to find the explanation of some of the undesirable dancing. A working man and girl go to a musical comedy. From their stuffy seats high up under the roof they look down upon the dancers on the stage. These are – so the program tells them – doing modern ball-room dancing. The man on the stage flings his partner about with Apache wildness; she clutches him around the neck and is swung off her feet. They spin swiftly or undulate slowly across the stage, and the program calls it a "Tango." The man and girl go away and talk of those "ball-room dances." They try the steps; they are novel and often difficult; they have aroused their interest. The result is that we find scores of young people dancing under the name of "One Step" or "Tango" the eccentric dances thus exaggerated and elaborated to excite the jaded audiences of a roof-garden or a music-hall.

There is no one to tell those young people that they are mistaken in their choice of the steps, that "society" does not do those dances. They hear hundreds of men and women denouncing the scandalous modern dances, and in their ignorance think that these are the only dances.

Let us, therefore, have dance-halls that are properly run, with instructors to teach the new dances, with a good floor and good music and a welcome for every one.

Let us have places of amusement where the fathers and mothers and even the little ones can come with the young people, and where they can look on and enjoy the healthy relaxation of their children.

Let the dance-halls become decent social centers where families can gather in sympathy and in understanding. There teach that it is better to dance correctly than to undulate round and round in a narrow circle and in a close embrace, misnaming this a Hesitation Waltz.

The One Step, the Hesitation, the Lame Duck, the Innovation, the Half and Half – all the new dances, in fact – have enough pretty steps to delight the hearts of girls and boys who want to show off. They are easy enough for even the awkward girl to learn, and they are good exercise and clean exercise for every boy.

I am delighted to find that the public schools are taking up dancing, and I believe that if every woman's club would give a free dance for the young people of the neighborhood once a week, with an instructor and a chaperon present, that they would do more good to the race than by discussing eugenics or by indulging in a flippant study of social economics.

Dancing is first and foremost a healthful exercise; it is pleasure; and it is an art that brings to the front courtesy, ease of manner, grace of body, and happiness of mind. It is for us to set this standard.

Many prominent citizens and some of our clergy have recently denounced modern dancing, believing in all sincerity that certain vulgar dances which they have witnessed are the models upon which general dancing must be based. Unfortunately, this is a case of the innocent suffering for the guilty, and it is our business and pleasure to prove that any sweeping condemnation of dancing as a pastime is not founded upon fact and that many have erred through ignorance rather than through intent. Let us, therefore, co-operate with our guardians of civic decency and aid them constructively in the elimination of the coarse, the uncouth, the vulgar, and the vicious. Let us establish once and for all a standard of modern dancing which will demonstrate that these dances can be made graceful, artistic, charming, and, above all, *refined.*

ELISABETH MARBURY.

NEW YORK, *March, 1914.*

2.   The dance hall depicted in the illustration that opens this chapter was in the New York City neighborhood of East Harlem, where there were about half a dozen such halls at the turn of the century. Around this time, Harlem had a long history as an affluent neighborhood at the edge of New York City (Alexander Hamilton had his home there), though southeastern Harlem was an enclave of Italian immigrants. The building of subway lines, a real estate boom, and the accelerating migration of African Americans to the area in the two decades after 1920 made Harlem a neighborhood in flux. By the end of the First World War, it was widely viewed as a ghetto, as well as the social and intellectual capital of black America.

Based on its location as described here and in the photo, what inferences can you draw about Aly's Dancing School and the people it attracted? How do the advertisements correspond to what Peiss says about dance halls? And how would you describe the relationship between the outside of the building by day and what might happen inside it at night?

3.   "What mattered in the dance hall – popularity, dancing ability, fashionable clothes, and male attention – was a modern style that promised independence, romance, and pleasure," Peiss writes in the final paragraph of this essay. Nevertheless, she concludes, not only did the realities of working-class life undercut such promise, but the very values of dance halls themselves ended

up doing at least as much harm as good. What do you think Peiss means when she asserts that the culture of dance halls "fused notions of female autonomy and pleasure with heterosexual relationships and consumerism?" Do you agree with Peiss that sex, freedom, and money still define women's lives? What, if any, are the alternatives?

Suggested Further Reading

Scholarly treatments of the dance hall culture Peiss analyzes in *Cheap Amusements* are relatively rare. One of the earliest is Paul G. Cressey's *The Taxi-Dance Hall; a Sociological Study of Commercialized Recreation and City Life* (Chicago: University of Chicago Press, 1932), a case study of Chicago. Lewis Ehrenberg's *Steppin' Out: New York Nightlife and the Transformation of American Culture, 1890–1930* (Chicago: University of Chicago Press, 1981) is the standard source on the role of dancing in the lives of more well-to-do people than Peiss portrays. Theater scholar Carol Martin analyzes a kindred phenomenon to turn-of-the-century dance halls in *Dance Marathons: Performing American Culture in the 1920s and 1930s* (Jackson: University of Mississippi Press, 1994). See also Nan Enstad, *Ladies of Labor, Girls of Adventure: Working Women, Popular Culture, and Labor Politics at the Turn of the Twentieth Century* (New York: Columbia University Press, 1999).

6
Moving Images

1870s	French scientist Etienne Jules Marey and British-born American photographer Eadweard Muybridge experiment with time-motion images
1893	Panic of 1893 plunges US into major economic depression
1893	Thomas Edison exhibits kinetoscope, a peep-show viewer, at the World Columbian Exposition in Chicago
1895–6	First movie projectors enter the market
1898–9	Spanish-American War (re-enactments exhibited at nickelodeons)
1908	New York Mayor George McClellan orders closings of 550 nickelodeons for code violations (a move successfully contested by film exhibitors)
1909	Motion Picture Patents Company, a cartel led by Edison, forms to dominate film industry
1912	Woodrow Wilson defeats Theodore Roosevelt and William Howard Taft to win presidency (1913–21)
1914–18	World War I (allows US to dominate world film production and distribution)
1915	Federal court declares Motion Picture Patents Company an illegal restraint of trade
1915	D. W. Griffith's *Birth of a Nation* released
ca.1920	Hollywood emerges as the US film capital

Introduction

From its beginnings and well into the nineteenth century, the core of American popular culture was print. To be sure, other kinds of sensory experience were important, among them musical and visual arts. But it was written words, far more than images or spoken words, that penetrated the nooks and crannies of everyday life, from the newspaper read at the breakfast table each morning to the novel read by candlelight in bed each night. In the twentieth century, by contrast, popular culture has been dominated by images. Words – whether formatted on paper, floppy disk, or posted at a website – continue to play a large role, especially as a building block for newer forms of popular culture (like television broadcasting). But it is the universal language of pictures – whether formatted in photographs, videotapes, or CD-ROMs – that defines our time in the shows we watch, the celebrities we follow, or in how important events are remembered. In an important sense, we live in a different world.

Actually, the reorientation of popular culture toward images has clear origins in the nineteenth century. Woodcuts and ink illustrations had long enhanced the appeal of chapbooks and newspapers, and the enormous commercial success of lithographers like Currier and Ives (see the illustration that opens chapter 2) suggests a widespread desire for Americans to bring visual art into their homes in the decades before the Civil War.

The advent of photography in the mid-nineteenth century was a turning point. A difficult and expensive process when first developed by a series of individuals in the 1820s and 1830s, photography became increasingly popular in the 1840s and 1850s, when family portraits and *cartes de visite* (card-sized photographs) became staples of middle-class life. Steady improvements in technology – and the stunning pictures taken by Matthew Brady and others during the Civil War – suggested the major role photography could play as a medium of mass communication. The 1880s invention of the half-tone process, whereby pictures could be reproduced via dots of ink in varying shades of gray, made it possible to include large numbers of photographs in any given issue of a newspaper or magazine. By the turn of the century, cartoons, comic strips, advertisements, and photographs were bulging out of newspapers, particularly the newfangled tabloid (easier for reading on streetcars and subways) and Sunday papers.

But the real watershed event in the creation of a new visual culture was the advent of a new mass medium: film. A neurological quirk of the human brain – the illusion of motion when a series of pictures are displayed in rapid motion – became the basis for a series of converging technological, commercial, and artistic trends that not only remade the map of popular culture but became central to American identity as a whole (indeed, movies have been our signature national export ever since the First World War, when they first captured the international market).

Movies didn't transform popular culture overnight; they were components of other kinds of entertainment (like vaudeville and amusement parks) for many years after their first appearance. Moreover, it took a while before moviegoing emerged in a form contemporary fans would recognize. The history of early film projection, for example, is marked by a series of fits and starts, and not until the 1920s was it possible to record sound as well as pictures on film and movies became a truly *multi*media experience. But some astute observers – among them immigrant Jews with names like Loew, Fox, and Warner, who founded companies that remain with us still – recognized early on that this new movie culture was no fleeting fad.

In this excerpt from his 1982 book *Media and the American Mind*, Mount Holyoke College historian Daniel Czitrom surveys the world of early film culture. Czitrom describes the technical, financial, and legal jockeying that characterized the early movie business. He also sketches the character of early films, filmmakers, and audiences – along with their critics. Movies, Czitrom asserts, marked a crucial moment in the emergence of modernity, and were a medium which, however harshly (and even justly) criticized, nevertheless represented the realization of a truly democratic culture in American life that crossed class, language, and other barriers.

American Motion Pictures and the New Popular Culture, 1893–1918

Daniel J. Czitrom

Projected motion picture photography became a reality in the 1890s, but the dream of throwing moving pictures on a screen stretched back at least three centuries. Various European inventors described and created "magic lanterns" (primitive slide projectors) as early as the mid-seventeenth century. But not until the early nineteenth century did Peter Mark Roget and others seriously consider the principle of persistence of vision, a concept fundamental to all moving pictures, drawn or photographed.

In the 1870s and 1880s several scientists engaged in the investigation of animal and human movement turned to photography as a research tool. The most important of these, Etienne Jules Marey of France and Eadweard Muybridge, an Englishman living in America, created varieties of protocinema that greatly advanced visual time-and-motion study. They also inspired inventors around the world to try their hand at constructing devices capable of producing the illusion of motion

Peeping time   Interior view of the Automatic Vaudeville at East 14th Street, New York City, ca.1905. This early movie arcade, dominated here by the kinetoscopes in the foreground, was owned by Adoph Zukor, an immigrant furrier who later installed a movie theater on the second floor and liked to watch the reactions of audiences. Zukor went on to become president of Paramount Pictures, a major Hollywood studio. *Photo by permission of the Museum of the City of New York*

photography. Most of these inventors, including Thomas Edison, took up motion picture work for quite a different reason than Marey and Muybridge: the lure of a profit-making commercial amusement.[1]

Early film historians and journalists chose to perpetuate and embellish the legend of Edison's preeminence in the development of motion pictures. In fact, as the painstaking and voluminous research of Gordon Hendricks has shown, the true credit for the creation of the first motion picture camera (*kinetograph*) and viewing machine (*kinetoscope*) belongs to Edison's employee, W. K. L. Dickson. Between 1888 and 1896, Dickson was "the center of all Edison's motion picture work during the crucial period of its technical perfection, and when others were led to the commercial use of the new medium, he was the instrument by which the others brought it into function." Edison himself admitted in 1895 that his reason for toying with motion pictures was "to devise an instrument which should do for the eye what the phonograph does for the ear"; however, his interest in motion pictures always remained subordinate to his passion for the phonograph.[2]

With the perfection of a moving picture camera in 1892, and the subsequent invention of the peep hole kinetoscope in 1893, the stage was set for the modern film industry. Previewed at the Columbian Exposition in Chicago during the summer of 1893, the kinetoscope could handle only one customer at a time. For a penny or a nickel in the slot, one could watch brief, unenlarged 35-mm black-and-white motion pictures. The kinetoscope provided a source of inspiration to other inventors; and, more importantly, its successful commercial exploitation convinced investors that motion pictures had a solid financial future. Kinetoscope parlors had opened in New York, Chicago, San Francisco, and scores of other cities all over the country by the end of 1894. The kinetoscope spread quickly to Europe as well, where Edison, revealing his minimal commitment to motion pictures, never even bothered to take out patents.[3]

At this time the Dickson-Edison kinetograph was the sole source of film subjects for the kinetoscopes. These early films were only fifty feet long, lasting only fifteen seconds or so. Beginning in 1893 dozens of dancers, acrobats, animal acts, lasso throwers, prize fighters, and assorted vaudevillians traveled to the Edison compound in West Orange, New Jersey. There they posed for the kinetograph, an immobile camera housed in a tarpaper shack dubbed the "Black Maria," the world's first studio built specifically for making movies.[4]

Although it virtually disappeared by 1900, the kinetoscope provided a critical catalyst to further invention and investment. With its diffusion all over America and Europe, the competitive pressure to create a viable motion picture projector, as well as other cameras, intensified. During the middle 1890s various people worked furiously at the task. By 1895, in Washington, DC, C. Francis Jenkins and Thomas Armat had discovered the basic principle of the projector: intermittent motion for the film with a period of rest and illumination in excess of the period of movement from frame to frame. In New York, Major Woodville Latham and his two sons, along with Enoch Rector and Eugene Lauste, contributed the famous *Latham loop*, which allowed the use of longer lengths of film. William Paul successfully demonstrated his *animatograph* projector in London in early 1896. The Frenchmen Auguste and Louis Lumière opened a commercial showing of their *cinematograph* in Paris in late 1895 – a remarkable combination of camera, projector, and developer all in one. W. K. L. Dickson and Herman Casler perfected their *biograph* in 1896, clearly the superior projector of its day and the foundation for the American Mutoscope and Biograph Company.[5]

Once again, the name of Edison is most closely associated in the popular mind with the invention of the first projection machine. Actually, the basis of the *Edison Vitascope*, first publicly displayed in New York on 24 April 1896, was essentially the projector created by Thomas Armat. The Edison interests persuaded Armat "that in order to secure the largest profit in the shortest time it is necessary that we attach Mr. Edison's name in some prominent capacity to this new machine... We should not of course misrepresent the facts to any inquirer, but we think we can use Mr. Edison's name in such a manner as to keep with the actual truth and yet get the benefit of his prestige."[6]

With the technology for the projection of motion pictures a reality, where were they to be shown? Between 1895 and 1905, prior to the nickelodeon boom, films were presented mainly in vaudeville performances, traveling shows, and penny arcades. Movies fit naturally into vaudeville; at first they were merely another novelty act. Audiences literally cheered the first exhibitions of the vitascope, biograph, and cinematograph in the years 1895 to 1897. But the triteness and poor quality of these early films soon dimmed the novelty and by 1900 or so vaudeville shows used films mainly as chasers that were calculated to clear the house for the next performance. Itinerant film exhibitors also became active in these years, as different inventors leased the territorial rights to projectors or sold them outright to enterprising showmen. From rural New England and upstate New York to Louisiana and Alaska, numerous visitors made movies a profitable attraction in theaters and tent shows. Finally, the penny arcades provided the third means of exposure for the infant cinema. Aside from their use of kinetoscopes, arcade owners quickly seized on other possibilities. Arcade patrons included a hard core of devoted movie fans, who wandered from place to place in search of films they had not yet seen. Some arcade owners bought, rented, or built their own projectors; they then partitioned off part of the arcade for screening movies. They acquired films from vaudeville managers who discarded them.[7]

The combination of the new audience and a growing class of profit-minded small entrepreneurs resulted in the explosion of store theaters (nickelodeons) after 1905. A supply of film subjects and equipment was necessary to meet the demand, and the first of several periods of wildcat development ran from 1896 to 1909. The three pioneer companies of Edison, Vitagraph, and Biograph in effect controlled the production of motion picture equipment, but a black market quickly developed. Each company that sprang up in these years became a manufacturer of instruments in addition to producing films. Many firms had long lists of patent claims, each arguing that it had a legal right to do business. Aside from the few real inventors and holders of legitimate patents, a good deal of stealing and copying of equipment took place. Lawsuits ran a close second to movies in production priorities. In 1909 the ten major manufacturers finally achieved a temporary peace with the formation of the Motion Picture Patents Company, a patent pooling and licensing organization. In addition to granting only ten licenses to use equipment and produce films, the Patents Company created the General Film Exchange to distribute films only to licensed exhibitors, who were forced to pay a two-dollar weekly fee. The immediate impetus for this agreement, aside from the desire to rationalize profits, offers one clue as to how early motion pictures became a big business. Edison and Biograph had been the main rivals in the patents struggle, and the Empire Trust Company, holder of two hundred thousand dollars in Biograph mortgage bonds, sent J. J. Kennedy (an executive and efficiency expert) to hammer out an agreement and save their investment.[8]

By 1909 motion pictures had clearly become a large industry, with three distinct phases of production, exhibition, and distribution; in addition, directing, acting, photography, writing, and lab work emerged as separate crafts. The agreement of 1909, however, rather than establishing peace, touched off another round of intense speculative development, because numerous independent producers and exhibitors openly and vigorously challenged the licensing of the Patent Company. In 1914, after five years of guerrilla warfare with the independents, the trust lay dormant; the courts declared it legally dead in 1917. Several momentous results accrued from the intense battle won by the innovative and adventurous independents. They produced a higher quality of pictures and pioneered the multireel feature film. Under their leadership Hollywood replaced New York as the center of production, and the star system was born. At the close of the world war, they controlled the movie industry not only in America, but all over the globe.[9]

Of all the facets of motion picture history, none is so stunning as the extraordinarily rapid growth in the audience during the brief period between 1905 and 1918. Two key factors, closely connected, made this boom possible. First, the introduction and refinement of the story film liberated the moving picture from its previous length of a minute or two, allowing exhibitors to present a longer program of films. One-reel westerns, comedies, melodramas, and travelogues, lasting ten to fifteen minutes each, became the staple of film programs until they were replaced by feature pictures around World War I. George Melies, Edwin S. Porter (*The Great Train Robbery*, 1903), and D. W. Griffith, in his early work with Biograph (1908 to 1913), all set the pace for transforming the motion picture from a novelty into an art.

Secondly, the emergence of the nickelodeon as a place devoted to screening motion pictures meant that movies could now stand on their own as an entertainment. These store theaters, presenting a continuous show of moving pictures, may have begun as early as 1896 in New Orleans and Chicago. In 1902 Thomas Tally closed down his penny arcade in Los Angeles and opened the Electric Theater, charging ten cents for "Up to Date High Class Moving Picture Entertainment, Especially for Ladies and Children." But the first to use the term *nickelodeon* were John P. Harris and Harry Davis, who converted a vacant store front in Pittsburgh in late 1905.[10]

News of their success spread quickly and spawned imitators everywhere. All over America adventurous exhibitors converted penny arcades, empty store rooms, tenement lofts, and almost any available space into movie theaters. Because no official statistics remain from those years, we must rely on contemporary estimates. By 1907 between three and five thousand nickelodeons had been established, with over two million admissions a day. In 1911 the Patents Company reported 11,500 theaters across America devoted solely to showing motion pictures, with hundreds more showing them occasionally; daily attendance that year probably reached five million. By 1914 the figures reached about 18,000 theaters, with more than seven million daily admissions totaling about $300 million.[11]

Perhaps more graphic (and accurate) than these national statistics, local surveys revealed the terrific popularity of movies, especially in the larger cities. Table 1 summarizes data from a number of contemporary estimates of movie attendance in eight cities during these years.[12]

Although data for smaller cities and towns is more scarce, what little we have suggests that the "nickel madness" was not limited to large urban centers. For example, in Ipswich, Massachusetts, an industrial town of six thousand in 1914, movie attendance was substantial among schoolchildren. Of 127 children in grades five through eight, 69 percent of the boys went once a week or more to the movies, as did 55 percent of the girls. Among 179 high school students, 81 percent attended moving picture shows, on the average of 1.23 times per week for boys and 1.08 for girls. A 1914 study of Springfield, Illinois (1910 population, 51,678) revealed that 813 of the 857 high school students interviewed went to the movies regularly. Forty-one percent of the boys and 30 percent of the girls attended at least seven times a month, whereas 59 percent of the boys and 53 percent of the girls attended at least four times a month. A similar survey in 1914 of four Iowa cities (Iowa City, Dubuque, Burlington, Ottumwa) questioned fourteen hundred high school students. It showed that 30 percent of the boys and 21 percent of the girls in these communities went to the movies at least seven times a

Table 1   Urban movie attendance, 1911–18

City	Population (1910)	Year	Weekly attendance	No. of theaters
New York	4,766,883	1911	1,500,000	400
Cleveland	560,663	1913	890,000	131
Detroit	465,766	1912	400,000	–
San Francisco	416,912	1913	327,500	–
Milwaukee	373,857	1911	210,630	50
Kansas City	248,381	1912	449,064	81
Indianapolis	233,650	1914	320,000	70
Toledo	187,840 (1915)	1918	316,000	58

month, with 60 percent of the boys and 45 percent of the girls going at least four times each month.[13]

This sudden and staggering boom in movie attendance evoked strenuous reactions from the nation's cultural traditionalists, those whose values and sensibilities had been shaped largely by some version of the doctrine of culture. Although the motion picture held out great promise for many of the traditionalists in the abstract, few of them could accept as positive advance the new popular culture and all it implied. Their consideration of motion pictures centered on three points, all interrelated: the context of exhibition, the nature of the audience, and the content of the films themselves.

All of the surveys of motion picture popularity, and indeed a large fraction of all discussions of the new medium, placed movies in a larger context of urban commercial amusements. Movies represented "the most spectacular single feature of the amusement situation in recent years," a situation that included penny arcades, dance academies and dance halls, vaudeville and burlesque theaters, pool rooms, amusement parks, and even saloons. Motion pictures inhabited the physical and psychic space of the urban street life. Standing opposite these commercial amusements, in the minds of the cultural traditionalists, were municipal parks, playgrounds, libraries, museums, school recreation centers, YMCAs, and church-sponsored recreation. The competition between the two sides, noted sociologist Edward A. Ross, was nothing less than a battle between "warring sides of human nature – appetite and will, impulse and reason, inclination and ideal." The mushrooming growth of movies and other commercial amusements thus signaled a weakness and perhaps a fundamental shift in the values of American civilization.

"Why has the love of spontaneous play," wondered Reverend Richard H. Edwards, "given way so largely to the love of merely being amused?" For those who spoke about "the moral significance of play" and preferred the literal meaning of the term *recreation*, the flood of commercial amusements posed a grave cultural threat. Most identified the amusement situation as inseparable from the expansion of the city and factory labor. Referring to the enormous vogue of the movies in Providence, Rhode Island before World War I, Francis R. North noted the "great alluring power in an amusement which for a few cents ... can make a humdrum mill hand become an absorbed witness of stirring scenes otherwise unattainable, a quick transference from the real to the unreal."

Commercial amusements tempted rural folk as well, and some writers argued that "the young people coming from the country form the mainstay of the amusement resorts." Frederick C. Howe warned in 1914 that "commercialized leisure is moulding our civilization – not as it should be moulded but as commerce dictates.... And leisure must be controlled by the community, if it is to become an agency of civilization rather than the reverse."

A scientific assessment of the situation, as attempted by the myriad of recreation and amusement surveys of the early twentieth century, seemed a logical first step. Beyond this, the drive for municipal supervision of public recreation and commercial amusements fit comfortably into the Progressive ethos of philanthropists, social workers, and urban reformers all over America. "In a word," asserted Michael M. Davis of the Russell Sage Foundation in 1912, "recreation within the modern city has become a matter of public concern; laissez faire, in recreation as in industry, can no longer be the policy of the state."[14]

What actually transpired in and around the early nickelodeons varied from theater to theater and city to city. On the whole they do not seem to have been an especially pleasant place to watch a show. A 1911 report made on moving picture shows by New York City authorities disclosed that "the conditions found to exist are such as to attach to cheap and impermanent places of amusement, to wit: poor sanitation, dangerous overcrowding, and inadequate protection from fire or panic." Despite the foul smells, poor ventilation, and frequent breakdowns in projection, investigators found overflow crowds in a majority of theaters. Managers scurried around their halls, halfheartedly spraying the fetid air with deodorizers and vainly trying to calm the quarrels and shoving matches that commonly broke out over attempts to better one's view. The overall atmosphere was perhaps no more rowdy or squalid than the tenement home life endured by much of the audience; but the nickelodeons offered a place of escape for its eager patrons.[15]

The darkness of the nickelodeon theater, argued some doctors and social workers, caused eye strain and related disorders: "Intense ocular and cerebral weariness, a sort of dazed 'good-for-nothing' feeling, lack of energy, or appetite, etc.," as one physician put it. The health problem melted into a moral one, as critics condemned the darkness. Declared John Collier at a child welfare conference, "It is an evil pure and simple, destructive of social interchange, and of artistic effect." Jane Addams observed that "the very darkness of the theater is an added attraction to many young people, for whom the space is filled with the glamour of love-making." Darkness in the nickelodeon reinforced old fears of theaters as heavens for prostitutes and places where innocent girls could be taken advantage of. John Collier asked: "Must moving picture shows be given in a dark auditorium, with all the lack of social spirit and the tendency to careless conduct which a dark auditorium leads to?"[16]

If the inside of the theaters was seamy, the immediate space outside could be severely jolting. Gaudy architecture and lurid, exaggerated posters were literally "a psychological blow in the face," as one writer put it. Sensational handbills, passed out among schoolchildren, vividly described movies such as *Temptations of a Great City:* "Wine women and gayety encompass his downfall. Sowing wild oats. See the great cafe scene, trap infested road to youth, and the gilded spider webs that are set in a great city after dark." Phonographs or live barkers would often be placed just outside the theater, exhorting passers-by to come in. Inside, the nickelodeon program varied from theater to theater. An hour-long show might include illustrated song slides accompanying a singer, one or more vaudeville acts, and an illustrated lecture, in addition to several one-reelers. But movies were the prime attraction.[17]

In the summer of 1909, while strolling in a provincial New England town, economist Simon Patten found the library, church, and schools, "the conserving moral agencies of a respectable town," all closed. In contrast to this literally dark side of town, Patten described the brighter side where all the people were. Alongside candy shops, fruit and nut stands, and ice cream parlors, Patten noted the throngs at the nickel theater:

Opposite the barren school yard was the arcaded entrance to the Nick-elodeon, finished in white stucco, with the ticket seller throned in a chariot drawn by an elephant trimmed with red, white and blue lights. A phono-graph was going over and over its lingo, and a few machines were free to the absorbed crowd which circulated through the arcade as through the street. Here were groups of working girls – now happy "summer girls" – because they had left the grime, ugliness, and dejection of their factories behind them, and were freshened and revived by doing what they liked to do.[18]

Here the contrast was more than symbolic. Like many others, Patten warned that the traditional cultural institutions needed to adapt quickly in the face of movies and other commercial amusements. They could compete only by transforming themselves into active and "concrete expressions of happiness, security, and pleasure in life."[19]

As for the nickelodeon program itself, everyone concurred that vaudeville was "by far the most pernicious element in the whole motion picture situation." Early projected motion pictures had found their first home in vaudeville houses during the 1890s. But with the rise of theaters devoted to motion pictures, the situation reversed itself. Exhibitors across the nation added vaudeville acts to their film shows as a novelty for attracting patronage in a highly competitive business. Not all movie houses included vaudeville acts on the bill; local demand, availability of talent, and other conditions dictated the exact format of the show. But vaudeville became enough of a commonplace in American nickelodeons for observers to agree that it was the most objectionable feature of them. Particularly in immigrant ghettos, where ethnic vaudeville remained popular until the 1920s, reformers feared the uncontrolled (and uncensorable) quality of the live performance. The singers, dancers, and dialect comics of vaudeville appalled and frustrated those who were struggling to regulate the burgeoning nickelodeon movement.

The mayor's committee in Portland, Oregon complained in 1914, for example, about the numerous shows "where decent and altogether harmless films are combined with the rankest sort of vaudeville. There is a censorship upon the films, but none at all on male and female performers, who in dialog, joke, and song give out as much filth as the audience will stand for." In 1910 an Indianapolis civic committee denounced the vaudeville performances in local movie theaters as unfit for any stage: "Almost without exception the songs were silly and sentimental and often sung suggestively." Robert O. Bartholomew, the Cleveland censor of motion pictures, could not believe some of the things he witnessed in that city's nickelodeons in 1913:

> Many verses of different songs have been gathered which would not bear printing in this report. Dancers were often seen who endeavored to arouse interest and applause by going through vulgar movements of the body. . . . A young woman after dancing in such a manner as to set off all the young men and boys in the audience in a state of pandemonium brought onto the stage a large python snake about ten feet long. The snake was first wrapped about the body, then caressed and finally kissed in its mouth.[20]

Nickelodeon vaudeville was usually cheap, almost impossible to regulate, and socially objectionable – to the authorities, if not to the audience. As a result, police harassment and stricter theater regulations were employed all over the country to exclude vaudeville from movie houses. By 1918 nearly all movie exhibitors had responded to external pressure and internal trade opinion by eliminating vaudeville. They were forced to concede what one exhibitor had written in a trade paper in 1909, that "a properly managed exclusive picture show is in a higher class than a show comprised partly of vaudeville."[21]

In every town and city the place of exhibition proved the most vulnerable point of the industry, a soft underbelly for critics to attack. New York's experience between 1908 and 1913 provides a rough historical model for what transpired all over the country as cultural traditionalists sought to control the sphere of exhibition. By 1908 over five hundred nickelodeons had appeared in New York, a large proportion of them in tenement districts. A city ordinance required only a twenty-five-dollar license for theaters with common shows (movies were so designated) that had a capacity below three hundred; the regular theater license of five hundred dollars was well above the means of average exhibitors, so they made certain that their number of seats remained below three hundred. At a stormy public meeting on 23 December 1908, prominent clergymen and laymen urged Mayor George McClellan to close the nickelodeons for a variety of reasons. These included violation of Sunday blue laws (the busiest day for the nickelodeon trade), safety hazards, and degradation of community morals. "Is a man at liberty," demanded Reverend J. M. Foster, "to make money from the morals of people? Is he to profit from the corruption of the minds of children?" The next day Mayor McClellan revoked the licenses of every movie show in the city, some 550 in all.

On Christmas day exhibitors, film producers, and distributors responded by meeting and forming the Moving Picture Exhibitors Association, with William Fox as their leader. The movie men successfully fought the order with injunctions, but the message was clear: some form of regulation was necessary. Marcus Loew began to ask various civic bodies for names of potential inspectors to investigate the theaters. It took several years, however, for New York to enact the first comprehensive law in the United States regulating movie theaters. The 1913 legislation included provisions for fire protection, ventilation, sanitation, exits, and structural requirements. Seating limits increased from three hundred to six hundred to provide exhibitors more funds for making improvements. Significantly, all vaudeville acts were banned from movie houses unless they met the stiffer requirements of regular stage theaters.[22]

Although movies contributed to the new web of commercial amusements, they obviously stood apart from them as well. Motion pictures presented a troubling paradox: they clearly departed from traditional forms of recreation, yet they were undoubtedly superior to dance halls and pool rooms. Their potential for uplift was enormous, especially when one considered the makeup of the audience. Contemporary observers never tired of stressing the strong appeal motion pictures held for the working classes and new immigrants. Vigorous movie-phobes thought it impossible to exaggerate "the disintegrating effect of the sensational moving picture." Those more sanguine about its possibilities agreed with publisher Joseph M. Patterson: "The sentient life of the half-civilized beings at the bottom has been enlarged and altered by the introduction of the dramatic motif, to resemble more closely the sentient life of the civilized beings at the top." Both sides agreed that precisely because of the special appeal movies had for these groups, as well as for children, one had an obligation to discover how and why the motion picture captured its enormous audience.[23]

The 1911 Russell Sage study of New York theaters estimated movie audiences in that city to be 72 percent working class. A 1914 study of how one thousand working men spent their leisure time concluded that the popularity of moving pictures was the one outstanding fact of the survey. Sixty percent of those questioned attended movies regularly; those working the longest hours spent the most time at the shows; and those who earned less than ten dollars per week went the most often.[24]

Most writers directly coupled the working-class response to the film with modern industrial conditions. Elizabeth B. Butler, in her classic 1909 study of working-class women in Pittsburgh, thought that grinding and monotonous factory labor radically changed recreation patterns: "Dulled senses demand powerful stimuli; exhaustion of the vital forces leads to a desire for the crude, for violent excitation. . . . In such circumstances, culture of hand or brain seems unattainable, and the sharing of our general heritage a remote dream." Using a prevalent distinction of the day, Butler noted that the working women of Pittsburgh "are spending their leisure, not using it." Thus, of the 22,685 women working in factories and stores, she found less than 2 percent involved with such centers of recreation as the YWCA, Business Women's Club, and sewing circles. The extent to which movies dominated the women's recreational life profoundly impressed Butler, and she vividly described a trip to the nickelodeon:

> I shall not soon forget a Saturday evening when I stood among a crowd of pleasure seekers on Fifth Avenue, and watched the men and women packed thick at the entrance of every picture show. My companion and I bought tickets for one of the five cent shows. Our way was barred by a sign, "Performance now going on." As we stood near the door, the crowd of

people waiting to enter filled the long vestibule and even part of the sidewalk. They were determined to be amused, and this was one of the things labelled "Amusement." They were hot and tired and irritable, but willing to wait until long after our enthusiasm was dampened and we left them standing in line for their chance to go in.[25]

Butler did not believe that motion pictures were inherently bad; indeed, the diversion they offered to work-weary women was essential. "Yet there should be possibility for constructive diversion. A diversion is needed which shall be a form of social expression, and with slighter toll from strength and income, be of lasting value to the body and spirit."[26]

Similarly, Margaret F. Byington's 1910 study of ninety households in the mill town of Homestead, Pennsylvania, also acknowledged the great popularity of movies. The nickelodeon was the only theater of any kind available in Homestead. Pittsburgh theaters were out of the reach of working-class families because of travel time and expense. "Many people, therefore, find in the nickelodeons their only relaxation. Men on their way home from work stop for a few minutes to see something of life outside the alternation of mill and home; the shopper rests while she enjoys the music, poor through it be, and the children are always begging for five cents to go to the nickelodeon. In the evening the family often go together for a little treat."[27]

Contemporary observers somewhat overstated both the class and ethnic factors in their analysis of movie audiences. Commercial amusements proved more commercial than they had ever dreamed. Thus, although the working classes made up the bulk of early audiences and provided the basic working capital for the new medium, efforts to woo the middle and upper classes began almost immediately. As Russell Merritt has shown, "The blue collar worker and his family may have supported the nickelodeons. The scandal was that no one connected with the movies much wanted his support – least of all the immigrant film exhibitors who were working their way out of the slums." Merritt's study of the early Boston movie trade shows that after 1908 virtually all new nickelodeons opened in business districts on the outer edges of slums and near white-collar shopping centers, where they hoped to attract middle-class patronage.[28]

Even before the rise of the feature film and the wave of new movie palaces built after 1914, two developments usually cited as correlative with the winning of the middle-class audience, movie men actively sought to leave the slums behind. In Chicago, for example, as early as 1908, the Swann Theater opened in a residential quarter at a cost of sixty-five thousand dollars, and it immediately attracted a large family trade. For five or ten cents, the theater ran an eighty-minute program of three one-reelers and several illustrated songs. "The policy of the house recognizes the eternal feminine as the great factor in determining the nature of any amusement enterprise; and the pictures shown are always carefully selected with the view of pleasing the ladies." Trade papers were filled with advice on how to improve the reputation of movies through higher prices, more attractive and carefully located theaters, and better films.[29]

The presence of large numbers of "undeveloped minds" in the nickelodeons – immigrants and children – evoked endless assertions about movies as a potential agent of Americanization and moral suasion. The notion that movies served to Americanize immigrants had more to do with wish fulfillment than reality. For one thing, perhaps a majority of films screened in early years were produced in Europe. The Americanization argument seems to have been largely another piece of ammunition in the battle to establish a censorship of films.

The image of ignorant immigrants and incorrigible youth uplifted by movies was a potent and reassuring one for social workers and civic leaders sympathetic to films. An anonymous poem entitled "A Newsboy's Point of View," written about 1910, typified this sentimental attitude. It purported to describe how a newsboy witnesses the father of his girlfriend giving up drink after they all see a film about the evils of alcohol. The poem is written in the urban slang appropriate for its narrator, a tough Irish urchin. A stock image of the Progressive imagination, the newsboy quotes his girl's father: "'I never knowed just what a bum I'd gone an' got to be / Until those movin' pitchers went an' showed myself to me.'" But the real revelation comes in the last stanza, as the newsboy reflects on a larger lesson:

> All what I see wit' me own eyes I known an' unnerstan's
> When I see movin pitchers of de far off, furrin' lan's
> Where de Hunks an' Ginnes come from – yer can betcher life I knows
> Dat of all de lan's an' countries, 'taint no matter where yer goes
> Dis here country's got 'em beaten – take my oat dat ain't no kid –
> 'Cause we learned it from de movin' pitchers, me an' Maggie did.[30]

A far more significant effect of the motion picture, particularly for children, was in the area of peer socialization. The act of moviegoing created an important new subculture centered outside of the home. Jane Addams astutely recognized this development. Although she actively involved herself in the community supervision of movies and theaters, Addams always looked upon this work as only a holding action. To the end of her life she remained ambivalent about the implications of motion pictures. Her response to the motion picture's growth in

Chicago reflected the uneasiness of even the most sympathetic traditionalists.

In the spring of 1907, responding to pressure from the *Chicago Tribune*, the city's police department set up a "nickel theater bureau" charged with investigating movie theaters and penny arcades. One detective, walking along Milwaukee Avenue, counted eighteen nickelodeons in a mile-and-a-half stretch. The *Tribune* and various social agencies were greatly agitated by both the large numbers of children at the shows and the large proportion of objectionable films: movies with scenes of robbery, murder, shoplifting, skirt-lifting, and bedrooms. At Hull House, Addams and her associates had observed the eagerness of the penniless children to attend the movies. At first the settlement tried to compete with commercial exhibitors, establishing its own moving picture show, probably in early 1907. "Although its success justified its existence," Addams discovered, "it was so obviously but one in the midst of hundreds that it seemed much more advisable to turn our attention to the improvement of all of them or rather to assist, as best we could, the successful efforts in this direction."[31]

Thus Hull House joined the Juvenile Protection Association, the Relief and Aid Society, and other civic groups in cooperating with the police censorship of "5 cent theaters, penny arcades, and other cheap amusement resorts where juveniles are taught depravity." Addams opposed any ordinances prohibiting children from attending theaters without an adult, arguing that these were unenforceable. "What is needed," she declared, "is a regulation of the theaters. They are useful in providing a place of amusement for those who cannot go to the regular theater and can be made instructive. Police regulation supplemented by the efforts of a citizen's committee will overcome any evil influence."[32]

Young people invariably attended shows in groups, "with something of the 'gang' instinct. . . . What is seen and heard there becomes the sole topic of conversation, forming the ground pattern of their social life. That mutual understanding which in another social circle is provided by books, travel, and all the arts, is here compressed into the topics suggested by the play." But how could this corrupt dramatic art and the crude music that went with it replace the true drama, the real theater, which was "the only place where they can satisfy that craving for a conception of life higher than that which the actual world offers them?"

It could not. Throughout her career Addams championed amateur drama as a vital expression of the "play instinct." Like so many others, she argued for more extensive public recreation as an alternative to the commercial exhibition of films: not only playgrounds, but also patriotic and ethnic festivals, folk dancing, children's theater. She was ahead of her time in her sensitivity to preserving immigrant cultures, and here again she lamented the tendency of movies to erase the ethnic heritage from the minds of so many children. Addams's views on recreation amounted to nothing less than a vision of multicultural communion based on the artistic expression of individuals. One could not achieve communion at the movies. "To insist that young people shall forecast their rose colored future only in a house of dreams, is to deprive the real world of that warmth and reassurance which it so sorely needs and to which it is justly entitled: furthermore we are left outside with a sense of dreariness, in company with that shadow which lurks only around the corner for most of us – a skepticism of life's value."[33]

Although both the exhibition milieu and the nature of the audience continued to trouble the cultural traditionalists, they realized that movies were here to stay. Municipal regulation of the theaters, along with the elimination of vaudeville, might improve the moral atmosphere of shows. However, in no way could the size of the audience and the intensity of its devotion be diminished by substituting alternative forms of cheap amusement. Regulation of the films themselves thus remained the focal point for social control.

The 1908 nickelodeon licensing struggle in New York City led directly to the first attempt at a comprehensive censorship of motion pictures, and this attempt was spearheaded by the movie industry itself. In March 1909 the movie exhibitors and producers in New York City requested the People's Institute, a civic and educational foundation, to organize the National Board of Censorship of Motion Pictures. Although administered by the People's Institute, the board was a self-regulating body; it comprised a general committee (electing its own members and an executive board) that formally elected people to the actual censoring committee. Essentially, the NBC was the first of several methods of voluntary trade regulation for the movie industry, with the exhibitors and producers footing the bill. The movie men clearly wanted to counter public criticism of their business, for the standing of each exhibitor and producer depended on every other. The creation of the board may also be viewed as another important method by which the industry could make motion pictures more palatable to the upper and middle classes, "to improve the average quality of the films in order that a larger and larger number of the total population [would] patronize motion pictures."[34]

Here the commercial realities of the movies forced the industry to seek the cooperation of the cultural traditionalists. The board continually defined its mission as the uplifting of both the films and the taste of the audiences; it claimed that its goal was the elimination of any need for censorship. It began with the premise that "the motion picture has become a public power and a moral and cultural influence which must be brought under social control." Hence it made sure that "these censors [were] cultured men and women, trained to look on the activities of life from the broad view of their social significance; . . . persons of culture and more or less prominent in social and other public life in New York – doctors, lawyers, clergymen, and, in fact, men and women of all kinds of activities."

The board presumed a very simple psychology at the core of the moviegoer's experience: "Those who are educated by the movies are educated through their hearts and their sense impressions and that sort of education sticks. Every person in an audience has paid admission and for that reason gives his attention willingly. . . . Therefore he gives it his confidence and opens the window of his mind. And what the movie says sinks in." The board's standards of judgment mostly concerned elimination of excesses in scenes dealing with sex, drugs, and crime, particularly prostitution. While keeping in mind the differences in local standards, it tried "to act on behalf of the general conscience and intelligence of the country in permitting or prohibiting a given scene on film." By 1914 the National Board of Censorship claimed to be reviewing 95 percent of the total film output in the United States; it either passed a film, suggested changes, or condemned a movie entirely. Mayors, police chiefs, some four hundred civic groups, and local censoring committees from all over the country subscribed to the board's weekly bulletin.[35]

Local censorship arrangements remained active despite the work of the national board. Compared to the national board, local censors felt a greater confidence in their absolute right and ability to distinguish between moral and immoral films. Local boards often attacked the national board as too lenient, and they fiercely defended the necessity for community control of the censorship power. They tended to judge films solely as an endless succession of potential morality plays. In Portland, Oregon, for example, the form instituted by the mayor's committee on motion pictures asked investigators of movie theaters to use the following criteria in judging films: "Estimate moral value: Good, bad, or without moral value. Does the wrong doer prosper? Is the way of the transgressor easy? Are the rascals held up for admiration? Are the virtues made sources of mirth?" In Pennsylvania the state censors defined the "standards of the board" in a totally negative fashion. The state board worked out an incredibly detailed list describing scores of scenes that it prohibited from films shown in Pennsylvania.[36]

Compared to the large number of people interested mainly in the social effects of motion pictures, writers who approached movies as an art form were a small circle before World War I. They stand out as a prophetic minority in their efforts to treat the new popular culture from an aesthetic perspective, but they frequently revealed the same assumptions as the traditionalists about the nature of "true culture." At first most critics assessed movies in relation to the art form to which they seemed closest: drama. Indeed, there was a great deal of cross-fertilization between movies and the theater in these early years, both in terms of personnel and in the stylistic fusion of realism and romanticism.[37] But this insistence on judging motion pictures as merely another category of drama blinded many critics to the early achievements of film artists such as Griffith, Chaplin, Sennett, Pickford, Ince, and others. The motion picture, argued Brander Matthews in 1917, can improve on standard theatrical melodrama and farce, but "comedy and tragedy are wholly beyond its reach, and equally unattainable by it are the social drama and the problem play."

Film was not one of the higher or more important forms of drama, Matthews asserted, because it could not combine intellectual cooperation, emotional appeal, and sense gratification, the three elements that made drama the most illustrious art. He grudgingly conceded that motion pictures might be a new art, but because they could not utilize the spoken word, they would never rival the drama. Matthews concluded condescendingly that, as film makers accepted the medium's limitations and began to develop its techniques, "the apparent rivalry between the drama and the moving picture will lessen, and each will be left in possession of its own special field."[38]

Theater critics in general had difficulty with movies as an art form, and their confusion is perhaps best summarized in the work of Walter P. Eaton. As early as 1909, Eaton cited what he perceived as a rise in movie audience taste: "They have come to demand real drama, pictures that tell a coherent, interesting story and tell it well, with genuine settings and competent actors." Several European *films d'art* were already raising people's awareness of acting, story construction, and dramatic unity. For Eaton, however, appreciation of the "canned drama" remained only a means to the true understanding of real drama. He ultimately viewed the improvement of movies merely as a method of rescuing theatrical drama: "When they are well planned and well played, it is quite possible that they can always fill a useful function, in leading the lower strata of society up toward an appreciation of true dramatic art, which is, after all, only brought to flower on the stage of a true theater, where actual men and women speak with the voices God gave them."[39]

Four years later, Eaton still distinguished between movies and "the real thing." The menace of the movies to dramatic art was overstated, he claimed, even if "talking pictures" became a reality. Eaton pointed to the "layers on layers of intelligence and taste in the public," and although movies appealed to the hoi polloi, true drama would always remain a province of the cultural elite. "Talking movies can never give to these people the deep emotional glow, the keen intellectual zest, the warm aesthetic satisfaction which comes from living, vital acting, from distinguished, witty speech, from all the complex and interblended technical problems of the drama brought triumphantly off." In 1914 he saw some hope in the rising popularity of the feature film. Here he found sustained narrative, more clearly allied to dramatic and pictorial art, demanding concentration of two hours or more. Movies such as *Queen Elizabeth* (featuring Sarah Bernhardt) and *The Prisoner of Zenda* (starring James K. Hackett), larger theaters, and higher admission prices brought a more dignified quality to the motion picture. This is precisely what independent film producers such as Adolph Zukor aimed at. Nevertheless, for Eaton feature pictures of famous plays had value only as feeders for live performances.[40]

Finally, by 1915, Eaton even renounced his former optimism that movies might act as a school of appreciation for drama, breeding new audiences for the financially troubled legitimate stage. The drama must take to the offensive and recapture the masses, its gallery, through a program of socialized theater. Only municipal playhouses and branch theaters could compete economically with the movies for the working-class audience. It was time for true drama to fight motion pictures, not accommodate them. "They have a cruel realism which at once dulls the imagination and destroys the illusive romance of the art. They are utterly incapable of intellectual content.... All poetry, all music, all flash of wit, all dignity of spoken eloquence, they can never know."[41]

As the movie industry turned away from the simple one- and two-reelers produced by the Patents Company members and moved toward full-length features and spectacles, so too did film slowly achieve an independent critical status. By World War I more and more newspapers, magazines, and trade publications began to employ full-time reviewers to consider the latest in film art. Aside from professional critics, though, increasing numbers of intellectuals and artists began to contemplate seriously the aesthetic possibilities that movies offered. They were excited because film seemed a truly popular art, one that entered to an amazing extent "into the daily thought of the masses." As a new medium of expression, movies had advantages over the drama. It liberated the narrative from constraints of time and space and gave the artist a greater ability to alter his point of view. Robert Coady, writing in the avant-garde little magazine *Soil*, defended the motion picture as "a medium of visual motion." Aesthetic censorship, the attempt to make movies simply imitate drama, would prove just as crippling as the legal kind. "There is a world of visual motion yet to be explored, a world the motion picture is opening up to us."[42]

The two most substantial early treatments of film aesthetics came from antipodal sources. One may be considered the fount of the psychological approach to film analysis. The other sought to somehow adapt the classical notions of beauty to a new democratic art. Hugo Munsterberg's psychological study, *The Photoplay*, wanted to establish the aesthetic independence of motion pictures. But Munsterberg, chairman of the philosophy department at Harvard, wished to combine aesthetic inquiry with an exploration of the psychological factors involved in the movies' appeal. His psychology owed more to Kant and the German idealist tradition than to Freud and the new psychoanalysis.

Munsterberg argued that understanding the psychology of the motion picture must precede consideration of its aesthetic and that this was crucial for appreciating its differences from other arts. Various aspects of the motion picture depended on illusion, for example, depth and movement. "Flatness is an objective part of the technical physical arrangement, but not a feature of that which we really see"; similarly, the motion that a spectator sees "appears to be a true motion, . . . yet is created by his own mind." Both depth and movement "come to us in the moving picture world, not as hard facts, but as a mixture of fact and symbol. They are present yet they are not in the things. We invest the impression with them."

The *close-up* "objectified in our world of perception our mental act of attention," and thereby gave art "a means which far transcend[ed] the power of any theater stage." The *cutback* (flashback) paralleled the close-up by objectifying the mental act of remembering. The technique of *cutting* in movies allowed the objective world to be molded by the interests of the mind: "Events which are far distant from one another so that we could not be physically present at all of them at the same time are fusing in our field of vision, just as they are brought together in our consciousness. . . . This inner division, this awareness of contrasting situations, this interchange of diverging experience in the soul, can never be embodied except in the photoplay." All of these techniques made the power of suggestion great in film; the subtle art of the camera had great potential for deeply touching the emotions and attitudes of the audience.

Once one comprehended the basic psychology of the movies, the aesthetic followed naturally. Art must transcend reality, not imitate it, showing us things and events perfectly complete in themselves. Motion pictures were well suited for this task. They told "the human story by overcoming the forms of the outer world, namely space, time, and causality, and by adjusting the events to the forms of the inner world, namely attention, memory, imagination, and emotion." Human action was thus freed from physical phenomena and transferred to the realm of the mind. This transferral, Munsterberg argued, explained the great popularity of movies and accounted for the aesthetic feeling they gave.

In elaborating his aesthetic, Munsterberg sounded a good deal like those cultural traditionalists who could accept film only as a means to an end; he saw film's greatest mission as aesthetic education. Although Munsterberg hailed the new art of film, his ideas in some ways resembled those of Matthew Arnold: "An enthusiasm for the noble and uplifting, a belief in duty and discipline of the mind, a faith in ideals and eternal values must permeate the world of the screen." Perhaps because he was so involved in discovering why the new medium was so powerful, Munsterberg worried about the average person's ability to handle it: "The people still have to learn the great difference between true enjoyment and fleeting pleasure, between real beauty and the mere tickling of the senses."[43]

In *The Art of the Moving Picture*, the poet Vachel Lindsay tried to outline "a basis for photoplay criticism in America"; it is memorable less for its success in forming a critical theory than for Lindsay's ebullience in extolling the movies on several levels. The book was really a prose poem, still remarkable today in its breadth of vision, urgent commitment, and naiveté. Enormously excited at being present at the creation of a new art, Lindsay predicted that the movies would evolve into a peculiarly American cultural form: "The possibility of showing the entire American population its own face in the Mirror Screen has at last come."

His method was to categorize various types of movies by comparing them with traditional art forms. Thus, "the Action Film is sculpture-in-motion, the Intimate Photoplay is painting-in-motion, [and the] Splendor Pictures [are] architecture-in-motion." These analogies gave Lindsay the opportunity to legitimize the art of film, and he reiterated the theme of its independence: "The photoplays of the future will be written from the foundation of the film. . . . The supreme photoplay will give us things that have been half expressed in all other mediums allied to it."

To a poet who once walked across the nation reciting and selling his work to anyone who might listen, the potential for "a democracy and a photoplay business working in daily rhythm" was dizzying. Movies might succeed where earlier art forms had failed. Lindsay invoked the fervor of his kindred spirit: "Whitman brought the idea of democracy to our sophisticated literati, but did not persuade the democracy itself to read his democratic poems. Sooner or later the kinetoscope will do what he could not, bring the nobler side of the equality idea to the people who are so crassly equal."

Although he discussed a large number of contemporary films, Lindsay thought the future of movies most worthy of attention. We were all in on the ground floor; Edison became the new Gutenberg, and the invention of the motion picture seemed as great an advancement as the beginning of picture writing. Ostensibly an attempt to carve out a theory of film criticism, Lindsay's book went far beyond this, affirming that "the density of America from many aspects may be bound up in what the prophet wizards among her photoplay wrights and producers mark out for her, for those things which a whole nation dares to hope for it may in the end attain."[44]

By the end of the Great War, the medium of motion pictures had established a new popular culture: a postprint confluence of entertainment, big business, art, and modern technology that catered to and drew its strength from popular taste. The new popular culture combined product and process, neither of which fit within the matrix of the old doctrine of culture. The achievements of film art could not be measured by traditional critical standards; they demanded their own aesthetic. The act of moviegoing became a powerful social ritual for millions, a new way of experiencing and defining the shared values of peer and family.

Motion pictures thus proved a medium of communication that touched everyday life far more viscerally and immediately than had the more heralded telegraph. Telegraphy rearranged perceptions of time and space with its instantaneous transmission of information. Movies altered patterns of leisure and created a new art form. The new popular culture, however, still found its locus outside of the home. By the 1920s radio broadcasting would combine the impact of these two previous breakthroughs in media development. As a result, the accumulated force of modern communication penetrated the American home itself.

Notes

1 The best account of the prehistory of the motion picture is in Kenneth MacGowan, *Behind the Screen: The History and Techniques of the Motion Picture* (New York: Delacorte Press, 1965), pp. 25–84. Also useful are Kurt W. Marek, *Archaeology of the Cinema* (London: Thames and Hudson, 1965); and Frederick A. Talbot, *Moving Pictures: How They are Made and Worked* (Philadelphia: J. B. Lippincott, 1912), pp. 1–29. On the specific contributions of Marey, Muybridge, and others, see Robert Sklar, *Movie-Made America* (New York: Random House, 1975), pp. 5–9; MacGowan, *Behind the Screen*, pp. 45–64.

2 Gordon Hendricks, *The Edison Motion Picture Myth* (Berkeley: University of California Press, 1961), p. 142. The Edison quotation is taken from his preface to W. K. L. Dickson and Antonia Dickson, *History of the Kinetograph,*

Kinetoscope, and Kinetophonograph (New York: n.p., 1895), the Dicksons' own history of the inventions.

3 On the success and wide geographical dispersion of kinetoscopes, see Gordon Hendricks, *The Kinetoscope* (New York: Beginnings of the American Film, 1966), pp. 64–9. These parlors often contained phonographs and other machine novelties. On the kinetoscope at the Chicago fair, see Robert Grau, *The Theater of Science: A Volume of Progress and Achievement in the Motion Picture Industry* (New York: Broadway Publishing Co., 1914), pp. 3–4; and Hendricks, *Kinetoscope*, pp. 40–5.

4 For descriptions of these early films and how they were made, see Dickson and Dickson, *History*, pp. 23–40; Hendricks, *Kinetoscope*, pp. 21–8, 70–97; Joseph H. North, *The Early Development of the Motion Picture, 1887–1900* (New York: Arno Press, 1973), pp. 1–26.

5 Gordon Hendricks, *Beginnings of the Biograph* (New York: Beginnings of the American Film, 1964); MacGowan, *Behind the Screen*, pp. 75–84; North, *Early Development*, pp. 23–33; Terry Ramsaye, "The Motion Picture," *Annals of the American Academy of Political and Social Science* 128 (November 1926): 1–19.

6 Norman C. Raff and Frank R. Gammon, two of Edison's business partners, to Thomas Armat, 5 March, 1896, in Terry Ramsaye, *A Million and One Nights: A History of the Motion Picture* (New York: Simon and Schuster, 1926), p. 224.

7 FILMS IN VAUDEVILLE: "Edison Vitascope Cheered," *New York Times*, 24 April 1896; Grau, *Theater of Science*, pp. 11–12; Benjamin B. Hampton, *History of the American Film Industry* (1931; reprint ed., New York: Dover Publications, 1971), pp. 12–14. ITINERANT EXHIBITORS: Grau, *Theater of Science*, pp. 28–33; North, *Early Development*, pp. 55–6; George Pratt, "No Magic, No Mystery, No Sleight of Hand," *Image* 8 (December 1959): 192–211. PENNY ARCADES: Lewis Jacobs, *The Rise of the American Film* (New York: Harcourt, Brace and Co., 1939), pp. 5–8; Grau, *Theater of Science*, pp. 11–16; Hampton, *History*, pp. 12–14.

8 Jacobs, *Rise*, pp. 52–66, 81–5; Hampton, *History*, pp. 64–82; Ramsaye, *Million and One Nights*, pp. 59–72. An important review of the activities of the Motion Picture Patents Company is Ralph Cassady, Jr., "Monopoly in Motion Picture Production and Distribution: 1908–1915," *Southern California Law Review* 32 (Summer 1959): 325–90.

9 The rise of the independents and their contributions to both film industry and film art is a whole story in itself. See Jacobs, *Rise*, pp. 51–94; Hampton, *History*, pp. 83–145; Anthony Slide, *Early American Cinema* (New York: A. S. Barnes, 1970), pp. 102–35.

10 Tally's advertisement reproduced in MacGowan, *Behind the Screen*, p. 128; Hampton, *History*, pp. 44–6; Jacobs, *Rise*, pp. 52–63.

11 I have compiled these figures from several sources, using the more conservative estimates where there is conflict. 1907: Joseph M. Patterson, "The Nickelodeon," *Saturday Evening Post* 180 (23 November 1907): 10; "The Nickelodeon," *Moving Picture World* 1 (4 May 1907): 140. 1911: Patents Company figures are in Cassady, "Monopoly in Motion Picture Production and Distribution," p. 363 (a little over half of these were licensed by the trust, paying the weekly two-dollar fee); William Inglis, "Morals and Moving Pictures," *Harper's Weekly* 54 (30 July 1910): 12–13. 1914: Frederic C. Howe, "What to do With the Motion Picture Show," *Outlook* 107 (20 June

1914): 412–16. Howe, chairman of the National Board of Censorship of Moving Pictures, estimated a daily attendance of between seven and twelve million; W.P. Lawson, "The Miracle of the Movie," *Harper's Weekly* 60 (2 January 1915): 7–9.

12 Statistics gathered from the following sources: US Department of Commerce, *Thirty-eighth Statistical Abstract of the United States* (Washington, DC: Government Printing Office, 1915). New York: Michael M. Davis, *The Exploitation of Pleasure: A Study of Commercial Recreation in New York* (New York: Russell Sage Foundation, 1911). Davis's careful study of the attendance at New York City theaters estimated 900,000 for Manhattan movie houses alone. Three years later the National Board of Censorship placed the New York daily attendance between 850,000 and 900,000 so the 1.5 million weekly figure for 1911 is probably low. Cleveland; Robert O. Bartholomew, *Report of Censorship of Motion Pictures* (Cleveland: n.p., 1913). Detroit: Rowland Haynes, "Detroit Recreation Survey" (1912), cited in Richard H. Edwards, *Popular Amusements* (New York: Association Press, 1915), pp. 50–1. San Francisco: "Public Recreation," *Transactions of the Commonwealth Club of California* (1913), cited in Edwards, *Popular Amusements*, pp. 16, 51. Milwaukee: Rowland Haynes, "Recreation Survey, Milwaukee, Wisconsin," *Playground* 6 (May 1912): 38–66. Kansas City: Rowland Haynes and Fred F. McClure, *Second Annual Report of the Recreation Department of the Board of Public Welfare* (Kansas City: n.p., 1912). Indianapolis: F. R. North, "Indianapolis Recreation Survey" (1914), cited in Edwards, *Popular Amusements*, p. 33. Toledo: J. J. Phelan, *Motion Pictures as a Phase of Commercialized Amusements in Toledo, Ohio* (Toledo: Little Book Press, 1919).

13 Howard R. Knight, *Play and Recreation in a Town of 6000: A Recreation Survey of Ipswich, Mass.* (New York: Russell Sage Foundation, 1914); Lee F. Hanmer and Clarence A. Perry, *Recreation in Springfield, Illinois* (New York: Russell Sage Foundation, 1914). The Iowa study was done by Irving King and is cited in Hanmer and Perry, *Recreation in Springfield*.

14 Edward A. Ross, Introduction to Richard H. Edwards, *Popular Amusements* New York: Associated Press, 1915), p. 5; Edwards, *Popular Amusements*, pp. 20–1, 133; Francis R. North, *A Recreation Survey of the City of Providence* (Providence: Providence Playground Association, 1912), p. 58; Belle L. Israels, "Recreation in Rural Communities," *Proceedings of the International Conference of Charities and Correction* (Fort Wayne: n.p., 1911), p. 105; Frederic C. Howe, "Leisure," *Survey* 31 (3 January 1914): 415–16; Davis, *Exploitation of Pleasure*, p. 4.

15 Raymond Fosdick, *A Report on the Condition of Moving Picture Shows in New York* (New York: n.p., 1911), p. 11. See also Charles de Young Elkus, "Report on Motion Pictures," *Transactions of the Commonwealth Club of California* 8 (1914): 251–72, a report on fifty-eight motion picture houses in San Francisco.

16 Dr. George M. Gould in the *Journal of the American Medical Association*, quoted in "Health," *Survey* 29 (15 February 1913): 677; John Collier, *The Problem of Motion Pictures* (New York: National Board of Censorship, 1910), p. 5; Jane Addams, *The Spirit of Youth and the City Streets* (New York: Macmillan Co., 1910), p. 86; John Collier, "Light on Moving Pictures," *Survey* 25 (1 October 1910): 801. See also Vice Commission of Chicago, *The Social Evil in Chicago* (Chicago: Gunthrop Warner, 1911), p. 247, for

claims that "children have been influenced for evil by the conditions surrounding some of these shows."

17 Davis, *Exploitation of Pleasure*, p. 54; Haynes and McClure, *Recreation Survey of Kansas City*, p. 78, quotes examples of the handbills. For further descriptions of what went on inside the nickelodeons, as well as the reasons for their rapid spread across the country, see the trade papers, for example: "Trade Notes," *Moving Picture World* 1 (30 March 1907): 57–8; Melville C. Rice, "The Penny Arcade as a Side Show," *The Nickelodeon* 1 (January 1909): 23; "Vaudeville in Picture Theaters," *The Nickelodeon* 1 (March 1909): 85–6. See also Edward Wagenknecht, *Movies in the Age of Innocence* (Norman: University of Oklahoma Press, 1962), Introduction.

18 Simon N. Patten, *Product and Climax* (New York: B. W. Huebsch, 1909), pp. 18–19.

19 Ibid., p. 28.

20 Collier, *The Problem of Motion Pictures*, p. 5; Grau, *Theater of Science*, pp. 19–20; Marcus Loew, "The Motion Picture and Vaudeville," in Joseph P. Kennedy, ed., *The Story of the Films* (Chicago: A. W. Shaw, 1927), pp. 285–300; William T. Foster, *Vaudeville and Motion Picture Shows: A Study of Theaters in Portland, Oregon* (Portland: Reed College, 1914), pp. 12–13; "Moving Pictures in Indianapolis," *Survey* 24 (23 July 1910): 614; Bartholomew, *Report of Censorship of Motion Pictures*, p. 14.

21 "Vaudeville or Not?" *The Nickelodeon* 1 (November 1909): 134. For an example of provaudevillian sentiment in the trade, see "The Elevation of Vaudeville," *Moving Picture World* 1 (18 May 1907): 164. See also Boyd Fisher, "The Regulation of Motion Picture Theaters," *American City* 7 (September 1912): 520–2; John Collier, "'Movies' and the Law," *Survey* 27 (20 January 1912): 1628–9.

22 "Say Picture Shows Corrupt Children," *New York Times*, 24 December 1908; "Picture Shows All Put Out of Business," *New York Times*, 25 December 1908; "Picture Show Men Organize to Fight," *New York Times*, 26 December 1908; "Mayor Makes War on Sunday Vaudeville," *New York Times*, 29 December 1908; Sonya Levien, "New York's Motion Picture Law," *American City* 9 (October 1913): 319–21. See also Sklar, *Movie-Made America*, pp. 30–1.

23 "'Movie' Manners and Morals," *Outlook* 113 (26 July 1916): 695; Patterson, "The Nickelodeon," p. 11; Ramsaye, "The Motion Picture." Good descriptions of the working-class audience at the movies can be found in Barton W. Currie, "The Nickel Madness," *Harper's Weekly* 51 (24 August 1907): 1246–7; Mary Heaton Vorse, "Some Picture Show Audiences," *Outlook* 97 (24 June 1911): 442–7; Lucy F. Pierce, "The Nickelodeon," *The World Today* 15 (October 1908): 1052–7.

24 Davis, *Exploitation of Pleasure*, table 8, p. 30; a table note explains: "The social groups considered were three – working class, business or clerical class, and leisure class. Costume and demeanor enabled the observer, after a little experience, to place his people quite readily." Charles Stelzle, "How One Thousand Working Men Spent Their Spare Time," *Outlook* 106 (4 April 1914): 722–66; this article summarizes the results of a Ph.D. dissertation done at Columbia University by George E. Bevans.

25 Elizabeth B. Butler, *Women and the Trades: Pittsburgh, 1907–1908* (New York: Charities Publication Committee of the Russell Sage Foundation, 1909), p. 333.

26 Ibid.

27 Margaret F. Byington, *Homestead: The Households of a Mill Town* (New York: Charities Publication Committee of the Russell Sage Foundation, 1910), p. 111.

28 Russell Merritt, "Nickelodeon Theaters 1905–1914; Building an Audience for the Movies," in Tino Balio, ed., *The American Film Industry* (Madison: University of Wisconsin Press, 1976), p. 65.

29 Charles F. Morris, "A Beautiful Picture Theater," *The Nickelodeon* 1 (March 1909): 65–7. On the desirability of finer theaters and their requirements for better pictures, see "The Modern Motion Picture Theater," *Motion Picture News* 8 (6 December 1913).

30 "A Newsboy's Point of View," included in Herbert A. Jump, *The Religious Posibilities of the Motion Picture* (New Britain, Conn.: n.p., 1910?). This item can be found in the National Board of Review of Motion Pictures Collection, 1911–26, NC 17, 225, Lincoln Center Theater Library, New York; Merritt, "Nickelodeon Theaters," pp. 64–5. For examples of those who were more sanguine about movies as a positive agent for assimilation, see Knight, "Americanization of the Immigrant Through Recreation," in *Play and Recreation in a Town of 6000*, pp. 60–5; Constance D. Leupp, "The Motion Picture as a Social Worker," *Survey* 24 (27 August 1910): 739–41; "The Moving Pictures and the National Character," *Review of Reviews* 42 (September 1910): 315–20.

31 "Censors Inspect Nickel Theaters," *Chicago Tribune*, 1 May 1907; Jane Addams, *Twenty Years at Hull House* (New York: Macmillan, 1910), p. 386.

32 "Social Workers to Censor Shows," *Chicago Tribune*, 3 May 1907.

33 Addams, *The Spirit of Youth*, pp. 86–7, 75–6, 103. For views late in life, see Jane Addams, *The Second Twenty Years at Hull House* (New York: Macmillan Co., 1930), especially the chapter on "The Play Instinct and the Arts."

34 *Report of the National Board of Censorship of Motion Pictures* (New York: National Board of Censorship, 1913), p. 6; *The Standards of the National Board of Censorship* (New York: National Board of Censorship, 1914?).

35 *Report of the National Board*, pp. 3–4; *Standards of the National Board*, pp. 3–5; W. P. Lawson, *The Movies: Their Importance and Supervision* (New York: National Board of Censorship, 1915), p. 6. For descriptions of the daily work of the National Board of Censorship, see Charles W. Tevis, "Censoring the Five Cent Drama," *The World Today* 19 (October 1910): 1132–9; Orrin G. Cocks, "Applying Standards to Motion Picture Films," *Survey* 32 (27 June 1914): 337–8.

36 Foster, *Vaudeville and Motion Picture Shows in Portland, Oregon*, p. 12; Pennsylvania State Board of Censorship, *Rules and Standards* (Harrisburg: J. L. L. Kuhn, 1918), pp. 15–17. See also Elkus, "Report on Motion Pictures," on the continuing need for local censorship.

37 See A. Nicholas Vardac, *Stage to Screen: Theatrical Method from Garrick to Griffith* (Cambridge: Harvard University Press, 1949); John R. Fell, "Dissolves by Gaslight: Antecedents to the Motion Picture in Nineteenth-Century Melodrama," *Film Quarterly* 23 (Spring 1970): 22–34. For contemporary discussions on this relationship, see Robert Grau, "The Motion Picture Show and the Living Drama," *Review of Reviews* 45 (March 1912): 329–36; Bennet Musson and Robert Grau, "Fortunes in Films: Moving Pictures in the Making," *McClure's* 40 (December 1912): 193–202.

38   Brander Matthews, "Are the Movies a Menace to the Drama?," *North American Review* 205 (March 1917): 451, 454.

39   Walter P. Eaton, "The Canned Drama," *American Magazine* 68 (September 1909): 495, 500.

40   Walter P. Eaton, "The Menace of the Movies," *American Magazine* 76 (September 1909): 55–60, and "A New Epoch in the Movies," *American Magazine* 78 (October 1914): 44.

41   Walter P. Eaton, "Class Consciousness and the 'Movies,'" *Atlantic Monthly* 115 (January 1915): 55.

42   Robert Coady, "Censoring the Motion Picture," *Soil* 1 (December 1916): 38. See also Clayton Hamilton, "The Art of the Moving Picture Play," *The Bookman* 32 (January 1911): 512–16; "A Democratic Art," *The Nation* 97 (28 August 1913): 193. Myron D. Lounsbury, " 'Flashes of Lightning': The Moving Picture in the Progressive Era," *Journal of Popular Culture* 3 (Spring 1970): 769–97, contains a useful analysis of two of the earliest regular film critics, Louis Reeves Harrison and Frank Woods.

43   Hugo Muensterberg, *The Photoplay: A Psychological Study* (New York: D. Appleton and Co., 1916), pp. 52, 71, 88, 106–7, 173, 228, 230.

44   Vachel Lindsay, *The Art of the Moving Picture* (New York: Macmillan Co., 1915), pp. 65–6, 206, 224, 7.

Consider the Source

1.   One figure who surfaces a number of times in Daniel Czitrom's discussion of movie culture is Jane Addams, one of the leading figures of the Progressive Era. Born in small-town Illinois in 1860, Addams was a child of privilege, restless, with a youth marked by extensive education and travel in Europe. But during one such trip in the late 1880s, Addams was inspired by the work of English settlement houses (or dormitory/social clubs) for the poor, particularly women and children. Returning to the United States, she founded such an establishment, Hull House, in a ramshackle Chicago mansion. Addams became world famous for her efforts on behalf of immigrants and other poor city residents, winning a Nobel Peace Prize in 1931.

      Unlike some other Progressives, who had a top-down style of reforming the nation's institutions, Addams was notable for her intimate knowledge of the people she helped and the problems they faced. Her keen powers of observation led her to think long and hard about how they used their free time. In this excerpt from her 1909 book *The Spirit of Youth and the City Streets*, Addams assesses the new medium of film. What is her stance toward movies? (It may be useful to compare and contrast it with Elisabeth Marbury's stance toward dance halls in chapter 5.) How valid is her distinction between movie-going and baseball? To what extent do the patterns she observed in young people a hundred years ago still apply to new immigrants in cities like Los Angeles and Houston?

Excerpts from *The Spirit of Youth* by Jane Addams (1909)

This spring a group of young girls accustomed to the life of a five-cent theater, reluctantly refused an invitation to go to the country for a day's outing because the return on a late train would compel them to miss one evening's performance. They found it impossible to tear themselves away not only from the excitements of the theater itself but from the gaiety of the crowd of young men and girls invariably gathered outside discussing the sensational posters.

A steady English shopkeeper lately complained that unless he provided his four daughters with the money for the five-cent theaters every evening they would steal it from his till, and he feared that they might be driven to procure it in even more illicit ways. Because his entire family life had been thus disrupted he gloomily asserted that "this cheap show had ruined his 'ome and was the curse of America." This father was able to formulate the anxiety of many immigrant parents who are absolutely bewildered by the keen absorption of their children in the cheap theater. This anxiety is not, indeed, without foundation. An eminent alienist of Chicago states that he has had a number of patients among neurotic children whose emotional natures have been so over-wrought by the crude appeal to which they had been so constantly subjected in the theaters, that they have become victims of hallucination and mental disorder. . . .

This testimony of a physician that the conditions are actually pathological, may at last induce us to bestir ourselves in regard to procuring a more wholesome form of public recreation. Many efforts in social amelioration have been undertaken only after such exposures; in the meantime, while the occasional child is driven distraught, a hundred children permanently injure their eyes watching the moving films, and hundreds more seriously model their conduct upon the standards set before them on this mimic stage.

Three boys, aged nine, eleven, and thirteen years, who had recently seen depicted the adventures of frontier life including the holding up of a stage coach and the lassoing of the driver, spent weeks planning to lasso, murder, and rob a neighborhood milkman, who started on his route at four o'clock in the morning. They made their headquarters in a barn and saved enough money to buy a revolver, adopting as their watchword the phrase "Dead Men Tell no Tales." . . . Fortunately for him, as the lariat was thrown the horse shied, and, although the shot was appropriately fired, the milkman's life was saved. Such a direct influence of the theater is by no means rare, even among older boys. Thirteen young lads were brought into the Municipal Court in Chicago during the first week that "Raffles, the Amateur Cracksman" was upon the stage, each one with an outfit of burglar's tools in his possession, and each one shamefacedly admitting that the gentlemanly burglar in the play had suggested to him a career of similar adventure.

In so far as the illusions of the theater succeed in giving youth the rest and recreation which comes from following a more primitive code of morality, it has a close relation to the function performed by public games. It is, of course, less valuable because the sense of participation is largely confined to the emotions and the imagination, and does not involve the entire nature. . . .

Well considered public games easily carried out in a park or athletic field, might both fill the mind with the imaginative material constantly supplied by the theater, and also afford the activity which the cramped muscles of the town dweller so sorely need. Even the unquestioned ability which the theater possesses to bring men together into a common mood and to afford them a mutual topic of conversation, is better accomplished with the one national game which we already possess, and might be infinitely extended through the organization of other public games.

The theater even now by no means competes with the baseball league games which are attended by thousands of men and boys who, during the entire summer, discuss the respective standing of each nine and the relative merits of every player. During the noon hour all the employees of a city factory gather in the nearest vacant lot to cheer their own home team in its practice for the next game with the nine of a neighboring manufacturing establishment and on a Saturday afternoon the entire male population of the city betakes itself to the baseball field; the ordinary means of transportation are supplemented by gay stage-coaches and huge automobiles, noisy with blowing horns and decked with gay pennants. The enormous crowd of cheering men and boys are talkative, good-natured, full of the holiday spirit, and absolutely released from the grind of life. They are lifted out of their individual affairs and so fused together that a man cannot tell whether it is his own shout or another's that fills his ears; whether it is his own coat or another's that he is wildly waving to celebrate a victory. He does not call the stranger who sits next to him his "brother" but he unconsciously embraces him in an over- whelming outburst of kindly feeling when the favorite player makes a home run. Does not this contain a suggestion of the undoubted power of public recreation to bring together all classes of a community in the modern city unhappily so full of devices for keeping men apart? . . .

. . .

As it is possible to establish a connection between the lack of public reaction and the vicious excitements and trivial amusements which become their substitutes, so it may be illuminating to trace the connection between the monotony and dullness of factory work and the petty immoralities which are often the youth's protest against them.

There are many city neighborhoods in which practically every young person who has attained the age of fourteen years enters a factory. When the work itself offers nothing of interest, and when no public provision is made for recreation, the situation becomes almost insupportable to the youth whose ancestors have been rough-working and hard-playing peasants.

In such neighborhoods the joy of youth is well nigh extinguished; and in that long procession of factory workers, each morning and evening, the young walk almost as wearily and listlessly as the old. Young people working in modern factories situated in cities still dominated by the ideals of Puritanism face a combination which tends almost irresistibly to overwhelm the spirit of youth. When the Puritan repression of pleasure was in the ascendant in America the people it dealt with lived on farms and villages where, although youthful pleasures might be frowned upon and crushed out, the young people still had a chance to find self-expression in their work. Plowing the field and spinning the flax could be carried on with a certain joyousness and vigor which the organization of modern industry too often precludes. Present industry based upon the inventions of the nineteenth century has little connection with the old patterns in which men have worked for generations. The modern factory calls for an expenditure of nervous energy almost more than it demands muscular effort, or at least machinery so far performs the work of the massive muscles, that greater stress is laid upon fine and exact movements necessarily involving nervous strain. But these movements are exactly of the type to which the muscles of a growing boy least readily respond, quite as the admonition to be accurate and faithful is that which appeals the least to his big primitive emotions. . . .

In vast regions of the city which are completely dominated by the factory, it is as if the development of industry had outrun all the educational and social arrangements.

The revolt of youth against uniformity and the necessity of following careful directions laid down by some one else, many times results in such nervous irritability that the youth, in spite of all sorts of prudential reasons, "throws up his job," if only to get outside the factory walls into the freer street, just as the narrowness of the school inclosure induces many a boy to jump the fence.

When the boy is on the street, however, and is "standing around on the corner" with the gang to which he mysteriously attaches himself, he finds the difficulties of direct untrammeled action almost as great there as they were in the factory, but for an entirely different set of reasons. The necessity so strongly felt in the factory for an outlet to his sudden and furious bursts of energy, his overmastering desire to prove that he could do things "without being bossed all the time," finds little chance for expression, for he discovers that in whatever really active pursuit he tries to engage, he is promptly suppressed by the police. . . .

The unjustifiable lack of educational supervision during the first years of factory work makes it quite impossible for the modern educator to offer any real assistance to young people during that trying transitional period between school and industry. The young people themselves who fail to conform can do little but rebel against the entire situation.

There are many touching stories by which this might be illustrated. One of them comes from a large steel mill of a boy of fifteen whose business it was to throw a lever when a small tank became filled with molten metal. During the few moments when the tank was filling it was his foolish custom to catch the reflection of the metal upon a piece of looking-glass, and to throw the bit of light into the eyes of his fellow workmen. Although an exasperated foreman had twice dispossessed him of his mirror, with a third fragment he was one day flicking the gloom of the shop when the neglected tank overflowed, almost instantly burning off both his legs. Boys working in the stock yards, during their moments of wrestling and rough play, often slash each other painfully with the short knives which they use in their work, but in spite of this the play impulse is too irrepressible to be denied. . . .

The discovery of the labor power of youth was to our age like the discovery of a new natural resource, although it was merely incidental to the invention of modern machinery and the consequent subdivision of labor. In utilizing it thus ruthlessly we are not only in danger of quenching the divine fire of youth, but we are imperiling industry itself when we venture to ignore these very sources of beauty, of variety and of suggestion.

2. The Automatic Vaudeville penny arcade depicted in the photograph that opens this chapter is empty. It was, however, located in the heart of a commercial district, and was often crowded with people. What kind of people

do you imagine visited it? (Are movie titles like *Peeping Jimmies* and *French High Kickers* any indication?) How would you compare it to arcades you might visit at a mall or amusement park today?

3. Czitrom notes that in the face of mounting criticism by politicians, reformers, and church groups, the early motion picture industry formed the National Board of Censorship of Motion Pictures to monitor and/or regulate film content. The NBC, as it was known, was only the first of a series of such organizations, among them the Motion Picture Producers and Distributors Association (founded in 1922), which currently rates movies G, PG, PG-13, R and NC-17. Why would the movie industry – or, for that matter, any commercial organization – voluntarily accept self-censorship? How effective is such regulation likely to be (and how are you defining "effective")?

4. "The achievements of film art could not be measured by traditional critical standards; they demanded their own aesthetic," Czitrom writes at the end of this piece (p. 152). What are some of those standards? How are they different from other media like theater and or the novel?

Suggested Further Reading

Unlike some of the other subjects covered in this book, it is not hard to find information on the origins and development of movies. Indeed, the problem is more a matter of narrowing a blinding array of choices. There are two books in particular, however, that have long been considered indispensable for students and scholars. As its title suggests, James Monaco's *How To Read a Film: The Art, Technology, Language, History, and Theory of Film and Media* (1977; New York: Oxford University Press, 1981) covers the introductory bases. In terms of American film history, Robert Sklar's *Movie-Made America: A Cultural History of American Movies* (1975; New York: Vintage, 1995) is widely considered the standard text. For more information on the material covered in this chapter in particular, see Terry Ramsay, *A Million and One Nights: A History of the Motion Picture Through 1925* (1954; New York: Touchstone, 1986); and Lary May, *Screening Out the Past: The Birth of Mass Culture and the Motion Picture Industry* (Chicago: University of Chicago Press, 1983). See also David Nasaw's *Going Out: The Rise and Fall of Public Amusements* (New York: Basic Books, 1993), which has a series of highly readable chapters on early movie culture.

7

Waves of Selling

1844	Samuel Morse successfully transmits first message by telegraph between Washington and Baltimore
1902	Italian inventor Guglielmo Marconi transmits wireless message across the Atlantic
ca.1907	Americans Reginald Fessenden and Lee DeForest separately transmit the human voice over radio waves
1912	Radio Act begins US government regulation of industry
1914–18	World War I (radio communication used in air, land, and sea operations)
1920s	Radio broadcasting emerges as entertainment medium
1926	National Broadcasting Company (NBC) created as first radio network
1928	Premiere of *Amos 'n' Andy* radio serial
1929	Stock market crash ushers in Great Depression
1932	Franklin Delano Roosevelt elected president (1933–45; gives "Fireside Chats" via radio)
1934	Creation of Federal Communications Commission to monitor radio and other electronic media
1939–45	World War II (covered by radio news)

Introduction

Until about 1920, the financial structure of popular culture was fairly simple. You want to see a show? Buy a ticket. You want to read a novel? Buy the book. Even forms of popular culture that were not solely supported by users, such as newspapers financed at least in part by advertising, were nevertheless acquired by readers who paid for them. While there were sometimes mediating institutions – public libraries supported by taxpayers, for example, might allow a person to read a book without paying for it directly – more often than not they limited or even denied access to popular culture (indeed, for much of American history public libraries saw themselves as providing *alternatives* to dime novels and other such fare).

The advent of modern radio broadcasting in the 1920s, with its emphasis on advertising-supported content, represented a significant departure from the old pop culture economic order. But this change was rooted in developments that had been underway for a long time. Advertising, after all, had long been a part of print culture; what really changed in the decades on either side of the First World War was the growing sophistication and growth of an advertising industry that placed new emphasis on consumer psychology and business organizations, like advertising agencies, that specialized in particular aspects of market capitalism.

In any event, the marriage between art and commerce represents an important chapter in the history of popular culture – and thus this book – not only because their relationship has always been important, but also because this particular point in that relationship would have lasting consequences for later media like television and the Internet. In an important sense, the future began here.

Technologically speaking, that future began when Samuel Morse's work on the telegraph in the 1830s and 1840s created the possibility of instantaneous communication between two points connected by a wire. The next step was to develop a process whereby the wire would be unnecessary. A series of European and American scientists (including Thomas Edison) investigated the subject; the Italian Gugliemo Marconi successfully built on their work and in 1897 formed a company backed by British financing to sell wireless telegraphy equipment for ships and lighthouses to communicate with each other via Morse code.

By 1910 it was possible to transmit the human voice by radio, with subsequent refinements over the next decade. It was during these years that the new medium became a popular activity for hobbyists, or "hams," who communicated with each other across long distances. For precisely this reason, however, the airwaves soon became crowded with a multitude of voices over a limited spectrum of radio frequencies.

Rapid innovations led to other applications for radio, notably by combatants in World War I. Meanwhile, large corporations were also showing an interest in radio. The American Telegraph and Telephone Company (AT&T) hoped it would have applications for long-distance telephony. General Electric (GE) saw a market in the manufacture of hardware for hams. So did the Radio Corporation of America (RCA). Through a complicated series of maneuvers, these companies pooled their patents in the early 1920s to form a cartel to dominate the manufacturing of radio equipment.

But would this be where the action was? A decade earlier, Thomas Edison and other entrepreneurs scrambled for control of motion picture projectors.

The real profits, as it turned out, were in the movies themselves, an insight that led savvy observers like Adolph Zukor and the Warner brothers to triumph over Edison and other hardware-minded rivals. A similar pattern was enacted in radio. In 1920, an executive at Westinghouse, a lagging competitor in the industry, noticed that an employee who was playing records over the airwaves in East Pittsburgh was attracting a lot of attention in the local press, as was a department store that was advertising radio receivers as a means to hear the music. In other words, what was valued here was not communication between two points, but rather transmissions from *one* source to *many* listeners – what came to be known as broadcasting. From this vantage point, it was owning radio *stations*, not selling ham radio *sets*, that mattered. The radio boom was on.

Many issues remained unresolved, however. While private companies were an important presence in radio stations, so were schools, churches, government agencies, and labor unions. Early radio broadcasting was a freewheeling – and very uneven – panoply of talk, music, drama and other kinds of entertainment generally offered for free: most radio stations had no source of income, and typically allocated no money to pay individuals who were as often as not thrilled to have an electronic soapbox. Imagining a radio world without such limitations, early promoters of the medium wondered: What kinds of programs did the public want? How could they be supported? Who could best provide them?

AT&T had some answers. Unlike GE and RCA, it had no real interest in hardware; what the company really wanted was for customers to, in effect, rent its technology for timed intervals, much in the way a person paid for the use of a telephone line to make a call. In August of 1922, a real estate company spent $50 for the right to broadcast a ten-minute advertisement on its AT&T's New York station, WEAF. A short while later, a department store paid for the station to broadcast some entertainment – in other words, it sponsored a program. In January of 1923, WEAF broadcast a concert that was simultaneously transmitted by wire to the Boston station WNAC, a development that signaled the feasibility of a series of affiliated stations, that is, a network. While here too there was uncertainty about different technological means of creating networks, the system of wired stations favored by AT&T emerged as the dominant model. In 1926 RCA joined with GE and Westinghouse to create the National Broadcasting Company (NBC), the first broadcasting network. It was followed less than a year later by the Columbia Broadcasting System, or CBS. A capitalist model for radio was being fine-tuned.

But would Americans buy it? As Brown University historian Susan Smulyan explains, it was by no means clear to proponents *or* opponents of this new model that they would. In this chapter from her 1994 book *Selling Radio: The Commercialization of American Broadcasting, 1920–1934*, Smulyan describes what she calls the strenuous "campaign for broadcast advertising" by promoters who had to overcome the skepticism not only of radio listeners, but of businesses and advertising agencies as well. In the end, the campaign was successful. But that success was by no means inevitable – and it is by no means inevitable that the advertising-dominated media culture we inhabit today is the only, or best, possible world.

Arguments Over Broadcast Advertising

Susan Smulyan

Eight hundred people entered *Radio Broadcast*'s 1925 contest, "Who Is To Pay for Broadcasting and How?" offering "ingenious" plans to charge for program listings, schemes for voluntary listener contributions, and even a call for government licensing. As the editors wrote, "suggestions there were of all kinds, and the problem of deciding which one of all the group was the best was not found at all easy." The winning entry sought a tax on vacuum tubes, as an "index of broadcast consumption," to be administered by a federal Bureau of Broadcasting. Despite the award, neither the *Radio Broadcast* editors nor the judges of the contest found much to praise in the winning entry, and they were especially critical of the large government role proposed for distributing the tax revenue. All agreed that "the last word has not been said on this subject."[1] Although radio broadcasting had existed for five years, a single idea of how it should be financed had not yet taken hold. The contest suggested a wealth of options, as broadcasters, listeners, and advertisers vied for control of the airwaves.

Early stations

While receiver manufacturers financed some of the earliest radio stations simply to boost their sales, other businesses founded stations to gain publicity or goodwill. Secretary of Commerce Herbert Hoover initially hoped that more businesses might be persuaded to finance radio stations, even though radio gave only an "intangible return" on

---

Advertising radio This 1926 sheet-music cover for the "Clicquot Fox Trot March" was sent to 50,000 radio listeners to promote Clicquot's sponsored program and its banjo orchestra (the company mascot is at the left). Note the way the bands of sun in the background resemble radio waves. *Photo courtesy of Susan Smulyan*

investment.[2] In his history of early radio, Erik Barnouw lists stations owned by a stockyard, a marble company, a laundry, and a poultry farm.[3] Such stations could be called commercial insofar as some of their programming related to the owner's products, yet they did not sell advertising time to other manufacturers.

While these stations provided models for how business could profit from radio, some financing proposals did not aim to profit the business

world. Voluntary contributions to stations from philanthropists or listeners, some observers believed, might keep broadcasting out of the
clutches of business. "A powerful station could be put up and operated
at a cost less than that required for a reasonable sized library," declared
an editorial in the first issue of *Radio Broadcast* magazine, adding that "a
properly conducted radio broadcasting station can do at least as great an
educational work as does the average library." The editorial predicted
"that many such stations will be operating in the next twenty-five
years."[4]

Public schools and universities seemed logical sources of financial
backing for stations operating in the public interest. Many colleges and
school districts did establish radio stations, often as part of their science
departments, enlisting teachers and students as performers. By 1925
ninety educational institutions held licenses to broadcast.[5]

A few city governments founded and supported radio stations to be
"operated for direct public benefit."[6] Promoters hoped that the first
municipal station, WNYC in New York, would provide an alternative
to privately owned stations that had begun accepting paid advertisements. Programming on WNYC, however, resembled that heard over
other New York stations. The police department broadcast alarms for
wanted criminals, and various city agencies presented talks, but WNYC
filled most of its broadcast hours with musical selections.[7] In 1926 a
newspaper article described WNYC's offerings as "not the most attractive in the metropolitan district by the furthest stretch of the imagination." The station's problems included taxpayers who "would resent any
lavish expenditure of talent" and "city officials" who "are not elected for
the purpose of giving nightly musical entertainment." One promoter of
radio advertising noted that, after broadcasting a year, WNYC could
"make a group picture of its usual audience on the City Hall steps."[8]
Despite its undistinguished programming, small audiences, poor
funding, and attacks by citizens' groups, WNYC survived (now independently), but it failed to provide much inspiration for other municipal
stations. It remained an interesting experiment rather than a genuine
alternative.

Despite the fact that the American government never levied taxes
specifically to pay for broadcasting, the federal government went on
the air early and stayed on. The US Department of Agriculture, for
example, produced programs ranging from weather and market reports
to household hints, broadcast by private and college stations in rural
areas. But the radio corporations lobbied heavily against any extension
of the federal role in broadcasting, always fearing a government takeover.
Some radio magazines promoted the funding of broadcasting through
taxes, highlighting the successful British system, but most listeners

seemed reluctant to begin paying for a service they already received free of charge.[9]

Stations approached ordinary listeners for financial support several times during the early 1920s. "The Radio Music Fund Committee" sought gifts to engage the best musical talent, artists "hopelessly beyond the appeal of gratuitous performances," to perform over WEAF in New York.[10] In a widely reported effort, Kansas City station WHB (owned by the Sweeney Auto School) sold tickets for an "invisible theater." Listeners received tickets and a program book for contributions of between one and ten dollars. "We are more than willing to spend money to operate the station," the manager noted, "but with musicians demanding $4 an hour and stage artists one-eighth their weekly salary...we believe it is only fair for those sharing the pleasure to pay a portion of the expenses."[11] Advocates of this strategy hoped that the financial support of listeners would keep broadcasting from being exploited by businesses whose aims were "not wholly compatible with the public interest."[12] The problem, one critic wrote, was that if all stations began soliciting funds, "their tin cups would have glistened before our eyes at every street-corner; they would have stood panting at our back doors like hungry dogs."[13]

None of the early experiments in financing radio stations, including commercial sponsorship, worked very well. Yet, as the *Radio Broadcast* contest showed, before 1925 broadcast advertising was considered just one of the options that seemed unsatisfactory. Observers could imagine broadcasting financed in a variety of ways, or even a mixed system with different stations funded in different ways. Before the advent of the networks, advertising stood out among the financing options only because it elicited the loudest protests and had the fewest supporters. The network system's need for large amounts of cash in order to rent wire lines suddenly gave broadcast advertising a privileged position. The networks had the money and energy to push for their choice among the financing plans, and push they did.

Opponents

In 1925 the editors of *Radio Age* noted that "the broadcasters who succumbed to the commercial influence are building up a monster who, like Frankenstein, will slay his creator."[14] Such anti-advertising rhetoric came from every group involved in early radio: listeners, critics, legislators, regulators, and broadcasters. Many critics adopted a hysterical tone when writing of radio advertising, using metaphors out of horror stories to describe the new mutant. Another radio magazine warned that advertising might "become an Old Man Of The Sea –

practically impossible to shake off once he got a good grasp" and concluded with a call for "a country-wide movement" with "definite,
speedy action" against it.[15] Despite these concerns about listener control
and the affect on programs, however, no "country-wide movement"
against radio advertising took hold in the early 1920s.

Many broadcasters wanted to dismiss advertising quickly and continue the search for a more practical solution to their economic problem.
They believed that "advertising by radio does not offer a solution to the
problem of making broadcasting self-supporting" and that advertising
presented "dangers to broadcasting" that might cause both radio and
advertising to fail.[16] Radio professionals worried that listeners would
grow disenchanted with the medium as its novelty faded. One article
noted that "bombastic advertising... cuts into the vitals of broadcast
advertising – its circulation – by creating an apathetic public, impairing
listener interest and curtailing the sale of receiver sets." This writer
named the worst fear of both the radio and advertising industries: once
a method for financing radio had been established, listeners might dislike
the solution and turn off their sets without allowing the industry sufficient time to reorganize. Fears that broadcast radio was a fad, and that
listeners would be easily alienated, remained widespread in the industry
until late in the 1920s and caused many professionals to distrust broadcast advertising.[17]

Early on, the advertising industry became concerned that listeners
might resent radio sponsorship and by extension reject all types of advertising. *Printer's Ink*, an advertising trade publication, argued that radio
advertising (along with "sky writing," "press agent dope," or any "disguised publicity") was against "good public policy," and that radio was
an "objectionable advertising medium." The magazine warned that "an
audience... wheedled into listening to a selfish message will naturally be
offended," and "its ill-will would be directed not only against the company that delivered the story, but also against the advertiser who chooses
to talk shop at such an inopportune time."[18] To a certain extent, print
advertisers and the advertising industry in general (represented by *Printer's Ink*) saw broadcast advertising as unwanted competition. But beyond
that, the often repeated comment that radio advertising, if unwanted,
would "probably die by itself in a short time" made advertisers worry that
if broadcast advertising failed, all advertising might suffer.[19]

Public attitudes toward broadcast advertising remained difficult to
discern, but several groups purporting to speak for listeners reinforced
the fears of broadcasters and advertisers. In 1924 the executive secretary
of the American Radio Association (ARA), an organization of listeners,
explained that "numerous complaints are being received from the radio
public which is objecting in increasing numbers to having its news,

music, and entertainment interspersed with advertising." The ARA believed that "pure and unadulterated advertising on radio" would be "disastrous to the trade itself."[20] Participants in the Fourth National Radio Conference agreed that the "listening public" found radio advertising "objectionable" and added that "advertising could be made detrimental to the interests of both the public and the broadcasting stations."[21]

Opponents claimed that listeners would be overlooked in programming decisions if advertising supported radio. The first editorial in *Radio Broadcast* magazine called on listeners "to exert their influence in such a way that the entertainment offered them is determined by themselves." At present, the 1922 editorial told listeners, they were "helpless" with regard to radio programming because "you have nothing to say about it, you pay nothing for it, and still more to the point, you have no rights in the matter at all."[22] These critics found inherent problems with any financial solution not based on listener support. "It is plain that the public must meet the cost of broadcasting if the benefit of broadcasting is to be public," warned *Outlook* magazine.[23] Other commentators pointed out that listeners lacked even the last refuge of the consumer, because broadcast advertising was harder to ignore than newspaper and magazine advertising.[24]

Emmanuel Celler, a New York congressman, parodied radio abuses in 1924 as he introduced a bill to control broadcast advertising:

> This is BLAA, broadcasting station of the Jumbo Peanut Company at Newark, New Jersey. You will now have the pleasure of listening to the "Walk Up One Flight Clothing Company's" orchestra. Their first number will be "You Don't Wear Them Out If You Don't Sit Down."

Celler found such gimmicks more than annoying. "Radio is of tremendous value for educational and amusement purposes," he believed, but "unless suitable measures are passed to steer it into proper channels we will, indeed, run amuck." Broadcast advertising, he argued, would damage radio programming by its very presence; it was "worthless stuff which interferes with instructive and informative broadcasting."[25]

Even Secretary Hoover, a believer in private control of most businesses, initially opposed broadcast advertising. At the First National Radio Conference in 1922, Hoover had found it inconceivable that "we should allow so great a possibility for service, for news, for entertainment, for education, and for vital commercial purposes, to be drowned in advertising chatter, or used for commercial purposes."[26] Two years later, he still maintained that the solution to the "problem of remuneration for broadcasting stations" was "the hardest nut in the bowl" to crack.[27]

The notion of "indirect advertising" helped Hoover and others overcome their distaste for pitching products over the air. Difficult to define,
indirect advertising permitted the airing of the sponsor's name, but no
"direct" selling. How such definitions translated into practice remained
even more puzzling. A *New York Times* reporter asked, "what is the
distinction between announcing an orchestra under the name of a well-
known brand of tea or coffee and actually talking about the tea or
coffee?"[28] By October 1924, during the Third National Radio Conference, Hoover had moved cautiously toward support of indirect advertising, maintaining that "the listeners will finally decide in any event."[29] A
year later, during the Fourth National Radio Conference, he spoke more
positively still of indirect advertising and approved of "unobtrusive
publicity" that would be "accompanied by a direct service and engaging
entertainment" rather than "unobtrusive advertising."[30] Indirect advertising, Hoover now believed, could strengthen small stations without
bothering listeners, involving the federal government, or hurting the
large corporations involved in radio.[31]

    Hoover's shift in opinion reflected the general indecision about how to
finance and regulate broadcasting, but his actions also sprang from his
free-market economic principles. The quintessential "scientific" business leader of the 1920s, Hoover approved of government involvement
in broadcasting principally to help radio companies rationalize their
young industry. He attacked the problems of radio as he did those of
the aviation and the electrical power industries: by working for the kind
of cooperation between government and business that would benefit
both sides and might also stimulate a lagging economy.[32] Hoover
believed that the radio industry should resolve the controversy regarding
advertising with the approval of its listeners and without government
interference. Such beliefs kept Hoover from acting aggressively to contain the growth of broadcast advertising.

    General public acceptance of broadcast advertising came only as a
result of the radio industry's sustained campaign to promote it. The early
promoters of broadcast advertising, aware that it was still considered
only one financing option among many, moved to make their strategy
look less commercial. Trying to sell the idea to a skeptical advertising
industry, they presented radio advertising as a "natural" outgrowth of
earlier experiments. The first historians of broadcasting took a similar
approach, pointing out that broadcasting in the United States had first
prospered because of a patent pool and because of the investments of
large receiver manufacturers. In addition, many businesses, including
feed and grain merchants, newspapers, department stores, and radio
set retailers, had founded radio stations primarily to generate publicity
for themselves. Such a view presented broadcast advertising as simply

a logical extension of the other early means of financing radio.[33] Later, historians and the radio industry alike preferred to overlook the hard work that had been necessary to sell radio as an advertising medium.

The Campaign for Broadcast Advertising

If all American broadcasting was, and had always been, essentially commercial, why the opposing outcry against broadcast advertising? Proponents of broadcast advertising tried to paper over the differences between the early "commercial" stations supported by private enterprises and the financing of all operations through the sale of airtime. They sought to convince skeptical listeners and advertisers that broadcast advertising could bring them all the benefits of radio without any costs. This view ignored the difference between one sponsor and hundreds. Programs on stations supported through the sale of time soon became selling vehicles only, while the advertisements took up more and more broadcast time. Many of those involved in early radio saw this difference quite clearly and remained outspoken in their dislike of broadcast advertising. Yet with the founding of the networks, the radio industry had to finance expensive wire rentals in order to provide national service. Advertising was the only financing alternative that had the potential to be hugely profitable. NBC therefore spearheaded a publicity and educational campaign to promote broadcast advertising, a campaign that further influenced radio's shape and content.

According to historian Susan Strasser, advertising professionals had used the military term "campaign" to refer to a coordinated series of promotional activities since the turn of the century.[34] The push to sell broadcast advertising looked exactly like any other early twentieth-century advertising campaign: advertising professionals drew on well-known promotional methods to create acceptance and demand for broadcast advertising. I have deliberately labeled this "the campaign for broadcast advertising" to describe the character and techniques of their efforts.

In addition to promoting radio advertising, the campaign aimed to convince advertisers that radio programs should be treated as products and marketed as such to listeners. In the process, it developed the concept that time, as well as space, could be bought and sold for commercial purposes. Radio advertising ended up reinforcing the advertising industry's theories about how advertising worked, and came to function exactly like advertising in other media. The changes in radio brought about by the selling of broadcast advertising culminated in the promotion of daytime programming. As part of their attempt to make broadcasting fit into preconceived notions about advertising, the promoters presented women in the home as a key audience for radio. Networks worked to sell daytime hours to sponsors by preparing special programs, and the entire broadcast day became commercialized.

Promoters

Most of those involved in advertising in the 1920s had little interest in radio at first. Yet the field of advertising, by then well established and carefully professionalized, included a few salesmen with a mixture of advertising, radio, and journalism or academic experience that made them suitable for promoting broadcast advertising. Their skills enabled them to present the network view of broadcast advertising to their fellow advertising professionals, the public, and potential advertisers.

Between 1927 and 1932 five advertising professionals produced books, and others a new magazine, designed to promote broadcast advertising.[35] The books and magazine articles outlined the theory and methods of successful radio sponsorship. Writing for a varied audience about a little-known subject, the promoters of broadcast advertising found the text-book approach convenient and powerful. This concentrated production of materials reflected both the continued resistance to broadcast advertising and the radio industry's determination to break down that resistance.

NBC kicked off the campaign with the appointment of Frank Arnold as director of development in 1926. The best-known proponent of broadcast advertising, Arnold had worked in merchandising, retailing, magazines, and as an advertising executive before he entered radio. Owen D. Young, chairman of NBC's board, believed Arnold could sell the "present and future opportunities of radio" to "the national advertiser and to the advertising agencies with whom he has been intimately connected for more than 20 years."[36] As "time salesman on an ambassadorial level," Arnold talked to NBC officials about advertising, delivered speeches to business groups about radio's potential (to avoid "arousing suspicion that what they were listening to was propaganda ... my general procedure was to tell the story and let the advertising use follow as an aftermath"), spoke about radio to the general public, organized the NBC promotion department, and even helped with audience mail.[37] In the fall of 1930 Arnold gave a series of thirteen lectures on "Radio Broadcast Advertising" to sixty-two students, each of whom paid $12.50, at City College of New York; he later published these lectures as a book, *Broadcast Advertising: The Fourth Dimension.* Arnold's call for "indirect" advertising, and his belief that "the time will never come when the programs of our great broadcasting systems will be 100% commercial," aimed to reassure those who worried about the increasing commercialization of the air.[38]

Edgar Felix and Orrin Dunlap also published early books advocating the use of radio in advertising. Like many young men during the years before World War I, both had become fascinated with radio, built transmitters and receivers, and "in the period from 1913 to 1915... spent a good deal of time wearing headphones."[39] Both studied electronics and radio more formally as part of their war service and, after completing college and graduate school, looked for jobs in radio. Soon both became professional promoters of radio, first working in advertising agencies and then writing about radio for a variety of publications. Felix edited the radio section of *Advertising and Selling* from 1927 to 1932, while Dunlap served for eighteen years as radio editor of the *New York Times*.[40] In their books, Felix's *Using Radio in Sales Promotion* and Dunlap's *Radio in Advertising*, both admitted that most listeners hated advertising.[41] But if sponsors followed the tips they provided, they maintained, radio advertising could prove successful. Felix's and Dunlap's combination of radio, advertising, and journalism experience made them particularly effective promoters.

Herman Hettinger had a different mix of experience: he trained as an economist and worked as a business school professor before he became a consultant to the radio industry. Hettinger wrote his doctoral dissertation on radio advertising and later alternated between teaching at the University of Pennsylvania's Wharton School of Finance and Commerce and working as the first director of research at the National Association of Broadcasters (a trade lobbying group), where he compiled radio advertising statistics.[42] Despite the use of statistics, charts, and economic analysis, Hettinger's dissertation, later published as *A Decade of Radio Advertising*, followed much the same format, made the same arguments, and reached many of the same conclusions as the previous more anecdotal treatments of radio advertising. Hettinger lacked the practical radio experience of Felix and Dunlap, but his teaching skills and economics background made his arguments persuasive. Like Arnold, Hettinger had worked for the radio industry, particularly that part of it dominated by the networks, and promoted its view of broadcast economics.

The Advertising Agency Looks at Radio, edited by Neville O'Neill, followed the formula of the Arnold, Dunlap, and Felix books, in which advertising professionals justified radio advertising to their colleagues. Seventeen essays, each contributed by a different agency executive, explained how agencies could plan and deliver a radio advertising campaign.[43] O'Neill's book, which advocated vigorous involvement by advertising agencies in radio and favored more direct advertising strategies, illustrated how far the campaign for broadcast advertising had already progressed by 1932.

All these authors and contributors also wrote for *Broadcast Advertising* magazine, which began in April 1929 and continued until absorbed by another journal in December 1932.[44] Based in Chicago, *Broadcast Advertising* maintained strong links with the professional organizations of the radio and advertising industries, publishing speeches delivered at the meetings of the National Association of Broadcasters and the American Association of Advertising Agencies.[45] It continued the promotional work begun in the textbooks by publishing case studies of successful radio advertising and directions for preparing commercial broadcast programs and advertisements.

The early promoters of radio advertising exhibited similar outlooks, career paths, methods of presentation, and concerns. Most had worked in both radio and advertising (or business) at a time when such a combination of experience was rare. They explained the mysteries of broadcasting in terms advertising professionals could understand. Their ties to the networks, and the trade associations dominated by the networks, reinforced their beliefs about the best method to finance radio and fueled their messianic zeal. Drawing on their knowledge of contemporary advertising theory and practice, they presented radio as a familiar, but improved, advertising medium. At the same time, they used a pedagogical approach to reach the public, employing slogans and metaphors to promote radio advertising. The proponents of broadcast advertising shifted their focus as the technology and organization of the radio industry developed, but their persuasive techniques, drawn from the larger advertising industry, remained the same.

Campaign Rhetoric and Strategies

In 1925 *Popular Radio* printed a listener's response to the portrayal, by the promoters of broadcast advertising, of radio as magical:

> There is one thing I hate to be called,
> Against it I boldly protest;
> It gives me a shiver
> A chill on the liver,
> To be hailed as "invisible guest."
>
> It's hard to imagine the ether,
> As crawling with bodiless hosts,
> But it gives me the creeps,
> When a voice from the deeps,
> Seeks to claim me as one of the ghosts.

When you call me "dear friend" or "dear fan,"
I'll tune in with fervor and zest,
But somehow I quiver,
And cannot but shiver,
When hailed as "invisible guest."[46]

This poem reveals that the promoters of broadcast advertising had adopted the language of 1920s print advertising, including the use of "magic," to present their case. They also invoked slogans and the appeal of "sincerity" to sell radio advertising, as if it were a product taken on by one of the agencies in which they had worked. Broadcast advertising's proponents also portrayed radio as a desirable sales medium by using words and concepts prevalent in theoretical writing about advertising in the 1920s.[47] Boosters bragged that radio could fulfill advertisers' needs by appealing to consumers' senses, providing control over the surrounding material, becoming an integral part of the advertising campaign, improving brand-name awareness, and involving dealers with the products.

From the beginning, the supporters of broadcast advertising used slogans that mirrored the "indirect" form of advertising they advocated for radio. Felix addressed the need for subtlety in writing slogans (because the "radio audience ... resents the slightest attempt at direct advertising") and described the case of the Happiness Candy Company, which in its announcement "got over the idea that their stores are conveniently located throughout New York, without resorting to a direct advertising statement, by working in the phrase that 'happiness is just around the corner from you.'" An announcement "to the effect that 'there is a Happiness Candy Store near you' would be neither so subtle nor so favorably remembered," according to Felix.[48] Slogans for radio advertising used the indirect approach both because promoters believed indirect selling worked better and because they sought to remind listeners of the proper form of radio advertising.

Many observers described the new financial arrangement represented by radio advertising as the "American System" of broadcasting, which provided "a rich variety of entertainment at the expense of the advertiser, instead of an anemic flow as in England at the expense of the set owner."[49] Support of broadcast advertising was treated almost as a matter of patriotic pride, while broadcast advertising itself was made to appear as a natural extension of a capitalist economy. By calling attention to radio's conventional and "American" financial structure, promoters aimed to defuse objections to the new system.[50]

Arnold claimed that he invented another slogan, "The Fourth Dimension of Advertising," to describe broadcast advertising, bragging that his slogan had "since become a classic." Advertisers, according to Arnold, had previously depended on the three advertising dimensions of newspapers, magazines, and billboards, and the addition of radio appealed to the sense of sound as well as sight. Arnold's phrase aligned radio with traditional advertising media and, at the same time, presented broadcast advertising as something out of science fiction.[51]

Such slogans joined a long list of metaphors used to describe radio, including many that emphasized its ability to make everyday objects special. Observers often described broadcasting as "traffic through the highways of the sky," for one example, with much ensuing discussion of policemen, local roads, and turnpikes.[52] In the promoters' rhetoric, radio advertising was American, but also fabulous; part of advertising, but also supernatural. Case studies detailing the success of broadcast advertising portrayed radio as fantastic, just as early print advertising copy had commonly portrayed new products as magical.[53] *Broadcast Advertising* magazine featured articles entitled "Radio's Magic Carpet: Extensive Printed Advertising Re-enforces Broadcast Campaign" (the article described advertising by a Persian rug manufacturer); "Putting Aladdin Lamps on the Air Puts Them into Farmers' Homes" and "The Cinderella of Broadcasting, Continuity, Is Paging the Fairy Prince."[54] Promoters also talked about radio's "invisible" audience; how radio magically allowed the advertiser to become a guest in a consumer's home; and the ability of radio advertising to "create an atmosphere" of "fashion and luxury and of Paris itself" for a perfume company. Radio became an "open sesame" to new prospects and broadcasting a "modern miracle."[55]

A continuing tension among competing appeals led advertising professionals to attribute fantastic and magical qualities to a product while at other times depending on "sincerity" or "naturalness" to sell the same object. During the early twentieth century, advertising trade journals often discussed "sincerity," as advertising theorists strove to legitimize their profession to the public, to the government, to other business leaders, and to themselves.[56] Sincerity also became an important trait of individual advertisements. Historian T.J. Jackson Lears noted that "sincerity had become at once a moral stance and a tactic of persuasion" and that advertisers wanted an individual advertisement to "be seamless, that its artifice be concealed, that it seemed straightforward and truthful."[57]

Proponents of broadcast advertising tried to convince listeners that radio was harmless at the same time as they presented it as magical. Presenting radio as a "sincere" medium enabled the promoters to begin emphasizing the compatibility of radio with the contemporaneous advertising industry. They moved quickly to present radio as a particularly

trustworthy form of communication. Dunlap wrote "that in some myst-
erious manner the air waves register not what the performer tries to
convey, but what he actually feels. There must be fundamental sincerity.
Artifices are baldly exposed."[58] Promoters thus aimed to place radio in a
category with other new technologies, principally photography, that were
considered incorruptible. The imposition of a machine was perceived to
give the information an additional veracity.[59] Radio, in the argument of
the promoters, could protect the listener/consumer by automatically
exposing lies; one article asserted that "nation-wide audience response
is so sensitive that no intelligent advertiser can long misuse this wonderful medium for mass communication."[60]

In addition to presenting radio as magical and trustworthy, promoters
of radio advertising chose other appeals from both contemporaneous
and older advertising practice to buttress their campaign. The new
emphases in the 1920s on the consumer rather than on the product,
and on vignettes that illustrated the benefits of product use, did not
lend themselves to the kind of indirect advertising then considered
proper for radio. As radio advertising became more direct, it focused
on putting the advertiser "side by side with the consumer" selling
"consumer satisfactions," as Roland Marchand has written.[61] Radio's
promoters found more useful material, however, in advertising theories
and practices from the decades before 1920. Old advertising concepts
tended to be layered on top of each other rather than discarded; advertising professionals used, and seemingly believed, even contradictory
theories.[62]

Principles of psychology and appeals to nonrational impulses had
entered advertising at the turn of the century. Concepts of association
and suggestion, which emphasized sense memory, especially influenced
early advertisers. Rather than describing a product, advertisements tried
to "control the action of the consumer at the time of purchase" by
associating a consumer need with an advertised product.[63] Advertisers,
according to Merle Curti, soon accepted the "non-rationality of human
nature" and emphasized texts and images that operated by "suggestion,
the use of forceful concrete details and pictures, by attention-arresting
stimuli, by playing on human sympathy, and by appeals to the
senses."[64]

Because descriptive advertising did not work well on radio, broadcasting's proponents embraced the concept of suggestive selling. They
presented radio as particularly well-suited to sensory appeals and
suggestive advertising, with music replacing the visual stimuli of
newspapers, magazines, and billboards. Case studies described successful radio programs that reminded listeners of the sponsor's product – the
"tinkling" and "refreshing" music of the Clicquot Club Eskimos to

suggest Clicquot Club soda, for example.[65] Radio advertisers held the consumer's attention for an entire half hour and so could more strongly influence buying decisions than advertisers in other media. Hettinger compared the radio program, which was constructed by the advertiser, to magazine pages conceived and written by the magazine staff, and concluded that radio advertising was more effective because "it enables the advertiser to select the type of entertainment most certain to appeal to that part of the public which he is most interested in reaching and to place it next to his own advertising message."[66] Through control of the material surrounding their sales pitch, radio advertisers tapped into consumers' nonrational impulses. Hettinger placed great importance on the atmosphere in which consumers received the advertisement, and believed radio offered advertisers a chance to influence that atmosphere. For example, the broadcaster should "study his musical program" to ensure that "the correct emotional state has been built up before his sales message is delivered, or whether the type of music and performing group chosen is in keeping with the emotional background or feeling-tone which he wishes his product to possess."[67] Much like other believers in radio's commercial utility, Hettinger advocated indirect advertising because it did not offend audiences, but he also presented indirect advertising positively as a way to influence consumers' emotions.[68]

As advertising grew more professionalized and complex in the 1920s, broadcasting promoters presented radio advertising as an integral part of any carefully planned advertising campaign, identifying specific tasks radio could perform. In particular, radio could help advertisers improve brand-name consciousness. By the 1920s a reliance on branded products was an important part of American mass marketing. Thus, promoters appealed to brand-name advertisers by emphasizing radio's ability to build a "name-consciousness." The sponsor's name could be used many times during a half-hour broadcast. Dunlap reported that one tire manufacturer told him "that the mention of the company's name twenty-four times in the continuity is possible in so unobtrusive a manner that he believes the audience is scarcely conscious of the repetition."[69] Arnold wrote that testing proved the "value of broadcast advertising as a means of obtaining trade-mark publicity," and speculated that radio succeeded because the trademark "seems more human and more real . . . through the radio message" than it did in cold print.[70] National advertising worked best for low-cost items to which a brand name could be affixed, and the manufacturers of these so-called "convenience goods" needed to be wooed to advertise on radio.[71]

Seeking to attract manufacturers of brand-name products led proponents of radio advertising to become interested in marketing strategies, since nationally marketed goods often faced distribution pro-blems.[72] Broadcasting propaganda repeatedly assured manufacturers that radio programs pleased dealers and helped ensure their cooperation. Arnold devoted a chapter, "Broadcasting Aids Distribution," to the subject, claiming that "broadcast advertising gives the distributor some-thing to talk about in addition to the merchandise itself."[73]

NBC emphasized the usefulness of radio advertising in stimulating dealer goodwill in a series of pamphlets for potential sponsors. One account noted that "radio listeners, prospective customers, and dealers are quite likely to be one and the same," and another that dealers "appreciate the Broadcast Advertising."[74] Another booklet, *Improving the Smiles of a Nation! How Broadcast Advertising Has Worked for Ipana Tooth Paste*, looked closely at "dealer cooperation." A manufacturer making a low-cost, low-margin, easily replicated product (such as tooth-paste), "had to persuade consumers to buy his brand at the same time he convinced dealers that they could profit by stocking it."[75] Radio, NBC declared, could help such an advertiser meet both objectives with a single advertisement – a sponsored radio program. The brochure began: "Radio has achieved the apparently impossible, by giving real personality to a toothpaste! . . . Ipana programs have secured . . . the will-ing support and cooperation of dealers . . . far beyond that obtained through any other medium."[76] Quotations from dealers' letters were included to support NBC's claim, with one dealer exclaiming, "We appreciate both the music of your Troubadours and also the increased sale of Ipana Tooth Paste. Your last program prompted us to give you one of our windows for display." "Broadcast advertising did this job for Ipana," the brochure continued, because "dealers are keenly inter-ested in the programs themselves. Aside from the entertainment which they personally enjoy in common with other listeners, they realize sales are going to benefit."[77] NBC hoped to convince advertisers that radio could double the advertising dollar by improving both marketing and sales.

Changes in Broadcasting

Promoters of broadcast advertising had boldly presented radio as a perfect advertising medium – exciting, natural, inherently "American," and sincere – which could improve brand-name consciousness and keep dealers happy. In order to increase radio time sales even further, promoters gradually sought to change radio programming to conform more closely to prevailing theories and practices of advertising. Broad-casters, especially those who had long participated in radio, still rarely thought of broadcasting in commercial terms. But radio needed to become fully commercialized before most advertisers would willingly use it to sell goods. During the late 1920s and early 1930s, therefore, promoters pushed broadcasters toward the use of advertising agencies to sell every broadcast hour as a product in and of itself; toward the standardization and professionalization of operations; and toward day-time programming targeted to women listeners.

The entrance of advertising agencies into radio program production resulted from a combination of propaganda and profit maximization. During the 1920s agencies had resisted radio as an advertising medium, and broadcasters tended to view them as competitors rather than potential allies. As late as 1933, Hettinger described agencies as "newcomers in the field of broadcast advertising," while an early historian of advertising, Ralph Hower, concluded that "the advent of radio gave the agencies much trouble and expense, without any considerable amount of gain in revenue to offset the new burden."[78] But the promoters of radio advertising believed agencies and broadcasters needed each other, particularly since agencies controlled most of the national advertising accounts. An advertising agency must give "this lusty new member [radio] a recognition fully commensurate with its present importance and future potentialities," as one *Broadcast Advertising* writer put it.[79] Although radio stations had, of necessity, initially served as their own producers, conceiving of programs and procuring talent, promoters recognized that programs designed by advertising agencies would be more effective as commercial vehicles than the shows developed by broadcasters.

In the introduction to his book, *The Advertising Agency Looks at Radio*, O'Neill remembered a National Association of Broadcasters convention where broadcasters asked, without a "blush, gulp, or stammer," what advertising agencies did. O'Neill wrote his book as an answer to that question.[80] *Broadcast Advertising* magazine published several sets of paired articles in which station managers and advertising agency executives patiently explained their points of view on broadcast advertising.[81] In addition to the promoters' efforts, networks also worked directly to involve advertising agencies. For example, NBC paid commissions whenever an agency client sponsored a radio show, whether or not the agency participated in the planning. NBC also loaned its employees to help establish radio departments within advertising agencies. These departments served as "propagandists" for the use of radio, especially since no other medium had its own dedicated sections.[82]

As long as the issue of commissions was unresolved, however, a stumbling block to agency participation in radio remained. Hard-won tradition permitted agencies to collect a 15 percent commission from the medium in which the agency placed an ad. Radio stations and networks paid commissions on the time purchases made by agencies, but often refused to pay a commission on the fees for performers. *Broadcast Advertising* explained that if an agency spent $1,000 to place ads in a magazine, its commission was $150. But "the same amount spent with a radio station may very possibly be split $500 for the time and $500 for the talent. In such cases the agency usually receives a commission on time only, or $75."[83] Station managers argued that agencies did little or nothing to deserve a commission on the talent used by a radio station and that agency-produced programs often failed to meet a station's highest standards.[84]

The issue of agency commissions on talent masked a larger question. Agencies believed that if they were to profit in radio, they needed to move into program production, hire performers, receive full commissions on advertising placed on the radio, and charge their clients higher fees for these extra services. The growing complexity of commercialized broadcasting – including the need to publicize radio programs, the increasing expense of more sophisticated programming, and the greater technical demands on station managers – added to the pressure on broadcasters to turn over programming to agencies. By the early 1930s "virtually all sponsored network programs were developed and produced by advertising agencies."[85] Local and independent stations continued to produce some programs, but agencies took over production of national sponsored programs. The effort by the promoters of broadcast advertising to involve advertising agencies in the business of radio was reinforced by the Depression era's economics – agencies wanted to protect their fragile profit margins, and stations needed to reduce their expenses.

The change in who produced radio programs brought changes in how broadcasters and advertisers thought about the programs and, eventually, changes in the programs themselves. Broadcasters considered programs as something for listeners to hear when they turned on the radio, while advertising professionals needed to think about what programs might make listeners *want* to turn on the radio.

Agencies had to assure their clients that large numbers of people heard particular radio programs. The appeal of a program could no longer be left to chance. One advertiser believed that "simply to broadcast and let it go at that... would be like hiring a theater and putting on a splendid show without telling anybody about it."[86] Promoters called for radio advertisers to publicize their programs, and warned broadcasters, "don't confuse product advertising with program advertising... when you advertise the program, talk about it, not the product." A radio sponsor needed to promote its program "within the advertiser's own organization, within his sales organization, within the ranks of his dealers and finally, among the consumers and potential consumers of his product."[87] Most writers agreed that if a program was to reach more than the "average number" of listeners, an advertiser needed to sell the show to its audience.

Merchandising suggestions included the use of newspaper and magazine advertisements and publicity; notices in trade papers; proper follow-up to listener letters; contests and special offers; window, counter, automobile, and outdoor displays; sales representatives' portfolios; broadsides; and booklets and leaflets. Case histories of successful merchandising abounded.[88] Such merchandising was aimed equally at the radio audience (the consumers) and at the advertisers' dealers and sales force. One company sent its sales representatives bulletins about their radio programs because "it was hard for you fellows to hear the program regularly," and the company wanted its sales force to point out the popularity of the program to dealers.[89]

According to these merchandising theories, a radio program was a product to be sold, and the ultimate aim was the commercialization of every aspect of radio. Dunlap wrote that a program "leads the horse to water," but it was merchandising that "makes it drink." A few promoters believed that attention should be paid first to the program because unless the program was good, "all other broadcast merchandising ideas might just as well have never been."[90] But the majority of those writing on the subject ignored program content in favor of merely listing merchandising methods. The merchandising of radio programs helped fuel a growing public perception of radio as commercialized, despite the large proportion of unsponsored programs still paid for by the networks and local stations throughout the early 1930s.

Radio's emerging commercialization made different demands on the broadcasting industry, especially with regard to the selling of time. The two networks quickly standardized both their arrangements with affiliated stations and the rates they charged advertisers. NBC and CBS paid their affiliates for broadcasting commercial programs sent over the network. NBC paid a flat rate that included production costs and line charges, but the CBS arrangement was more complicated and varied from station to station based on a complex formula and on negotiation. NBC charged affiliated stations for providing unsponsored programs, while CBS gave the programs free but asked the stations to pay line charges.[91] By the early 1930s both networks provided potential advertisers with elaborate printed rate cards outlining charges for combinations of affiliated stations at various times.[92]

Standardization of time selling by local stations came more slowly. A 1931 *Broadcast Advertising* article bemoaned the confusion in local stations' rates by describing a "practical example":

Mr. Jones wishes to learn the cost of one minute announcements daily for one month over a certain group of stations. Referring to present rate schedules, this is what he finds: Station A gives only fifty-word announcements; Station B gives only 200-word announcements; Station C gives only two-minute announcements; Station D, no quotation; Station E quotes by the word; Station F, "rates on application"; Station G quotes minimum of thirty-nine announcements; Station H quotes minimum of seventy-five announcements.[93]

At its 1932 convention the National Association of Broadcasters approved a standard radio advertising contract for use by member stations. The contract covered issues such as program cancellation by either broadcaster or advertiser, interruptions, use of announcers, and deadlines for program material.[94]

Despite variations among local station practices, affiliation with a network and the commercialization of operations brought a new way of thinking about time. One observer wrote that "a statue of radio Thespis would assuredly be blind and with a stopwatch in one hand, or perhaps in each."[95] Unlike the first radio performers, who were urged to fill as much time as they could, a singer on an early network show remembered that "timing was the sword of Damocles hanging over our heads. We could not be ten seconds overtime without infringing on another sponsor's territory."[96] To the promoters of broadcast advertising, the new importance of time in radio must have suggested a growing acceptance of broadcasting's commercialization.

The development of radio advertising recapitulated aspects of the growth and professionalization of the larger advertising industry. The first national print advertisers had not known the circulations of the widely scattered newspapers in which they advertised. Daniel Pope noted that "until well into the new century, agents and advertisers bought literally billions of dollars of advertising space – worrying all the while – without a reliable idea of how many copies of the publications they were using actually were printed or reached customers." Uncertainty about the size and composition of the audience increased the participation of advertising agencies in the advertising process, as uneasy clients turned to professionals with specialized knowledge. The movement of advertising agencies from space brokers to advertisement producers to marketing advisers had been completed by the 1920s, when the process reoccurred in broadcast advertising.[97] Early radio advertisers also lacked information about audience size and were therefore reluctant to use the medium. Contests and premiums designed to attract mail helped gauge the number of listeners. But the growing participation of advertising agencies in broadcasting also helped rationalize the process and calm the fears of advertisers.

Radio Advertising to Women

One of the principal arguments for radio advertising was that it enabled advertisers to reach consumers with messages of home and family at the moments when they were enjoying both. An executive announced that "American businessmen, because of radio, are provided with a latchkey to nearly every home in the United States."[98] To take the final step in the commercialization of broadcasting, promoters worked to build a loyal female radio audience that would regularly listen to radio at home during the day. Promoters had to make daytime broadcasting attractive to advertisers in order for radio to turn a profit and in order to fit broadcasting into advertising objectives that posited a day-long audience. With increased sales of time over the networks in the early 1930s, promoters could foresee a moment when they would run out of evening time to sell. The effort to develop radio advertising directed toward women shows how the campaign to promote broadcast advertising ultimately affected both programming content and broadcasting practice.

Promoters faced several cultural and technological barriers in their efforts to convince advertisers to sponsor radio programs aimed at women. Some advertisers resisted using the home – seen both as a women's workplace and as a space set apart from the harsh economic realities of the marketplace – as a site for consumption. Radio's existence in real time – listeners could not put a radio program aside, like a magazine, for a moment when it would not intrude on housework or the family circle – added to advertisers' reluctance to invade the home with this new medium. Radio also maintained, in the minds of many broadcasters and listeners, the image of a boy's toy and a male-controlled entertainment medium.

The first radio schedules did not include daytime programming at all. Radio reception was better at night, and distant signals came in clearly only after sunset. As late as 1924, "successful broadcasting during the daylight hours" remained a "question which is occupying . . . the attention of radio engineers," as they struggled with unexplained static and fading.[99] Station managers scrambled to fill the few evening hours with amateur performers and happily ignored daytime programming.

Men had monopolized early radio listening. One needed some technical skill to assemble a radio in the early 1920s and to tune the set properly once it was assembled – skills many American men had learned as hobbyists before World War I and in the armed forces during the war, and then had passed on to their sons.[100] Of course some women did learn about radio and constantly amazed their male counterparts with their abilities. For example, *Radio World* magazine published an early column, "Radio and the Woman," written by Crystal D. Tector, and students at Wellesley College studied radio technology in physics class and had their photographs published in a radio magazine to prove it.[101] As transmitters became more powerful and receivers more sensitive, daylight broadcasting became easier, but the idea persisted of radio as an evening, family, and father-controlled entertainment.

The promoters of broadcast advertising took particular interest in radio's role in the home and family, which had become dominant advertising themes. In print advertising, manufacturers presented their products as contributors to domestic bliss and strongly related family happiness and well-being to intelligent consumption. Historian Otis Pease notes that American advertisers aimed to sell "an entire pattern of consumption" centered on the home, and "advertisers increasingly invaded that allegedly private sphere, the family." The emerging consumer culture would be based on what T. J. Jackson Lears has called a new "domestic ideal."[102]

To remind the advertising industry that broadcasting provided a rich opportunity for those interested in home- and family-based appeals, promoters constantly described radio and radio advertisers as "guests in the home." Frank Arnold (using a rather alarming image of radio as an invasive rather than invited medium) went so far as to write:

> Then came radio broadcasting, utilizing the very air we breathe, and with electricity as its vehicle entering the homes of the nation through doors and windows, no matter how tightly barred, and delivering its message audibly through the loud speaker wherever placed. For the first time in the history of mankind, this dream of the centuries found its realization. In the midst of the family circle, in moments of relaxation, the voice of radio brings to the audience its program of entertainment or its message of advertising.[103]

Women's roles as wives and mothers made them pivotal figures in the new advertising theories. Marchand notes that, by the 1920s, male advertising professionals believed they were "engaged primarily in talking to women."[104] Prospective advertisers, however, tended to believe that radio drew a smaller audience during the day because women working in the home were too busy to sit down and listen. As late as 1932, several women wrote of turning on the radio only after their housework was done, and then listening only while they did their sewing.[105] Network programmers therefore aimed to devise formats that would appeal to reluctant advertisers and draw female listeners.

The first daytime radio programs aimed at women – produced for local and regional stations before the networks were established – presented short sponsored talks by representatives of companies that produced goods or services women purchased. Broadcasters saw the programs as an integral part of women's "working day," a time when they could introduce housewives to products "whose chief appeal is to women and which need some interpretation."[106] The programs were instructional, so that women would not feel they were taking time from their busy schedules merely to enjoy light entertainment; instead they would listen to become better wives and mothers. For example, Anna J. Peterson, "our radio mother," broadcast menus and recipes in 1925 for the People's Gas Light and Coke Company over KYW, Chicago. In 1926 Buttericks presented a talk over WJZ, New York, on the "making of winter attire."[107]

After the networks made regular national radio programming possible, broadcasters continued to look for programs that could be presented to advertisers as directly related to women's work in the home. Rather than taking a homemaker away from her chores, educational programs could instruct women in the use of a sponsor's product, and could allow the sponsor to advertise in both the commercials and the program for the same price. Advertisers and broadcasters found a willing ally in the home economics profession, which gladly took up the challenge of using radio to teach women how to shop and do housework more efficiently.[108] The radio home economists also fit well with the contemporary view of using advertising to educate consumers. The advertising industry in the 1920s had found the use of "experts" particularly useful; consumers were made to feel insecure and then were offered advice about what products would bring them a feeling of security.[109] Besides "expertise," radio instructors could provide "warmth," an attribute broadcasters hoped would overcome advertisers' fears about barging into listeners' homes uninvited. One such "authority," broadcasting over WOR in New York City, wrote that women consumers could find the answers to their questions in many places but preferred the "human contact and little more personal touch which they receive when we of the air talk to them."[110]

Identifying an expert as a real person proved an important element of fostering this "personal touch." Three of the best-known experts who went on the air to instruct and sell to American women were Aunt Sammy (Uncle Sam's wife), Betty Crocker, and Ida Bailey Allen. Their programs pioneered formats designed to overcome advertisers' objections to selling to women over the radio. On October 4, 1926, fifty women in fifty radio stations across the country first became "Aunt Sammy" by reading identical scripts prepared by US Department of Agriculture home economists. In that initial fifteen-minute broadcast, Aunt Sammy:

> recited a stanza of doggerel verse, told several jokes, explained how to select and care for linoleum for the kitchen floor, directed how to roast wienies the "modern" way, how to use vinegar left over from a jar of pickles, and how to put up a cucumber relish, defined what a vitamin was, enumerated the five foods essential to the daily diet, listed "what foods should be taken from dishes with fingers," and ended by offering the menu for the day – meat loaf with brown gravy, scalloped potatoes, carrots or beets, fresh sliced tomatoes and lemon jelly dessert.[111]

Aunt Sammy became a hit and remained popular. During the Depression, her cookbook helped listeners get through what she called "these days of thrift."[112]

Broadcasters loved USDA programs such as "The Housekeeper's Chat," which featured Aunt Sammy. They cost little, filled hours unpopular with sponsors, and at the same time helped prove to potential advertisers that similar programs could draw an audience. The large number of listener requests for Aunt Sammy's printed recipes proved that women were listening to her program, and thus encouraged those trying to convince sponsors to invest in daytime programs. While her programs discussed no brand-name products, Aunt Sammy, like the home economist she was, explained and introduced "modern" and "improved" consumer goods of particular use to rural women.[113] She showed how a familiar and friendly "individual" could appeal to women listeners while instructing them in their household duties.

Another fictional character, Betty Crocker, had a more particular message for her listeners: to buy General Mills products. The company invented Crocker to answer questions for consumers by mail, and it soon launched regional cooking schools in which Crocker clones demonstrated the full range of General Mills products. The company founded one of the first radio stations, WCCO in Minneapolis, and the home economists who portrayed Crocker eagerly took to the airwaves to spread their ideas to a larger audience. At first, different Betty Crockers broadcast from various stations, but after the advent of network radio one woman speaking from the Minneapolis studio could be heard in many cities. General Mills remained convinced that its instructional radio program helped sell its products, and Betty Crocker long provided a model for other sponsors in combining instruction with the promotion of particular products.[114]

Trained as a dietician and working as a cooking school instructor and cookbook author, Ida Bailey Allen was one of the first nonfictional experts approached by broadcasters to give morning radio talks. After the formation of CBS, when radio time became more expensive, Allen wondered "how in the world I could finance broadcasts to the entire country." An executive at the company that published Allen's cookbooks suggested that she handle the problem like a magazine by selling segments of the program to interested sponsors.[115] CBS agreed to air Allen's program, "The National Homemaker's Club," and by 1930 she had her own radio studio, test kitchen, beauty boudoir, living room, and elaborately decorated executive offices with daily fresh flowers, all intended to serve as models for her listeners.[116] Allen's magazine-style radio format lured advertisers by giving them a chance to sponsor portions of programs without a major commitment of time or money. Companies that made products with low unit costs could afford to buy small blocks of radio time without the expense of sponsoring an entire program.

Aunt Sammy, Betty Crocker, and Ida Bailey Allen all showed that broadcasters could design programs to overcome advertisers' objections to daytime radio. Moreover, these models illustrated programming forms the networks would adopt and market to completely commercialize the broadcast day. One approach was to gather various short sponsored talks together in a magazine program, like Ida Bailey Allen's. The networks would then sell airtime for commercials and assure advertisers that a network home economist would provide a relevant talk to appear directly preceding their message.[117] This may well have been the first attempt to sell "spot advertisements." The networks thus developed these early daytime shows to appeal specifically to advertisers, presaging the later form taken by all commercial broadcasting.

As late as 1932, however, broadcasters were still encountering problems selling their daytime hours. Although the commercialized broadcasting system dominated by the networks was in place, only one-third of network programming was commercially sponsored. Mornings came close to the evening level, with 29.5 percent of the hours paid for by advertisers, but in the afternoons only 11.8 percent of the broadcast hours were sold.[118] An NBC internal memo from 1933 called daytime broadcasting a "hodge-podge arrangement" and recommended greater thought and structure for the daytime schedule.[119] For the next five years, NBC made a special attempt to encourage advertisers to buy daytime hours, publishing pamphlets entitled "Wake Up to Daytime Possibilities"; "Sell the Housewife and You Sell All"; "At Least 72.9% of the Women Are at Home at Any Given DAYTIME Hour. Tell Them . . . You'll Sell Them!"; and "28.9% of All NBC Sponsored Programs Are DAYTIME Programs: Daytime Is Sales Time."[120]

Having made a beginning at selling morning hours for instructional programs, the networks strove to convince more sponsors to buy time in the afternoons. "Soap operas" – serial melodramas sponsored by detergent manufacturers – quickly came to dominate the afternoon hours. One inspiration for the soaps were the skits presented during the morning instructional shows. Characters such as Uncle Ebenezer and nephew Billy sometimes joined Aunt Sammy, as did Finicky Florine and Percy DeWallington Waffle, fussy eaters who drove their mothers crazy.[121] Soap operas followed the criteria proven successful in the morning instructional shows: they featured recurring characters using products, lasted fifteen minutes rather than the evening's usual half-hour, and were sold to companies that manufactured something women bought routinely without consultation. Other factors, notably the soap companies' advertising needs during the Depression and the success of continuing evening dramas such as "Amos 'n' Andy" and "The Rise of the Goldbergs," also influenced the emergence of the afternoon soaps.[122] But networks based the soap operas on a marketing concept – that women, a perfect audience for advertisers, were best reached in their homes by radio – that had, over the previous ten years, been tested and sold to advertisers by those who had a stake in fully commercialized broadcasting. Expenditures for daytime radio advertising more than doubled between 1935 and 1939, and daytime radio finally began to be profitable.[123]

Radio advertising to women was a tough sell, but one that the broadcast industry had to make so that radio conformed to other ideas about advertising prevalent in the 1920s, when many advertising professionals came to think of women as the chief consumers.[124] The eventual acceptance, by broadcasters and advertisers, of daytime radio programs directed at women marked the conclusion of the campaign to promote broadcast advertising. The promoters had succeeded both in convincing advertisers that radio was a useful advertising medium able to reach consumers in their homes, and in convincing broadcasters that all programming should be available for sponsorship. In the process, the form and content of radio programming changed. The promoters presented all such changes as improvements, just as they presented broadcast advertising as "natural." In truth, the evolutionary adaptations in radio programming – such as the movement from local amateur musicians to nationally celebrated vaudeville performers – brought both gains and losses to radio listeners.

Notes

1 Zeh Bouck, "Can We Solve the Broadcasting Riddle?" *Radio Broadcast* 6 (April 1925): 1040–3; "The Decision in the 'Who Is To Pay for Broad-

casting?' Contest," *Radio Broadcast* 6 (February 1925): 736. See also Halsey D. Kellog, Jr., "Who Is To Pay for Broadcasting – And How: The Plan Which Won *Radio Broadcast*'s Prize of $500," *Radio Broadcast* 6 (March 1925): 864. For another contest, see "Prize Offered for Best Solution of Broadcasting Problem," *Radio World* 5 (29 March 1924): 29. For other contemporary discussions of the issue, see "Thought Waves from the Editorial Tower," *Radio Age* 1 (October 1922): 17; Waldemar Kaempffert, "Who Will Pay for Broadcasting? A Frank and Searching Outline of Radio's Most Pressing Problem and the Possible Ways of Solving It," *Popular Radio* 2 (December 1922): 236–46.

2   "Experts Foresee End of Present Easy Broadcasting Arrangements," *New York Times*, 18 May 1924, Section 8, 3.

3   Erik Barnouw, *A Tower in Babel: A History of Broadcasting in the United States to 1933* (New York: Oxford University Press, 1966), 99.

4   J. H. Morecroft, "Radio Currents: An Editorial Interpretation," *Radio Broadcast* 1 (May 1922): 3. See also J. H. Morecroft, "The March of Radio: Who Will Endow Broadcasting?" *Radio Broadcast* 10 (January 1927): 257–8. Robert J. Landry, *This Fascinating Radio Business* (New York: Bobbs-Merrill Company, 1946), 44–5; Philip Rosen, *The Modern Stentors: Radio Broadcasters and the Federal Government, 1920–1934* (Westport, Conn.: Greenwood Press, 1980), 68; J. H. Morecroft, "The March of Radio: Great Minds Still Disagree on Broadcasting Payment," *Radio Broadcast* 5 (August 1924): 304. For another editorial call for stations supported by philanthropy, see "Broadcasting from the Editor's Chair," *Radio Digest* 26 (January 1921): 61.

5   "Experts Foresee End," *New York Times;* S. E. Frost, Jr., *Education's Own Stations* (Chicago: University of Chicago Press, 1937), 4.

6   James C. Young, "Radio – The Voice of the City," *Radio Broadcast* 6 (January 1925): 448.

7   Saul N. Scher, "An Old City Hall Tradition: New York's Mayors and WNYC," *Journal of Broadcasting* 10 (Spring 1966): 138; Logbook 1 of Radiophone WNYC: Municipal Station City of New York, 5 July 1924–10 December 1924, Museum of the City of New York. See also Grover Whalen, "Radio Control," *The Nation* 119 (23 July 1924): 90; "CONY Sought as Letters of City's Station," *Radio World* 5 (19 April 1924): 35; Irving Foulds Luscombe, "WNYC: 1922–1940 – The Early History of a Twentieth-Century Urban Service" (Ph.D. diss., New York University, 1968); Milton Nobel, "The Municipal Broadcasting System: Its History, Organization and Activities" (MPA thesis, City College of New York, 1953); "History of WNYC," unpublished publicity pamphlet, WNYC, New York. For a description of municipal broadcasting in Chicago, see "The City of Chicago in Radio," *Radio Age* 1 (July–August 1922), 7. I want to thank Betsy Smulyan for her help in researching the WNYC logbook.

8   For "not the most attractive," see newspaper clipping, 26 June 1926, WNYC scrapbook, WNYC, New York. For "resent lavish expenditure," see Dudley Siddall, "Who Owns Our Broadcasting Stations?" *Radio Broadcast* 6 (February 1925): 707–8. For "group picture," see Edgar H. Felix, *Using Radio in Sales Promotion* (New York: McGraw-Hill, 1927), 44.

9   For an example of network propaganda against federal support of broadcasting, see M. H. Aylesworth, "Radio's Accomplishment," *Century* (June 1929): 216, and Bouck, "Can We Solve the Broadcasting Riddle?" For

an example of the listener's point of view (albeit heavily influenced by the radio industry), see J. H. Morecroft, "The March of Radio," *Radio Broadcast 7* (May 1925): 39.

10 Rothafel and Yates, *Broadcasting: Its New Day*, 149; "Success Promised," *Radio World 5* (19 April 1924): 26. For a similar plan, see "A Scheme for Paying Artists for Broadcasting," *Popular Radio 2* (September 1922): 71–2.

11 "Broadcaster Asks Listeners To Pay," *New York Times*, 26 March 1924, 22; J. H. Morecroft, "The March of Radio: Voluntary Contributions for Radio Programs," *Radio Broadcast 5* (July 1924): 220; Rothafel and Yates, *Broadcasting: Its New Day*, 150–3.

12 "Radio – The New Social Force," *Outlook 136* (19 March 1924): 456–7.

13 Jennie Irene Mix, "The Listeners' Point of View: Who Will Pay for Broadcasting?" *Radio Broadcast 4* (April 1924): 479; Rothafel and Yates, *Broadcasting: Its New Day*, 150.

14 "Radio Editorials," *Radio Age 4* (May 1925): 4.

15 Joseph H. Jackson, "Should Radio Be Used for Advertising?" *Radio Broadcast 2* (November 1922): 76.

16 Rothafel and Yates, *Broadcasting: Its New Day*, 156. See also "Advertising Takes Its Place in Radio Programs," *Radio Age 5* (July 1925): 67; J. C. McQuiston, "Advertising by Radio: Can It and Should It Be Done?" *Radio News 4* (August 1922): 232.

17 E. J. Van Brook, "How Bombastic Advertising Can Be Suppressed," *Broadcast Advertising 1* (July 1929): 18. See also H. Gernsback, "Future Developments of Radio," *Radio News 5* (March 1924): 1221.

18 "Radio, An Objectionable Advertising Medium," *Printer's Ink 8* (February 1923): 175–6.

19 Bruce Bliven, "How Radio Is Remaking our World," *Century 108* (July 1924): 149.

20 "Radio Men Oppose 'Ad' in Programs," *New York Times*, 2 April 1924, 8.

21 Fourth National Radio Conference, *Proceedings of the Fourth National Radio Conference and Recommendations for Regulation of Radio* (Washington, DC: Government Printing Office, 1925), 18.

22 J. H. Morecroft, "Radio Currents: An Editorial Interpretation," *Radio Broadcast 1* (May 1922): 1.

23 Stuart Chase, "An Inquiry into Radio," *Outlook 148* (18 April 1928): 617.

24 Jackson, "Should Radio Be Used for Advertising?" 75.

25 "Celler Would Curb Radio Advertising," *New York Times*, 24 March 1924, 24.

26 Marvin Robert Bensman, "The Regulation of Radio Broadcasting by the Department of Commerce" (Ph.D. diss., University of Wisconsin, 1969), 113.

27 Ibid., 233–4.

28 R. D. Heinl, "Problems the Conference Must Face," *New York Times*, 13 September 1925, Section 11, 2.

29 Third National Radio Conference, *Recommendations*, 4.

30 Fourth National Radio Conference, *Proceedings*, 5.

31 Glenn Johnson, "Secretary of Commerce Herbert Hoover: The First Regulator of Broadcasting" (Ph.D. diss., University of Iowa, 1970), 152, 277. For Hoover's flip-flop on government support, see Samuel L. Rothafel and Raymond F. Yates, *Broadcasting: Its New Day* (New York: Century, 1925), 159; "Topics of the Times: He Feels a Need for Action," *New York*

Times, 23 November 1924, Section 18, 5; "Hoover Advocates Tax on Radio Sales," *New York Times*, 22 December 1924, Section 20, 1; "Topics of the Times: He Did Not Propose a Radio Tax," *New York Times*, 25 December 1924, Section 16, 15; J. H. Morecroft, "The March of Radio: Hoover Not for a Radio Sales Tax," *Radio Broadcast* 6 (March 1925): 898. For a pro-tax position, see Raymond Francis Yates, "Shall We Have a Federal Radio Tax?" *Radio News* 5 (January 1924): 867, 976–7.

32 David Burner, *Herbert Hoover: A Public Life* (New York: Alfred A. Knopf, 1979), 163; Ellis Hawley, "Herbert Hoover and Economic Stabilization, 1921–22," in Ellis Hawley, ed., *Herbert Hoover as Secretary of Commerce: Studies in New Era Thought and Practice* (Iowa City: University of Iowa Press, 1981), 60; Joan Hoff Wilson, *Herbert Hoover: Forgotten Progressive* (Boston: Little, Brown & Company, 1975), 112; C. M. Jansky, "The Contribution of Herbert Hoover to Broadcasting," *Journal of Broadcasting* 1 (Summer 1957): 241–9; Herbert Hoover, *The Memoirs of Herbert Hoover: The Cabinet and the Presidency* (New York: Macmillan Company, 1952), 139–48; Edward F. Sarno, Jr., "The National Radio Conferences," *Journal of Broadcasting* 13 (Spring 1969): 189–202.

33 For contemporary writing that presents radio as essentially commercial, see John Wallace, "The Listeners' Point of View: Communication," *Radio Broadcast* 9 (May 1926): 38–9; Austin C. Lescarboura, "How Much It Costs To Broadcast," *Radio Broadcast* 9 (September 1926): 367–71; "Is All Broadcasting Advertising?" *Radio Broadcast* 8 (January 1926): 398; James C. Young, "How Will You Have Your Advertising?" *Radio Broadcast* 6 (December 1924): 245–6; Hugo Gernsback, "Who Pays for Radio Broadcasting?" *Radio News* 7 (November 1925): 585; Raymond Francis Yates, "The Broadcast Listener: The Broadcasting of Advertising," *Popular Radio* 8 (July 1925): 90. For examples of historians adopting this view, see Alfred N. Goldsmith and Austin C. Lescarboura, *This Thing Called Broadcasting* (New York: Henry Holt, 1930), 48; Paul Schubert, *The Electric Word: The Rise of Radio* (New York: Macmillan, 1928), 219.

34 Susan Strasser, *Satisfaction Guaranteed: The Making of the American Mass Market* (New York: Pantheon, 1989), 93–5.

35 In discussing the campaign I've concentrated on the following books: Frank A. Arnold, *Broadcast Advertising: The Fourth Dimension* (New York: J. Wiley and Sons, 1931); Orrin Elmer Dunlap, *Radio in Advertising* (New York: Harper and Brothers, 1931); Edgar Felix, *Using Radio in Sales Promotion* (New York: McGraw-Hill, 1927); Herman S. Hettinger, *A Decade of Radio Advertising* (Chicago: University of Chicago Press, 1933); Neville O'Neill, ed., *The Advertising Agency Looks at Radio* (New York: D. Appleton and Company, 1932); and one magazine, *Broadcast Advertising*, published in Chicago between April 1929 and December 1932.

36 Frank Arnold, "The Reminiscences of Frank Arnold," Oral History Research Office, Columbia University, New York, 15.

37 Barnouw, *A Tower in Babel*, 192; Arnold, "Reminiscences," 20, 50, 65.

38 Arnold, *Broadcast Advertising*, 40, 54–5.

39 Edgar Felix, "The Reminiscences of Edgar Felix," Oral History Research Office, Columbia University, New York, 6.

40 "Our Respects To: Major Edgar Herbert Felix," *Broadcasting* 27 (30 October 1944): 38–40; Barnouw, *A Tower in Babel*, 28–9; "We Pay Our Respects To: Orrin Elmer Dunlap, Jr.," *Broadcasting* 23 (5 October 1942): 37.

41   Dunlap, *Radio in Advertising*, 104; Felix, *Using Radio in Sales Promotion*, 9.
42   *National Cyclopedia of American Biography*, 1977, s.v. "Hettinger, Herman
     Strecker." See also "We Pay Our Respects To: Herman Strecker Hettinger,
     Ph.D.," *Broadcasting* 11 (15 December 1936): 49.
43   O'Neill, *The Advertising Agency Looks at Radio*, v.
44   Frank A. Arnold, "High Spots in Broadcast Techniques: Procedures in
     Broadcast Advertising That Are Foreign to the Uninitiated," *Broadcast
     Advertising* 1 (May 1929): 6–7, 31; Orrin E. Dunlap, "Gauging Listener
     Interest in Radio Broadcasts: Methods Used by Advertisers to Determine
     Public's Opinion," *Broadcast Advertising* 1 (August 1929): 17–22; Howard
     Angus, "Preparation of Commercial Copy Is Hardest Task of Radio Adver-
     tiser," *Broadcast Advertising* 4 (December 1931): 7–8; Angus, "The Impor-
     tance of Stars in Your Radio Program," *Broadcast Advertising* 4 (February
     1932): 12, 26–7; Angus, "Intelligent Broadcast Merchandising," *Broadcast
     Advertising* 5 (August 1932): 8, 20–2; L. Ames Brown, "Broadcast Adver-
     tising – Its Possibilities and Limitations: Mass Psychology Plays Important
     Part in Radio Advertising," *Broadcast Advertising* 1 (April 1929): 22–9;
     Brown, "Broadcasting Is Vigorous, Effective, Successful," *Broadcast Adver-
     tising* 3 (June 1930): 3–4, 18, 20; Brown, "The Development of Radio as an
     Advertising Medium: A Report of Changing Concepts," *Broadcast Advertis-
     ing* 4 (June 1931): 5–6, 26–30; Charles F. Gannon, "The Agency's Place in
     American Broadcasting," *Broadcast Advertising* 4 (August 1931): 15, 28; M.
     A. Hollinshead, "Recordings: Their Place in Broadcasting," *Broadcast
     Advertising* 4 (July 1931): 5–7, 22–6; H. H. Kynett, "The Agency's Needs
     in Broadcasting," *Broadcast Advertising* 3 (July 1930): 8–9, 32; Kynett,
     "Spot Broadcasting as Viewed by the Advertising Agency," *Broadcast
     Advertising* 3 (December 1930): 14–18, 40–2; Hubbell Robinson, "How
     True Detective Mysteries, Broadcasting Dramatized Sample Stories, Won
     Half a Million New Readers in Less Than a Year," *Broadcast Advertising* 2
     (March 1930): 10–12.
45   "NAB Committees Make Constructive Reports: Embrace Legislation,
     Ethics, Commercial Broadcasting," *Broadcast Advertising* 2 (November
     1929): 23, 26–7; "Broadcasters Talk about Rates and Representatives at
     San Francisco Meeting," *Broadcast Advertising* 4 (October 1931): 20–1,
     54–60; L. Ames Brown, "Broadcasting Is Vigorous, Effective, Successful:
     An Address Delivered before the Annual Convention of the AAAA," 3–4,
     18–20.
46   "The 'Invisible Guest,'" *Popular Radio* 8 (September 1925): 273.
47   On the beliefs of those who worked in the industry about how advertising
     worked in the 1920s, see Roland Marchand, *Advertising the American
     Dream: Making Way for Modernity, 1920–1940* (Berkeley: University of
     California Press, 1985).
48   Felix, *Using Radio in Sales Promotion*, 216.
49   Arnold, *Broadcast Advertising*, 85.
50   Henry Adams Bellows, "A Defense of the American System of Broadcast-
     ing," *Broadcast Advertising* 4 (July 1931): 16–17, 44; Arnold, *Broadcast
     Advertising*, 85; Hettinger, *Decade of Radio Advertising*, viii.
51   Arnold, *Broadcast Advertising*, xviii, 38–44.
52   William Boddy, "The Rhetoric and Economic Roots of the American
     Broadcasting Industry," *Cine-Tracts* 2 (Spring 1979): 38–40. I am grateful
     to Sally Stein for calling Boddy's work to my attention.

53 For example, AT&T had claimed that the telephone provided a "Sixth Sense – The Power of Personal Projection," and advertisements for radio receiving sets stressed their "magical" capabilities. See T. Jackson Lears, "Some Versions of Fantasy: Toward a Cultural History of American Advertising, 1880–1920," *Prospects: The Annual of American Cultural Studies* 9 (1984): 349–406.

54 "Radio's Magic Carpet: Extensive Printed Advertising Re-enforces Broadcast Campaign," *Broadcast Advertising* 1 (July 1929): 5–10, 23–6; E. A. Fellers, "Broadcasting Barn Dances Sells Kerosene Lamps: Putting Aladdin Lamps on the Air Puts Them into Farmers' Homes," *Broadcast Advertising* 2 (December 1929): 18–20, 34; Showalter Lynch, "The Cinderella of Broadcasting, Continuity, Is Paging the Fairy Prince," *Broadcast Advertising* 3 (January 1931): 11, 30–1.

55 Arnold, *Broadcast Advertising*, 21, 44; Dunlap, *Radio in Advertising*, 7; Harrison J. Cowan, "Broadcasting a Perfume: Methods Pursued in Bourjois' 'Evening in Paris' Campaign," *Broadcast Advertising* 2 (October 1929): 1–5, 30–2; Harry C. Butcher, "The Sponsor's Place in Broadcasting," *Broadcast Advertising* 3 (November 1930): 10–11, 22, 24.

56 The most organized attempt to present advertising as sincere and trustworthy was the Truth in Advertising movement of the Progressive era. See Daniel Pope, *The Making of Modern Advertising* (New York: Basic Books, 1983), 202–26.

57 T. J. Jackson Lears, "The Rise of American Advertising," *Wilson Quarterly* 7 (Winter 1983): 157. See also T. J. Jackson Lears, "From Salvation to Self-Realization: Advertising and the Therapeutic Roots of the Consumer Culture, 1880–1930," in *The Culture of Consumption*, eds. T. J. Jackson Lears and Richard Fox (New York: Pantheon, 1983), 20; and T. J. Jackson Lears, "Some Versions of Fantasy: Toward a Cultural History of American Advertising, 1800–1920," *Prospects: The Annual of American Cultural Studies* 9 (1984): 368.

58 Dunlap, *Radio in Advertising*, 139.

59 Alan Trachtenberg, with Amy Weinstein Meyers, *Classic Essays on Photography* (New Haven, Conn.: Leete's Island Books, 1980), 1–108; Marchand, *Advertising the American Dream*, 149–53; Judy Babbitts, " 'To See Is To Know': Stereographs Educate Americans about East Asia, 1890–1930" (Ph.D. diss., Yale University, 1987). I want to thank Judy Babbitts for this insight.

60 O'Neill, *The Advertising Agency Looks at Radio*, 3.

61 Marchand, *Advertising the American Dream*, 13–24.

62 Stephen Fox's tracing of the cycles of advertising practice from hard sell to soft sell and back again, demonstrates that different approaches never vanish, just go in or out of favor. See Stephen Fox, *The Mirrormakers* (New York: Vintage Books, 1984).

63 A. Michael McMahon, "An American Courtship: Psychologists and Advertising Theory in the Progressive Era," *American Studies* 3 (Fall 1972): 9. See also Otis Pease, *The Responsibilities of American Advertising: Private Control and Public Influence, 1920–1940* (New Haven, Conn.: Yale University Press, 1958), 20–6; Stephen Richard Shapiro, "The Big Sell – Attitudes of Advertising Writers about Their Craft in the 1920's and 1930's" (Ph.D. diss., University of Wisconsin, 1969), 43, 53, 227.

64 Merle Curti, "The Changing Concept of 'Human Nature' in the Literature of American Advertising," *Business History Review* 41 (Winter 1967): 347.
65 Hal Johnson, "We Made the Program Fit the Product," *Broadcast Advertising* 2 (March 1930): 6–8; "Reproduce Product's Tempo in Program, Says Woolley," *Broadcast Advertising* 4 (May 1931): 26, 28; Robert T. Colwell, "The Program as Advertisement," in O'Neill, *The Advertising Agency Looks at Radio*, 22–41.
66 Hettinger, *Decade of Radio Advertising*, 23.
67 Ibid., 14.
68 Ibid., 3–40.
69 Dunlap, *Radio in Advertising*, 110–11.
70 Arnold, *Broadcast Advertising*, 112.
71 On the history of branding, see Strasser, *Satisfaction Guaranteed*, 29–57 and passim. On convenience goods, see Pope, *Making of Modern Advertising*, 46–8; Michael Schudson, *Advertising, the Uneasy Persuasion: Its Dubious Impact on American can Society* (New York: Basic Books, 1984), 97–8.
72 Pope, *Making of Modern Advertising*, 92–6; Strasser, *Satisfaction Guaranteed*, 21–3, 57–88.
73 Arnold, *Broadcast Advertising*, 97.
74 National Broadcasting Company, *Making Pep and Sparkle Typify a Ginger Ale*, 18. See also National Broadcasting Company, *Selling Goods, Selling Service, Selling the Consciousness of a Great Ideal: The Broadcast Advertising of Cities Service Company*, 1928, p. 11, Box 3, Folder 6, E. P. H. James Papers (hereafter cited as James Papers), Mass Communications History Center, Wisconsin State Historical Society, Madison.
75 Pope, *Making of Modern Advertising*, 94.
76 National Broadcasting Company, *Improving the Smiles of a Nation! Advertising Has Worked for the Makers of Ipana Tooth Paste*, 1928, Broadcast Pioneers Library, Washington, DC, 5.
77 Ibid., 15.
78 Hettinger, *Decade of Radio Advertising*, 162. On agency reaction, see M. O. Hastings, "You're Not Quite Ready for That As Yet!" *Broadcast Advertising* 1 (April 1929): 10; "Should Stations Pay Commission on Talent? Broadcasters and Advertising Agencies Express Varying Views," *Broadcast Advertising* 3 (September 1930): 6–7, 22; Ralph However, *The History of an Advertising Agency: N. W. Ayer & Son at Work, 1869–1949* (Cambridge, Mass.: N. W. Ayer & Son, 1949), 168.
79 Gordon Best, "Radio Has Brought a New Responsibility to Advertising Agencies," *Broadcast Advertising* 5 (July 1932): 6. See also Roy S. Durstine, "Function of the Agency in Broadcast Advertising," *Broadcast Advertising* 1 (June 1929): 29.
80 O'Neill, *The Advertising Agency Looks at Radio*, v.
81 Ray R. Morgan and H. K. Carpenter, "West Coast Advertising Man's Complaint 'Let's Get Down to Business' Is Answered by Eastern Station Manager 'All Right – Let's,' " *Broadcast Advertising* 3 (August 1930): 6–8, 22, 26; "Should Stations Pay Commission on Talent?" *Broadcast Advertising* 3 (September 1930): 6–7, 22; "A Station-Agency Symposium: What the Station Wants from the Agency" and "How Can We Improve Radio? What the Agency Wants from the Station," *Broadcast Advertising* 5 (April 1932): 4–5, 24–7. See also John Benson, "The Advertising Agency and

Broadcasting," *Broadcast Advertising* 3 (January 1931): 4; John Benson, "Radio's Advertising Problems May Be Solved Jointly by Broadcasters and Agencies," *Broadcast Advertising* 4 (January 1932): 5, 42–6.

82 Mark Woods, "The Reminiscences of Mark Woods," Oral History Research Office, Columbia University, New York, 21, 29.

83 "Should Stations Pay Commission on Talent?" 6.

84 Morgan and Carpenter, "West Coast Advertising Man's Complaint," 6–8, 22, 26; William S. Hedges, "Agencies and Broadcasters Should Cooperate," *Broadcast Advertising* 3 (July 1930): 5–6, 28, 30; "Should Stations Pay Commission on Talent?" 6–7, 22. See also A. A. Cormier, "What the Radio Station Wants from the Agency," *Broadcast Advertising* 3 (December 1930): 19–20; "A Station-Agency Symposium: What the Station Wants from the Agency," *Broadcast Advertising* 5 (April 1932): 4.

85 Barnouw, *A Tower in Babel*, 239. See also J. Fred McDonald, *Don't Touch That Dial: Radio Programming in American Life, 1920 to 1960* (Chicago: Nelson-Hall, 1979), 31–3.

86 "Merchandising a Radio Campaign,: How Carson Pirie Scott and Company Sold Their Dealers on the Bobolink Broadcasts," *Broadcast Advertising* 3 (October 1930): 6.

87 For "don't confuse," see Russell Bryon Williams, "In Radio, It Pays To Advertise," *Broadcast Advertising* 5 (June 1932): 23. For "within the advertiser's own organization," see Harry Shinnick and Irwin Borders, "Merchandising in Its Relation to Radio," in O'Neill, *The Advertising Agency Looks at Radio*, 153.

88 Shinnick and Borders, "Merchandising in Its Relation to Radio," 155–70; Bernard Grimes, "How Radio Programs Are Merchandised," *Printer's Ink* 155 (25 June 1931): 53–6; "Merchandising the Radio Program," *Printer's Ink* 156 (23 July 1931): 118; "Chain Advertisers To Use Listener Magazines," *Broadcast Advertising* 5 (June 1932): 26; Dunlap, *Radio in Advertising*, 189–212; Hettinger, *Decade of Radio Advertising*, 276–88.

89 "How Quaker Products Company 'Sells' Radio to Salesmen," *Broadcast Advertising* 1 (July 1929): 14. See also E. P. H. James, "Why Dealer Cooperation Is Important," *Broadcasting* 3 (January 1933): 11.

90 For "leads the horse to water," see Dunlap, *Radio in Advertising*, 189. On program quality, see Howard Angus, "Intelligent Broadcast Merchandising Means Building a Good Program and Exploiting It in Every Way Possible," *Broadcast Advertising* 5 (August 1932): 8.

91 "Here's an Explanation of Chains' Financial Arrangements with Affiliated Stations," *Broadcast Advertising* 5 (October 1932): 13.

92 Arnold, *Broadcast Advertising*, "Appendix G: General Rate Card of National Broadcasting Co., Inc., as of July 19, 1931," 232–6; Arnold, *Broadcast Advertising*, "Appendix J: General Rate Card of Columbia Broadcasting System, Inc., as of June 1, 1931," 249–53; Dunlap, *Radio in Advertising*, "Appendix A: National Broadcasting Company, Inc., Rate Card, May 1, 1931," 302–9; Dunlap, *Radio in Advertising*, "Appendix B: Columbia Broadcasting System, Rate Card No. 10," 310–18.

93 Ted Hill, "Let's Standardize Our Rate Cards," *Broadcast Advertising* 4 (September 1931): 18–19, 26.

94 "Broadcasters Strengthen Ranks To Resist Outside Domination," *Broadcast Advertising* 15 (December 1932): 12–13.

95   Goldsmith and Lescarboura, *This Thing Called Broadcasting*, 98.

96   Jessica Dragonette, *Faith Is a Song: The Odyssey of an American Artist* (New York: David McKay Company, 1951), 104.

97   Pope, *The Making of Modern Advertising*, 168, 139–43.

98   Arnold, *Broadcast Advertising*, xv.

99   Ray A. Sweet, "Daylight Broadcasting," *Radio News* 5 (June 1924): 1727–1821.

100 On the first wave of boy enthusiasts, who by the 1920s were teaching their sons about radio, see Susan Douglas, *Inventing American Broadcasting* (Baltimore: Johns Hopkins University Press, 1987), 187–215.

101 Crystal D. Tector, "Radio and the Woman" *Radio World* 1 (20 May 1922): 20. See also subsequent issues, (3 June 1922): 14; (17 June 1922): 15; (15 July 1922): 15; (29 July 1922): 15; (5 August 1922): 15; and (12 August 1922): 15. "At Wellesley College," *Radio Broadcast* 7 (July 1925): 336. For other examples, see "The Autobiography of a Girl Amateur: Being a True Account of the Trials and Tribulations of a Lady Member of the Honorable Body of 'Hams,'" *Radio Amateur News* 1 (March 1920): 490; Marianne C. Brown, "One of the Gang," *Radio News* 3 (September 1920): 148; Abbye M. White, "Hearing North America," *Radio Broadcast* 3 (September 1923): 421; S. R. Winters, "A Lady (Radio) Bug," *Radio News* 4 (July 1922): 52; Alfred M. Caddell, "A Woman Who Makes Receiving Sets," *Radio Broadcast* 4 (November 1923): 29.

102 Otis Pease, *The Responsibilities of American Advertising* (New Haven: Yale University Press, 1958), 34; Lears, "From Salvation to Self-Realization," 23. See also Dolores Hayden, *The Grand Domestic Revolution: A History of Feminist Designs for American Homes, Neighborhoods, and Cities* (Cambridge, Mass.: MIT Press, 1981), 283–86; Stuart Ewen, *Captains of Consciousness: Advertising and the Social Roots of the Consumer Culture* (New York: McGraw-Hill, 1976), 113–24.

103 Arnold, *Broadcast Advertising*, 42.

104 Marchand, *Advertising the American Dream*, 66.

105 Claudine MacDonald to John Royal, 15 January 1932, Box 15, Folder 25, NBC Papers (hereafter cited as NBC Papers), Mass Communications History Center, Wisconsin Historical Society, Madison.

106 Mary Loomis Cook, "Programs for Women," in O'Neill, *The Advertising Agency Looks at Radio*, 132.

107 Nena Wilson Badenoch, "Meet Our Radio Mother," *Radio Age* 4 (February 1925): 33; "WJZ: Facts for Feminine Fans," *WJZ Program Guide*, 18 December 1926, Box 1, Folder 7, James Papers.

108 William D. Jenkins, "Housewifery and Motherhood: The Question of Role Change in the Progressive Era," in Mary Kelley, ed., *Woman's Being, Woman's Place: Female Identity and Vocation in American History* (Boston: G. K. Hall, 1983), 142–53. See also Susan Strasser, *Never Done: A History of American Housework* (New York: Pantheon, 1982), 202–23; Laura Shapiro, *Perfection Salad: Women and Cooking at the Turn of the Century* (New York: Farrar, Straus, and Giroux, 1986); Emma Seifert Weigley, "It Might Have Been Euthenics: The Lake Placid Conferences and the Home Economics Movement," *American Quarterly* 26 (March 1974): 79–96.

109 Jean Gordon and Jan McArthur, "Interior Decorating Advice as Popular Culture: Women's Views Concerning Wall and Window Treatments, 1870–1920," *Journal of American Culture* 9 (Fall 1986): 15–16; Warren

Susman, *Culture as History: The Transformation of American Society in the Twentieth Century* (New York: Pantheon, 1984), 201. Roland Marchand writes that "the inadequacy ascribed to women was only one salient example of the wider public incompetence that advertisers assumed, and sought to reinforce, by their constant celebration of experts." See Marchand, *Advertising the American Way*, 350–1.

110 Marjorie Presnell, "Women Strong for Home Hints," *Radio Digest* 24 (February 1930): 51.

111 Martin Grief, "Introduction," in Ruth Van Deman and Fanny Walker Yeatman, *Aunt Sammy's Radio Recipes* (New York: Universe Books, 1975), n. p.

112 Ibid. The U.S. Department of Agriculture still has in print a selection of "Aunt Sammy's Radio Recipes" as Home and Garden Bulletin No. 215, available from the US Government Printing Office, Stock Number 001–000–03523.

113 On the USDA's efforts to teach farm families to consume, see Mary Neth, "Preserving the Family Farm: Farm Families and Communities in the Midwest, 1900–1940" (Ph.D. diss., University of Wisconsin, 1987), particularly chapter 8.

114 James Gray, *Business without Boundary: The Story of General Mills* (Minneapolis: University of Minnesota Press, 1954) 177–8. See also "National Exchange of Radio Recipes," *Radio Age* 4 (December 1925): 29; "Thousands of Cooking Students Are Graduated in Our Homes," *Radio World* 8 (23 January 1926): 31; Pauline Chestnut, "Recipes via Radio," *Radio Digest* 26 (January 1926): 80.

115 Florence Roberts, "Radio Reminiscences," *Radio Digest* 26 (April 1931): 53.

116 "New Women's Hour on CBS," *Radio Revue* 1 (30 January 1930): 47; Eve M. Conradt-Eberlin, "Real Homemaking in the Studio," *Radio Digest* 25 (June 1930): 78.

117 See "The Woman's Magazine of the Air" 2 (15 August 1930); 3 (1 September 1930); 4 (15 September 1930); 5 (1 October 1930); and 6 (15 October 1930) in Box 5, Folder 79, James Papers. For another example of a magazine program, see the "Women's Radio Revue" as described in internal NBC memos, such as J. V. McConnell to D. C. Williams, 13 August 1931 and 2 December 1931, and Christine MacDonald to John Royal, 15 January 1932, with listener comments, Box 15, Folder 25, NBC Papers; National Broadcasting Company, "The Woman's Radio Revue: Let Us Join the Ladies: They Buy about 85% of Everything That Goes into the Home," 15 April 1931, Box 2, Folder 8, James Papers.

118 Hettinger, *Decade of Radio Advertising*, 201.

119 Niles Trammel to John Royal, 23 August 1933, Box 90, Folder 9, NBC Papers.

120 Pamphlets in Box 4, Folder 1, James Papers. See also Halsey D. Kellog and Abner G. Walters, "How To Reach Housewives Most Effectively," *Broadcasting* (15 April 1932): 7, 31.

121 Marleen Getz Rouse, "Daytime Radio Programming for the Homemaker, 1926–1956," *Journal of Popular Culture* 12 (Fall 1979): 317. See also "Exploiting Women's Interest in People To Create an Interest in Products: Sponsors of Morning Broadcasts Find Success with 'Human Interest' Skits," *Broadcast Advertising* 5 (July 1923): 200.

122 Robert C. Allen, *Speaking of Soap Operas* (Chapel Hill: University of North Carolina Press, 1985), 96–121.
123 MacDonald, *Don't Touch That Dial*, 233.
124 Marchand, *Advertising the American Dream*, 66–9.

Consider the Source

1. In 1930, *Radio Revue* magazine published a poem by an anonymous radio listener irritated with the presence of advertising over the airwaves. It was called "Sponsoritis." The following is one stanza from the poem:

> It's thriving like a healthy weed
> Or fungus newly grafted
> And mercenaries sow the seed
> Wherever sound is wafted
> The artists rave and grow morose
> Because of laryngitis
> And "fans" then get a stronger dose
> Of this same SPONSORITIS

What does this writer's use of an extended organic metaphor (weed, fungus, seed) suggest about the nature of advertising? How does the notion of a "newly grafted fungus" situate the poem historically? In what sense is it new? Grafted from what?

2. When you listen to a radio program or watch a television show, you might plausibly conclude that the show or program you're tuning into is the product the radio or television station sells: after all, the more people that watch it, the more money it can charge for commercials. In fact, however, most media outlets do not quite operate under this premise. Instead, it is the *audience* that is the product. The customer for a network or station is not the person who listens to or watches a show, but rather *advertisers* – that is, those who, unlike ordinary viewers, actually pay them for producing programming. Stations and networks take money from sponsors, and in return promise them a certain number or kind of people will be tuned in when their commercials are broadcast (if later ratings show they failed to deliver on this promise, they must offer additional advertising time to compensate the difference). How significant is the difference between viewing an audience rather than programming as the product a station sells? What kind of impact might it have on the kinds of programming you get on television and radio? (Consider, for example, pay-per-view programming on cable television versus a prime-time show on the WB or ABC.)

3. "Who pays for radio?" Susan Smulyan asks at the end of the book from which this chapter was taken. "All of us – radio listeners and television viewers, children, adults, PBS and Fox viewers, college radio station listeners and talk-show callers – continue to pay for the system used to finance American broadcasting." In what sense *do* we pay? Is that cost too high? What are the costs of some alternatives? Consider, for example, the implications of listener-supported, or government-owned, radio stations.

Suggested Further Reading

The titan in the field of broadcasting scholarship is Erik Barnouw, the author of a massive three-volume history published by Oxford University Press: *A Tower in Babel: A History of Broadcasting in the United States to 1933* (1966), *The Golden Web: A History of Broadcasting in the United States, 1933–1953* (1968), and *The Image Empire: A History of Broadcasting in the United States from 1953* (1970). These three books have been usefully condensed into a one-volume edition, *Tube of Plenty: The Evolution of American Broadcasting* (first issued in 1975 and revised in 1982 and 1990). See also the *Historical Dictionary of American Radio*, edited by Donald G. Godfrey and Frederic A. Leigh (Westport, Conn.: Greenwood, 1998). For an exhaustive account of the struggle over advertising and commercialized radio, see Robert McChesney, *Telecommunications, Mass Media, and Democracy: The Battle for Control of U.S. Broadcasting, 1928–1935* (New York: Oxford University Press, 1993).

8
The Firmament of Stardom

1915	Francis Albert Sinatra born in Hoboken, New Jersey, to Italian immigrant parents
1930s	Bing Crosby premier American pop singer on radio, records, and movies during the Great Depression
1937	Sinatra takes job as singing waiter at New Jersey nightclub and begins ascent as a pop singer
1941	Bombing of Pearl Harbor brings US into World War II
1944	Sinatra causes riot at Columbus Day shows at Paramount Theater in New York City
1945	Dropping of atomic bombs on Japan ends World War II
1947–50	Cold War prompts investigations of alleged Communists (including Sinatra)
1951	Sinatra divorces first wife to marry Ava Gardner amid plummeting popularity (the two divorce in 1955)
1953	Sinatra begins comeback by appearing in *From Here to Eternity*, for which he wins Academy Award
1954–60	Sinatra releases series of albums – including *In the Wee Small Hours* (1955) and *(Sinatra Sings for) Only the Lonely* (1958) – that cement his reputation
1960–1	John F. Kennedy elected president; Sinatra raises campaign funds and organizes Inaugural Gala
1963	Kennedy assassinated
1998	Sinatra dies at age 82

Introduction

"The American Dream" is one of the most familiar – and powerful – phrases in the US national lexicon. Jubilant athletes declaim it following championship games. Aspiring politicians invoke it as the basis of their candidacies.

Otherwise sober businessmen cite achieving it as the goal of their enterprises. The term seems like both the most lofty as well as the most immediate component of an American identity, a birthright far more meaningful and compelling than terms like "democracy," "constitution," or even "United States."

And yet for all its seeming simplicity and appeal, the American Dream is also a very complicated concept. For one thing, the opportunities the phrase implies also impose costs all the more painful for rarely being recognized, much less discussed. The unfulfilled yearnings of Jimmy Stewart's character in *It's a Wonderful Life* are never quite erased by that movie's happy ending. The failure of countless social reforms in the United States, which founder on the confidence of individual citizens that *they* will be the ones who overcome the odds and get rich, is one of the great themes of American politics. And we've all heard stories about celebrities who find themselves overwhelmed by the very success they so fiercely pursued – and attained.

Moreover, even if one assumes success is both obtainable and worthwhile, there is no *one* American Dream; rather, there are many American *Dreams*. Religious freedom, a college education, homeownership – at different points in US history, Americans have worked toward these or other aspirations. Most of the time, they have been relatively modest, even anonymous, in doing so. Indeed, the legitimacy of the American Revolution and the republic on which it stands was specifically premised on the possibility of pursuing happiness, variously defined, on a mass scale.

There are, however, some American Dreams that are notable for both their scope and visibility. In the eighteenth century, such dreams often took the form of statesmanship, as in the grand achievements – and reputations – of people like Benjamin Franklin and George Washington. In the nineteenth century, the emblematic American Dream was the creation of grand industrial empires along the lines of John Rockefeller and Andrew Carnegie. In the twentieth century, though, the characteristic realm of the American Dream has been popular culture. The possibility of a poor girl from a small town becoming transformed into a Hollywood princess on the silver screen seems to embody our notion of an individualistic democracy far more than, say, an equal distribution of economic resources.

Other chapters in this book have looked at popular culture from what might be termed a structural standpoint – describing types, technology, economics, and audiences. This one, by contrast, looks at it as a personal experience: what it means to devote one's life to popular culture; the process by which one becomes a star; the costs of such stardom; and how much difference an individual's choices can make. The focus of this inquiry is a case study of Frank Sinatra (1915–98), a man many Americans, particularly those born before the Second World War, would regard as the greatest all-around entertainer of the twentieth century.

Over the course of his long life, Sinatra was truly a multimedia star of radio, television, and movies. First and foremost, however, he was a singer, both on stage and in recording studios. Legendary for his unique – but lastingly influential – style of improvised vocal phrasing, he was also a pioneer in his release of thematically unified record albums like *In the Wee Small Hours* (1955) and *Songs for Swingin' Lovers* (1956). In a career that spanned from the late 1930s to the late 1990s, Sinatra was alternately a chaste teen idol, a randy playboy, a depressed loner, an arrogant lout, and a powerful entertainment impresario. He was both larger than life and all too human – qualities that made him a compelling popular icon.

This previously unpublished essay, part of a work-in-progress entitled *The House I Live In: Frank Sinatra and American Identity*, explores these facets of Sinatra's life and career in terms of an American Dream he so vividly embodied. Situating him in the broader context of his time (a time, it is argued, that is still very much ours), it traces the possibilities and limits of that Dream for Sinatra – and perhaps for our own dreams as well.

Fool's Paradise: Frank Sinatra and the American Dream

Jim Cullen

Frank Sinatra has a sledgehammer in his hands, and he is furious. He swings away, the blows landing on newly hardened concrete. (Do his hands feel the vibration of the handle as the sledgehammer pounds the ground? Does he notice his valet, George Jacobs, witnessing his rage? Would he care?) Sinatra is destroying the heliport he's just had built in the grounds of his house in Palm Springs.[1]

It was supposed to be Jack's house – or, at any rate, the house Jack lived in when he left the White House for the west coast. Three years before, when he was running for president, he had visited, and Sinatra had installed a plaque on the door of the guest room: "John Fitzgerald Kennedy Slept Here."[2] In the months that followed, Sinatra had been one of Kennedy's most visible and effective supporters. Using his extensive contacts in entertainment, he had organized Kennedy's spectacular Inaugural Gala, and had served as Jacqueline Kennedy's escort at the event. Perhaps more importantly, he had served as a conduit for JFK's

Portrait of the artist as a young heartthrob A 1943 publicity photo of
Frank Sinatra, whose gorgeous voice, signature bowties, and expressive face
("Those cheekbones!...Like a young Lincoln," sculptor Jo Davidson once
said) made him a star. Before Elvis, before the Beatles, before Ricky Martin,
there was "Sinatratrauma." *Photo from the Collection of the New-York Historical
Society*

mistresses, notably Judith Campbell [Exner], whom Kennedy shared
with Sam Giancana, the notorious organized crime chieftain.[3]
    Now, in the winter of 1962, Kennedy is well into the first of what he
hopes will be a two-term presidency. Sinatra, for his part, expects their
friendship to continue. To that end – but without any formal request that
he do so – he's made extensive renovations in his home: separate cot-
tages for the president and the Secret Service; a dining room for about

40 guests; 25 extra phone lines; enough cable to support teletype services; a switchboard to handle the incoming communications traffic; a heliport to serve air traffic. He's even installed a flagpole like the one at the Kennedy compound on Cape Cod so that he can fly the presidential flag when the president arrives for a weekend visit in March and a vacation in June.

But Kennedy never does. He defers to his brother Robert, who insists JFK cannot go. The reason, in a word, is Giancana. In late February of 1962, Attorney General Kennedy receives information from FBI director J. Edgar Hoover showing Judith Campbell has not only been calling the White House, but also Giancana and fellow mobster Johnny Roselli. (In Hoover's mode of operations, this intelligence is as likely to be a covert threat – I've got dirt on you people – as it is a matter of passing data up the chain of command.) No one at the Justice Department yet knows for sure that Sinatra is the connecting link between Giancana, JFK, and Campbell, but a series of bureau reports document personal calls by Giancana – the focus of a major investigation of organized crime – to Sinatra's unlisted phone number. These reports also claim that Giancana has been a frequent guest at Sinatra's house in Palm Springs. This in itself is a reason that Robert Kennedy says JFK can't go there: the president cannot politically afford to be entertained by a man who also hosts gangsters.[4] His brother reluctantly agrees. The presidential party will instead stay with (Republican) Bing Crosby, who also has a house in Palm Springs. Security considerations are the official reason given for changing the previously announced plan to stay with Sinatra.

The president delegates his brother-in-law, Peter Lawford, a member of the so-called "Rat Pack" (Sinatra had changed its name to the "Jack Pack" during the 1960 campaign), to give Sinatra the news. One result of the conversation is that Sinatra wields a sledgehammer. Another is that he shoots the messenger: Lawford is literally written out of two movies in which he is to appear with Sinatra, who refuses to speak to him ever again. Twenty years later, upon learning that Lawford and his wife were in the audience for a show at the Sands Hotel, Sinatra delegates two security guards to remove him from the premises. "Mr. Sinatra refuses to perform until you are gone," he is told.[5]

Sinatra's response to JFK is milder, though it's clear damage has been done. Upon his arrival in California at the end of March, Kennedy asks Lawford how Sinatra has taken the news. "Not very well," Lawford replies. "I'll make it up to him," Kennedy responds. He calls Sinatra and invites him to Crosby's for lunch. Sinatra declines. Too busy, he explains. He's on his way to Los Angeles to visit some friends (one of whom, Marilyn Monroe, will soon be an intimate of the Kennedy brothers).

The bloom is off the rose. In May, Sinatra sends the president a birthday gift, which Kennedy acknowledges in a thank-you note. In August, Sinatra telegraphs his readiness to send a print of *The Manchurian Candidate* if desired. But Kennedy, who will soon be faced with mortal limits himself, keeps his distance. Sinatra does not attend his funeral. He does call the White House to offer his condolences (the call is taken by Lawford's wife, Patricia, JFK's sister).[6] But for all intents and purposes, Sinatra's stay in Camelot is over by the spring of 1962. In 1968, he supports Hubert Humphrey, not Robert Kennedy, for the presidency.

"The thing was this: Frank was hurt," Sammy Davis Jr. told Sinatra biographer Randy Taraborelli decades later.

> He thought it was chickenshit, the whole goddamn thing. And for the president to stay at Bing's, well, that looked to Frank like a slap in the face. A Republican! In other words, it looked to Frank like Kennedy was saying "I'd rather stay *anywhere* than with you." I think Frank felt like the whole thing was designed to humiliate him, and you know what, pal? I fucking agree. I do. The way Frank helped the Kennedys, man, that whole thing they did was *cold*.[7]

Other perhaps more neutral observers were less outraged by what happened. "Why the fuck would the president stay with Sinatra?" Giancana said at the time. "He ain't crazy."[8] One might argue that appearances notwithstanding, simple loyalty might have led the Kennedy people to stand by those who helped them get where they were. But as Giancana – a man whose work behind the scenes in Chicago allegedly secured JFK's razor-thin electoral margin – could testify, this was not the Kennedy style. The real problem, one can easily infer him arguing, was that Sinatra had trouble accepting his dispensability.

Which leads to what I regard as an interesting question: How did Frank Sinatra come to see himself as a man entitled to consort with Kennedys and kings (from Martin Luther King to the royal family of Monaco)?[9] Twenty years before, he was "a little guy from Hoboken" thrilled to shake President Roosevelt's hand during a last-minute visit to the White House.[10] Clearly, he had come a long way since then. Unlike FDR, JFK was a contemporary of Sinatra's, and while Sinatra clearly admired Kennedy, their relationship was at least initially reciprocal – and Sinatra may have even had more to offer the senator than vice versa. But the issue goes deeper than personal contacts or generational protocols; it has more to do with Sinatra's apparent belief that he could pretty much go, do, and act as he pleased with anyone he wanted to. By the early 1960s, this assumption – undoubtedly rooted in actual experience – was so strong that learning otherwise, even from the President of the United States, was infuriating.

But when did this assumption actually take root? When he began singing at the Rustic Cabin, a small New Jersey nightclub, in the 1930s? When the girls began screaming at the Paramount in the 1940s? When his comeback was secure in the 1950s? No doubt all these turning points contributed toward shaping his outlook. But I suspect that the series of thoughts and experiences that led him to wield a sledgehammer that March day originated much earlier at a relatively unprepossessing house in Hoboken, New Jersey. The real groundbreaking took place there.

> He didn't dream. He said, "I'm gonna do it. I'm gonna get across this river. I'm gonna go there [New York City] and make a name for myself."
> – Tina Sinatra on her father's youth in Hoboken[11]

> As I left the theater, with the shriek of young lungs still ringing in my ears, I was bothered by a strange discovery – that you could become a public idol simply by looking young, sad, and undernourished, then by skimming off a certain amount of your misery and pouring it into a microphone.
> – Journalist Jack Long after a Sinatra performance, 1943[12]

It may be a perverse tribute to the elasticity of the American Dream that by the early twentieth century Martin Sinatra would adopt an Irish name – O'Brien – as a means of upward mobility. Of course, he probably didn't think about his situation exactly this way. For the young Sicilian immigrant, it was probably more a matter of common sense: there was no way an aspiring boxer was ever going to get into a gym, never mind a ring, with a name like Sinatra. Perhaps he was aware that there was a time when people with names like "Kennedy" had been regarded with the same degree of disdain and dismay as Italians like him. Perhaps he could anticipate a time when there would be those (Puerto Ricans? Koreans?) who would take their place at the bottom of the pecking order along with a fixed underclass of Negroes. But he probably didn't spend a lot of time thinking about it.

Not much came of Marty O'Brien's boxing career. Still, the O'Brien name continued to have its uses, particularly when wielded by his bride, the Genoan-born Natalie "Dolly" Garavante, who apparently did most of the family's thinking. It was she who, as a major backstage player for the Democratic party in Hoboken, orchestrated Marty's appointment as a city fireman. It was she who, after borrowing money from her mother, opened a saloon she named "Marty O'Brien's" (this during Prohibition). And it was she who, when her only child was born in December of 1915, made sure he had an Irish godfather, Frank Garrick, to someday get him a job for the *Jersey Observer*. Garrick got him hired to bundle papers, but when young Francis was fired for posing as a sports-writer, Dolly never forgave Garrick for failing to get the paper to take him back.

You get the idea: Francis owes a lot of what he became to Dolly. Part of this is sheer economic privilege. Later in life Sinatra would emphasize the gritty urban milieu of his youth, but without underestimating the insularity and widespread poverty that surrounded him, it must never-theless be said that he lived a life of relative affluence. In 1932, with the Depression at its height, the Sinatras moved into a four-story $13,400 house (a price tag of affluent Westchester County proportions). Young Frank, an only child, had so many pairs of pants that he had the nickname of "Slacksey O'Brien." But the advantages in life that Dolly gave Frankie were not just material; they had more to do with instilling a sense of confidence that would lead a high school drop-out to believe he could pass himself off as a sportswriter, and to later make both his high school and journalistic "experiences" fixtures of his official publicity biography. Here, truly, was a child with great expectations.

Still, an ambitious mother will only get any child so far, particularly a child who, much to that mother's dismay, was indifferent about educa-tion and lacked an obvious channel for yearnings that remained inchoate well into his adolescence. Anyone reading a Sinatra biography looking for a childhood incident that would foreshadow his future will be largely disappointed; while there are scattered references to him singing to friends or at family gatherings, there's little here to distinguish such an activity from a passion for baseball or a knack for drawing. Most accounts of his youth emphasize Dolly's and Martin's skepticism about their son's growing interest in a singing career (they hoped he would attend the nearby Stevens Institute and become an engineer). Though Dolly eventually bought him a sound system and a car to allow him to pursue his avocation, one suspects this had less to do with her belief that he could become a singing star – who, after all, could really make a living doing that? – than it did her long-standing strategy of making sure her son had enough money in his pocket to treat, and thus make, plenty of friends.

The epiphany, virtually everyone agrees, took place in the spring of 1935 when the nineteen-year-old Sinatra took his girlfriend, Nancy Barbato, to see Bing Crosby, the premier popular singer of his day. Crosby's appeal had less to do with the pure beauty of his voice than his ability to exploit the cultural possibilities of new technology, specifi-cally that of the microphone. By singing in a smooth, subtly modulated voice – a style that came to be known as "crooning" – Crosby distin-guished himself from more powerful vocalists like Al Jolson and Sophie

Tucker, who attained their pre-eminence as "belters" who could project their voices to the far corners of a room. Moreover, Crosby's image matched his singing style: that of an elegantly dressed, pipe-smoking man of leisure. Ironically, the effect of Crosby's understated image on young Frank Sinatra was electrifying. "When I saw that guy on stage," he reputedly told Nancy, "something happened to me. It was like I was really up there, not Crosby. I've got to be that singer." As the magazine writer who related this anecdote explained, "Probably a thousand other youngsters who heard Crosby that night painted the same mental picture – themselves in the spotlight, thrilling millions. But Sinatra was the one out of a thousand with the courage to chase the rainbow."[13]

Courage, certainly: there's a lot to be said for that. But it's also worth considering the particular rainbow Sinatra was chasing. It had its own arc, and one can confidently say that had be been born in a different place or time it would have been situated – and chased – differently. As his chroniclers tirelessly assert, Frank Sinatra was very much man of his time. What time was that? My answer, despite the fact that he is dead and buried, is now.

Why is Sinatra "now," when did "now" begin, and why hasn't "now" ended? To put it simply, I believe the basic texture of modern American life emerged during Sinatra's youth, that he embodied it with unusual clarity, and that its contours, despite its myriad variations, remain largely in place. Far more than extraordinary events of his childhood (like the stock market crash of 1929) or the leading figures of his era (like the so-called Lost Generation of Ernest Hemingway and F. Scott Fitzgerald), there's something accessibly familiar about the rhythms of everyday life in the years following World War I, a time known by those who lived it as the "New Era."

That familiarity is almost palpable, for example, in this description of a day in the life of the fictional John Smith, "a typical citizen of this restless republic," written by an ad agency copywriter in 1928, when Sinatra was twelve years old:

> Yanked out of bed by an alarm clock, John speeds through his shave, bolts down his breakfast in eight minutes, and scurries for a train or the street car. On the way to work his roving eye scans, one after another, the sport page, the comic strips, several columns of political hokum, and the delectable details of the latest moonshine murder.
>
> From eight to twelve, humped over a desk in a skyscraper, he wrestles with his job to the accompaniment of thumping typewriters, jingling telephones, and all the incessant tattoo of twentieth century commerce. One hour off for a quick lunch, a couple of cigarettes, and a glamorous glance at the cuties mincing down the boulevard. Jangling drudgery again from one until five. Then out on the surging streets once more.

Clash, clatter, rattle and roar! Honk! Honk! Honk! Every crossing jammed with traffic! Pavements fairly humming with jostling crowds! A tingling sense of adventure and romance in the very air! Speed – desire – excitement – the illusion of freedom at the end of the day! The flashing lights of early evening – Clara Bow in Hearts Aflame! Wuxtry! Wuxtry! – Bootlegger Kills Flapper Sweetheart! Clickety-click, clickety-click – John Smith homeward-bound, clinging to a strap and swiftly skimming through the last edition.[14]

The point of this little tableau was to illustrate the fast pace of life in the New Era. What may first strike a reader now, however, is how quaint it all seems – the virtual bragging about technology that is now common-place, if not obsolete (alarm clocks, skyscrapers, typewriters); the dated slang and references ("hokum," "wuxtry," movie star Clara Bow); behavior that was once racy but is now regarded as distasteful, if not unacceptable (cigarette smoking, alcohol consumption, leering at women). Moreover, this sketch was not as fully representative as it was clearly meant to be; a "typical citizen," if there is any such person, did not necessarily live in a city, ride a subway, work in a skyscraper, or even have a lunch hour. Ironically, perhaps, what it most accurately depicts is the provincialism inherent in this writer's assumption that he can render a "typical" American experience.

Such limits notwithstanding, there nevertheless does seem to be much in this description that not only rings true of what many observers at the time and since have observed of the 1920s, but also in the way John Smith's life resembles that of, say, his granddaughter Juanita Smith. The essential shape of the day shows striking similarity to ones experienced today: a morning routine followed by a rush-hour commute to work, with a subsequent workday punctuated by daily rituals that culminate in a trip home and "an illusion of freedom." One can grasp the funda-mental continuity of John's and Juanita's time by imagining alternatives on either side of the temporal divide: these are not people who begin their day by milking cows or drawing water from a well, nor do they put food on the table by telecommuting from computer terminals in their homes or attached to their clothing.

Perhaps more importantly, John's and Juanita's lives are also paralleled in the extraordinary range of the mass media in suffusing their days. Driving home from work, Juanita may be less likely to get her news from a newspaper than by listening to the radio – a medium that came into its own in the 1920s – but the content of what she absorbs, right down to the sensational murder trials and entertainment news, is much the same in its intense, but fleeting, interest. Even the evocative phrase "jangling drud-gery" continues to describe the combination of hectic activity and numb-ing repetition that characterizes the workday lives of most Americans.

Changes in family life were also important. While women gained the right to vote in 1920, it was the developments that occurred in the domestic sphere – smaller families, more sexual freedom, and the replacement of servants by labor-saving devices like vacuum cleaners and washing machines – that were more obviously transformative. While it is possible to overstate the impact of the changes (not all young women were gin-swilling flappers; labor-saving devices were accompanied by rising housekeeping standards),[15] one nevertheless senses that the *issues* of the time gave rise to assumptions and language that have been with us ever since. In *Only Yesterday*, his history of the 1920s published in 1931, journalist Frederick Lewis Allen noted that "married women who were encumbered with children and could not seek jobs consoled themselves with the thought that home-making and child-rearing were really 'professions' after all."[16] One does not have to strain very hard to find an identical sentiment expressed today – or to find women, like Dolly Sinatra, who left much of their childcare in the hands of others while they made their way in a so-called "man's world."

If women were increasingly going into the outside world, that outside world was also increasingly coming into the home via new communications technologies like radio, record players, and telephones. What is significant here is not the technology itself – radio broadcasting, like other technological innovations such as automobiles, were developed well before the 1920s – but rather the way these once cutting-edge inventions had become a part of everyday life on a mass scale.

What is also significant is the *way* this technology became part of everyday life: through a fully mature mass-market industrial capitalism. Chain retailing, buying on credit, and especially the rise of pervasive national advertising came into their own in the 1920s. Nothing better illustrates the impact of this new consumer culture than the development of radio, a crucial medium in the rise of Sinatra's idol, Bing Crosby. Originally developed for its shipping and naval uses for wireless communication between two points, the nascent broadcast industry was a patchwork quilt of stations and programming run by churches, unions, and other institutions at the start of the decade. But the use of wired networks created for private profit, as well as the use of advertising to pay for programming, not only quickly became the dominant way of structuring the industry and its programs – like the soap opera, an entertainment genre that got its name from its sponsor – but also laid down the political, organizational, and financial tracks that would be followed by television (in its infancy in the 1920s) and even the Internet.

These social, economic, and technological developments also had a decisive impact on American values. Until around the time Sinatra was born, the United States was predominately a culture of *production:* its social values (for example, the Puritan work ethic), material conditions (an abundance of raw materials), and economic realities (like relatively high labor costs, which fostered technological innovation as well as the immigration of intellectual capital from abroad), helped create a society in which making things was paramount. Starting in the 1920s – the first decade where more Americans lived in cities than in rural areas – the United States became a culture of *consumption:* as many government and business leaders recognized, the future success of capitalism depended on the nation's ability to absorb its incredible productive capacity via buying, spending, using up. Indeed, it was precisely the difficulty in absorbing this capacity that was widely blamed for the advent of the Great Depression.

This new culture of consumption had important psychological ramifications that reached deep into the roots of mass consciousness. In the words of cultural historian Warren Susman, a society that once placed emphasis on *character* now prized *personality.* "Character" has a moral connotation; it suggests the essential nature of an individual in a way that transcends surface appearances. But "personality" suggests the allure of precisely such surface appearances, whether via the acquisition of cosmetics or a newly styled automobile (Alfred Sloan's General Motors Corporation was finally able to beat Henry Ford at his assembly-line game in the 1920s by subtly changing his models every year).

Here again, the example of Crosby is instructive. While he no doubt had to work hard to establish himself, a large part of Crosby's appeal was that he made it all seem so easy. He was one of the first modern celebrities – a man famous in large measure for being famous, and one whose fame allowed him to seemingly effortlessly cross into media like film and television even though his primary claim to fame was music. As a young man, Sinatra smoked a pipe and wore a hat in conscious emulation of his hero (upon finding a picture of Crosby in his room, an exasperated Dolly threw a shoe at her son and called him a bum). What he wanted, very clearly, was to become a show-business personality just like Crosby.

And he did – to a point. But for Frank Sinatra, character nevertheless remained a destiny that would push him significantly farther than Crosby. One can hear this in one thing Sinatra pointedly did *not* copy from Crosby: his style of singing. "I was a big fan of Bing's," he later told his daughter. "But I never wanted to sing like him, because every kid on the block was boo-boo-booing like Crosby. I wanted to be a different kind of singer. And my voice was higher anyhow and I said, 'That's not for me.' "[17] To that end, Sinatra cultivated a more expressive approach. It was comparatively mild to what came later in his career, but was distinctive enough to win him attention, and, eventually, accolades.

Of all the mysteries in Frank Sinatra's career, few are more perplexing than the nature of his talent. To put it simply: how was it that a man who could not read music should be celebrated as an unparalleled interpreter of popular song? How did someone with virtually no formal training come to be seen as a musician's musician, winning the admiration of geniuses like Duke Ellington and Miles Davis? Actually, in the context of American popular music, these seeming anomalies are less contradictory than they might appear; musical ability is often as much about instinct as it is about training, and it is likely that much of Sinatra's originality came precisely from the absence of formal models to follow. Moreover, much of what made him unique had less to do with music *per se* than drama, specifically his much-celebrated ability to convey emotion and conviction. In other words, Sinatra was a great actor with music long before he became an occasionally convincing actor with a script.

And yet, for that very reason, it is almost possible to believe that he wasn't really an artist but rather a celebrity pretending to be one. After all, anyone can be a singer, and the difference between one who sings well and one who does not very often has less to do with hard work than a roll of the genetic dice. The many musicals in which young Sinatra appeared, often as an ordinary-guy loser who would periodically break into song, could almost reinforce this belief that there was nothing to it. It's almost as if his presence there is random, and that you too could be in that spotlight, thrilling millions.

In fact, of course, Sinatra worked extremely hard. Indeed, even if you factor out the elements in his personality that effectively disqualified him from the mellow, Bing Crosby school of effortless poise – his almost compulsive work ethic, that legendary temper – Sinatra's cool public image could never wholly disguise his energy, even his edge. As William Herndon said of his law partner Abraham Lincoln, his ambition was a little engine that knew no rest.

That ambition emerged from the mists of his childhood shortly after the Crosby concert in 1935, when Sinatra made his first serious effort to break into show business by trying out for the *Major Bowes and his Original Amateur Hour*, a nationally broadcast radio show. ("Round and round she goes," went Bowes's signature slogan, referring to the wheel of fortune, "and where she stops nobody knows.") It's not clear whether it was Bowes's inspiration or Dolly's machinations that led him to join another auditioning group, the Three Flashes, which as a result of Sinatra's involvement was rechristened the Hoboken Four. The group took first place on the September 8 show, and were invited to tour with a series of other acts in Bowes's national company. Sinatra stayed on until the bullying of other group members led him to quit at the end of the year.

Marty Sinatra was disappointed in his 19-year-old son: here was one more failed bid for self-sufficiency. But for Frank the Hoboken Four had never been much more than a necessary detour on the road to becoming a solo act. As usual, Dolly supported him. "The two of you are driving me nuts," she said of the fighting between father and son. "Frankie wants to sing, Marty. Jesus Christ, let him sing, will ya?" Once more, it appears, Mother Knew Best.[18]

The next stage in Sinatra's career began in 1937 when a song promoter named Hank Sanicola became his unofficial manager and got him a job waiting tables and singing with the house band at the Rustic Cabin, a club in Englewood, New Jersey, right on the shore of the Hudson. But even Dolly was dubious about this idea:

> His salary was only fifteen dollars a week, and I used to give him practically twice that so he could pick up the tabs of his friends when they dropped in. When he got a five dollar raise, I told him "This isn't getting me anywhere. It would be cheaper to keep you at home." "Mama," he said, "it's going to roll in someday. I'm going to be big time." He always believed that.[19]

While the Rustic Cabin was hardly a major musical showcase, it offered a number of crucial advantages to Sinatra. One was its strategic location near the George Washington Bridge, which provided him easy access to the most important New York City venues, where he could learn what was going on. The other was that the Rustic Cabin had a direct radio wire to radio station WNEW in Manhattan, where the house band could be heard on weekly Saturday Dance Parade broadcasts. This, in turn, brought important band leaders like Jimmy Dorsey to the Rustic Cabin, who then saw Sinatra for themselves.

Not that these people always liked what they saw or heard. "He was such a nuisance, hogging the mike all the time and singing every chorus when he was only supposed to do an occasional vocal," a musician who worked with him later told Kitty Kelly. "Finally we started taking the microphone away from him. We ridiculed him because he just wasn't that good." Sinatra, however, kept at it, picking up a vocal coach and rejecting any criticism. "When we'd tell him how bad he was, he'd get furious and start cursing and swearing at us. 'Son of a bitch,' he'd yell. 'You bastards wait. One of these days you're going to pay to hear me sing. You just wait.' "[20]

Sinatra's first important true believer was Harry James, a trumpeter who had left Benny Goodman's band to start his own. He was looking for a singer – a role which, in those days, was secondary to featured players like bandleaders themselves – and thought Sinatra sounded promising. Sinatra signed on and began touring with James in June of

1939. But the band struggled to make ends meet. When, six months later, the much more prestigious Tommy Dorsey sought Sinatra's services with a long-term contract, James let him go with a handshake. Dorsey himself would not be quite so accommodating.

Sinatra remained with Dorsey for the next two years. In that time, his status rose steadily from a visible member of Dorsey's ensemble to a featured vocalist. He appeared in a number of films with the band, was named outstanding male vocalist by the bellwether *Billboard* and *Downbeat* magazines, and became a fixture on the pop scene with records like "I'll Never Smile Again" and "I'll Be Seeing You."

In 1942, Sinatra, now 26, began making his first solo recordings. This was the direction he wished to take – a path cleared by Crosby – but it was by no means clear that anyone, never mind Sinatra himself, could make the transition from a band vocalist to a pop singer. Moreover, Dorsey was not particularly interested in making it easy for Sinatra to leave. He ultimately agreed to do so, but not before claiming a third of his gross earnings for the next ten years (protracted negotiations the following year between Dorsey, Sinatra's agent, and his new record company, Columbia, untangled him from such onerous terms).

He had momentum now. Most of it came from adolescent girls – "bobby-soxers," as they were called for their distinctive apparel – whose growing adulation of the singer was described as "Sinatratrauma" and "Sinatramania" in mass media voracious for content. The climax occurred on in his first solo appearance on December 30, 1942, when he appeared as an "extra added attraction" to Benny Goodman's Band at New York's Paramount Theater. "Who the hell is Frank Sinatra?" Goodman asked upon learning of the addition to the program, which featured the Bing Crosby movie *Star-Spangled Rhythm*. Goodman soon found out. The screaming, applauding, and urine-stained seats made clear that Frank Sinatra, wearing his signature bowtie, had arrived. In fact, the girls refused to leave when the show was over, preventing the next scheduled performance from getting underway. ("Whatever he stirred beneath our barely budding breasts, it wasn't motherly," one bobby-soxer later reminisced.)[21] Theater management resorted to showing the dullest films they could find in the hope of getting the audience to leave.

With an army of managers, publicists, and promoters, Sinatra pushed on, expanding his dominions. A series of nightclub appearances at New York's Riobamba Club and the Waldorf-Astoria in 1943 established his appeal with older, more serious audiences. His appointment as a host of the weekly radio show *Your Hit Parade* made him a household word across the country. Signed to Metro-Goldwyn-Mayer, the most prestigious of the movie studios, he prepared for his first major musical, *Anchors Aweigh*, by learning how to dance under the tutelage of Gene Kelly.

But his core constituency remained the bobby-soxers. On Columbus Day of 1944, tens of thousands of them rioted at the Paramount, where Sinatra returned for a series of performances, and where the refusal of those with seats to vacate them led to the arrival of the police. By now, all the adulation generated by "The Voice," as he was known, had become familiar, alternately amusing and irritating to those who constantly heard about it. Others, however, were perplexed, even troubled. In a piece for *The New Republic* shortly after the Columbus Day riot, writer Bruce Bliven groped to understand what all the fuss was about:

> My strongest impression was not that Frankie means so much to the bobby-socksers, as that everything else means so little. Our civilization no doubt seems wonderful to the children of half-starved, dictator-ridden Europe; our multiplicity of gadgets is the envy of the world. And yet, if I read the bobby-socksers aright, we have left them with a hunger still unfulfilled: a hunger for heroes, for ideal things that do not appear, or at least not in sufficient quantities, in a civilization that is so busy making things and selling things as ours. Whatever else you may say of the adoration of The Voice, it is a strictly non-commercial enterprise, a selfless idolatry which pays its 75 cents at the box office and asks in return only the privilege of being allowed to ruin its vocal chords. Perhaps Frankie is more important a symbol than most of us are aware.[22]

In retrospect, of course, most of us *are* aware that Frankie was an important symbol, but we are no more able to fix exactly what he was a symbol *of* than Bliven was. As he suggests, it has something to do with the longing engendered by the very promise of American life, the incalculable price dreams exact by the mere fact of their (often ill-formed) existence. "It was the war years, and there was a great loneliness," Sinatra has said in explanation of his own appeal, but while that sounds poetic and true as far as it goes, it's too clichéd and incomplete to really be a satisfying answer. Yes, as Sinatra explained, he surely was "the boy in every corner drugstore, the boy who'd gone off to war."[23] But even so, why did that loneliness persist for so many years even after the boys had come home (hadn't it long preceded their departure)? And even if that loneliness had come and gone, why was *Sinatra* the voice of it?

My own guess is that Sinatra had an unusually clear understanding of this loneliness, which has something to do with the sense of isolation that results when you have high hopes in a land where you are told anything is possible, and where, no matter what you do, the perception of plenty always seems most vividly in view somewhere *else*. Sinatra was literally the voice of these hopes, and had inhabited them with an intensity that few of us have the stomach for. Because, let's face it: dreams wear you down. Even if you have confidence, talent, opportunity, energy, courage, and luck – things I've spent the last few pages tracing – there's no guarantee that you'll get what you want, or that you'll be satisfied once you do.

Indeed, even after achieving more fame, wealth, and admiration than any sane person could ever hope for, Sinatra – like many before and after him – seemed to regard mere success as somehow unworthy of serious consideration. "Happy? I don't know," Sinatra once responded to a query about the early days. "I wasn't *un*happy, let's put it that way. I never had it so good. Sometimes I wonder whether anybody had it like I had it, before or since. It's was the damnedest thing, wasn't it? But I was too busy ever to know whether I was happy or even to ask myself."[24]

More than anything else, it was Sinatra's busy-ness – his legendary work ethic that cut through the culture of personality he came of age in – that was cornerstone of his success. And that busy-ness, in turn, rested on an assumption that his (often remarkably focused) actions would make a difference as to the outcome of his life. The American Dream has been many different things to many different people in the last four centuries, but its inexhaustible ends have tended to obscure its indispensable means: a sense of agency. Not everyone can become a star, but those who do usually believe that will is the engine of success. "Luck is fine, and you have to have luck to get the opportunity," Sinatra once told columnist Earl Wilson. "But after that, you've got to have talent and know how to use it."[25] There's little doubt where the emphasis is here. But as Sinatra would learn, luck and opportunity (not to mention to actions of others) continue to haunt even those most intent on banishing them from the dominions of fortune.

It had now been a decade since Sinatra went to that Crosby concert. Reading about it in the space of a few minutes can obscure that it really was a fairly long time, and there must have been long moments, especially in those early years, when it would have been hard even for Sinatra himself to believe he was going to get to that place he had never been but knew he wanted to go. At some point he must have sensed that he had caught a wave, one that would carry him from a sea of pure potential straight to the shore of recognized achievement (and once there, he would just keep going). And while he might not be happy, but he could at least ride out his personal demons. One thing was certain: there was no going back.

He kept saying, "My career is over. I'm fucking washed up, and now I have to go out and face these people – the same goddamn people who aren't buying my records, who aren't seeing my movies."
– Sinatra bodyguard Jimmy Silvani, quoting Sinatra backstage at the Copacabana, 1950[26]

He couldn't sing. Frank Sinatra was onstage for his third show of the evening at the Copacabana in New York City on April 26, 1950 when he lost the power to do what he did best. "No words would come out – absolutely nothing – just dust," he later told his daughter. "I was never so panic-stricken in my whole life. I remember looking at the audience, there was a blizzard outside, about seventy people in the place – and they knew something serious had happened. There was absolute silence – stunning, absolute silence." Sinatra looked at pianist Skitch Henderson, whose face was white with fear. "Finally I turned to the audience and whispered into the microphone 'Good night,' and walked off the floor."[27] The problem was attributed to bleeding in Sinatra's vocal cords. He canceled the rest of the engagement to regain his voice, and did. But there was a serious question about how much that mattered. For in the eyes of many observers – and even Sinatra himself – his career was finished.

The stages of Sinatra's fall from commercial grace seem to have occurred as imperceptibly as his meteoric rise. To all outward appearances, he was still at his peak in 1945, when he appeared in *The House I Live In*, a movie short promoting social tolerance, and he was the lead star (with higher billing than Gene Kelly) in *Anchors Aweigh*. In addition to receiving a special Academy Award for his work in *House* in 1946, Sinatra enjoyed a string of top-ten hits and was named "America's Favorite Male Singer" in *Downbeat* magazine.

Still, there were signs of slippage. In 1945 Sinatra was dropped from *Your Hit Parade*; although he had come to hate the drudgery of hosting the radio program, he found it doubly irritating to be replaced by opera star Lawrence Tribbett.[28] He returned to the show in 1947, but by that point his output of hit singles had noticeably declined to one that year ("Mam'selle") and none in 1948. Meanwhile, a new group of singers like Frankie Laine and Johnny Ray were attracting attention that had generally been Sinatra's five years before. And while some of his movies – notably *Take Me Out to the Ball Game* (1949), another musical with Kelly – continued to perform at the box office, most of his films in the second half of the decade were regarded as middling at best by critics and moviegoers. By the time of his Copacabana engagement in 1950, there was an established public perception that Sinatra was not quite the celebrity he had been during the war. Indeed, Sinatra took the gig in part because he needed the money, and the mental and physical stresses of multiple shows a night over a period of weeks was no doubt a major factor in the vocal health of a not-quite-so-young 34-year-old who simply lacked the effortless ability he exuded a decade earlier.

Sinatra's fall from grace can plausibly be attributed to shifts in public taste and a real decline in the quality of his singing (though the latter, as I plan to make clear later, is a partial explanation at best). Strictly speaking, these were both matters beyond his control. But the most important cause of his fall may well have been his own personal conduct. In part, this was a matter of comeuppance by those who had been neglected – and, all too often, abused – during his rise, and who were now only too happy to see him fall. A Columbia Records engineer said of Sinatra's recording sessions at mid-century:

> It was pathetic. Sinatra would open his mouth and nothing would come out but a croak. Usually, when a singer is in bad shape, we can help him by extending his notes with an echo chamber. But Sinatra was one of the meanest men we ever worked for, so we engineers and musicians just sat on our hands and let him go down.[29]

However widespread or fair such comments may have been, they were essentially a private matter concerning Sinatra's workday world. Far more problematic was public behavior that could be witnessed – and reported. Rumors over Sinatra's involvement in organized crime can be dated to 1947, when he visited the notorious gangster Lucky Luciano in Havana. Long fascinated by gangsters, Sinatra ate, gambled, and even posed for pictures with Luciano and fellow crime chieftains Carlo Gambino, Vito Genovese, Joe Bonanno, and others. Columnist Robert Ruark, of the Scripps–Howard chain, after seeing Sinatra in Havana, wrote:

> The curious desire to cavort among the scum is possibly permissible among citizens who are not peddling sermons to the nation's youth and may even be allowed to a mealy-mouthed celebrity if he is smart enough to confine his social tolerance to a hotel room. But Mr. Sinatra, the self-confessed savior of the country's small fry, by virtue of his lectures on clean living and love-thy-neighbor, his movie shorts on tolerance, and his frequent dabblings into the do-good department of politics, seems to be setting a most peculiar example.[30]

As the tone of such comments suggests, Sinatra was not especially popular with some in the media, particularly those conservative writers and publishers under the control of the powerful Hearst syndicate. Few were more powerful – and more contemptuous of Sinatra – than Lee Mortimer, who taunted him mercilessly. (In fact, Sinatra had only taken the stage that painful night at the Copa in April of 1950 after five previous cancellations because Mortimer had bet club owner Jack Entratter $500 that he wouldn't show again.) Mortimer, who described Sinatra's fans as "imbecilic, moronic, screaming-meemie autograph kids," was also the primary source of unconfirmed reports in a dossier the FBI compiled on him. Sinatra, aware of this, threatened Mortimer with violence, and considered planting stories that he was gay (Morti-mer's FBI contact, Clyde Tolson, was rumored to be FBI chief J. Edgar Hoover's lover). On April 8, 1947, Sinatra saw Mortimer at Ciro's, an exclusive Hollywood nightclub, and accosted him as he left. Calling Mortimer "a fucking homosexual," he punched him, and continued to slug away as two of Sinatra's bodyguards held the writer down. "Next time I see you, I'll kill you, you degenerate!" he allegedly said. Mortimer had Sinatra arrested, and sued him for $25,000. Sinatra claimed Morti-mer had called him a "dago," but under pressure from MGM studio chief Louis B. Mayer, he retracted that allegation and settled out of court. Though he would later atone for the act by paying a visit to publisher William Randolph Hearst himself, Sinatra would be viewed for the rest of his life as a man prone to resort to violence when he felt he was crossed – a perception that would only be augmented in barely concealed incidents that would continue to surface in the media for decades to come.[31]

But Sinatra's biggest offense against a public he had so assiduously cultivated was probably his now-legendary love affair with Ava Gardner. Sinatra had married Nancy Barbato in 1939, and she had borne him a daughter the following year who figured prominently in shaping his public image as a husband and father. In truth, of course, Sinatra had never been a traditional family man, not only because a mid-century celebrity lifestyle largely foreclosed that possibility, but also because it was a more or less open secret that Sinatra was a notorious womanizer (in the memorable words of Dean Martin, "When Sinatra dies, they're giving his zipper to the Smithsonian").[32] For the most part, how-ever, Sinatra kept his sexual activity from the prying eyes of gossip columnists.

Ava Gardner, however, was different. By most accounts, she was truly the love of his life. Moreover, the thrice-married Gardner was something of a larger-than-life figure herself who was not always inclined to dis-cretion even when Sinatra was (there's a salty edge to her 1992 auto-biography that distinguishes it from the typical Hollywood memoir).[33] This is not the place for a detailed examination of their romance, not only because its highlights – which include abortions, possible suicide attempts, gunplay, and highly public temper tantrums – have been covered in detail elsewhere, but also because there are parts of it that can never (and probably *should* never) be known to anyone but the now-dead principals. Sinatra's relationship with Gardner matters here, how-ever, to the degree it affected the course of his career. In terms of his commercial power, that impact was largely negative. His long and highly publicized struggle to obtain a divorce from Nancy in the late 1940s, his short and stormy marriage to Gardner from 1951 to 1953, and his protracted and also highly public separation and divorce from Gardner from 1953 to 1955 all considerably damaged Sinatra's public image, and consolidated a view of him as a mercurial and irresponsible celebrity who simply rode roughshod over social rules most Americans felt compelled to honor. Perhaps only Ingrid Bergman, whose relationship with film director Roberto Rossellini scandalized the nation at around the same time, attracted more censure than Sinatra and Gardner did.

Ironically, however, Gardner may well have been the pivotal figure in rescuing Sinatra from a future of disdainful oblivion. By the time of their marriage she had far more cultural cachet than he did, thanks to her work in films like *The Snows of Kilimanjaro* (1952), *Mogambo* (1953), and *The Barefoot Contessa* (1954). A celebrated beauty in a Hollywood culture that took good looks for granted, she used that power to make studio executives want to keep her happy. When Sinatra learned a movie was going to be made from James Jones's 1951 novel *From Here to Eternity*, he began lobbying hard for the part of the defiant but doomed Angelo Maggio. Harry Cohn, head of Columbia Studios, which was making the movie, was initially unmoved by the prospect. But Gardner played a role in bringing him around. "You know who's right for that part of Maggio, don't you?" she told Cohn after finagling a dinner invitation with him. "That son-of-a-bitch husband of mine, that's who. If you don't give him this role, he'll kill himself." Cohn reluctantly agreed to a screen test, and asked Sinatra to "call off the dogs, and Ava too."[34]

He got the part in *From Here to Eternity*, which was released with great fanfare generally and for Sinatra specifically in late 1953. It proved to be a turning point, not only in Hollywood (where he won an Academy Award for Best Supporting Actor in 1954), but also in the music industry, where he had been wholly absent from the charts since 1951. From the mid-1950s on, Sinatra became a man "who took up permanent residence in his success," in the evocative words of John Lahr.[35] Occasionally, one could get glimpses of the ravaged figure Sinatra had been at his nadir in films like *Young At Heart* (1954), where he played a songwriter down on his luck, or in *The Man with the Golden Arm* (1955), in which he played a heroin addict with almost harrowing credibility. But for the most part, even that door would shut by the end of the 1950s, as his film work became ever more complacent, and his far more interesting music took on a more aggressively masculine edge. "When he was down and out, he was so sweet," Gardner said toward the end of their relationship. "But when he got back on top again, it was hell. Now that he's successful again, he's become his old arrogant self. We were happier when he was on the skids."[36]

Henceforth, Sinatra would play a man in control so effectively that it often seemed even he himself was convinced of his omnipotence. So it must have been all the more shocking when his friend Jack "Chicky Boy" Kennedy would teach him otherwise in that breezy way Sinatra himself, despite decades of trying, could never quite master.

> I think he solved it – whatever he was going through – by keeping it inside of him and filing it, putting it aside to use later in his art.
> – Sammy Davis, Jr. on Sinatra's fall and later comeback[37]

The most dramatic point in the history of an American Dream is not its moment of conception. Nor is it the moment of realization, or (as some might suppose) that moment *just before* it is realized. Rather, it is that essential moment of adversity when the attainability – or perhaps even worse, the legitimacy – of the Dream is called into serious question. It is at moments like these that the true costs of dreaming begin to come into focus: of energy not allocated to other purposes, of potential disappointment that has accumulated in direct proportion to hope. It is also the time when crucial questions – like the difference between growing up and giving up, between being admirably persistent and being dismayingly pathetic – become honestly confusing. You begin to find out (without really intending to ask, and without really wanting to find out) who you really are: a person of real, but limited, talent; a self-deceived poseur; someone of accomplishment whose achievements, as it turns out, are not as important as they seemed; or perhaps one happy with – and maybe even humbled by – success.

Confronted with such possibilities or realities, some will strike the tent of aspiration, wisely striking a bargain for what seems attainable. Others will hold out at least a while longer, insecure with the new knowledge that stakes are now higher than ever. Some will learn from their experiences, and others will descend into mindless self-destruction – like wielding a sledgehammer against concrete. The really amazing thing, though, is the way any person seems to remain capable of either in lives that, to invoke Sinatra's contemporary Yogi Berra, are never quite over until they're over.

When Sinatra entered Columbia Recording Studios on March 27, 1951, his career had just about bottomed out. The label hadn't dropped him yet, but the writing was on the wall. This was the period in his life when he was producing his most embarrassing work – a time when, in collaboration with Columbia executive Mitch Miller, he recorded novelty songs like "The Huckle Buck" and "Mamma Will Bark" that generated ridicule perhaps most vociferously from Sinatra himself.

And yet – as those who have examined Sinatra's work closely have long noted – mid-century was also a major artistic turning point in his career. In 1951, for example, Sinatra recorded "The Birth of the Blues," a remarkable musical snapshot that captured the fluidity of his youthful voice as well as the more assertive style that would characterize his Capitol work and more than compensate for any loss of vocal purity in the next decade. Confident yet melancholy, clearly patterned on the blues and yet bearing the stamp of his own inimitable style, "The Birth of the Blues" almost single-handedly illustrates the difference between Sinatra's commercial decline and artistic decline. Here, quite simply, is a hitless pop singer near the height of his powers.

In my mind, however, the actual summit was reached on this March night. Sinatra was reputedly miserable. His wife Nancy was refusing to give him a divorce, and a notably unsympathetic Gardner, who had a weakness for Spanish bullfighters, was making it clear to Sinatra that she would not wait indefinitely to get married. Interestingly, the song scheduled for the evening's session was one – the only one, in fact – for which Sinatra claimed a songwriting credit. It was called "I'm a Fool to Want you."[38]

To borrow a term of psychoanalysts, the tone of "I'm a Fool to Want You" was "overdetermined" before he ever sang a note. Arranger Alex Stordahl opened the song with dark, almost weeping strings, a mood augmented by haunting backup vocals. When Sinatra himself begins to sing, the emotion escalates even as the arrangement recedes; the intensity he brings to the words takes the feeling beyond heartsickness into bona fide grief. The death in question is not that of a relationship, but rather the self-respect of a man who hates himself for what he has become. Mere words can't express this loathing: you have to hear it to believe it. Although a composer and lyricist also worked on the song (and probably were the primary writers), it seems unusually apropos for Sinatra to receive songwriting credit for "Fool": his contribution is utterly unmistakable.

One of the more remarkable aspects of "Fool" is that it does not simply capture a powerful inner experience. It also charts a trajectory of emotion from resistance to capitulation. At first, the singer acknowledges that indulging his longing is counterproductive. But by the bridge of the song, there's a slippage between past and present, and it becomes increasingly clear that its lovelorn protagonist has not gotten over the relationship. In the end, he lapses into a capitulation made all the more awful for the self-knowledge that accompanies it: "Pity me: I need you." Never before and never again would Sinatra sing with the tremulous intensity that he sings these words – especially "need" – and the song ends with this character confessing that while he knows it's wrong, he simply can't go on without his lost love.

"Frank was worked up," Ben Barton, the head of his music company, later said. "So worked up he couldn't do more than one take. But that take was so tremendous it didn't need more than one."[39] Indeed, an emotionally overwrought Sinatra reputedly fled the studio that night.

It has been customary in (mostly brief) discussions of "I'm a Fool to Want You" to emphasize the obvious autobiographical dimensions of the song – as indeed I've done here. But such an approach, however valid and useful, also has the effect of obscuring the nature of Sinatra's achievement. The really striking thing about "Fool" is not that Sinatra was able to spontaneously express his pain in song (this underestimates the decades of applied passion and discipline that Sinatra brought to the studio that night). Nor is it that "Fool" is an especially intelligent or insightful piece of music (considered solely on the basis of lyrics or music in isolation, it would undoubtedly seem both melodramatic and trite).

Here's what's really great about the song – and, by extension, much of Sinatra's best music: a kind of emotional honesty that closes a gap between people. The protagonist of "Fool" has no lesson or advice to offer; indeed, the unresolved ending is part of what makes it so harrowing. And yet for reasons that aren't entirely clear, a powerfully rendered rendition of an inner life, even an anguished one, can bring comfort to those with whom it is shared: You are not alone. You are not alone in your feeling of deprivation, and perhaps more importantly, you are not alone in feeling foolish for wanting things you had no real right to expect, but could not help but want anyway. The best popular music makes the world a bigger place, not simply by validating common feelings (though that inevitably is what attracts most listeners), but also by illuminating an unseen community and tapping the wellsprings of empathy.

In short, Sinatra's performance in "I'm a Fool to Want You" is a profoundly creative act, one that falls more into the realm of character than personality. He took the pain of an unrealized longing and shaped it not only into an experience that could be shared, but one whose beauty transcends the pain that inheres in it. Maybe it isn't surprising that as Sinatra grew older, he seemed to become increasingly less interested in performing such productive work. Destroying things is sometimes an easier way to deal with frustration than making things.

So we probably shouldn't blame him for wielding that sledgehammer. It's enough that some of the time, anyway, he gave us a love that's there for others too.

Notes

1 Kitty Kelly, *His Way: The Unauthorized Biography of Frank Sinatra* (1986; New York: Bantam, 1987), p. 329. While Kelly is a problematic source whose accuracy and authority have been questioned in some quarters (particularly by partisans of Sinatra), the planning and subsequent cancellation of President Kennedy's visit to Frank Sinatra's house in Palm Springs is a staple of all major Sinatra biographies. The specific details vary, though all – with one exception – agree that the result was "a big Sinatra tantrum," in the words of a "longtime associate" quoted by J. Randy Taraborelli, *Sinatra: Behind the Legend* (New York: Birch Lane Press, 1997), p. 267. The exception is Nancy Sinatra, who, as usual, offers a less dramatic account in *Frank Sinatra: My Father* (1985; New York: Pocket Books, 1986). Yet even she acknowledges the event was "a disappointment in Dad's life" (p. 157). The sledgehammer incident is attributed to Jacobs, who personally witnessed it and later described it to Peter Lawford, the bearer of the bad news and the focus of Sinatra's rage in the aftermath of the affair. Lawford, in turn, was interviewed by Kelly in 1984. Regardless of which of these accounts are most credible, I believe all support the basic point I'm trying to make here: that by 1962, Frank Sinatra believed himself to be a man with virtually unlimited access to privilege in American life, and that he was deeply hurt when it became apparent that this was not the case. I use the sledgehammer to make this point because it seems so, well, poetically apt.
2 Sinatra, p. 155.
3 Though shrouded in controversy and misinformation – Judith Campbell Exner herself disavowed her 1977 memoir *My Story*, claiming fear of retribution – a basic Giancana–Campbell–Sinatra–Kennedy connection has now been largely accepted by those who have studied both Sinatra and Kennedy extensively. For a good brief overview of the matter, see Taraborelli, pp. 221–3.
4 For versions of this story from the Kennedys' perspective, see Peter Collier and David Horowitz, *The Kennedys: An American Drama* (New York: Summit Books, 1984), pp. 294–5 and Richard Reeves, *President Kennedy: Profile of Power* (New York: Simon & Schuster, 1993), pp. 292–3.
5 Taraborelli, pp. 267–8. "I tried several times to apologize for whatever it was that I had done to Frank, but he has not spoken to me for over twenty years," Peter Lawford told Kitty Kelly in 1983. "He wouldn't take my phone calls and wouldn't answer my letters. Wherever I saw him at a party or in a restaurant, he just cut me dead. Looked right though me with those cold blue eyes like I didn't exist." Lawford talked about the problem with Sinatra's daughter Tina, who encouraged him to keep trying, but to no avail (Kelly, p. 592).
6 Earl Wilson, *Sinatra: An Unauthorized Biography* (New York: Macmillan, 1976), pp. 171–2; Taraborelli, p. 268.
7 Taraborelli, p. 268.
8 Taraborelli, p. 267.
9 Sinatra held a fund-raiser for Martin Luther King in the early 1960s; his ties to Monaco stem from his friendship with (future princess) Grace Kelly, which took root during their work together in the 1956 film *High Society*.

10   Sinatra's 1944 meeting with Franklin Delano Roosevelt has been widely documented. For one such account, see Taraborelli, pp. 69–71.

11   John Lahr, *Sinatra: The Artist and the Man* (New York: Random House, 1997), p. 4.

12   Jack Long, "Sweet Dreams and Dynamite," *The American*, September 1943 (included in *Legend: Frank Sinatra and the American Dream*, ed. Ethlie Ann Vare [New York: Boulevard Books, 1995], p. 9).

13   Ibid., p. 13.

14   Roland Marchand, *Advertising and the American Dream: Making Way for Modernity, 1920–1940* (Berkeley: University of California Press, 1985) p. 3.

15   For more on the role of technology in housekeeping standards, see Susan Strasser, *Never Done: A History of American Housework* (New York: Pantheon, 1982).

16   Frederick Allen, *Only Yesterday: An Informal History of the 1920's* (1931; New York: Harper & Row, 1964), p. 81.

17   Sinatra, p. 13.

18   Dolly Sinatra quoted in Taraborelli, p. 23.

19   Dolly Sinatra quoted in Kelly, p. 45.

20   Quoted in Kelly, pp. 45–6.

21   Martha Weinman Lear, "The Bobby Sox Have Wilted, but the Memory Remains Fresh," *New York Times*, October 13, 1974, sec. 2, p. 12.

22   Bruce Bliven, "The Voice and the Kids," *The New Republic*, 6 November 1944, p. 593.

23   Quoted in Taraborelli, p. 55.

24   Quoted in Taraborelli, p. 56.

25   Quoted in Wilson, p. 117.

26   Taraborelli, p. 115.

27   Sinatra, p. 73. "I thought for a fleeting moment that the unexpected pantomime was a joke," Henderson is quoted by Kitty Kelly without attributing a source. "But then he caught my eye. I guess the color drained out of my face when I saw the panic in his" (Kelly, pp. 165–6).

28   Wilson, p. 77.

29   Quoted in Kelly, p. 168.

30   Kelly, p. 134.

31   Sinatra's assault on Mortimer has been widely recounted; I've relied principally on Wilson, pp. 69–76 and Taraborelli, pp. 92–5. Kitty Kelly based her knowledge of a Sinatra–Hearst meeting on an interview with Hearst's grandson John Hearst. See Kelly, pp. 139–40, 575. Years later, a drunken Sinatra found Mortimer's grave and urinated on it. See Lahr, p. 43.

32   Martin quoted in Wilson, p. 140.

33   Ava Gardner, *Ava: My Story* (New York: Bantam, 1992).

34   Sinatra, pp. 94–6; Taraborelli, p. 147.

35   Lahr, p. 52.

36   Gardner, quoted in Kelly, p. 225.

37   Davis, quoted in Sinatra, p. 91.

38   For factual background on "I'm a Fool to Want You," see Ed O'Brien with Robert Wilson, *Sinatra 101: The 101 Best Recordings and the Stories Behind Them* (New York: Boulevard Books, 1996), p. 33.

39   Arnold Shaw, *Sinatra: Twentieth Century Romantic* (New York: Holt, Rinehart & Winston, 1968), p. 145.

Consider the Source

1. Published in two volumes between 1835 and 1840, Alexis de Tocqueville's
Democracy in America has long been celebrated by students of American
history and culture as a uniquely shrewd – and often stunningly prescient –
analysis of US life. An aristocratic Frenchman, Tocqueville had come to the
United States in 1831 in an official government capacity to study the American
prison system along with his friend Gustave de Beaumont. What began as a
narrow sociological investigation, however, quickly became an extended med-
itation on the costs and benefits of American democracy, which Tocqueville
sensed would be a harbinger of changes that would soon sweep Europe as
well. To that end, he surveyed American geography, politics, manners, and
other subjects to see what lessons could be learned from the US experience.

The following extract comes from the second volume of *Democracy in
America,* which focuses on largely social dimensions of American life. Although
he never actually uses the term "American Dream" – it would apparently not
be coined until historian James Truslow Adams used it in his own 1931 book
The Epic of America – Tocqueville was clearly thinking of something like it. How
does he view the "restless" spirit of Americans? How does he explain their
"strange melancholy?" Do Tocqueville's observations accord with the portrait
of Sinatra drawn in this chapter? Do they accord with your own experience?
Why or why not?

"Why the Americans are so Restless in the
Midst of their Prosperity," from Vol. II of
Democracy in America by Alexis de Tocqueville
(1840)

In certain remote corners of the Old World you may still sometimes
stumble upon a small district that seems to have been forgotten amid the
general tumult, and to have remained stationary while everything around
it was in motion. The inhabitants, for the most part, are extremely
ignorant and poor; they take no part in the business of the country and
are frequently oppressed by the government, yet their countenances are
generally placid and their spirits light.

In America I saw the freest and most enlightened men placed in the
happiest circumstances that the world affords; it seemed to me as if a

cloud habitually hung upon their brow, and I thought them serious and almost sad, even in their pleasures.

The chief reason for this contrast is that the former do not think of the ills they endure, while the latter are forever brooding over advantages they do not possess. It is strange to see with what feverish ardor the Americans pursue their own welfare, and to watch the vague dread that constantly torments them lest they should not have chosen the shortest path which may lead to it.

A native of the United States clings to this world's goods as if he were certain never to die; and he is so hasty in grasping at all within his reach that one would suppose he was constantly afraid of not living long enough to enjoy them. He clutches everything, he holds nothing fast, but soon loosens his grasp to pursue fresh gratifications.

In the United States a man builds a house in which to spend his old age, and he sells it before the roof is on; he plants a garden and lets it just as the trees are coming into bearing; he brings a field into tillage and leaves other men to gather the crops; he embraces a profession and gives it up; he settles in a place, which he soon afterwards leaves to carry his changeable longings elsewhere. If his private affairs leave him any leisure, he instantly plunges into the vortex of politics; and if at the end of a year of unremitting labor he finds he has a few days' vacation, his eager curiosity whirls him over the vast extent of the United States, and he will travel fifteen hundred miles in a few days to shake off his happiness. Death at length overtakes him, but it is before he is weary of his bootless chase of that complete felicity which forever escapes him.

At first sight there is something surprising in this strange unrest of so many happy men, restless in the midst of abundance. The spectacle itself, however, is as old as the world; the novelty is to see a whole people furnish an exemplification of it.

Their taste for physical gratifications must be regarded as the original source of that secret disquietude which the actions of the Americans betray and of that inconstancy of which they daily afford fresh examples. He who has set his heart exclusively upon the pursuit of worldly welfare is always in a hurry, for he has but a limited time at his disposal to reach, to grasp, and to enjoy it. The recollection of the shortness of life is a constant spur to him. Besides the good things that he possesses, he every instant fancies a thousand others that death will prevent him from trying if he does not try them soon. This thought fills him with anxiety, fear, and regret and keeps his mind in ceaseless trepidation, which leads him perpetually to change his plans and his abode.

If in addition to the taste for physical well-being a social condition be added in which neither laws nor customs retain any person in his place, there is a great additional stimulant to this restlessness of temper. Men will then be seen continually to change their track for fear of missing the shortest cut to happiness.

It may readily be conceived that if men passionately bent upon physical gratifications desire eagerly, they are also easily discouraged; as their ultimate object is to enjoy, the means to reach that object must be prompt and easy or the trouble of acquiring the gratification would be greater than the gratification itself. Their prevailing frame of mind, then, is at once ardent and relaxed, violent and enervated. Death is often less dreaded by them than perseverance in continuous efforts to one end.

The equality of conditions leads by a still straighter road to several of the effects that I have here described. When all the privileges of birth and fortune are abolished, when all professions are accessible to all, and a man's own energies may place him at the top of any one of them, an easy and unbounded career seems open to his ambition and he will readily persuade himself that he is born to no common destinies. But this is an erroneous notion, which is corrected by daily experience. The same equality that allows every citizen to conceive these lofty hopes renders all the citizens less able to realize them; it circumscribes their powers on every side, while it gives freer scope to their desires. Not only are they themselves powerless, but they are met at every step by immense obstacles, which they did not at first perceive. They have swept away the privileges of some of their fellow creatures which stood in their way, but they have opened the door to universal competition; the barrier has changed its shape rather than its position. When men are nearly alike and all follow the same track, it is very difficult for any one individual to walk quickly and cleave a way through the dense throng that surrounds and presses on him. This constant strife between the inclination springing from the equality of condition and the means it supplies to satisfy them harasses and wearies the mind.

It is possible to conceive of men arrived at a degree of freedom that should completely content them; they would then enjoy their independence without anxiety and without impatience. But men will never establish any equality with which they can be contented. Whatever efforts a people may make, they will never succeed in reducing all the conditions of society to a perfect level; and even if they unhappily attained that absolute and complete equality of position, the inequality of minds would still remain, which, coming directly from the hand of God, will forever escape the laws of man. However democratic, then, the social state and the political constitution of a people may be, it is certain that every member of the community will always find out several points about him which overlook his own position; and we may foresee that his looks will be doggedly fixed in that direction. When inequality of conditions is the common law of society, the most marked inequalities do not strike the eye; when everything is nearly on the same level, the slightest are marked enough to hurt it. Hence the desire of equality always becomes more insatiable in proportion as equality is more complete.

Among democratic nations, men easily attain a certain equality of condition, but they can never attain as much as they desire. It perpetually retires from before them, yet without hiding itself from their sight, and in retiring draws them on. At every moment they think they are about to grasp it; it escapes at every moment from their hold. They are near enough to see its charms, but too far off to enjoy them; and before they have fully tasted its delights, they die.

To these causes must be attributed that strange melancholy which often haunts the inhabitants of democratic countries in the midst of their abundance, and that disgust at life which sometimes seizes upon them in the midst of calm and easy circumstances. Complaints are made in France that the number of suicides increases; in America suicide is rare, but insanity is said to be more common there than anywhere else. These are all different symptoms of the same disease. The Americans do not put an end to their lives, however disquieted they may be, because their religion forbids it; and among them materialism may be said hardly to exist, notwithstanding the general passion for physical gratification. The will resists, but reason frequently gives way.

In democratic times enjoyments are more intense than in the ages of aristocracy, and the number of those who partake in them is vastly larger: but, on the other hand, it must be admitted that man's hopes and desires are oftener blasted, the soul is more stricken and perturbed, and care itself more keen.

2.　Take a close look at the publicity photo of Frank Sinatra that opens this chapter. What specific components in this portrait do you find especially striking? Do you find him appealing? Can you imagine why hordes of teenage girls would?

3.　Before reading this essay, what impressions did you have of Frank Sinatra? Did it confirm or challenge those assumptions? Are there celebrities today you would compare with him? On what basis?

Suggested Further Reading

Frank Sinatra's life and work have been examined in great detail, and the notes to this chapter include many of the more important sources. Earl Wilson's

Sinatra (New York: Macmillan, 1976) is the first major biography, and Wilson was one of the few writers with long-term access to his mercurial subject. The personal authority of Nancy Sinatra's *Frank Sinatra: My Father* (New York: Pocket Books, 1986) is somewhat offset by its understandable bias. Like many of her books, Kitty Kelly's *His Way: The Unauthorized Biography of Frank Sinatra* (New York: Bantam, 1986) is highly controversial; extensively reported but incompletely documented, Kelly uncovers facts no other writer does, but devotes much more space to unflattering anecdotes than an evaluation of Sinatra's work. Much more appreciative is Pete Hamill's brief memoir/essay, *Why Sinatra Matters* (Boston: Little, Brown, 1998), an often insightful first-person account. Two edited collections, Ethlie Ann Vare's *Legend: Frank Sinatra and the American Dream* (New York: Boulevard, 1995) and (especially) Steven Petkov and Leonard Mustazza's *The Frank Sinatra Reader* (1995; New York: Oxford University Press, 1997) are compelling collections of primary sources such as reviews, profiles, and memoirs of Sinatra.

9
The Age of Television

1884	Invention of Nipkow disk by German engineer Paul Nipkow pioneers scanning of images
1927	American inventor Philo T. Farnsworth applies for key patents in early television technology
1939	Radio Corporation of America (RCA) demonstrates television at New York World's Fair
1941–5	World War II (television technology diverted to radar)
1945	Capture of German tape recorders at end of World War II paves way for alternative to live broadcasting
1950–4	*Your Show of Shows* airs, featuring the comedy of Carl Reiner and other comedians in variety-show format
1951	NBC launches *Today* show
1952	Dwight Eisenhower elected president (1953–61)
1954	Cold War "Red Scare" abates after Senator Joseph McCarthy appears on live television
1960	Kennedy–Nixon debates carried live on national television
1961	*The Dick Van Dyke Show* premieres
1963	Coverage of Kennedy assassination on television
1970s	Spread of cable television offers more programming options
1989–98	Network run of *Seinfeld*, perhaps the last sitcom with a broad national audience

Introduction

In the second half of the twentieth century, television broadcasting was the supreme medium in popular culture. Its reach was virtually universal, and it demonstrated a resilient capacity to both encompass and extend its predecessors, from its transformation of vaudeville into the variety show in the

1950s to its integration with rock-and-roll in the rise of music video in the 1980s. While there are signs that its primacy is waning (a splintered audience amid the proliferation of ever more specialized channels; the challenge posed by the Internet), at the start of the twenty-first century television broadcasting remains the closest thing we have to a center in the sprawling world of popular culture.

Television's immediate roots lie in radio. Unlike with radio, however, there was relatively little confusion about how television would be used, and the victory of commercial interests in radio gave those interests an insuperable advantage in shaping this newer form of broadcasting. As early as the 1920s, key figures at radio networks – like David Sarnoff, the former telegraph operator and eventual NBC president – were imagining picture shows beamed to American homes and paid for by advertising.

This future, however, took a while to arrive. The usual wrangling over patents and financing that characterized earlier media also marked the rise of television. The American government, meanwhile, was concerned about the interlocking interests of RCA, GE, Westinghouse and AT&T, and the Justice Department brokered a 1933 arrangement that broke up their direct collaboration (a similar intervention in 1941 resulted in NBC divesting itself of some holdings to create the American Broadcasting Company, or ABC). Television was further delayed by the advent of World War II, when many of the people who worked on it were channeled into working on radar technology instead. The gathering momentum of television-set manufacturing and television-station licensing was again disrupted in the early 1950s, when interference problems and the outbreak of the Korean War led the government to suspend further licensing. Not until the mid-1950s did the new medium finally attain critical mass.

When it did, its impact was tremendous. Seemingly overnight, television went from a technological novelty to an essential household staple. Even the poorest Americans eventually had television sets, and virtually everyone indulged in speculation about the ways the new medium would utterly change American life forever.

Television also had a dramatic impact on other media. Movie attendance dropped precipitously in the 1950s, and nervous Hollywood studios focused their energy on huge epic extravaganzas to provide a sense of spectacle television could not. (This strategy remains in place, though movie executives softened their early hostility to television once they realized they could sell broadcast rights to old films at a huge profit.) Radio, which had been a staple of American households, changed its focus away from expensive live entertainment to recorded music and news that could be heard in the car or at work. And print journalism became more specialized and localized as pictures – which, beginning in the late 1950s, could be recorded on various kinds of videotape – increasingly took the place of thousands of words.

Television soon became the repository of a series of popular culture genres (and the target of criticism such genres had always received, intensified by complaints about the blandness that typically resulted when attempting to appeal to an extremely broad national audience). Westerns, science fiction, soap operas and other kinds of programming, many of which originated on radio, soon filled the airwaves. One kind of show, however, was notable not only for its durable appeal, but also in the way it became established in the popular mind as the particular province of television: the situation comedy, or "sitcom." Sitcoms, which derived from old radio serials like the wildly popular *Amos 'n' Andy*, can be defined as regularly scheduled shows that feature ongoing characters rooted in a particular setting (like a suburban home). Usually slotted into 30-minute segments that allocated 8 minutes for commercials, theme music, and credits, these light dramas proved endlessly adaptable in reflecting the warp and woof of contemporary American life, from the domesticated sentimentality *of The Adventures of Ozzie and Harriet* (1952–66), to the arch urbanity of *Seinfeld* (1989–98).

In this chapter from his 1989 book *Comic Visions: Television Comedy and American Culture*, television historian David Marc explores the high tide of the sitcom (and television, and, for that matter, the United States itself) by taking a close look at *The Dick Van Dyke Show* (1961–6) and its broader cultural context. For Marc, sitcoms generally and this sitcom in particular are revealing – if distorted – mirrors of our national life. Viewed casually from the perspective of 40 years later, the suburban idyll of the show's two main characters, Rob and Laura Petrie, seems almost exotic in its simplicity, even naïveté, about ethnicity, sexuality, and class. But, as Marc suggests, the show documents a series of struggles and compromises that are by no means unknown in our own time.

The Making of the Sitcom, 1961

David Marc

I was driving my car downtown from New Rochelle, wondering what grounds do I stand on that no one else stands on? I thought I am an actor and writer who worked on the Sid Caesar shows.

– Carl Reiner[1]

I don't want to be an artist; I'm a good writer.

– "Rob Petrie"[2]

Any discussion of the American transmogrification of *la condition humaine* into consumer lifestyle could do worse than to begin with an examination of *The Dick Van Dyke Show*. In terms of the evolution of prime time, the show's portrayal of suburban life in the Northeast

On with the show   Dick Van Dyke (standing), Morey Amsterdam, and Rose Marie of the *Dick Van Dyke Show* at work producing comedy for television (note the set in the foreground). The sitcom was the brainchild of Carl Reiner, who brought the medium into new terrain by effacing the line between home and work – as well as fiction and reality. *Photo by permission of Michael Ochs Archive, Venice, California*

Corridor bridges the gap between the idealized We Like Ike nuclear family homeownership epics of the fifties (*Father Knows Best, The Stu Erwin Show, Leave It to Beaver*) and the stagflation-era designer social comedies of the seventies, such as the Norman Lear and MTM productions. Since completing its five-year CBS production run in 1966, *Dick Van Dyke* has proven itself to be what the syndication industry likes to call an "evergreen," having achieved continuous play in many important markets, both in the United States and around the non-Communist world. Moreover, it is perhaps the only emphatically New Frontier sitcom ever produced by television – a domestic video wall painting of those politically ebullient thousand days.

In the early sixties, television was coming into its own as an oracle supplying narrative continuity to even the most preposterous of situations. John F. Kennedy, the handsome instant New World aristocrat, and Nikita Khrushchev, the pithy proletarianized Old World peasant, were an iconic diplomatic dynamic duo, the likes of which has not since presided over the lives of the viewing audience. Both superpower button men were well made for television, carrying mythic baggage laden with elements of action-adventure, romance, and comedy. Here were the living precipitates of a century of Western politics: representing capitalism, a prince of an immigrant Boston dynasty with roots in urban ward-heeling and Prohibition; and in the corner to the left, a pauper who had lent a hand in the overthrow of the Romanovs, fought the Nazis in Kiev, denounced the cult of the personality before the Twentieth Party Congress, and lived to tell the tales with relish.

Neither head of state was camera shy. World-class adventurers who were not reluctant to exploit their triumphant, even grandiose personalities, each in his own way savored the unprecedented opportunities afforded by television for intimate mass exposure. The dashing young senator from Massachusetts appeared as Edward R. Murrow's guest star on *Person to Person*, accepting compliments from his future US Information Agency director on the charm of his Boston apartment, the graciousness of his New York wife, and (though the term had yet to leap forth from psychology textbooks into television discourse) his entire "lifestyle."[3] Khrushchev, in New York to attend the opening of the fifteenth session of the United Nations General Assembly, went uptown, the world press in tow, to take a lunch with Fidel Castro at the Hotel Theresa in Harlem. With dozens of international leaders present – Eisenhower, Nehru, Nkrumah, Tito, to name just a few – he stole the show at the United Nations by taking off his shoe and banging it on the desk in spontaneous protest of capitalist–imperialist propaganda (a breach of parliamentary procedure for which the Soviets would be slapped with a $10,000 fine by Secretary-General Dag Hammarskjöld).[4]

The News had only recently become important enough to rate a daily coast-to-coast half-hour at suppertime and the two superpower leaders stood behind events – Harvard and the Ukraine, touch football and tractors, proto-Mr. Goodbar and bald, fat grandpa – as the compellingly colorful players in what had mushroomed into the postmodern multi-media contest of world affairs. They battled. They compromised. They closed missile gaps. They engaged in cultural exchange. They sought "peaceful coexistence." Their dueling images offered a bonus of heightened intensity to those viewers brave enough or mad enough to notice the stakes.

Ironically, this colorful cold-war programming met with early and abrupt cancellation. *The Dick Van Dyke Show* was barely into its third season in prime time when Kennedy was murdered under circumstances still not fully clear to the public; less than a year later Khrushchev was unceremoniously issued a one-way ticket to Palookagrad by a Central Committee not amused to see Lenin's heir struggling with the West to gain entry into Disneyland. "JFK" and "K," as New York *Daily News* headlines had once so familiarly called this unlikely pair of hundred-megaton godfathers, gradually achieved the distance of "slain President John F. Kennedy" and "former Soviet Premier Nikita Khrushchev," fading from daily electric screen life into the sanctity of history books. By the end of the decade, the magic had faded to the grim political five o'clock shadows of Nixon and Brezhnev.

Carl Reiner, the *The Dick Van Dyke Show*'s creator, was still hard at work on his as yet unsold sitcom even as the hatless Kennedy was swearing allegiance to the US Constitution on Earl Warren's Bible, an event carried simultaneously by all three networks. A survivor of the "golden age" of live TV comedy-variety, Reiner had worked for Sid Caesar as both on-screen second banana and uncredited staff writer during most of the 1950s. Reiner's new show, his first effort at series authorship, was a timely swan song for the dying genre in which he – and others, including Woody Allen, Neil Simon, and Larry Gelbart – had made their professional marks. In this and several ways *The Dick Van Dyke Show* is a revealing use of network television as a medium of personal expression; its autobiographical depth rivals that of [Jackie] Gleason's *Honeymooners*.

A native of the Bronx, Carl Reiner was not an unfamiliar face in America during the pioneer years of network telecasts. His prime-time acting credits can be traced back as far as 1948, when he played the role of a comic photographer in ABC's *The Fashion Story*, an obscure experimental sitcom set each week in the context of a fashion show (an idea that would lie dormant for over thirty-five years before turning up again as an eighties action-adventure concept in such series as *Cover Up* and

Miami Vice). He became best known, however, for his sketch performances as a regular member of Caesar's comedy-variety repertory troupes
on *Your Show of Shows* (NBC, 1950–4), *Caesar's Hour* (NBC, 1954–7),
and *Sid Caesar Invites You* (ABC, 1958).

Like Caesar, Reiner was a second-generation upwardly mobile
Westchester homeowner with a consciousness minted in a Jewish New
York City Depression childhood.[5] Members of what Jimmy Breslin
would one day call "the bridge and tunnel crowd," both artists had
crossed the river to take up their show-business vocations in the fabled
midtown Manhattan culture complex. In *A Walker in the City*, Alfred
Kazin explores the psychosocial distance between neighborhood life in
the boroughs of New York and cosmopolitan engagement in Manhattan.
But Carl Reiner, Neil Simon, Mel Brooks, Selma Diamond, and the
other hungry young writers who had come to early television from the
Bronx and Brooklyn triangularized this mythic geography to a third
point, a place, perhaps, of less interest to the Irving Howe crowd – the
affluent bedroom town on the parkway several exits beyond the last stop
of the subway. The ongoing blackout sketches that Caesar performed
with Imogene Coca (and later Nanette Fabray), Howard Morris, and
Reiner – minidomesticoms with titles such as "The Hickenloopers" and
"The Commuters" – exploited the self-amused peccadilloes of emerging
alrightnik culture in post-World War II America: dented fenders, forgotten anniversaries, wives with charge accounts, impossible in-laws, the
darned plumbing, and so on. If there could be no poetry after Auschwitz,
there could at least be New Rochelle.[6]

Though comedy-variety stars such as Caesar, Milton Berle, Martha
Raye, Jack Carter, and Jackie Gleason are often credited with having sold
many American families their first TV sets during the wonder years of
video, the comedy-variety show was already withering on the vine as the
fifties drew to a close. As early as 1957–8, not a single example of such
programming could be found in Nielsen's Top Ten, even as the Western
(enjoying what proved to be its own brief moment in the sun) placed five
programs in the charmed circle that season. With the television audience
now roughly equivalent to the population at large, the economic stakes
of prime-time telecast had suddenly risen steeply and no top was in sight.
The ad agencies became increasingly anxious to assert quality control
over the TV product. Spontaneity and uniqueness of occasion and
performance – precisely those qualities that were potentially most satisfying in a comedy-variety show – came to be viewed as liabilities. Seed
money was attracted by the rationalized system of film production. In
terms of comedy, that meant the sitcom.

The mighty fell quickly: the 1957–8 season was the first of the decade
to open without Sid Caesar on the prime-time schedule. Let go by NBC,

the desperate star went hat in hand to ABC and made a deal with the last-place network for a new, live Sunday night show – a stubborn attempt to retain the purity of the genre within the limits of a half-hour (*Your Show of Shows* had run ninety minutes in prime time). Furthermore, the revival would reunite Caesar in comedy blackout sketch performance with Imogene Coca, his original costar from *Your Show of Shows*, whose own career had also suffered in the comedy-variety crash.[7] With as much fanfare as ABC could muster, *Sid Caesar Invites You* premiered as a midseason replacement in January 1958; it was canceled, however, after only thirteen weeks, unable to outpoint the anthology dramas of *General Electric Theater with Ronald Reagan* in the 9 P.M. time slot.

Milton Berle – "Mr. Television" – who had signed a thirty-year contract with NBC in 1951, found himself earning his keep as host of *Jackpot Bowling* for the network in 1960. His 1974 autobiography contains bitter reflections on the death of the genre that had helped make both Berle and TV household items: "Seven solid years of live television when it was really live, seven years of going seven days a week trying to make each week's show better, bigger, and funnier than the week before – and for what? To end up axed, out.... I was really working my way down to the depths."[8]

Berle was not the only comedy-variety Brahmin headed for a game-show mike. Jackie Gleason, whose comedy-variety hour was cut in half by CBS in 1957–8 and then canceled altogether at the end of the season, left television completely to try his hand at Hollywood movies for the next several years. When the "Great One" attempted a grand return to CBS prime time in 1961, it was as the emcee of *You're in the Picture*, a game show, which in spectacular Gleason style flopped after a single telecast. Similarly, Ernie Kovacs, who had hosted game shows for Dumont [an early television network] before achieving critical acclaim as commercial television's greatest comedy-variety artist, found himself back in the moderator's chair as host of *Take a Good Look* (ABC, 1959–61).

Even an injection of promising new talent could not revive the genre. Bob Newhart's comedy album *The Button-Down Mind of Bob Newhart* had made him the hottest young stand-up in America in 1960. Described by the New York *Times* that summer as a "rising young comedian who specializes in satire,"[9] Newhart was essentially a monologist who preferred sitting on a stool with an imaginary telephone in his hand (in the style of Shelley Berman or Mort Sahl) to running around on a vaudeville set with a seltzer bottle. The comedian had won network interest by stealing the 1959 *Emmy Awards Show* with his takeoff on an officious TV director going through a dry run of Khrushchev's arrival in the United States. CBS approached Newhart first, hoping to bolster its weak Thursday evening schedule with a fresh face. The network, however, dropped out at the last minute. Its reasoning offers a glimpse at how low confidence had fallen in comedy-variety. Lee Rich, who had been engineering the CBS deal for Benton and Bowles, explained, "Considering the time period we had lined up for the show [it would have faced *The Untouchables* and *You Bet Your Life with Groucho Marx*], we reconsidered and decided not to take the risk."[10]

NBC, the network that had traditionally been most closely associated with comedy-variety, took a more optimistic view. Perhaps, it was thought, this type of program could rebound in the hands of a relatively sophisticated humorist who might attract a new viewership. But *The Bob Newhart Show*, premiering in the fall of 1961, went nowhere. It was quietly canceled at the end of its first season, losing out in the ratings to representational dramas (*Naked City* and *The U.S. Steel Hour*) on the other two networks. Newhart disappeared from national television, only to reemerge twenty years later as a sitcom star. With the failure of the Newhart show, the handwriting was on the wall for comedy-variety. Except for a few hangers-on – most notably Red Skelton – the presentational showcases enjoyed by the pioneer comedians had pretty much become a thing of the past. The few hours of comedy-variety left in prime-time passed into the painfully mellow hands of singers such as Andy Williams and Perry Como.

By the turn of the decade, the prime-time network game show seemed to be the last refuge for a comedian who wished to work on national television without donning the mask of a sitcom character. The model for success in this now extinct genre was clearly Groucho Marx's *You Bet Your Life*. Though billed as a quiz show, the program was a thinly disguised talking-heads vehicle for the comedian's talents as a witty raconteur, a talk show that eschewed the pretense of being one. In terms of production control, *You Bet Your Life* was filmed in sixty-minute sessions and then edited down to thirty-minute episodes, affording a greater degree of quality control than could be exercised over live comedy-variety.[11] Though Groucho was apparently at liberty to go after the incredible collection of Southern California wild life that took the stage as quiz-show contestants on *You Bet Your Life*, any remarks that violated network, agency, or sponsor sensibility could be put to rest on the cutting-room floor, just as in a sitcom. Groucho had synthesized the talk show and the quiz show, much as Jack Benny had synthesized the sitcom and the comedy-variety show. *You Bet Your Life* had been a consistent ratings winner for NBC television since 1950, when it had crossed over from network radio.

In the fall of 1958, thirty-five-year-old Carl Reiner had read the situation accurately and was ready to make a career move. Like Berle,

Gleason, and Kovacs, he turned first to the prime-time game show, replacing Monty Hall as the host of a CBS series, *Keep Talking*: "The players . . . were divided into two teams of three each. The emcee gave each player a different secret phrase, which the player was then required to incorporate into a story. After the phrase had been used the emcee would stop the story and ask the other team what the phrase was."[12] The show was one of several attempts to rehabilitate the scandal-tainted quiz-show genre as a celebrity parlor game which was so much fun to watch that the audience would fail to notice that no cash prizes were on the line. Regulars included Elaine May, Joey Bishop, Peggy Cass, Paul Winchell, and Morey Amsterdam. In less than a year, however, Reiner was himself replaced by the rapidly ascending Merv Griffin.

That same year, Reiner also completed *Enter Laughing*, a nostalgic autobiographical coming-of-age-in-the-city novel. David Kokolowitz, Reiner's innocent, idealistic first-person narrator, is an apprentice sewing-machine repairman living with his parents in a Bronx apartment. The action focuses on his effort to transform himself into Don Coleman, sophisticated Manhattanite and Broadway actor. Early in the story, after a seemingly disastrous audition, the hapless though politically prescient Kokolowitz comments, "As I left the Lyric Theater, I felt that my chances of [getting the part] were as slim as my chance of becoming the first non-Protestant President of the United States."[13] The novel was adapted for the Broadway stage by Joseph Stein in 1963 and Reiner himself directed a 1967 film version.

But Reiner's cash project in the period immediately following the demise of TV comedy-variety was a situation comedy that he had been developing under the working title of "Head of the Family." Whereas *Enter Laughing* had been a memoir of Bronx adolescence dissolving into Manhattan worldliness, Reiner would build the fictive order of the new sitcom from his experience as a Manhattan artist seeking to establish adult mainstream assimilated domesticity in New Rochelle. The autobiographical roots of the work were clear: the author had cast himself in the lead role of Rob Petrie, head staff writer for a live New York comedy-variety show titled (at that point) "The Alan Sturdy Show."[14] The name "Sturdy" was an anglicized compromise of the Yiddish word *Shtarker* ("big bruiser"), a reference to the six-foot, two-inch Sid Caesar, a man who, in Mel Brooks's words, "was considered a giant among Jews." Rob would be married to a former dancer who had given up her career as an artist to be his wife; Reiner was in fact married to a former painter. The Petries would have a son; the Reiners had a son (Rob Reiner, who grew up to play Meathead in *All in the Family*). The Petries would live at 448 Bonnie Meadow Road in New Rochelle; the Reiners lived at number 48. The narrative line, like the sitcom auteur, would commute between the mythic poles of downtown show biz and winding-lane family life. "It was actually what my wife and I were doing," recalls Reiner.[15]

The comic relationship of stage and hearth was, of course, nothing new in American culture. It provided, for example, the narrative framework that tied together the song-and-dance numbers of the Judy Garland–Mickey Rooney musicals directed by Busby Berkeley in the thirties and forties. In terms of television situation comedy, the "show-biz family" had always been a strong subgenre. Burns and Allen refused to distinguish between home and theater; their home was a theater. Danny Thomas and Desi Arnaz had masked themselves as Danny Williams and Ricky Ricardo, professional nightclub entertainers, which, in fact, both had been before transforming themselves into sitcom stars. Chief, perhaps, among the advantages of building a storyline on this premise was that it allowed presentational forms of entertainment – singing, dancing, even stand-up comedy – to be worked into the episodes of otherwise representational programs: a Cuban number for Ricky, a ballad for Danny, a few yarns for George.

In *The Adventures of Ozzie and Harriet* show biz and middle-class family life were revealed as emphatically compatible. Ozzie Nelson's duties as a bandleader made so few demands upon him that he was left free virtually twenty-four hours a day to play golf, improve the house, and otherwise cultivate himself as a source of ethical inspiration for his wife and children. His son Rick's budding career as a rock-and-roll singer was encouraged as a positive opportunity for both Rick and the family, even though rock-and-roll in the 1950s still had a long way to go before achieving the status of American family music. As portrayed by the Nelsons in *Ozzie and Harriet*, there was indeed no business like show business.

In *I Love Lucy*, however, the relationship is not quite so congenial. Lucy was frankly jealous of Ricky's show-biz career. The Ricardos lived in the East Sixties in a residential neighborhood that was close enough to the midtown entertainment world so that Lucy could get over to the Tropicana quickly. However, the nightclub is territory verboten to wife Lucy by her bandleader husband. She plots and schemes to find a way out of her drab routine domestic life and into one of Ricky's "shows." With her friends the Mertzes, retired vaudevillians who own the apartment building and who themselves yearn for the roar of the greasepaint, Lucy is often stuck at home for most of an episode, emerging only in the climatic segment to sneak onto the stage of the Tropicana for the grand finale. Even though she is funny – to both the on-screen nightclub audience and the television viewer – her attempt to cross over from neighborhood (urban provincial) life into the cosmopolitan world of show business is revealed as both ridiculous and futile. She is funny, but incompetence is the source of her humor. The audience, which watches television and knows professional entertainment when it sees it, laughs at Lucy Ricardo, not with her: she sings in an opera sketch with a horrendous voice. She dances in a bebop routine with a crazed jitterbug who throws her all over the stage like a sack of potatoes. She gets stage fright and forgets her lines. As the episode ends she is, in quick order, reminded of her rightful place, forgiven by her exasperated but loving husband, and sent back to Little Ricky and the roast.

In "Head of the Family," however, Reiner would tap his own memory to strive for a new autobiographically based realism that would eschew the fantastic extremes of the Nelsons and the Ricardos. "I was examining my life and putting it down on paper," Reiner claims. He was trying to create "the first situation comedy where you saw where the man worked *before* he walked in and said, 'Hi, honey, I'm home!' "[16] The fact that the place where the man worked happened to be a network television production company seemed perfectly normal to Reiner, who had spent over a decade doing just that. The paradigms of Reiner's life – ethnicity and assimilation, urbanity and suburbanity, presentationalism and representationalism – would be the mythic resources from which the show would be refined.

Reiner's dedication to "Head of the Family" led him past the conventional wisdom that guides TV show creators: instead of completing just a pilot script, he went ahead and – with no money or guarantee of any kind – wrote scripts for thirteen series episodes. "This would be a nucleus, a bible, for anybody who would help write it after that. It would guard against supposition; everything would be spelled out."[17] Clearly, the author was envisioning more than syndication residuals.

Harry Kalcheim, Reiner's agent, took the material to Peter Lawford, the "Rat Pack" film actor who was then attempting to establish himself as a television producer. Lawford was the husband of Patricia Kennedy, the sister of Senator John F. Kennedy, who was at that moment neck deep in his race for the US presidency. Joseph P. Kennedy, the patriarch of the clan, was keeping close watch over all activities of family members during this crucial period. He demanded to read the sitcom script before sanctioning Kennedy involvement. "Everything the Kennedy money went into had to be approved by him," recalls Reiner.[18] After a weekend of careful study at the family's Hyannis Port retreat, the elder Kennedy gave the venture a resounding thumbs-up. He was so enthusiastic about "Head of the Family" that he not only granted the go-ahead to Lawford, but agreed to personally finance the production of the pilot.

Kennedy, of course, was no stranger to the mass-entertainment industry, having been deeply involved in Hollywood during the interwar years. He had owned FBO, a major distributing company, and for a time he had even served as chairman of the board of the Keith-Albee-Orpheum theater chain. Kennedy had also had his share of experience playing the angel. In 1925 he had personally backed his intimate friend Gloria Swanson in the ill-fated *Queen Kelly*, a nonstudio production directed by the difficult Erich von Stroheim. Though costs ran in excess of $1 million (mostly out of Kennedy's pocket), the film was never released in the United States.[19]

On July 19, 1960, the pilot episode of "Head of the Family" appeared on *Comedy Spot*, a "Failure Theatre" summer replacement anthology series that CBS was using to showcase would-be sitcoms.[20] On the strength of Reiner's reputation, the New York *Times* placed a star next to its listing of the show, denoting "a program of unusual interest" (the network competition consisted of *Arthur Murray's Dance Party* and *Colt. 45*). The dramatis personae, especially Rob's colleagues at the office, had a decidedly New York flavor: Rob Petrie (Carl Reiner), Laura Petrie (Barbara Britton), Ritchie (Gary Morgan), Sally Rogers (Sylvia Miles), Buddy Sorrell (Morty Gunty), and Alan Sturdy (Jack Wakefield).

In *Watching TV*, a season-by-season history of American television, Harry Castleman and Walter Podrazik describe the "Head of the Family" pilot: "Petrie and his wife Laura had to convince their son Ritchie that his father's job was as interesting and important as those of the other kids' fathers. To prove his point, Rob brought Ritchie to the office to see firsthand how valuable he was.... The format seemed workable, the cast adequate, and the writing mildly clever."[21]

Though there was some sponsor interest, the series was not picked up by CBS. For one thing, situation comedy seemed to be in eclipse in 1960. Only one new sitcom had premièred during the 1959–60 season, *Love and Marriage*, which starred William Demarest as an aging music publisher who hated rock and roll and had little patience for his hipper-than-thou son-in-law and partner. NBC canceled it almost immediately. Westerns were the hot properties as the election of 1960 rolled around, with *Gunsmoke*, *Wagon Train*, and *Have Gun, Will Travel* finishing win, place, and show in the Nielsen Top Ten for two consecutive seasons. Reiner fully believed that "Head of the Family" had died a quiet death in a bad sitcom market.

Kalcheim, however, was not so sure. In September 1960 he persuaded Reiner to meet with another of his clients, Sheldon Leonard. Though a fellow New York Jew, Leonard had followed a different path into show business. A theater graduate of Syracuse University, Leonard first found a career in B movies in the forties as a stock

Runyonesque gangster heavy, but then jumped to the production end in the television era, where he achieved phenomenal success. In 1953 he had joined Danny Thomas's production company as executive producer of *Make Room for Daddy* (later retitled *The Danny Thomas Show*) and the show had been running ever since. More recently, he had sold a new sitcom to CBS, *The Andy Griffith Show*, which was set for a fall 1960 premier.

The Reiner–Leonard relationship was that of student to mentor. Leonard tutored Reiner in the fine points of cranking out situation comedy (as opposed to comedy-variety), giving him license to roam the Thomas production facilities and observe the day-to-day operations of making a narrative TV series. Asked for his opinion on the all-but-moribund "Head of the Family" pilot, Leonard remembers being "torn between a desire to be helpfully honest and a desire to be tactful. . . . The only thing I could say was 'Carl, you're not right for what you wrote for yourself.' I believe that if recast, the show would have every chance of making it. Do you mind if I try to rewrap the package?"[22] After some initial reluctance, Reiner accepted this judgment and Leonard was hired to direct a new pilot.

The shortlist of candidates to replace Reiner in the role of Rob Petrie consisted of two thirty-five-year-old nationally familiar (but not yet star) performers, both midwesterners by birth: Johnny Carson and Dick Van Dyke. The Iowa-born, Nebraska-bred Carson had been a television personality since 1951, when he had hosted *Carson's Cellar*, a local Los Angeles satire program in which the comedian riffed on the day's head-lines, much as he would in his *Tonight Show* monologues years later. The show drew the attention of several West Coast comedy giants, including Red Skelton and Groucho Marx, both of whom willingly appeared as unpaid guests to help out the young comedian. In 1953, Skelton gave Carson his big break, hiring him to write the stand-up monologues with which he opened his weekly CBS show; in less than two years, the network decided to try Carson in a comedy-variety hour of his own. Johnny, however, proved not ready for prime time. The only TV series ever actually titled *The Johnny Carson Show* was dumped at the end of its first season. As Reiner and Leonard began their search for a new Rob Petrie, Carson was biding his time, building an "F Score" with the daytime audience as host of the game show *Who Do You Trust?* (formerly *Do You Trust Your Wife?*) on ABC.[23]

Dick Van Dyke seemed, on paper, the underdog in the competition. A native of West Plains, Missouri, he had started out in the forties by opening his own advertising agency in Danville, Illinois. Moving over to the performance end of the business, he gradually built a prime-time resumé that offers an eclectic panorama of 1950s television: a summer as host of *CBS Cartoon Theater starring Heckle and Jeckle*; a season as a regular on Mike Stokey's *Pantomime Quiz*; a dramatic role opposite George C. Scott on *The U. S. Steel Hour*; two guest spots as a hillbilly private on *The Phil Silvers Show*; and a brief stint as comic relief on *The Andy Williams Show*. TV stardom, however, eluded Van Dyke. Unable to find a suitable format in television for his considerable talents as a physical comedian, he turned his efforts away from the medium in 1959 and scored a tremendous smash on Broadway in the musical comedy *Bye Bye, Birdie*.

Leonard, however, strongly favored the gangly, pratfalling Van Dyke to the mesomorphic, wisecracking Carson, despite Johnny's greater public recognition factor. He had envisioned Rob Petrie as the kind of guy who is not "too glamorous to be sharing your living room with,"[24] and following this logic, Carson's relative fame worked against him; the newer the face, the better, as far as Leonard was concerned. He had also imagined Rob as someone who "doesn't want to get up in front of an audience, but who can perform in a room at a party."[25] In this respect, Van Dyke's proven abilities in musical comedy offered distinct advantages for the presentation of nonnarrative performance art in what amounted to a backstage sitcom. While Carson could do stand-up, some yeoman's party magic, and a bit of ventriloquism, Van Dyke could sing, dance, do pantomime, and play broad slapstick. Leonard sent Reiner to New York to see *Bye Bye, Birdie*, and the issue was settled. Van Dyke received permission from his Broadway producer for time off to go to the West Coast and shoot the pilot.

As Sheldon Leonard had predicted, the cast change proved to be the key to getting the series on the air. But the significance of recasting Rob Petrie from a Bronx-born Jew to a heartland gentile surely could not have been lost on an author who had so self-consciously set out to produce an autobiographical work. Carl Reiner had never worn his Jewishness on his sleeve. He had in fact played the ethnically nondescript "interviewer" of Sid Caesar's "German Professor" on many occasions. The low-key (assimilated?) nature of his style can be seen perhaps most plainly when Reiner performs with the hyperactive Mel Brooks. On *The 2000-Year-Old Man* record albums (which contain not only the title cuts, but a wide variety of sketches) Reiner characteristically plays the "American" straightman to Mel Brooks's howling ghetto *mishuganeh*.

By what logic had Leonard come to the conclusion that "if recast, the show would have every chance of making it?" After ten years in front of the camera, Reiner's competence as a television performer could not have been the issue. Was there an unspoken agenda to the change in personnel? It has been suggested that Berle and Caesar in particular had proved "too Jewish" for the vastly expanded television audience of 1960.

Was Leonard's new plan to sell "Head of the Family" based on the WASPing of Rob Petrie?

As the series unfolded it was obvious that Rob's background had been thoroughly reimagined to reflect the life of the actor who now played the role. In flashback episodes, we learn that the comedy writer is a native of Danville, Illinois;[26] that he met Laura, a dancer with a USO troupe, while serving in the army; that Rob and Laura lived as newlyweds in Joplin, Missouri, before moving to New York. Whereas in "Head of the Family," the Rob character had played a Carl Reiner to the Buddy character's Mel Brooks, in *The Dick Van Dyke Show*, the relationship was removed one more level: Rob played the Middle American to Buddy's Jewish New Yorker.

The transformations in ethnic cosmology brought about by Van Dyke's assumption of the lead role is a subject that has apparently never been broached in print. In *The Dick Van Dyke Show: Anatomy of a Classic*, the only book ever devoted to the program, Ginny Weissman and Coyne Sanders go into otherwise exhaustive detail about the mechanics of recasting the series, but completely ignore the issue of ethnicity. There is no mention at all of it in an interview that Reiner and Leonard gave to *Television Quarterly* in 1963, at the height of the show's popularity.[27] The newspaper and magazine reviewers of the day were similarly silent on the subject.

Leonard, with his excellent sitcom track record, had little trouble in placing the revamped show on the CBS prime-time schedule. In the early sixties, advertising agencies tended to control blocks of time on network television and had great leverage in making program decisions. Using his liaison with the Benton and Bowles agency (which handled the sponsor accounts for both *Danny Thomas* and *Andy Griffith*), Leonard obtained an assurance from Procter and Gamble that the retailing giant "would back any pilot I chose."[28] A company, Calvada Productions (*C*arl Reiner, Sheldon *L*eonard, Dick *Va*n Dyke, *Da*nny Thomas), was formed to produce the show, with each partner to receive a percentage of the profits. Thomas, who provided much of the financing for the new pilot out of his own pocket, was to receive the lion's share.

As for the name of the program, it was generally agreed that "Head of the Family" would be abandoned so as not to confuse the series with the Kennedy-backed pilot of the previous summer. Several titles that referred to Rob's dual management functions in the office and at home were considered. "Double Trouble" was adopted as a working title at one point, but was dropped in favor of "All in a Day's Work." In the end, however, Leonard reverted to form. *The Danny Thomas Show* and *The Andy Griffith Show* had both done quite well for him and the new sitcom was christened *The Dick Van Dyke Show*.

Like the television industry itself, Reiner (under the tutelage of Sheldon Leonard) had made the transition from the blackout sketch vaudeville of live East Coast comedy-variety to the prerecorded, studio-edited filmed drama of West Coast situation comedy. He was one of the very few who did this successfully. Caesar, Berle, Coca, and other golden-age stars attempted periodic comebacks, but to no avail. Imogene Coca's *Grindl* (NBC, 1963–4) was a particularly ambitious sitcom in which Coca, playing the title role of a housemaid, was afforded generous opportunities to perform pantomime bits and other types of high-tone physical shtick. Unfortunately *Grindl* was programmed against *The Ed Sullivan Show* during a season that included appearances by half the groups in the British invasion – the Beatles and the Rolling Stones among them – and it never had a chance.

While the fifties comedy-variety performers frantically tried to retool for the brave new prime time that Madison Avenue was inventing for the sixties, the best golden-age writers abandoned the medium, using their TV resumés to gain entrance into the relatively genteel circles of popular theater and cinema. After penning several "Sergeant Bilko" scripts for his friend Nat Hiken's *Phil Silvers Show*, Neil Simon headed for Broadway and became the most widely produced playwright of the century – some say of history. Woody Allen and Mel Brooks dabbled in stand-up performance, but soon began new careers as movie directors and, eventually, producers. Each of the three won a national audience by focusing his lower-middle-class Brooklyn Jewish sensibility on a different social circle: Simon created a theater of consumer realism that made him a comic plaintiff voice for New York middle-class *arrivistes*. Allen, with his *shiksas* and poetesses, became the bard of the uptown condominium cosmopolitans. Brooks, apparently knowing no shame, continued to cultivate the scatological excesses of the schoolyard.

Ironically, Reiner – who had been both performer and writer during the comedy-variety era – accomplished his feat of network survival by creating a nostalgic West Coast sitcom about the life of a New York comedy-variety writer. In the bargain, he was forced to reinvent his Bronx persona in the image of a tall, skinny gentile who had grown up next to the Mark Twain National Forest in Howell County, Missouri. Leonard, the bicoastal mastermind of this transmutation, apparently mixing up his midwestern states, once referred to Van Dyke as "an Indiana Baptist."[29]

The Dick Van Dyke Show pilot went into production on a soundstage at the Desilu Cahuenga complex in January 1961. The "three-camera system," which Desi Arnaz had originated for *I Love Lucy*, was used. This system synthesized film, theater, and video techniques so that a live audience, in effect, attended the filming of a short movie that was shot with three stationary cameras and then cut in an editing room. In April,

CBS chose to pick up the series without a preseason airing of the pilot; full-scale episode production began on June 20. Reiner's original writing staff consisted of the team of Jerry Belson and Garry Marshall; in subsequent seasons another team, Bill Persky and Sam Denoff, was added, along with several contributing free-lancers. The half-hour, black-and-white show premiered that fall in the Tuesday 8 P.M. slot, hammocked between *Marshall Dillon* (reruns of the old half-hour *Gunsmoke*) and *The Many Loves of Dobie Gillis*. The competition was *Bachelor Father* on ABC and the second half of *Laramie* on NBC.

Each episode of *The Dick Van Dyke Show* opens in a fashion that makes it recognizable as a turn-of-the-decade nuclear-family sitcom: an instrumental musical theme plays on the soundtrack as the members of the family gather together in the house. The signature scene of *Dick Van Dyke*, however, distinguishes itself in several ways. Most fifties suburban domesticoms opened with brief but potent establishing shots of the exterior of the family home. These suburbopastoral house portraits emphatically underscore the family's unbearably secure upper-middle-class status. No such shot, however, is offered of the Petrie house. Their class status must be gleaned instead from the more subtle connotations of interior decoration: their contemporary sectional sofa; their quasi-modern *objects d'art*; their breakfast counter; their elaborate but unused woodstore fireplace. In this way, the Petrie living room transcends the traditional sitcom standard of family comfort, introducing notions of personal taste. The signature sequence then departs even further from fifties sitcom custom: instead of just dad, mom, and offspring, the picture is extended beyond blood members to include Rob's office co-workers, Buddy and Sally – a Jew and an unmarried career woman.

Rob enters the living room (his and yours) through the front door, emerging from behind the superimposed series title, as it is vocally announced. The white-collar dignity of his suit and tie is immediately betrayed by a slapstick pratfall over the ottoman. (Later, this was self-reflexively revised so that Rob enters and *avoids* tripping over the ottoman.)[30] He is greeted and surrounded, first by Laura and Ritchie, who approach Rob from the viewer's right, and then by Buddy and Sally, who follow from the left. The show-business world, as symbolized by the pratfall (or nonpratfall) and the joke writers, is resolved into the domestic world of wife, child, and spacious but warm living room. All constitute one big happy family – only forty-five minutes from Broadway. Though Rob is a "real character," in the midwestern sense of that phrase, his soul is "out here" in the New Rochelle house, among the prosperous eight-cylinder families – and not "down there" among the Others of Manhattan.

There is a kind of curious narrative anomaly embedded in this opening. What, a regular viewer might ask, are Buddy and Sally, city-dwelling Others, members of minorities, doing in the idyllic Middle American house? They seem somehow to be waiting for Rob to come home from the office. The typewriter sitting on the coffee table (foreground, viewer's left) suggests that a work session is about to take place, but this is something that never happens in the course of the 158 episodes. The scene might as easily have been shot at the office, with Laura and Ritchie dressed for a visit. The use of the living room, however, establishes the show's cosmic priorities: family, blood, and home constitute both the alpha and the omega of Rob's consciousness; city, art, and commerce, while important, are, in the final analysis, only transitory experience. Though the series will spend more time at the office than other family sitcoms, it proclaims itself no less a family sitcom than *Donna Reed* or *Danny Thomas* by reaffirming the primacy of family life.

Much like the New Frontier, the show viewed in reruns a quarter-century later waxes and wanes as a series of promises and compromises. Fresh and unconventional styles are used to package familiar morals in what evolves as an upbeat saga of a bright, fast-track couple playing by the rules and making it. The power – and the possibilities of power – all belong to a youngish middle-aged white male hero, an unpretentious college graduate of liberal sensibility who makes good money in a creative position with a Madison Avenue industry. A modern guy riding the wave of late-twentieth-century technocracy, Rob outranks the older, more experienced writers on *The Alan Brady Show* staff by virtue of his college diploma. Luckily, his political outlook is just as up-to-date. "Head writer" is only a title to Rob; he is careful to treat Buddy and Sally as equals and valued collaborators at all times. Perhaps he is satisfied to simply make more money than they do.

Laura (Mary Tyler Moore) is Rob's sitcomic Jackie, a talented beauty who has given up any number of possibilities in life to pilot the family station wagon. With their pointedly youthful good looks, with their emphatically *moderne* suburban detached single-family dwelling, with a respect for art and Kultur that is topped only by a love of show business and what it can do for you, the Petries were perhaps the last sitcom couple who could simultaneously take for granted their unnamed (and, on television unnamable) white, middle-class, heterosexual advantage and still manage to exhibit a kind of quasi-sophistication and personal warmth that imply sympathy for civil rights and possibly even advocacy of welfare-state measures.

The politically progressive feel of the show is due in part to the inclusion of black actors as extras in crowd scenes at public places and private events, such as museums and parties. Reiner was by no means the first sitcom producer to attempt to integrate his cast. Nat Hiken had always included one or more black soldiers in Sergeant Bilko's platoon on *The Phil Silvers Show* (CBS, 1955–9) and several black officers in the police squad of *Car 54, Where Are You?* (NBC, 1961–3). *Car 54*, premiering the same season as *The Dick Van Dyke Show*, was perhaps the most integrated series that had ever appeared on network television. Regulars included Officer Anderson (Nipsey Russell) and Officer Wallace (Frederick O'Neal) and many episodes of the series, which took place in the Bronx, featured black extras and walk-ons. But *Dick Van Dyke*, unlike the Hiken shows, was about suburban family life and even token integration stood out as extraordinary.

In "A Show of Hands," Rob and Laura are to go to a banquet to accept an award for Alan Brady from the Committee on Interracial Unity. Before leaving the house, however, they accidentally dye their hands indelibly black while helping Ritchie make a costume. Embarrassed, they wear white gloves, but take them off when they are reminded by their hosts that truth is the only path to human understanding and therefore world harmony. In "That's My Boy??," Rob recounts the birth of Ritchie in flashback. A series of events influences Rob to believe that the hospital has given them the wrong baby, switching Ritchie Petrie of Room 206 with Richie Peters of Room 208. Rob calls the Peters family and tells them what he thinks has happened. Punchline? The Peters walk in – and they are black. Though blacks are otherwise never seen on sixties sitcoms as guest stars, Godfrey Cambridge appeared on *The Dick Van Dyke Show* as secret agent Harry Bond in "The Man from My Uncle," a 1966 spy-spoof episode.

Could Rob or Laura have voted for Nixon in 1960 or Goldwater in 1964? Could Carl Reiner have voted for them? (The Petries and the Reiners might well have parted ways, however, in 1952 and 1956.) While an identifiable if tepid political statement is implicit in Reiner's casual integration of middle-class blacks into the series mise-en-scène, Reiner is more explicit on other, perhaps less controversial themes. One of the recurring leitmotifs in *Dick Van Dyke* is a kind of status-based tension between art and mass entertainment. Artists who work in relatively low-return media – painters, poets, independent filmmakers – are almost always treated skeptically. At the same time, the pursuit of money by the commercial artist is tied to common sense, love of family, and humane social values, all of which are embodied in Rob, who is utterly valorized. *Artistes* who show up on *The Dick Van Dyke Show* can expect rough treatment.

In "I'm No Henry Walden," Rob is mysteriously invited to a charity cocktail party where all the other guests are poets, playwrights, novelists, critics, and assorted literati given to avant-garde hyperbole. Everycouple

Rob and Laura are completely out of place. The "serious" writers turn out to be nothing but a bunch of intolerable snobs who can't even get Rob's name straight, no matter how many times he introduces himself. When he mentions that he is a TV writer, they are aghast, one of the guests exclaiming, "Why I don't even own a television machine." Doris Packer, who was typed as one of the great sitcom snobs for her stunning performance as Chatsworth Osborne, Jr.'s mother in *Dobie Gillis*, plays the party's hostess, Mrs. Huntington. She introduces the "Petrovs" to Yale Samsden (Carl Reiner), "one of our budding British anti-existentialists." Reiner, with a goatee and a virtually incomprehensible Oxbridge accent, launches into a crazed exegesis on "the state of American culture in our times." Phrases such as "plethora of the mundane" and "atrophy of the brain" emerge from his otherwise brilliantly incoherent rantings. "Verisimilitude," Yale warns in a backhanded swipe at the sitcom, "must be stamped out."

Henry Walden, as the name suggests, is a "true" poet conjured from America's nineteenth-century literary heritage. He is brought by Reiner to *The Dick Van Dyke Show* much as Kennedy had produced Robert Frost for his inauguration. The snowy-haired Walden, who has not been seen for most of the episode, appears at the end to right the wrongs that have been done to Rob. Unlike his snotty friends, he is a Whitmanian appreciator of mass culture, an unabashed fan of *The Alan Brady Show*. He even proves his sincerity by reciting the complete career resumés of Buddy and Sally. (Interestingly, we learn that Buddy, like Morey Amsterdam, had once had his own comedy-variety show and that Sally had been a gag writer for Milton Berle.) The real reason he invited Rob to the party was to ask him to collaborate on a TV documentary on the history of American humor from the Revolutionary War to the present. When Rob protests that he knows nothing about American history, Walden assures him, "Don't worry, I know all about that stuff. I need someone who knows television."

The episode ends with the same group of snobs from the party gathered at Mrs. Huntington's Park Avenue apartment to watch the documentary on a "television machine" that has been placed in the living room just for the occasion. Henry Walden reads the writers' credits aloud at the end of the broadcast and the literati are forced by the revered poet to recognize Rob's talent – and the "validity" of television as an art. Poor Henry Walden, however, must remain with the entourage of pseudointellectuals; he is dependent on their patronage. Rob, on the other hand, is lucky to be "no Henry Walden" but a self-sufficient breadwinner with a beautiful wife who can choose his own friends.

In "Draw Me a Pear" (a risqué pun on "pair"), Rob and Laura take art classes from a devious female painter who praises Rob's work in an attempt to seduce him. Laura sees through the ruse from the start, but wishing to appear modern, she tells her husband to do "whatever makes you happy, darling." The seductress-in-smock invites Rob into the city for "private lessons" at her Greenwich Village studio. After giving him a phony line about "freeing himself from his inhibitions," she makes her move. Instructing Rob to feel her face with one hand while sketching it with the other, she fondles Rob's fingers with her mouth, an extraordinarily frank bit for an early sixties sitcom. Perhaps more extraordinary, the sexually aggressive home wrecker is not made to seem either excessively evil or pathetic. Her personality flaw is revealed as deviousness, not hypersexuality. The conclusion, however, is strictly fifties: Rob tells Laura in the coda, "It's a good thing I'm such a good boy." (A variation on this episode can be seen in "Teacher's Petrie," in which Laura's creative writing teacher betrays similarly lecherous designs on her.)

Perhaps the most sarcastic dig at noncorporate artists takes place in "October Eve," in which Reiner once again caricatures the *artiste*, this time playing the role of Serge Carpetna, a Russian painter – complete with goatee, beret, and insufferable ego. Many years ago, Laura had commissioned Carpetna, then an unknown, to do a painting of her for $50. Though she had posed for him fully clothed, the artist had taken license to paint her as a nude. Enraged, Laura attempted to destroy the canvas by throwing black paint on it. But Carpetna, we learn, has restored the painting. It shows up in a swank New York gallery with a $5,000 price tag attached to it.

In a flashback sequence, Laura tells the story of the painting to Rob, apologizing for having kept it a secret from him for all these years. We see Laura's reaction as she gazes at Carpetna's image of her nude body for the first time. Though her outrage is presented as the only reasonable attitude in such a situation, the arrogant artist shows no understanding for her middle-class morality. In a stereotypical display, he calls her a "peasant" and tells her to "go back to New Rochelle, land of peasants."

Realizing that Laura owns the painting by virtue of the $50 she paid for it long ago, Rob decides to go down to the city to confront the artist in his Greenwich Village studio. The maestro is hard at work on a new masterpiece – with squirt guns. When Carpetna learns the reason for Rob's visit, he throws a tantrum, threatening to knock Rob in the head before allowing him to destroy his work of art. Revealing sensitivity and fairness, however, even as he seeks to protect his own interests, Rob offers Carpetna a deal: the Petries will forgo their ownership of the painting if they can pick the buyer. The "happy" ending has the artist selling his painting to a reclusive South American millionaire who will place it in his Brazilian mountaintop retreat. As if this is not enough, an extra potshot is added after the climax. Carpetna does a new painting of Laura, which he promises will not be a nude. Keeping his word, he creates a Marcel Duchamp-like "portrait" in which no one can even find Laura. The *artiste*, unlike the TV writer and most people, simply cannot comprehend the "normal" human preference for simple representationalism. Carpetna would no doubt agree with Yale Samsden that "verisimilitude must be stamped out."

The caricaturing of artists (as well as intellectuals) is a convention of the pre-1970s sitcom that is by no means limited to *The Dick Van Dyke Show*. Male artists are usually portrayed as either effeminate or lecherous; female artists, as either sexually maladjusted or just downright daffy. But the fact that Rob himself is a writer gives a certain edge to Reiner's obsession. There is a plea for identification with Rob's relatively down-to-earth attitude. The audience is asked to accept the TV writer as one of the bourgeois crowd. Rob is a writer the way Jerry Helper (Jerry Paris), his next-door neighbor, is a dentist. There are no callings in New Rochelle, just professions. Each man democratically pays off his auto loan with the same green money. Ironically, the signature credits sequence concludes each week with the superimposition of an episode title across the Petrie living room, a flourish that in sitcom terms suggests no small artistic pretension. Who does Reiner think he is, Quinn Martin?[31]

With the seemingly divided world of the commuter given continuity and coherence by Rob's ability to maintain a single consciousness at both ends of his daily trip on the New Haven Railroad, the notion of the artist as marginal person is disputed. The avant-gardists down in the city of art are provocative, but they are too self-important to be the cognoscenti of a democracy. Let them jump off the deep end, as is their right; Rob, the American poet, seeks the center. It is left up to him, the man with the mortgage, to be the divine literatus of posturban society. Rob – the male, the breadwinner, the homeowner, the artist, the manager, the Middle American – is the hub of all of the drama's dynamic human relationships.

The lack of emphasis on parenting problems in *The Dick Van Dyke Show* was another factor that helped create the penumbra of sophistication that still surrounds the series twenty-five years later. Compared to children on other Sheldon Leonard shows – *Danny Thomas* and *Andy Griffith* – Ritchie Petrie is the sitcom's answer to the neglected child. As is the case with *I Love Lucy*, the plots tend to focus on adult problems, often excluding the couple's son completely. When Little Ricky does appear in an *I Love Lucy* episode, however, he is often trotted out in grand style, wearing miniature Xavier Cugat outfits, playing the bongos, and joining dad in a chorus of "Babalu." Ritchie (Larry Mathews) rarely if ever gets such attention. He is occasionally used as a font of cute remarks, but his personality and his consciousness remain largely unexplored. His problems are presented only to the extent that they allow the viewer to see how Rob and Laura react to them. Besides being obedient and painfully well adjusted (or perhaps because of these things) he is pretty much of a nebbish. The screaming apple-of-my-eyeism that so thoroughly dominated the genre during this period was absent from the show.

Robert S. Alley has argued that the classic domesticoms of the fifties, which are often ridiculed today as ideological fossils of a conformist conservative era, actually contain many highly relevant – and in some cases quite liberal – political and social messages, especially in the area of parent–child relations.[32] For example, sitcom children are never spanked or physically punished. Instead, they are reasoned with in a calm but firm manner as prescribed by Dr. Spock, who, according to Laura in one episode, "is a genius [and] knows everything."[33] Parents who practice this progressive method will be rewarded with a Beaver or a Wally. Parents who do not can expect an Eddie Haskell or a Lumpy Rutherford.

The child-rearing philosophy of the Petries is perhaps best illustrated in the episode "Girls Will Be Boys," in which Ritchie is repeatedly harassed and beaten up by a female classmate, Priscilla Darwell, at school. Having been taught by his parents never to hit a girl under any circumstances, he refuses to retaliate, choosing instead to suffer the pain of emasculation. Under his mother's concerned and sympathetic questioning, he breaks down and reveals his shame. Rob goes to see the girl's father, but Priscilla, in a perfect little party dress, looking like Patty McCormack in *The Bad Seed*, politely denies having ever hit Ritchie and, as far as Mr. Darwell is concerned, the matter is settled. Rob, whose sense of fair play transcends his paternal pride, is equally impressed by the performance and is perfectly willing to believe that his son is the liar – until an impeccable eyewitness (Jerry and Millie's son Freddie) bears Ritchie out. The attacks continue, and this time Laura goes to see Mrs. Darwell. She turns out to be an even worse parent than her husband. She refuses to believe that her little girl is even capable of such behavior and suggests that Laura try giving Ritchie some sweets to get him to tell the truth. Dumbfounded and enraged at such parental irresponsibility, Rob and Laura give Ritchie permission to defend himself.

Tension builds as Rob and Laura wait for Ritchie to get back from school; Rob has come home from work early that day just to be there. Comic harmony is breathlessly restored as the twenty-two-minute drama winds to its conclusion. We learn that Ritchie was too embarrassed to tell his parents that all the little girl ever wanted from him was a kiss. Refusing to hit a girl despite parental permission, he gives in and kisses her, ending the attacks. As in "October Eve," a bit of overkill is added after the climax: Priscilla tells Ritchie's classmates about the kiss and some boys tease Ritchie and start a fight with him. He promptly beats up all three of them. Hearing the story, Rob is devilishly delighted; he sees both his virility and his values redeemed in such good, old-fashioned male horseplay.

As the show's increasing ratings gained credibility for him at CBS, Reiner gradually became freer to leave behind parent–child situations and give more attention to the Rob–Laura and Rob–office plots he favored. By the fifth season, Ritchie had all but disappeared from the show, and quite frankly, not much was lost. In general, Reiner proved to be far more interesting and original at the office than in the home.

Morey Amsterdam and Rose Marie play the roles of comedy writers Buddy Sorrell and Sally Rogers strictly by The Method. Both had been stars of radio and early TV who made phoenixlike comebacks on the *Van Dyke* show. Amsterdam was born in Chicago in 1914. A cello-playing prodigy, he gained admission to college before the age of fifteen but chose to devote himself to show business, achieving national stature as a popular comedy-variety figure in the late forties and early fifties. He was known for his theme song, "Yuk-a-Puk," which he played on the cello as punctuation for the one-liners of his stand-up routine (a style of pre-sentation made perhaps more famous by Henny Youngman and his violin). Along with Youngman, Jack Carter, Milton Berle, and several others, Amsterdam had been one of a rotating circle of comedians who had hosted *The Texaco Star Theater* before Berle won the job for himself in 1948. He had his own show, *The Morey Amsterdam Show*, on CBS and then Dumont in the late forties; its supporting cast included pre-Norton Art Carney and pre-*Valley of the Dolls* Jacqueline Susann, whose hus-band, Irving Mansfield, was the show's producer. In 1950, Amsterdam returned to NBC as the Monday and Wednesday host of *Broadway Open House*, the first late-night network talk-variety show, an ancestor of *The Tonight Show*. Once again, however, he was passed over for an NBC top spot when the network gave the show to Jerry Lester on a Monday-through-Friday basis. As comedy-variety went into its tailspin in the latter part of the decade, Morey Amsterdam began what seemed to be a descent into game-show oblivion, appearing as a regular on no less than five prime-time network games, including *Keep Talking*, which Reiner had briefly hosted.

"Baby" Rose Marie, as she had been known when she began her career singing on network radio at the age of three, was a frequent guest on comedy-variety programs. She had been a regular on *The Ina Ray Hutton*

Show (NBC, 1956), a short-lived summer replacement series that retains the distinction of having been the only program in prime-time history to have had an all-female cast, featuring Ina Ray and Her All-Girl Band. The show's subtitle was "No Men Allowed" and, indeed, not a single man ever appeared on camera during its ten-week run on Wednesday evenings. Rose Marie's game-show credits included *Pantomime Quiz*, a long-running charades vehicle that had also featured Dick Van Dyke for a time. More recently, she had tried her hand at sitcom work, playing the role of Bertha the Secretary on *My Sister Eileen* (CBS, 1960–1).

Buddy and Sally, though toned down considerably by the constraints of genre, medium, and period, evocatively conjure visions of Mel Brooks and Selma Diamond in a Max Liebman writers' room. Known as "the human joke machine," Buddy is the acknowledged master of the one-liner – the wiseguy comic from the streets of neighborhood New York. The stuffy and officious Mel Cooley (Richard Deacon), Alan Brady's bald producer and brother-in-law, is the natural butt of Buddy's obsess-ive schoolyard rank-out prowess. Buddy's Jewishness is for the most part implicit, though it is freely acknowledged upon occasion. In "The Ugliest Dog in the World," Rob brings a street mutt to the office and Buddy feeds it a corned beef sandwich. When Rob tries to give the dog some milk, Buddy protests:

Buddy: That ain't kosher. For him it's cream soda or nothing.
Sally: Rob, he's trying to kill that dog.
Rob: No, he's trying to convert him.

In "There's No Sale Like Wholesale," Buddy uses what F. Scott Fitz-gerald had once called "gonnexions" to get Rob and Laura a fur coat at a wholesale price. The most "Jewish" episode of all, however, is "Buddy Sorrell – Man and Boy," in which the middle-aged comedy writer corrects an injustice of his poverty-stricken Brooklyn youth by finally taking bar mitzvah lessons. In the last few minutes, the bar mitzvah itself is presented (in English), complete with synagogue, congregation, and a yarmulke-clad Dick Van Dyke. The rabbi even refers to Buddy by his Jewish name: Moshe Selig Sorrell. Occurring as it does in the final months of the series production run, the episode seems like a whimsical revisiting of some of the autobiographical material that Reiner had been forced to abandon to put the sitcom on the air back in 1961. Amster-dam's organic *toomler* delivery makes him the surviving vessel of Jewish-ness in the otherwise mainstreamed narrative. "I *am* Buddy," he once told an interviewer.[34]

By contrast, Sally Rogers shows no hint of ethnicity. The archetypal sitcom career woman of the pre-Mary Richards era, her significance radiates strictly from gender. Sally's lack of a husband hangs over her like a dark cloud, adding an element of pathos that is lacking in any of the other characters. Rob and Laura frequently fix her up with blind dates, but her aggressive "unfeminine" style makes her unfit for each of these potential mates. Her one steady boyfriend is Herman Glimsher (Bill Idelson), a pathetic mama's boy whose widowed mother takes full advantage of his oedipal problems.

The "Sally episodes" take on a familiar pattern. In "Like a Sister," she misjudges the affections of guest star Vic Damone, who plays a singer named Vic Vallone. In "Jilting the Jilter," comedian Fred White (Guy Marks) tries to marry Sally as a cheap source of gags for his stand-up nightclub routine. In another episode, Rob's brother, Stacy (Jerry Van Dyke), comes for a visit and dates Sally in order to get over his shyness so he can propose to the woman he really wants to marry. In "Dear Sally Rogers," Sally appears on a network talk show and shamelessly solicits marriage proposals by mail. It is not unusual for a Sally episode to end with a tear in her eye; she has a cat named Mr. Henderson.

There is something inescapably off-center about the sitcom relationship of Buddy and Sally. Appearing together frequently at social functions, they might easily be mistaken for husband and wife. It is easy to speculate, however, on why Reiner and Leonard chose not to marry them. For one thing, Sally is not Jewish. Mixed marriages, then as now, were not considered sitcom fare.[35] On the other hand, if Sally was written as a Jewish character, a Jewish majority on *The Alan Brady Show* writing staff would violate another type of marketing wisdom. With Sally a single woman, Reiner retained the comic prerogatives of Sally's self-effacing spinster jokes as well as a dependable plotting device that accounted for more than a half-dozen episodes.

Buddy's wife, Pickles (Joan Shawlee; later Barbara Perry), though often mentioned as the butt of his one-liners, is rarely seen on screen. Yet, the fact that Buddy has a wife obviates speculation about his sexuality. Sally, by contrast, is the female eunuch, unfulfilled and philosophical about her lot in life. She is typical of the pre-1970s sitcom career woman in this way. In *Our Miss Brooks* (CBS, 1952–6), Eve Arden is an English teacher who spends most of her time at Madison High futilely trying to gain the romantic attentions of Mr. Boynton, a colleague in the Biology Department. Ann Sothern carried this archetype into two series: *Private Secretary* (CBS, 1953–7) and *The Ann Sothern Show* (CBS, 1958–61). The structural supposition of both programs was that she worked for a living in lieu of marriage, which was valorized as the principal or "real" goal of any woman. In the latter show, she plays an assistant hotel manager who is passed over for promotion in favor of an outside man. The new boss is played by none other than Don Porter, the same actor who had played Sothern's boss in the earlier series. Most of the episodes are built on her attempts to "snare" the man who has taken the job that was rightfully hers.

Sally is slightly better off than the Eve Arden and Ann Sothern characters in that her career is meaningful to her, but she is still very much the victim of male domination. Though officially a full member of *The Alan Brady Show*'s writing staff, she does all the typing while Buddy lies on the couch and Rob paces the center of the room. In the two-part episode "The Pen Is Mightier than the Mouth" / "My Part-time Wife," Sally makes an appearance on *The Stevie Parsons Show* (*Steve* Allen, Jack *Paar*, Johnny *Carson*). She is a big hit on the late-night talk show and takes an indefinite leave from her job to become one of Stevie's regulars. Rob and Buddy find themselves unable to function without Sally around to keep the office in order and do the typing. Sally, however, gives up her big chance to become a star by purposely getting into an argument with Stevie Parsons when he makes a crack about *The Alan Brady Show* on the air. She dutifully returns to her place at the typewriter in the office, learning the old sitcom lesson that a solid place in a warm gemeinschaft is worth more than anything the flashy gesellschaft can ever offer – a lesson still frequently taught in the genre.

The show's three regular women characters offer a constellation of sitcomic female figures. Laura is offered as the heroic center point of identification. Beautiful and capable, talented and motivated, she has found a comfortable and rewarding place in the world. If she is defined by her husband, at least it can be said that she has made the most enviable "catch" of the men in the series. Alan Brady is wealthy and a star, but he is arrogant and egotistical. Buddy may be funny, perhaps even funnier than Rob, but he is socially adolescent and physically endomorphic. Mel, as producer of the show, technically outranks Rob, but he is a fawning sycophant who has made his way in the world by nepotism. Next-door neighbor Jerry Helper is a successful dentist – a professional – but he is bland and ordinary. Rob stands out as the perfect blend of the domestic (loyal, loving, caring) and the artistic (funny, handsome, creative). That Laura gave up her career as a dancer is less important than the fact that she could have been a dancer, had she wanted to be anything other than Rob's wife and the mother of his children.

Her commitment to her choice is made clearest in "To Tell or Not to Tell." The episode begins with a typical *Dick Van Dyke* party scene at the Petrie home. The well dressed, middle-class, racially integrated guests are entertained first by Buddy and Sally, who do one of their Catskills song-and-dance comedy routines, and then by Rob, who does a few pantomime impressions. Next, however, we are treated to a rare performance by Laura, who, in capri pants, does some post-Martha Graham gallivanting around the living room to the accompaniment of bongo drums on the phonograph. Mel is so impressed by Laura's work that he asks her to fill in for an injured dancer on *The Alan Brady Show*. Buddy warns Rob not to let Laura do it: "You'll be eating frozen dinners." But Rob is too progressive to take authoritarian measures and so decides to let Laura make her own decision: "I think I know what my wife wants." The episode concludes with Laura's being offered a job as a regular dancer on the weekly network TV show.

"I always wondered if I could make it again as a dancer," Laura tells Rob, "but I don't want to be a dancer, I want to be your wife." She then adds a complaint about the aches and pains of dancing, but this is only an ameliorating gesture that serves as minimal ironic counterpoint to Laura's heavy-handed denial of ego. Laura's decision is very much in the official spirit of the times. As Theodore Sorensen has written, "Providing a normal life for her children and peaceful home for her husband was only one of Jacqueline Kennedy's contributions to the Kennedy era, but she regarded it as her most important. 'It doesn't matter what else you do,' she said, 'if you don't do that part well, you fail. . . . That really is the role which means the most to me, the one that comes first.' "[36]

Millie Helper (Ann Morgan Guilbert) helps define Laura as a "modern" woman by offering the contrast of a familiarly zany sitcom hausfrau. Millie's talents in life are strictly domestic. She is hyperemotional and unable to function outside her prescribed role. When any chance for individual attention or distinction is thrust upon her, she is unable to accept it, as in "Coast to Coast Big Mouth," an episode in which Millie is picked out of the audience to be a contestant on a game show, but falls to pieces with stage fright and gives her opportunity away to Laura. Millie functions as a sidekick, a kind of sounding board for Laura, allowing her to verbalize her feelings about Rob. She is a second banana lacking the dignity, however, of an Ethel Mertz, who at least gets to be Lucy's partner in middle-class deviance. Ann Morgan Guilbert handles the role with great skill, calling attention to Laura's calm, reasonable, and relatively cosmopolitan tone with her own mah-jongg game shrillness. Is Millie a recent émigré from the Bronx? Once again the marketing concerns of the medium seem to be masking a parochial subtext.

If Millie is a house mouse, Sally is a bull in a china shop. Too assertive, too aggressive, too willing to use her "unfeminine" powers, Sally is the career woman whom Laura wisely chose not to be. She suffers much more for her excess than Millie suffers for her passivity. The only men who can accept her are her coworkers; they know how to harness her sexually ambiguous eccentricities for productive purposes. Some of the single men Sally encounters are emasculated by her

verbal powers; others can only see her as a source of the valued com-
modity of humor. None can accept her as a woman. Both Sally and
Millie are static and incomplete compared to Laura. The balance of
female sitcom power would not shift decisively toward career women
until the 1970s.

The critic John Cawelti has written that the development of a popular
genre occurs as various authors synthesize the genre's familiar characteristics ("conventions") with innovative characteristics that freshen,
surprise, and recontextualize ("inventions").[37] *The Dick Van Dyke
Show* lends itself to this kind of schematic view of generic evolution
quite well. Perhaps more than any sitcom that preceded it, the series
incorporated an eclectic variety of elements from the sitcom canon
while adding significant innovations in plot content and structure. The
homogenous suburban family at home is familiar; the heterogeneous
extended family at the office is new. The broad, physical comedy of
Van Dyke is right out of *I Love Lucy*; the sophisticated early sixties
dialogue is unique.

Symmetrical, premodernist morality-tale plotting may be built right
into the formal constraints of situation comedy, but Reiner and the half-
dozen writers he collaborated with over the course of the show – Sam
Denoff and Bill Persky, Ben Joelson and Art Baer, David Adler, Lee
Erwin – at least had the virtue of being self-conscious about their
didacticism. The commitment to achieving a modicum of racial integration and ethnic representation distinguishes the sitcom from other early
sixties prime-time hits such as *The Beverly Hillbillies* and *The Flintstones*.
A viewer who doubts the relative "hipness" of *The Dick Van Dyke Show*
might remember that *Hazel* (NBC, 1961–5; CBS, 1965–6) was exactly
contemporaneous with it.

Dick Van Dyke, it should be noted, had not been an instant hit. Facing
a strong Western (*Laramie*) and a sitcom featuring teenagers (*Bachelor
Father*), the show struggled in its original 8 P.M. Tuesday night time
slot, not winning Nielsen numbers among the preadult viewers who
dominate that period. Wisely, Sheldon Leonard and Danny Thomas
lobbied the network tenaciously and the show was moved at midseason
to a later slot, 9:30, on Wednesdays. This did the trick. Having finishing
fifty-fourth during its first season, the show catapulated into the Nielsen
Top Ten the following year, finishing ninth in 1962–3, third in 1963–4,
seventh in 1964–5, and sixteenth in its final season.

It is worth noting that the cancellation of *The Dick Van Dyke Show* was
never ordered by CBS, but rather by Carl Reiner. Having watched too
many of his old colleagues from the comedy-variety days overstay their
welcome on network television, Reiner, with the approval of the cast,
decided to bow out gracefully while still on top. The exact timing of this

rare sitcom suicide (future examples would include *The Mary Tyler Moore Show* and *M*A*S*H*) was most likely tied to a CBS policy decision to go over to an "all-color" prime-time schedule in 1966–7. *The Dick Van Dyke Show* had been shot in black and white and the expense of gearing up for such a radical technological production change could not be justified for a limited run.

The decision to voluntarily end the show rather than wait for the inevitable but otherwise unpredictable network ax gave Reiner the opportunity to create a macrocosmic climax to the five-year, seventy-nine-hour narrative. In "The Last Chapter," Rob reveals to Laura that he has finished an autobiographical novel that he has been working on for the last five years. Laura sits down to read it, providing a flashback framework for a series of sentimental "greatest hits" scenes recapitulating the show's etiology: the marriage of Rob and Laura, the birth of Ritchie, and so on. The episode and the series reach completion as all the members of the cast – Buddy, Sally, Mel, Alan, and Ritchie (possibly a double; he speaks no lines and is seen only in profile) – join Rob and Laura in the Petrie living room:

Rob (to Laura):   You want to hear a bit of good news? I heard from the publisher today. . . . He *hates* it. He said it reminds him of about fifty other books.

Buddy (ecstatic):   One editor said it stunk.

Laura: Then why is everyone so happy?

Rob: Because Alan read it and he loved it.

Alan: What do I know from style?

Rob: Alan wants to produce it as a television series . . . Alan is going to play me.

Sally: The three of us are going to write it. Leonard Delshold is going to produce it.

(Close-up of Rob and Laura embracing and kissing.)

Reiner's bone to pick with the genteel traditional arts remains a primary theme to the bitter end. It doesn't matter that editors and other such pretentious creatures reject Rob's work. Alan likes the book, and though he knows nothing about "art," whatever that is, he will make a sitcom out of it and that means fame and fortune, success and redemption. Such are the consolations for the unappreciated writers who make the millions smile.

Perhaps more impressively, Reiner achieves elliptical closure for the series in this final episode. The narrative had commenced six years previously as an autobiographical work, with Carl Reiner playing Rob. The role was then taken over by Dick Van Dyke who became Rob in the eyes of the world; Carl Reiner, meanwhile, became Alan Brady. Rob/

Dick Van Dyke then writes an autobiography, which Alan decides to produce as a television series. In the new series, Alan/Carl Reiner will play the part of Rob/Dick Van Dyke, who, in turn, will write the show. Or, as Weissman and Sanders put it, "*The Dick Van Dyke Show* was complete, indeed 'coming around full circle': Carl Reiner (as Alan Brady) would portray Rob Petrie – in essence, himself – in a television situation comedy, as Reiner had done in *Head of the Family* years before, which then became *The Dick Van Dyke Show*."[38] In any case, Reiner has a last laugh, exiting as the Rob he had originally wanted to be.

Despite the commercial success of *The Dick Van Dyke Show*, it inspired no spin-offs or even any obvious imitators. Instead, shows such as Paul Henning's *The Beverly Hillbillies* and William Asher's *Bewitched* (and their spin-offs and imitators) came to dominate the sitcom throughout the sixties. This is not surprising. As the sixties hit civil rights and Vietnam in high gear, the very concept of sophistication was suddenly up for grabs and the networks sought to retain as high a degree of least-objectionability in this polarized atmosphere as possible. The sitcom, a representational art committed to harmony and consensus, found refuge in visions of America's premetropolitan past and fantasies of witches, genies, and nannies who could do the vacuuming by magic. The legacy of *The Dick Van Dyke Show* would not be redeemed until the 1970s, when shows such as *All in the Family*, *M*A*S*H*, and especially *The Mary Tyler Moore Show* would revise and revive the genre as a historically based comedy of American manners.

Notes

1 As quoted in Ginny Weissman and Coyne Steven Sanders, *The Dick Van Dyke Show* (New York: St. Martin's, 1983), p. 1.
2 "Draw Me A Pear," *The Dick Van Dyke Show* (CBS, October 20, 1965).
3 See Daniel Czitrom and David Marc, "The Elements of Lifestyle," *Atlantic Monthly*, May 1985, pp. 16–20.
4 See Roy Medvedev, *Khrushchev*, trans. Brian Pearce (New York: Anchor, 1983), pp. 153–5.
5 Caesar was born several miles away from Reiner in inner-city Yonkers.
6 For a dimmer view of Jewish suburban flight, see Philip Roth, *Goodbye, Columbus and Five Short Stories* (Boston: Houghton Mifflin, 1959), especially "Eli, the Fanatic" and "Goodbye, Columbus."
7 *The Imogene Coca Show* (NBC, 1954–5) was a pathetic casualty of the conflict between comedy-variety and situation comedy. The show premiered as a kind of autobiographical sitcom modeled after *The Jack Benny Program*. After two weeks it was changed into a comedy-variety showcase composed of blackout sketches, stand-up routines, and Broadway-style production numbers. Three months later, it reverted to a sitcom format. The show was not renewed for a second season.

8 Milton Berle, with Haskel Frankel, *Milton Berle: An Autobiography* (New York: Delacorte, 1974), p. 3.
9 Val Adams, "Newhart to Star in CBS-TV Show," New York *Times*, July 11, 1960.
10 Ibid., July 13, 1960.
11 Tim Brooks and Earl Marsh, *The Complete Directory to Prime Time Network TV Shows*, 3rd ed. (New York: Ballantine, 1985), p. 937.
12 Ibid., p. 446.
13 Carl Reiner, *Enter Laughing* (New York: Simon and Schuster, 1958), p. 5.
14 According to show-business legend, "Sturdy" became "Brady" after Morey Amsterdam observed that "Alan Sturdy" could be mistaken for "Alan's dirty." See Weissman and Sanders, p. 2.
15 Ibid.
16 Ibid.
17 Ibid.
18 Ibid., p. 5.
19 See Garry Wills, *The Kennedy Imprisonment* (Boston: Atlantic Monthly, 1982), pp. 66–7.
20 The term "Failure Theatre" was used by Robert Klein on *Late Night with David Letterman* to describe programs like *Comedy Spot* (NBC, July 24, 1986).
21 Harry Castleman and Walter Podrazik, *Watching Television: Four Decades of American Television* (New York: McGraw-Hill, 1982), p. 150.
22 Weissman and Sanders, pp. 5–6.
23 F Score, or "Familiarity" Score, is computed by the Performer Q company of Port Washington, New York. Each year the company does an extensive survey that attempts to rate the public's familiarity with TV performers (actors, game-show hosts, athletes, anchormen, etc.) by asking a sample group to identify pictures. These scores are then used by the networks and production companies in casting decisions.
24 Ibid., p. 6.
25 Ibid.
26 The sitcom is inconsistent on the point of Rob's hometown. In one episode, an old high school girlfriend from Danville shows up looking for an audition with Alan Brady. In another episode, Rob's parents come from Danville to visit. But in yet another episode, a male school friend (played by Jack Carter) appears and the two reminisce about their childhood in Westville, which seems like a composite of West Plains, Missouri (where Van Dyke grew up), and Danville, Illinois (where he moved as a young man to seek his fortune).
27 "Comedy on Television: A Dialogue," *Television Quarterly*, Summer 1963, pp. 93–103.
28 Weissman and Sanders, p. 17.
29 Ibid., p. 58.
30 A third opening, used only during the first half of the first season, differs completely from these: we see abstract still photographs of the cast members with the theme music playing.
31 Martin was the highly successful producer of such action series as *Barnaby Jones*, *The F.B.I.*, *The Streets of San Francisco*, and *Cannon*. His signature was the introduction of each segment after each commercial as "Act I," "Act II," etc. There was even an "Epilogue."

32   Robert S. Alley, address, University of Iowa International Television Symposium, Iowa City, Iowa, April 25, 1985.

33   "The Last Chapter," *The Dick Van Dyke Show*, June 1, 1966.

34   Weissman and Sanders, p. 26.

35   The first notable attempt at a Jewish–Gentile sitcom marriage was *Bridget Loves Bernie* (CBS, 1972–3).

36   Theodore Sorensen, *Kennedy* (New York: Harper and Row, 1965), p. 381.

37   See John G. Cawelti, "The Concept of Formula in the Study of Popular Literature," *Journal of Popular Culture*, 3 (1969), pp. 381–90.

38   Weissman and Sanders, p. 85.

Consider the Source

1. In reconstructing the origins and production of *The Dick Van Dyke Show*, David Marc relies on a variety of sources, ranging from historical accounts of the Kennedy administration to Carl Reiner's reminiscences of his childhood in the 1958 book *Enter Laughing*. In the following excerpts from her memoir *After All*, by contrast, one of the show's stars, Mary Tyler Moore – a beloved actor who headlined her own sitcom in the 1970s – offers a description of the show that appears to rely heavily on her own memory. In what ways does Moore's account correspond to Marc's? Are there any places where they differ in terms of interpretation or emphasis? Who do you regard as more credible? On what basis?

Excerpts from *After All* by Mary Tyler Moore (1995)

Carl's original vision had most of the show based in the writer's office, with home scenes kept to a secondary level. This was a big change for situation comedies. In the past you were never really sure about just what it was that Daddy did for a living. Domesticity was the mainstay of television comedy.

This look at the character's – Rob Petrie's – work was also distinguished by revealing a behind-the-scenes view of writing for a variety show. It was generally considered bad form to reveal any of the magic that was show business. But Carl used his experiences as a writer on *The Sid Caesar Show* as the drawing board for building Rob Petrie and humanizing the television industry.

Carl had written the original pilot and first six episodes of what is now *The Dick Van Dyke Show* for himself as Rob. I don't think there's any question that Carl could have carried it. He would have been a less vulnerable Rob, and maybe that's why CBS urged him to continue the project but not as its star. At that time it was also thought that being Jewish, and expecting the greater TV audience to identify with that family, was asking too much. In 1961, everyone at CBS was challenged enough just dealing with the unexpected exploration of Rob's office life, without having to deal with cultural experimentation as well. . . .

What a careful and restrained version of the Petries' life Carl had to write. And yet he broke ground in every area. If there was one thing the critics pointed to, it was the freshness of this show's style. Rob was a wonderful husband – well, as good as he could be, sleeping in obligatory twin beds. When we did the flashback stories of Ritchie's birth, the word "pregnant" was not allowed to be used. Come to think of it, it's amazing that Laura got pregnant at all, given the circumstances of the bed setup.

I immediately caused a stir in my style of dress. I wore pants. TV wives didn't do that. They wore full-skirted, floral-print dresses with high heels, even while vacuuming! My comedic insecurities pushed me to take a stand on something, and this seemed a reasonable issue. I may not have known jokes, but I knew what young wives were wearing. I was a young wife, and I wore pants.

Everyone I talked to agreed that it was appropriate – that's what their wives wore. But here again, television hadn't quite caught up with the times. And so it was, at my own suggestion, that in a long line of situation-comedy wives, I would be the first to disdain the costume of old and opt for what were then called Capri pants and flats.

2.   How would you describe Marc's tone in this essay? Is he funny? If so, why – and where? If not, why not? What does your reaction to the writing here suggest about your own tastes and standards?

3.   Marc notes that Carl Reiner's irritation with elite artists and intellectuals is a recurring motif in the show, one deftly embodied in Rob Petrie's epigraph: "I don't want to be an artist; I'm a good [television] writer." To what extent do you believe television is still looked down upon, even within the world of popular culture? To what extent is such a perception simple snobbery?

4.   ". . . the Petries were perhaps the last sitcom couple who could simultaneously take for granted their unnamed (and, on television unnameable) white, middle-class, heterosexual advantage and still manage to exhibit a kind of quasi-sophistication and personal warmth that imply sympathy for civil rights and possibly even advocacy of welfare-state measures," Marc writes in a

notably complex sentence (p. 252). Given what you know about what happened to the United States in the 1960s (and what followed), what do you think he means by it?

Suggested Further Reading

As with film and radio, the literature on television is voluminous. And as with radio, a good starting point is the three-volume (or one-volume abridgment) history of broadcasting by Erik Barnouw cited in "Consider the Source" in chapter 7. Other important work on the situation comedy and its contexts includes David Marc's *Demographic Vistas: Television in American Culture* (Philadelphia: University of Pennsylvania Press, 1984); Darrell Y. Hamamoto, *Nervous Laughter: Television Situation Comedy and Liberal Democratic Ideology* (New York: Praeger, 1989); Lynn Spigel, *Make Room for TV: Television and the Family Ideal in Postwar America* (Chicago: University of Chicago Press, 1992). See also Robin R. Means Coleman, *African American Viewers and the Black Situation Comedy: Situating Racial Humor* (New York: Garland, 1998).

10

Hip-Hop Nation

1915–45	Migration of African Americans – and their music – from the South to North and West
1945–50	Bebop jazz emerges as an alternative to dominant jazz styles
1956	Elvis Presley becomes "King of Rock- and-Roll" by drawing on African-American musical idioms
1964	"British Invasion" of Beatles, Rolling Stones, and others, inspired by black traditions
1972–4	Watergate crisis envelops Nixon presidency
1974–80	Disco becomes dominant genre of popular music
1979	Independent entrepreneur Sylvia Robinson releases the Sugar Hill Gang's "Rapper's Delight"
1980	Ronald Reagan elected president (1981–9)
1982	Grandmaster Flash and the Furious Five release "The Message"
1986	Run DMC finds crossover success with Aerosmith's "Walk this Way"
1989	Berlin Wall falls
1989	MTV premieres *Yo! MTV Raps*
1992	Los Angeles riots
1996	Shooting of Tupac Shakur intensifies criticism surrounding gangsta rap
1998–9	Monica Lewinsky scandal damages Clinton presidency (1993–2001)

Introduction

For most young Americans, rap music is not really about American history – it's about American life right now. Not everybody loves it, but anyone born in the last 25 years of the twentieth century experiences it as an-ever present soundtrack over the airwaves, in advertising, at sporting events, and on movie screens. Chapbooks may come, and dime novels may go, but for the foreseeable future, this moment belongs to rap.

In an important sense however, rap – and the hip-hop culture of dance and graffiti with which it is also associated – are profound historical phenomena that represent the latest chapter in the saga of a black Atlantic Diaspora that encompasses Africa, the Caribbean, and the Americas. That saga, which began in slavery and includes encounters with Western Christianity, industrial capitalism, and an ongoing struggle for equality, has been marked by grief and triumph. It has also been a deeply pluralistic experience, integrating black, white and everything in between. The African-American experience is now recognized as an indispensable ingredient in our national heritage, the strand in the tapestry that more than any other distinguishes the popular culture of the United States as truly American. And it is music – especially African-American music – that stands as one of our great contributions to world civilization.

That said, the story of African-American music in the United States can also be characterized as an ongoing effort on the part of black Americans to make art they could truly call their own in environments where they had virtually nothing else they could. Yet even this ambition was subject to exploitation. A series of cultural forms first developed by disenfranchised African Americans have been so thoroughly absorbed – and in commercial terms, at least, it would not be too strong to say stolen – by privileged white ethnic groups. Minstrelsy was an early example of this. The cakewalk, a late nineteenth-century dance craze that supposedly lampooned black pretensions to style, but which was originally invented by slaves satirizing *white* pretentiousness, is another. In the twentieth century, jazz emerged from the hothouse environment of New Orleans and for a number of decades became the dominant style of popular music. When it did so, a series of jazz musicians in the late 1940s, among them titans like John Coltrane and Miles Davis, developed bebop, a highly arcane jazz style resistant to popular white appeal. Meanwhile, a number of other black musicians began refining another style, rock-and-roll, which took the world by storm in the 1950s. (Predictably, rock emerged in the excitement surrounding Elvis Presley, an undeniably gifted singer who had the decisive advantage of not having black skin.) For the next 30 years, rock became the universal language for American youth, a brash cultural outcast that seized center stage.

As early as the late 1970s, however, rock's successor was taking shape. First emerging in the New York City borough of the Bronx, rap represented the marriage of the Jamaican tradition of spoken wordplay, or "toasting," and cheap American recording technology (turntables, drum machines, synthesizers, and sampling of old songs in new contexts). Pioneering rappers like the Sugar Hill Gang and Grandmaster Flash and the Furious Five captured the imaginations of urban black young people (and hip white observers like Blondie, whose 1980 hit single "Rapture" demonstrated just how quickly outsiders could hop on the bandwagon). Like jazz and rock before it, rap was widely ridiculed and attacked as a bad influence on youth. But like them, too, it has proved to be a durable cultural force in American life that has earned respect as a means of artistic expression and a source of inspiration in other media, forms, and genres of popular culture.

The following piece is the opening chapter of *Black Noise: Rap Music and Black Culture in Contemporary America*, by Tricia Rose, a scholar of history and African studies at New York University. Given the rapid pace of change in popular music in general and rap in particular, this 1994 essay is inevitably dated. But it is both a deft summation of rap's past and a revealing snapshot of the time when it was written – which is another way of saying it's an evocative piece of history. And as the history of a time that is still unfolding, it seems like an apt work of scholarship with which to conclude this book.

Voices from the Margins: Rap Music and Contemporary Black Cultural Production

Tricia Rose

Public Enemy's "Can't Truss It" opens with rapper Flavor Flav shouting "Confusion!" over a heavy and energetic bass line. The subsequent lyrics suggest that Flavor Flav is referring to lead rapper Chuck D's story about the legacy of slavery, that it has produced extreme cultural confusion. He could just as easily be describing the history of rap. Rap music is a confusing and noisy element of contemporary American popular culture that continues to draw a great deal of attention to itself. On the one hand, music and cultural critics praise rap's role as an educational tool, point out that black women rappers are rare examples of aggressive pro-women lyricists in popular music, and defend rap's ghetto stories as real-life reflections that should draw attention to the burning problems of racism and economic oppression, rather than to questions of obscenity. On the other hand, news media attention on rap seems fixated on instances of violence at rap concerts, rap producers' illegal use of musical

Reproduced from *Black Noise: Rap Music and Black Culture in Contemporary America*. © 1994 by Tricia Rose, Wesleyan University Press, by permission of University Press of New England.

Taking the stage Agent Attitude, Flavor Flav, and Chuck D of Public Enemy live in its heyday. The band's militancy – typified by its 1990 anthem "Fight the Power" – attracted enormous excitement, admiration, and condemnation as rap emerged as the dominant idiom of popular music at the end of the twentieth century. *Photo by permission of Michael Ochs Archive, Venice, California*

samples, gangsta raps' lurid fantasies of cop killing and female dismemberment, and black nationalist rappers' suggestions that white people are the devil's disciples. These celebratory and inflammatory aspects in rap and the media coverage of them bring to the fore several long-standing debates about popular music and culture. Some of the more contentious disputes revolve around the following questions: Can violent images incite violent action, can music set the stage for political mobilization, do sexually explicit lyrics contribute to the moral "breakdown" of society, and finally, is this really *music* anyway?

And, if these debates about rap music are not confusing enough, rappers engage them in contradictory ways. Some rappers defend the work of gangster rappers and at the same time consider it a negative influence on black youths. Female rappers openly criticize male rappers' sexist work and simultaneously defend the 2 Live Crew's right to sell misogynist music. Rappers who criticize America for its perpetuation of racial and economic discrimination also share conservative ideas about personal responsibility, call for self-improvement strategies in the black community that focus heavily on personal behavior as the cause and solution for crime, drugs, and community instability.

Rap music brings together a tangle of some of the most complex social, cultural, and political issues in contemporary American society. Rap's contradictory articulations are not signs of absent intellectual clarity; they are a common feature of community and popular cultural dialogues that always offer more than one cultural, social, or political viewpoint. These unusually abundant polyvocal conversations seem irrational when they are severed from the social contexts where everyday struggles over resources, pleasure, and meanings take place.

Rap music is a black cultural expression that prioritizes black voices from the margins of urban America. Rap music is a form of rhymed storytelling accompanied by highly rhythmic, electronically based music. It began in the mid-1970s in the South Bronx in New York City as a part of hip hop, an African-American and Afro-Caribbean youth culture composed of graffiti, breakdancing, and rap music. From the outset, rap music has articulated the pleasures and problems of black urban life in contemporary America. Rappers speak with the voice of personal experience, taking on the identity of the observer or narrator. Male rappers often speak from the perspective of a young man who wants social status in a locally meaningful way. They rap about how to avoid gang pressures and still earn local respect, how to deal with the loss of several friends to gun fights and drug overdoses, and they tell grandiose and sometimes violent tales that are powered by male sexual power over women. Female rappers sometimes tell stories from the perspective of a young woman who is skeptical of male protestations of love or a girl who has been involved with a drug dealer and cannot sever herself from his dangerous lifestyle. Some raps speak to the failures of black men to provide security and attack men where their manhood seems most vulnerable: the pocket. Some tales are one sister telling another to rid herself from the abuse of a lover.

Like all contemporary voices, the rapper's voice is embedded in powerful and dominant technological, industrial, and ideological institutions. Rappers tell long, involved, and sometimes abstract stories with catchy and memorable phrases and beats that lend themselves to black soundbite packaging, storing critical fragments in fast-paced electrified rhythms. Rap tales are told in elaborate and ever-changing black slang and refer to black cultural figures and rituals, mainstream film, video and television characters, and little-known black heroes. For rap's language wizards, all images, sounds, ideas, and icons are ripe for recontextualization, pun, mockery, and celebration. Kool Moe Dee boasts that each of his rhymes is like a dissertation, Kid-N-Play have quoted Jerry Lee Lewis's famous phrase "great balls of fire," Big Daddy Kane brags that he's raw like sushi (and that his object of love has his nose open like a jar of Vicks), Ice Cube refers to his ghetto stories as "tales from the darkside," clearly referencing the television horror show with the same name. Das Efx's raps include Elmer Fud's characteristic "OOOH I'm steamin'!" in full character voice along with a string of almost surreal collagelike references to Bugs Bunny and other television characters. At the same time, the stories, ideas, and thoughts articulated in rap lyrics invoke and revise stylistic and thematic elements that are deeply wedded to a number of black cultural storytelling forms, most prominently toasting and the blues. Ice-T and Big Daddy Kane pay explicit homage to Rudy Ray Moore as "Dolomite," Roxanne Shante toasts Millie Jackson, and black folk wisdom and folktales are given new lives and meanings in contemporary culture.

Rap's stories continue to articulate the shifting terms of black marginality in contemporary American culture. Even as rappers achieve what appears to be central status in commercial culture, they are far more vulnerable to censorship efforts than highly visible white rock artists, and they continue to experience the brunt of the plantationlike system faced by most artists in the music and sports industries. Even as they struggle with the tension between fame and rap's gravitational pull toward local urban narratives, for the most part, rappers continue to craft stories that represent the creative fantasies, perspectives, and experiences of racial marginality in America.

Rap went relatively unnoticed by mainstream music and popular culture industries until independent music entrepreneur Sylvia Robinson released "Rappers Delight" in 1979. Over the next five years rap music was "discovered" by the music industry, the print media, the fashion industry, and the film industry, each of which hurried to cash in on what was assumed to be a passing fad. During the same years, Run DMC (who recorded the first gold rap record *Run DMC* in 1984), Whodini, and the Fat Boys became the most commercially successful symbols of rap music's sounds and style.

By 1987, rap music had survived several death knells, Hollywood mockery, and radio bans and continued to spawn new artists, such as Public Enemy, Eric B. & Rakim, and L. L. Cool J. At the same time, women rappers, such as MC Lyte and Salt 'N' Pepa, encouraged by Roxanne Shante's early successes, made inroads into rap's emerging commercial audience. Between 1987 and 1990 a number of critical musical and industry changes took place. Public Enemy became rap's first superstar group, and media attention to its black nationalist political articulations intensified. The success of De La Soul's playful Afrocentricity, tongue in cheek spoof of rap's aggressive masculinity and manipulation of America's television culture encouraged the Native Tongues wing of rap that opened the door to such future groups as A Tribe Called Quest, Queen Latifah, Brand Nubian, and Black

Sheep. Ice-T put the Los Angeles gangsta rap style on the national map, which encouraged the emergence of NWA, Ice Cube, Too Short, and others.

At the industry level, the effects of rap's infiltration were widespread. Black filmmaker Spike Lee's commercially successful use of b-boys, b-girls, hip hop music, and style in the contemporary urban terrain as primary themes in *She's Gotta Have It* and *Do the Right Thing* fired up Hollywood's new wave of black male ghetto films, most notably, *Colors*, *New Jack City*, *Boyz N the Hood*, *Juice* and *Menace II Society*. By 1989, MTV began playing rap music on a relatively regular basis, and multi-million unit rap sales by the Beastie Boys, Tone Loc, M.C. Hammer and Vanilla Ice convinced music industry executives that rap music, for all of its "blackness" in attitude, style, speech, music, and thematics, was a substantial success with white teenagers.

Rap's black cultural address and its focus on marginal identities may appear to be in opposition to its crossover appeal for people from different racial or ethnic groups and social positions. How can this black public dialogue speak to the thousands of young white suburban boys and girls who are critical to the record sales successes of many of rap's more prominent stars? How can I suggest that rap is committed culturally and emotionally to the pulse, pleasures, and problems of black urban life in the face of such diverse constituencies?

To suggest that rap is a black idiom that prioritizes black culture and that articulates the problems of black urban life does not deny the pleasure and participation of others. In fact, many black musics before rap (e.g., the blues, jazz, early rock'n' roll) have also become American popular musics precisely because of extensive white participation; white America has always had an intense interest in black culture. Consequently, the fact that a significant number of white teenagers have become rap fans is quite consistent with the history of black music in America and should not be equated with a shift in rap's discursive or stylistic focus away from black pleasure and black fans. However, extensive white participation in black culture has also always involved white appropriation and attempts at ideological recuperation of black cultural resistance. Black culture in the United States has always had elements that have been at least bifocal – speaking to both a black audience and a larger predominantly white context. Rap music shares this history of interaction with many previous black oral and music traditions.

Like generations of white teenagers before them, white teenage rap fans are listening in on black culture, fascinated by its differences, drawn in by mainstream social constructions of black culture as a forbidden narrative, as a symbol of rebellion. Kathy Ogren's study of jazz in the

1920s shows the extensive efforts made by white entertainers and fans to imitate jazz music, dance styles, and language as well as the alarm such fascination caused on the part of state and local authority figures. Lewis Erenberg's study of the development of the cabaret illustrates the centrality of jazz music to the fears over blackness associated with the burgeoning urban nightlife culture. There are similar and abundant cases for rock 'n' roll as well.[1]

Fascination with African-American culture is not new, nor can the dynamics and politics of pleasure across cultural "boundaries" in segregated societies be overlooked. Jazz, rock 'n' roll, soul, and R&B each have large devoted white audience members, many of whom share traits with Norman Mailer's "white negroes," young white listeners trying to perfect a model of correct white hipness, coolness, and style by adopting the latest black style and image. Young white listeners' genuine pleasure and commitment to black music are necessarily affected by dominant racial discourses regarding African Americans, the politics of racial segregation, and cultural difference in the United States. Given the racially discriminatory context within which cultural syncretism takes place, some rappers have equated white participation with a process of dilution and subsequent theft of black culture. Although the terms dilution and theft do not capture the complexity of cultural incorporation and syncretism, this interpretation has more than a grain of truth in it. There is abundant evidence that white artists imitating black styles have greater economic opportunity and access to larger audiences than black innovators. Historical accounts of the genres often position these subsequently better known artists as the central figures, erasing or marginalizing the artists and contexts within which the genre developed. The process of incorporation and marginalization of black practitioners has also fostered the development of black forms and practices that are less and less accessible, forms that require greater knowledge of black language and styles in order to participate. Bebop, with its insider language and its "willfully harsh, anti-assimilationist sound" is a clear example of this response to the continuation of plantation system logic in American culture.[2] In addition to the sheer pleasure black musicians derive from developing a new and exciting style, these black cultural reactions to American culture suggest a reclaiming of the definition of blackness and an attempt to retain aesthetic control over black cultural forms. In the 1980s, this re-claiming of blackness in the popular realm is complicated by access to new reproduction technologies and revised corporate relations in the music industry.

In a number of ways, rap has followed the patterns of other black popular musics, in that at the outset it was heavily rejected by black and white middle-class listeners; the assumption was that it would be a short-lived fad; the mainstream record industry and radio stations rejected it; its marketing was pioneered by independent entrepreneurs and independent labels; and once a smidgen of commercial viability was established the major labels attempted to dominate production and distribution. These rap-related patterns were augmented by more general music industry consolidation in the late 1970s that provided the major music corporations with greater control over the market. By 1990 virtually all major record chain-store distribution is controlled by six major record companies: CBS, Polygram, Warner, BMG, Capitol-EMI, and MCA.[3]

However, music industry consolidation and control over distribution is complicated by three factors: the expansion of local cable access; sophisticated and accessible mixing, production, and copying equipment; and a new relationship between major and independent record labels. In previous eras when independent labels sustained the emergence of new genres against industry rejection, the eventual absorption of these genres by larger companies signalled the dissolution of the independent labels. In the early 1980s, after rap spurred the growth of new independent labels, the major labels moved in and attempted to dominate the market but could not consolidate their efforts. Artists signed to independent labels, particularly Tommy Boy, Profile, and Def Jam continued to flourish, whereas acts signed directly to the six majors could not produce comparable sales. It became apparent that the independent labels had a much greater understanding of the cultural logic of hip hop and rap music, a logic that permeated decisions ranging from signing acts to promotional methods. Instead of competing with smaller, more street-savvy labels for new rap acts, the major labels developed a new strategy: buy the independent labels, allow them to function relatively autonomously, and provide them with production resources and access to major retail distribution.[4] Since the emergence of Public Enemy and their substantial cross-genre success in the late 1980s, rappers have generally been signed to independent labels (occasionally black owned and sometimes their own labels) and marketed and distributed by one of the six major companies. In this arrangement, the six majors reap the benefits of a genre that can be marketed with little up-front capital investment, and the artists are usually pleased to have access to the large record and CD chain stores that would otherwise never consider carrying their work.

In the 1980s, the trickle-down effect of technological advances in electronics brought significantly expanded access to mixing, dubbing, and copying equipment for consumers and black market retailers. Clearly, these advances provided aspiring musicians with greater access to recording and copying equipment at less expense. They also substantially improved the market for illegal dubbing of popular music for street-corner sale at reduced cost. (Illegally recorded cassette tapes cost approximately $5.00, one-half the cost of label issues.) These lower quality tapes are usually sold in poorer, densely populated communities where reduced cost is a critical sales factor. Rap music is a particularly popular genre for bootleg tapes in urban centers.[5]

Even though actual sales demographics for rap music are not available, increasing sales figures for rap musicians (several prominent rap artists have sales over 500,000 units per album), suggest that white teenage rap consumers have grown steadily since the emergence of Public Enemy in 1988.[6] Middle-class white teenage rap consumers appear to be an increasingly significant audience. This can be inferred from location sales via market surveys and Soundscan, a new electronic scan system installed primarily in large, mostly suburban music chain stores. It is quite possible, however, that the percentage of white rap consumers in relation to overall sales is being disproportionately represented, because bootleg street sales coupled with limited chain music store outlets in poor communities makes it very difficult to assess the demographics for actual sales of rap music to urban black and Hispanic consumers. In addition to inconsistent sales figures, black teen rap consumers may also have a higher pass-along rate, that is, the rate at which one purchased product is shared among consumers. In my conversations with James Bernard, an editor at *The Source* (a major hip hop culture magazine with a predominantly black teen readership), *The Source's* pass-along rate is approximately 1 purchase for every 11–15 readers. According to Bernard, this rate is at least three to four times higher than the average magazine industry pass-along rate. It is conceivable, then, that a similar pass-along rate exists among rap music CD and cassette consumption, especially among consumers with less disposable income.

Cable television exploded during the 1980s and had a significant effect on the music industry and on rap music. Launched in August 1981 by Warner Communications and the American Express Company, MTV became the fastest growing cable channel and as [Reebee] Garofalo notes, "soon became the most effective way for a record to get national exposure."[7] Using its rock format and white teen audience as an explanation for its almost complete refusal to play videos by black artists (once pressure was brought to bear they added Michael Jackson and Prince), MTV finally jumped on the rap music bandwagon. It was not until 1989, with the piloting of "Yo! MTV Raps" that any black artists began to appear on MTV regularly. Since then, as Jamie Malanowski reports, " 'Yo MTV Raps' [has become] one of MTV's most popular shows, is dirt cheap to produce and has almost single-handedly dispelled the giant tastemaking network's reputation for not playing black artists."[8]

Since 1989, MTV has discovered that black artists in several genres are marketable to white suburban teenagers and has dramatically revised its formatting to include daily rap shows, Street Block (dance music), and the rotation of several black artists outside of specialized-genre rotation periods. However, MTV's previous exclusion of black artists throughout the mid-1980s, inspired other cable stations to program black music videos. Black Entertainment Television (BET), the most notable alternative to MTV, continues to air a wide variety of music videos by black artists as one of its programming mainstays. And local and syndicated shows (e.g., "Pump It Up!" based in Los Angeles and "Video Music Box" based in New York), continue to play rap music videos, particularly lower budget, and aggressively black nationalist rap videos deemed too angry or too antiwhite for MTV.

MTV's success has created an environment in which the reception and marketing of music is almost synonymous with the production of music videos. Fan discussions of popular songs and the stories they tell are often accompanied by a reading of the song's interpretation in music video. Music video is a collaboration in the production of popular music; it revises meanings, provides preferred interpretations of lyrics, creates a stylistic and physical context for reception; and valorizes the iconic presence of the artist. Can we really imagine, nonetheless understand, the significance of Michael Jackson's presence as a popular cultural icon without interpreting his music video narratives? The same holds true for Madonna, Janet Jackson, U2, Whitney Houston, Nirvana, and Guns n' Roses, among others. The visualization of music has far-reaching effects on musical cultures and popular culture generally, not the least of which is the increase in visual interpretations of sexist power relationships, the mode of visual storytelling, the increased focus on how a singer looks rather than how he or she sounds, the need to craft an image to accompany one's music, and ever-greater pressure to abide by corporate genre-formatting rules.

The significance of music video as a partner in the creation or reception of popular music is even greater in the case of rap music. Because the vast majority of rap music (except by the occasional superstar) has been virtually frozen out of black radio programming – black radio representatives claim that it scares off high-quality advertising – and because of its limited access to large performance venues, music video has been a crucial outlet for rap artist audiences and performer visibility. Rap music videos have animated hip hop cultural style and aesthetics and have facilitated a cross-neighborhood, cross-country (transnational?) dialogue in a social environment that is highly segregated by class and race.

The emergence of rap music video has also opened up a previously nonexistent creative arena for black visual artists. Rap music video has provided a creative and commercially viable arena where black film, video, set design, costume, and technical staff and trainees can get the crucial experience and connections to get a foot in the world of video and film production. Before music video production for black musicians, these training grounds, however exploitative, were virtually inaccessible to black technicians. The explosion of music video production, especially black music video, has generated a pool of skilled young black workers in the behind-the scenes nonunion crews (union membership is overwhelmingly white and male), who are beginning to have an impact on current black film production.

Shooting in the Ghetto: Locating Rap Music Video Production

Rap video has also developed its own style and its own genre conventions. These conventions visualize hip-hop style and usually affirm rap's primary thematic concerns: identity and location. Over most of its brief history (rap video production began in earnest in the mid-to-late 1980s), rap video themes have repeatedly converged around the depiction of the local neighborhood and the local posse, crew, or support system. Nothing is more central to rap's music video narratives than situating the rapper in his or her milieu and among one's crew or posse. Unlike heavy metal videos, for example, which often use dramatic live concert footage and the concert stage as the core location, rap music videos are set on buses, subways, in abandoned buildings, and almost always in black urban inner-city locations. This usually involves ample shots of favorite street corners, intersections, playgrounds, parking lots, school yards, roofs, and childhood friends. When I asked seasoned music video director Kevin Bray what comprised the three most important themes in rap video, his immediate response was, "Posse, posse, and posse. . . . They'll say, 'I want my shit to be in my hood. Yeah, we got this dope old parking lot where I used to hang out when I was a kid.' "[9] The hood is not a generic designation; videos featuring South Central Los Angeles rappers such as Ice Cube, Ice-T, and NWA very often capture the regional specificity of spatial, ethnic, temperate, and psychological facets of black marginality in Los Angeles, whereas Naughty by Nature's videos feature the ghetto specificity of East Orange, New Jersey.[10]

Rappers' emphasis on posses and neighborhoods has brought the ghetto back into the public consciousness. It satisfies poor young black people's profound need to have their territories acknowledged, recognized, and celebrated. These are the street corners and neighborhoods that usually serve as lurid backdrops for street crimes on the nightly news. Few local people are given an opportunity to speak, and their points of view are always contained by expert testimony. In rap videos, young mostly male residents speak for themselves and for the community, they speak when and how they wish about subjects of their choosing. These local turf scenes are not isolated voices; they are voices from a variety of social margins that are in dialogue with one another. As Bray points out, "If you have an artist from Detroit, the reason they want to shoot at least one video on their home turf is to make a connection with, say, an East Coast New York rapper. It's the dialogue. It's the dialogue between them about where they're from."[11]

However, the return of the ghetto as a central black popular narrative has also fulfilled national fantasies about the violence and danger that purportedly consume the poorest and most economically fragile communities of color. Some conservative critics such as George Will have affirmed the "reality" of some popular cultural ghetto narratives and used this praise as a springboard to call for more police presence and military invasionlike policies.[12] In other cases, such as that of white rapper Vanilla Ice, the ghetto is a source of fabricated white authenticity. Controversy surrounding Ice, one of rap music's most commercially successful artists, highlights the significance of "ghetto blackness" as a model of "authenticity" and happiness in rap music. During the winter of 1989, Vanilla Ice summoned the wrath of the hip-hop community not only by successfully marketing himself as a white rapper but also by "validating" his success with stories about his close ties to black poor neighborhoods, publicly sporting his battle scars from the black inner city. According to *Village Voice* columnist Rob Tannenbaum, Robert Van Winkle (aka Vanilla Ice) told Stephen Holden of the *New York Times* that "he 'grew up in the ghetto,' comes from a broken home, hung out mainly with blacks while attending the same Miami high school as Luther Campbell of 2 Live Crew, and was nearly killed in a gang fight." Yet, in a copyrighted, front-page story in the Dallas *Morning News*, Ken P. Perkins charges, among other things, that Mr. Van Winkle is instead a middle-class kid from Dallas, Texas.[13] Vanilla Ice's desire to be a "white negro" (or, as some black and white hip-hop fans say, a Wigger – a white nigger), to "be black" in order to validate his status as a rapper hints strongly at the degree to which ghetto-blackness is a critical code in rap music. Vanilla Ice not only pretended to be from the ghetto, but he also pretended to have produced the music for his mega-hit "Ice, Ice Baby." In keeping with his pretenses, he only partially credited – and paid no royalties to – black friend and producer Mario Johnson, aka Chocolate(!), who actually wrote the music for "Ice, Ice Baby" and a few other cuts from Vanilla's fifteen times platinum record *To the Extreme*. After a lengthy court battle, Chocolate is finally getting paid in full.[14]

Convergent forces are behind this resurgence of black ghetto symbolism and representation. Most important, the ghetto *exists* for millions of young black and other people of color – it is a profoundly significant social location. Using the ghetto as a source of identity – as rapper Trech would say, if you're not from the ghetto, don't ever come to the ghetto – undermines the stigma of poverty and social marginality. At the same time, the ghetto badman posture-performance is a protective shell against real unyielding and harsh social policies and physical environments. Experience also dictates that public attention is more easily drawn to acts, images, and threats of black male violence than to any other form of racial address. The ghetto produces a variety of meanings for diverse audiences, but this should not be interpreted to mean that intragroup black meanings and uses are less important than larger social receptions. Too often, white voyeuristic pleasure of black cultural imagery or such imagery's role in the performance of ghetto crisis for the news media, are interpreted as their primary value. Even though rappers are aware of the diversity of their audiences and the context for reception, their use of the ghetto and its symbolic significances is primarily directed at other black hip-hop fans. If white teen and adult viewers were the preferred audience, then it wouldn't matter which ghetto corner framed images of Trech from rap group Naughty by Nature, especially as most white popular cultural depictions of ghetto life are drained of relevant detail, texture, and complexity. Quite to the contrary, rap's ghetto imagery is too often intensely specific and locally significant, making its preferred viewer someone who can read ghettocentricity with ghetto sensitivity.

The fact that rappers' creative desires or location requests are frequently represented in music videos should not lead one to believe that rappers control the music video process. Music video production is a complex and highly mediated process dictated by the record company in what is sometimes a contentious dialogue with the artists' management, the chosen video director, and video producer. Even though the vast majority of the music video production budget is advanced from the artists' royalties (rap video budgets can range from a low $5,000 to an unusual $100,000 with an average video costing about $40,000), the artist has very little final decision-making control over the video process. Generally speaking, once the single is chosen, a group of music video directors are solicited by the record company, management, and artist to submit video ideas or treatments, and an estimated budget range is projected. After listening to the rapper's work, the video directors draft narrative treatments that usually draw on the rap artists' desires, strengths, lyrical focus, and the feel of the music while attempting to incorporate his or her own visual and technical strengths and preferred visual styles. Once a director is selected, the treatment and budget are refined, negotiated, and the video is cast and produced.[15]

In the first few years of rap video production, the record companies were less concerned about music video's creative process, leaving artists and directors more creative decision-making power. As rappers developed more financial viability, record companies became increasingly invasive at the editing stage, going even so far as to make demands about shot selection and sequencing. This intervention has been facilitated by record companies' increasing sophistication about the video production process. Recently, record companies have begun hiring ex-freelance video producers as video commissioners whose familiarity with the production process aids the record company in channeling and constraining directors, producers, and artist decisions. For veteran music video director Charles Stone, these commercial constraints define music video, in the final analysis, as a commercial product: "Commercial expectations are always an undercurrent. Questions like, does the artist look good, is the artist's image being represented – are always a part of your decision-making process. You have to learn how to protect yourself from excessive meddling, but some negotiation with record companies and artist management always takes place."[16]

With rap's genre and stylistic conventions and artists' desires flanking one side of the creative process and the record company's fiscal and artist management's marketing concerns shoring up the other, music video directors are left with a tight space within which to exercise their creativity. Still, video directors find imaginative ways to engage the musical and lyrical texts and enter into dialogue with the rappers' work. For Bray and other directors, the best videos have the capacity to offer new interpretations after multiple viewings, they have the spontaneity and intertextuality of the music, and most importantly, as Bray describes, the best videos are "sublime visual interpretations of the lyrics which work as another instrument in the musical arrangement; the music video is a visual instrument." Sometimes this visual instrumentation is a thematic improvisation on the historical point of reference suggested by the musical samples. So, a cool jazz horn sample might evoke a contemporary refashioning of a jazz club or cool jazz coloring or art direction. Stone often relies on text and animation to produce creative interpretations of musical works. "Using word overlay," Stone says, "is particularly compatible with rap's use of language. Both are candid and aggressive uses of words, and both play with words' multiple meanings." His selective and unconventional use of animation often makes rappers seem larger than life and can visually emphasize the superheroic powers suggested by rappers' lyrical delivery and performance.

Satisfying the record companies, artists, and managers is only half the battle; MTV, the most powerful video outlet, has its own standards and guidelines for airing videos. These guidelines, according to several frustrated directors, producers, and video commissioners, are inconsistent and unwritten. The most consistent rule is the "absolutely not" list (that some people claim has been subverted by powerful artists and record companies). The "absolutely not" list includes certain acts of violence, some kinds of nudity and sex, profanity and epithets (e.g., "nigger" or "bitch" no matter how these words are being used). The list of censored words and actions expands regularly.

Independent video producer Gina Harrell notes that the process of establishing airing boundaries takes place on a case-by-case basis. MTV is frequently sent a rough cut for approval as part of the editing process to determine if they will *consider* airing the video, and often several changes, such as word reversals, scene cuts, and lyrical rewrites, must be made to accommodate their standards: "Afterwards, you wind up with very little to work with. There is so much censorship now, and from the other end, the record company's video commissioners are much more exacting about what they want the end result to be. It has extended the editing process and raised production costs. Basically, there are too many cooks in the kitchen." There is, not surprisingly, special concern over violence: "The cop issue has really affected rap music video. You can't shoot anybody in a video, you can hold up a gun, but you can't show who you're pointing at. So you can hold up a gun in one frame and then cut to the person being shot in the next frame, but you can't have a person shooting at another person in the same frame.[17] Even so, many artists refuse to operate in a self-censoring fashion and continue to push on these fluid boundaries by shooting footage that they expect will be censored.

MTV's sex policies are equally vague. Although MTV has aired such a video as Wrecks-N-Effect's "Rumpshaker," whose concept is a series of closeup and sometimes magnified distortions of black women's bikini-clad gyrating behinds and breasts, it refused to allow A Tribe Called Quest to say the word *prophylactic* in the lyrical soundtrack for the video "Bonita Applebum," a romantic and uncharacteristically emotionally honest portrayal of teen desire and courtship. MTV denied Stone's request to show condoms in the video, even though the song's mild references to sex and his video treatment were cast in safe sex language. Given the power of cultural conservatives to "strike the fear of god" in music industry corporations, most video producers and directors are bracing themselves for further restrictions.

Rap music and video have been wrongfully characterized as thoroughly sexist but rightfully lambasted for their sexism. I am thoroughly frustrated but not surprised by the apparent need for some rappers to craft elaborate and creative stories about the abuse and domination of young black women. Perhaps these stories serve to protect young men from the reality of female rejection; maybe and more likely, tales of sexual domination falsely relieve their lack of self-worth and limited access to economic and social markers for heterosexual masculine power. Certainly, they reflect the deep-seated sexism that pervades the structure of American culture. Still, I have grown weary of rappers' stock retorts to charges of sexism in rap: "There are 'bitches' or 'golddiggers' out there, and that's who this rap is about," or "This is just a story, I don't *mean anything* by it." I have also grown impatient with the cowardly silence of rappers who I know find this aspect of rap troubling.

On the other hand, given the selective way in which the subject of sexism occupies public dialogue, I am highly skeptical of the timing and strategic deployment of outrage regarding rap's sexism. Some responses to sexism in rap music adopt a tone that suggests that rappers have infected an otherwise sexism-free society. These reactions to rap's sexism deny the existence of a vast array of accepted sexist social practices that make up adolescent male gender role modeling that results in social norms for adult male behaviors that are equally sexist, even though they are usually expressed with less profanity. Few popular analyses of rap's sexism seem willing to confront the fact that sexual and institutional control over and abuse of women is a crucial component of developing a heterosexual masculine identity. In some instances, the music has become a scapegoat that diverts attention away from the more entrenched problem of redefining the terms of heterosexual masculinity.

Rap's sexist lyrics are also part of a rampant and viciously normalized sexism that dominates the corporate culture of the music business. Not only do women face gross pay inequities, but also they face extraordinary day-to-day sexual harassment. Male executives expect to have sexual and social access to women as one of many job perks, and many women, especially black women, cannot establish authority with male coworkers or artists in the business unless they are backed up by male superiors. Independent video producers do not have this institutional backup and, therefore, face exceptionally oppressive work conditions. Harrell has left more than one position because of recurrent, explicit pressure to sleep with her superiors and finds the video shoots an even more unpredictably offensive and frustrating terrain:

> For instance, during a meeting with Def Jam executives on a video shoot, a very famous rapper started lifting up my pants leg trying to rub my leg. I slapped his hand away several times. Later on he stood onstage sticking his

tongue out at me in a sexually provocative way – everyone was aware of what he was doing, no one said a word. This happens quite a bit in the music business. Several years ago I had begun producing videos for a video director who made it clear that I could not continue to work with him unless I slept with him. I think that women are afraid to respond legally or aggressively, not only because many of us fear professional recriminations, but also because so many of us were molested when we were children. Those experiences complicate our ability to defend ourselves.[18]

These instances are not exceptions to the rule – they are the rule, even for women near the very top of the corporate ladder. As Carmen Ashhurst-Watson, president of Rush Communications (a multimedia offshoot of Def Jam Records) relates: "The things that Anita Hill said she heard from Clarence Thomas over a four-year period, I might hear in a morning."[19]

Mass media outlets need to be challenged into opening dialogue about pervasive and oppressive sexual conditions in society and into facilitating more frank discussion about sexist gender practices and courtship rituals. The terms of sexual identities, sexual oppression, and their relationship to a variety of forms of social violence need unpacking and closer examination. Basically, we need more discussions about sex, sexism, and violence, not less.

MTV and the media access it affords is a complex and ever-changing facet of mass-mediated and corporation-controlled communication and culture. To refuse to participate in the manipulative process of gaining access to video, recording materials, and performing venues is to almost guarantee a negligible audience and marginal cultural impact. To participate in and try to manipulate the terms of mass-mediated culture is a double-edged sword that cuts both ways – it provides communication channels within and among largely disparate groups and requires compromise that often affirms the very structures much of rap's philosophy seems determined to undermine. MTV's acceptance and gatekeeping of rap music has dramatically increased rap artists' visibility to black, white, Asian, and Latino teenagers, but it has also inspired antirap censorship groups and fuels the media's fixation on rap and violence.

Commercial marketing of rap music represents a complex and contradictory aspect of the nature of popular expression in a corporation-dominated information society. Rap music and hip-hop style have become common ad campaign hooks for McDonald's, Burger King, Coke, Pepsi, several athletic shoe companies, clothing chain stores, MTV, anti-drug campaigns, and other global corporate efforts ad nauseam. Rap music has grown into a multimillion-dollar record, magazine, and video industry with multiplatinum world renowned rappers, disc jockeys, and entertainers. Dominating the black music charts, rap music and rap music cousins, such as Hip House, New Jack Swing (a dance style of R&B with rap music rhythms and drum-beats), have been trendsetters for popular music in the US and around the world. Rap's musical and visual style have had a profound impact on all contemporary popular music. Rock artists have begun using sampling styles and techniques developed by rappers; highly visible artists, such as Madonna, Janet Jackson, and New Kids on the Block wear hip-hop fashions, use hip-hop dances in their stage shows and rap lyrics and slang words in their recordings.

Yet, rap music is also Black American TV, a public and highly access-ible place, where black meanings and perspectives – even as they are manipulated by corporate concerns – can be shared and validated among black people. Rap is dependent on technology and mass reproduction and distribution. As Andrew Ross has observed, popular music is cap-able of transmitting, disseminating, and rendering "visible 'black' mean-ings, *precisely because of*, and not in spite of, its industrial forms of production, distribution, and consumption."[20] Such tensions between rap's highly personal, conversational intimacy and the massive institu-tional and technological apparatuses on which rap's global voice depends are critical to hip hop, black culture, and popular cultures around the world in the late twentieth century. Inside of these commer-cial constraints, rap offers alternative interpretations of key social events such as the Gulf War, The Los Angeles uprising, police brutality, censor-ship efforts, and community-based education. It is the central cultural vehicle for open social reflection on poverty, fear of adulthood, the desire for absent fathers, frustrations about black male sexism, female sexual desires, daily rituals of life as an unemployed teen hustler, safe sex, raw anger, violence, and childhood memories. It is also the home of innovat-ive uses of style and language, hilariously funny carnivalesque and chit-lin-circuit-inspired dramatic skits, and ribald story telling. In short, it is black America's most dynamic contemporary popular cultural, intellec-tual, and spiritual vessel.

Rap's ability to draw the attention of the nation, to attract crowds around the world in places where English is rarely spoken are fascinating elements of rap's social power. Unfortunately, some of this power is linked to US based cultural imperialism, in that rappers benefit from the disproportionate exposure of US artists around the world facilitated by music industry marketing muscle. However, rap also draws interna-tional audiences because it is a powerful conglomeration of voices from the margins of American society speaking about the terms of that posi-tion. Rap music, like many powerful black cultural forms before it, resonates for people from vast and diverse backgrounds. The cries of pain, anger, sexual desire, and pleasure that rappers articulate speak to hip hop's vast fan base for different reasons. For some, rappers offer symbolic prowess, a sense of black energy and creativity in the face of omnipresent oppressive forces; others listen to rap with an ear toward the hidden voices of the oppressed, hoping to understand America's large, angry, and "unintelligible" population. Some listen to the music's powerful and life-affirming rhythms, its phat beats and growling bass lines, revelling in its energy, seeking strength from its cathartic and electric presence. Rap's global industry-orchestrated (but not industry-created) presence illustrates the power of the language of rap and the salience of the stories of oppression and creative resistance its music and lyrics tell. The drawing power of rap is precisely its musical and narrative commitment to black youth and cultural resistance, and nothing in rap's commercial position and cross-cultural appeal contradicts this fact. Rap's margin(ality) is represented in the contradictory reaction rap receives in mainstream American media and popular culture. It is at once part of the dominant text and, yet, always on the margins of this text; relying on and commenting on the text's center and always aware of its proximity to the border.

Rap music and hip-hop culture are cultural, political, and commercial forms, and for many young people they are the primary cultural, sonic, and linguistic windows on the world. After the Los Angeles riots, author Mike Davis attended an Inglewood Crip and Blood gang truce meeting in which gang members voiced impassioned testimonials and called for unity and political action. Describing their speeches, Davis said: "These guys were very eloquent, and they spoke in a rap rhythm and with rap eloquence, which I think kind of shook up the white television crews." Later, he noted that the gang truce and the political struggles articulated in that meeting were "translated into the [hip-hop] musical culture." Hip hop, Davis concluded, "is the fundamental matrix of self-expression for this whole generation."[21]

Notes

1   See Kathy J. Ogren, *The Jazz Revolution: Twenties America and the Meaning of Jazz* (New York: Oxford University Press, 1989); Lewis A. Erenberg, *Steppin' Out: New York Night Life and the Transformation of American Culture, 1890–1930* (Chicago: University of Chicago Press, 1981); Nelson George, *The Death of Rhythm and Blues* (New York: Pantheon, 1988); Leroi Jones, *Blues People: The Negro Experience in White America and the Music That Developed from It* (New York: Morrow Quill, 1963), for discussions on the politics of black music in the United States.
2   Jones, *Blues People*, p. 181.

3 Russell Sanjek and David Sanjek, *American Popular Music Business in the 20th Century* (New York: Oxford University Press, 1991).
4 Reebee Garofalo, "Crossing Over: 1939–1989," in Janette L. Dates and William Barlow, eds., *Split Image: African Americans in the Mass Media* (Washington, DC: Howard University Press, 1990), pp. 57–121.
5 At the last three annual New Music Seminars in New York, panels were devoted to the issue of bootleg record sales and their effect on rap music sales.
6 Although some evidence suggests that more adults are buying rap music, rap is still predominantly consumed by teenagers and young adults. See Janine McAdams and Deborah Russell, "Rap Breaking Through to Adult Market," *Hollywood Reporter*, 19 September 1991, pp. 4, 20. Chuck D and Ice-T have claimed that white teenagers consume approximately 50 to 70 percent of rap music. Ice-T claims that "more than 50 percent are going to white kids. Black kids buy the records, but the white kids buy the cassette, the CD, the album, the tour jacket, the hats, everything. Black kids might just be buying the bootleg on the street. It's only due to economics." Alan Light, "Ice-T," *Rolling Stone*, 20 August 1992, pp. 31–2, 60. My research has yielded no source for these statistics other than speculation. Furthermore, these rappers may be specifically referring to their fan base; Ice-T and Public Enemy are both known for mixing rock and rap, making it more likely that white consumers would be drawn to their work.
7 Garofalo, "Crossing Over," p. 108. See also Serge Denisoff, *Inside MTV* (New Brunswick, N.J.: Transaction Books, 1987).
8 Jamie Malanowski, "Top Hip Hop," *Rolling Stone*, 13 July 1989, pp. 77–8.
9 Rose interview with Kevin Bray, 18 March 1993. Kevin Bray has directed many rap videos, some of which are quite well-known and highly regarded, including: "Strobe Light Honey" and "Flavor of the Month" for Black Sheep; "All for One" for Brand Nubian; "Not Yet Free" for The Coup; "The Creator" and "Mecca and the Soul Brothers" for Pete Rock and C. L. Smooth; "I've Got the Power" for Chill Rob G; and "I Got To Have It" for Ed O. G. and the Bulldogs.
10 Of course, rap videos narrate other themes and situate rappers in other settings and locations. Probably, the next most frequent rap music video theme features the objectification of young women's bodies as a sign of male power. Some rap videos are explicit political and social statements, others are comic displacements of rappers from familiar surroundings, and increasingly, rap videos feature abstract props and images that deploy fewer location-specific settings. However, no other concept or location is as recurrent and emotionally significant as the depiction of one's home turf and posse.
11 Rose interview with Bray.
12 George F. Will, "Therapy from a Sickening Film," *Los Angeles Times*, 17 June 1993, p. B7. This article reviews the Hughes brothers' debut film, *Menace To Society*.
13 Rob Tannenbaum, "Sucker MC," *Village Voice*, 4 December 1990, p. 69. See Stephen Holden's "Pop Life" column, *New York Times*, 17 October 1990, p. C17, for published details of the fabricated biography. After the Perkins story and others, Ice's publicist significantly revised the bio, admitting that Vanilla Ice had actually grown up in both Miami and Dallas and deleted all references to Luther Campbell. Although fabricated artist biographies are not uncommon, Vanilla Ice's claims are particularly far from

the truth and, as Tannenbaum points out, insulting to poor black communities.

14 John Shecter, "Chocolate Ties," *The Source*, July 1993, p. 18.
15 Special thanks to producer Gina Harrell for her help in explaining this process.
16 Interview with Charles S. Stone III, 15 July 1993. Stone, who has been directing music videos, especially rap music videos, for several years is especially known for his creative use of animation and humor in his video treatments and concepts. Some of his more prominent and well-respected videos include "The Choice is Yours" for Black Sheep (which won MTV's and *The Source's* best rap video awards for 1992); "911 is a Joke" for Public Enemy; "Bonita Applebum" and "I Left My Wallet In El Segundo" for A Tribe Called Quest; "Blackman" for Tashan; "Funny Vibe" for Living color; and "Sassy" for Neneh Cherry (featuring Guru).
17 Rose interview with Gina Harrell, March 20, 1993. Harrell is an experienced video producer who has worked on dozens of music videos, commercials, and other projects.
18 Ibid.
19 See Tricia Rose interview with Carmen Ashhurst-Watson in Andrew Ross and Tricia Rose, eds., *Microphone Fiends: Youth Music & Youth Culture* (New York: Routledge, 1994).
20 Andrew Ross, *No Respect: Intellectuals and Popular Culture* (New York: Routledge, 1989), p. 71.
21 Cindi Katz and Neil Smith, "L. A. Infitada: Interview with Mike Davis," *Social Text*, no. 33, 19–33, 1993.

Consider the Source

1. In her 1999 memoir *Ladies First: Revelations of a Strong Woman*, hip-hop (and screen) star Queen Latifah describes how she chose her stage name. As you read her explanation, consider the values that lead her not simply to choose "Queen" and "Latifah" but also the very decision to choose a name in the first place. In what sense is Queen Latifah African? In what sense is she American? And how does she define the term "ultimate woman?"

Excerpts from *Ladies First* by Queen Latifah (1999)

For me, *Latifah* was freedom. I loved the name my parents gave me, Dana Elaine Owens. But I knew then that something as simple as picking a new name for myself would be my first act of defining who I was – for myself and for the world. *Dana* was daughter. *Dana* was sister. *Dana* was student, friend, girl in the 'hood. But *Latifah* was someone else. She would belong only to me. It was more than a persona. Becoming Latifah would give me the autonomy to be what I *chose* to be – without being influenced by anyone else's expectations of what a young girl from Newark is supposed to be. Or what she is supposed to do. Or what she is supposed to want.

My cousin Sharonda had a book of Muslim names, with the meaning listed next to each one. So Sharonda and I went through the book to see if we could find something for us...

Sharonda's father, my uncle Sonny, was a Muslim. He had a younger daughter whose name was Latifah. I thought that name was beautiful. I loved the way it sounded, how it just rolled off my tongue. So I was already feeling that name, but when I read what it meant, I knew that was me. *Latifah*: "Delicate, sensitive, kind." Yeah, that was me...

The people in my world may have been perceiving me as something else, but inside I felt delicate, sensitive, and kind. I knew who I was inside, and I wanted to show a bit of that on the outside – with my name.

The "Queen" didn't come until a decade later.

... Around this time, the late 1980s, the conflict in South Africa was coming to a head. Nelson Mandela was still imprisoned, and the United States was pressuring companies to divest their interests in the country that made *apartheid* a household world. My mother and I would get into deep discussions about the plight of the South African women and talk about how segregation and racism were alive and kicking right here – in the very country that was opposed to apartheid in a nation halfway around the world. My mom and I revered those African women we didn't know, because they seemed to be so close to the most royal ancestors of all time. Before there was a queen of England, there were Nefertiti and Numidia. The African queens have a unique place in world history. They are revered not only for their extraordinary beauty and power but also for their strength and for their ability to nurture and rule the continent that gave rise to the greatest civilizations of all time. These women are my foremothers. I wanted to pay homage to them. And I wanted, in my own way, to adopt their attributes.

So "Queen" seemed appropriate. Queen Latifah. When I said it out loud, I felt dominant. I was proud. When I said "Queen," it was like saying "woman." *Queen* became synonymous with *woman* for me – the way every woman should feel or should want to feel.

Queen is the ultimate woman.

2. Describe Rose's stance toward hip-hop culture. Is she a detached observer? An immersed participant? What clues can you gather from her prose?

3. "Some rappers have equated white participation [in rap] with a process of dilution and subsequent theft of black culture," Tricia Rose writes. "Although the terms dilution and theft do not capture the complexity of cultural incorporation and syncretism, this interpretation has more than a grain of truth to it." Who would you cite as examples of this kind of theft? (Rose cites Vanilla Ice; are there less obvious examples?) Can you think of any white or Latino rappers who would not fit such a description? On what basis?

4. How much – or how little – has rap changed in the last decade? What newer aspects of rap music or video are not covered here? How important are they – and in what sense?

Suggested Further Reading

The literature of rap music is growing rapidly, though most of it is ephemeral. Some of the more important scholarly (or scholarly-minded) studies include Houston A. Baker, Jr., *Black Studies, Rap, and the Academy* (Chicago: University of Chicago Press, 1993); William Eric Perkins, editor, *Droppin' Science: Critical Essays on Rap Music and Hip Hop Culture* (Philadelphia: Temple University Press, 1996), and Nelson George, *Hip Hop America* (New York: Viking, 1998).

Index